INTERNATIONAL LAW AND DIPLOMACY

INTERNATIONAL LAW AND DIPLOMACY

Dr C Chatterjee

LL.M (Cambridge), LL.M, Ph.D (London)

Barrister

LONDON AND NEW YORK

Paperback edition, with revisions, published 2010
by Routledge
Albert House, 1-4 Singer Street, London EC2A 4BQ

Simultaneously published in the USA and Canada
by Routledge
711 Third Avenue, New York, NY 10017

Routledge is an imprint of the Taylor & Francis Group, an informa business

© Dr Charles Chatterjee

The right of Dr Charles Chatterjee to be identified as author of this work has been asserted by him in accordance with sections 77 and 78 of the Copyright, Designs and Patents Act 1988.

All rights reserved. No part of this book may be reprinted or reproduced or utilised in any form or by any electronic, mechanical, or other means, now known or hereafter invented, including photocopying and recording, or in any information storage or retrieval system, without permission in writing from the publishers.

Trademark notice: Product or corporate names may be trademarks or registered trademarks, and are used only for identification and explanation without intent to infringe.

First published by Routledge 2007

British Library Cataloguing in Publication Data
A catalogue record for this book is available from the British Library

Library of Congress Cataloging in Publication Data
Chatterjee, C. (Charles)
　International law and diplomacy/C. Chatterjee. – p. cm.
　Includes bibliographical references and index.
　1.　Diplomacy. 2. Foreign relations administration. 3. International law. I. Chatterjee, C. II. Title
JZ1405.C43 2007
341.3/3-dc22

2007279157

ISBN13: 978-1-85743-384-5 (hbk)
ISBN13: 978-1-85743-586-3 (pbk)
ISBN13: 978-0-203-83065-9 (ebk)

Typeset in Plantin and Optima by AJS Solutions, Huddersfield - Dundee

Printed and bound in Great Britain by MPG Books Group

In loving memory of my parents

CONTENTS

		Page
List of Cases		xvi
Introduction		xxi

Chapter 1
Certain Essential Terms

1.1	Introduction	1
1.1.1	Belligerency	1
1.1.2	Buffer State	1
1.1.3	Calvo Doctrine	2
1.1.4	Casus Belli	2
1.1.5	Casus Foederis	2
1.1.6	Cold War	3
1.1.7	Comity	3
1.1.8	Concordat	3
1.1.9	Condominium	3
1.1.10	Contadora Group	4
1.1.11	Consular Invoice	4
1.1.12	Coup d'état	4
1.1.13	Démarche	5
1.1.14	Denunciation	5
1.1.15	Depositories	6
1.1.16	Détente	7
1.1.17	Diplomatic Asylum	8
1.1.18	Diplomatic Relations	8
1.1.19	Domino Theory	10
1.1.20	Envoys	10
1.1.21	Estrada Doctrine	10
1.1.22	Exequatur	10
1.1.23	Extradition	11
1.1.24	Formal Apology	13
1.1.25	Franchise du quantier or jus quareteriorum	14
1.1.26	Full Powers	14
1.1.27	Governments in Exile	15
1.1.28	Hot Pursuit	15

		Page
1.1.29	Incognito Travelling	16
1.1.30	In Dubio Mitius	17
1.1.31	Internationally Injurious Acts of Diplomatic Envoys	17
1.1.32	Inter-temporal Law	17
1.1.33	Juges Consuls or Consuls Marchands	18
1.1.34	Jus Cogens	18
1.1.35	Laissez-passer	18
1.1.36	Lateran Treaty of 1929	18
1.1.37	Monroe Doctrine	19
1.1.38	Nemo Plus Juris Transferre Potest Quam Ipse Habet	19
1.1.39	Notarial Act	20
1.1.40	Plenipotentiary	20
1.1.41	Plenipotentiary Conference	20
1.1.42	Procès-verbal	20
1.1.43	Plurilingual Treaties	20
1.1.44	Protocol	21
1.1.45	Punctationes	21
1.1.46	Rapporteur	21
1.1.47	Rapproachment	21
1.1.48	Recognition de facto	22
1.1.49	Recognition de jure	22
1.1.50	Regents	22
1.1.51	Res Extra Commercium	22
1.1.52	Reservations	22
1.1.53	Right of Expatriation	24
1.1.54	Servitudes	24
1.1.55	Territorial Asylum	25
1.1.56	Travaux Préparatoires	26
1.1.57	Uti Possidetis Juris	27
1.1.58	Vatican City in International Law	27
1.1.59	Veto	28
1.1.60	Volte face	28
1.1.61	Warships in Foreign Waters	28
1.2	Conclusions	29

		Page

Chapter 2
A Brief Account of the Historical Growth and Development of Diplomatic Relations

2.1	Introduction	30
2.2	A Brief Account of Historical Growth and Development of Diplomatic Relations	31
2.3	Conclusions	35

Chapter 3
Sovereignty

3.1	Introduction	36
3.2	Meaning and Characteristics of Sovereignty	36
3.3	Types of Jurisdiction	49
3.3.1	The Territoriality Principle	50
3.3.2	The Nationality Principle	53
3.3.3	The Passive Personality Principle	54
3.3.4	The Protective Principle	54
3.3.5	The Universality Principle	55
3.4	Extension of Jurisdiction by means of Treaties	55
3.5	Abuse of Sovereignty	58
3.6	The Extraterritorial Application of EC Competition Law	62
3.7	Conclusions	63

Chapter 4
Ethics in Diplomacy

4.1	Introduction	66
4.2	Is there anything called *"international morality"*?	68
4.3	Ethics in Diplomacy and Politics of Diplomacy	70
4.4	What role may Ethics in Diplomacy play in restraining Politics of Diplomacy?	73
4.5	Is Multilateral Diplomacy totally short of ethics?	75
4.6	Conclusions	77

Chapter 5
Diplomacy and Diplomats

5.1	Introduction	80

		Page
5.2	What is Diplomacy?	80
5.3	What are the attributes of an Ideal Diplomat?	82
5.4	Diplomatic Studies and International Law	84
5.5	Functions of a Diplomat	85
5.6	Conclusions	87

Chapter 6
Bargaining Power

6.1	Introduction	90
6.2	What is Bargaining Power?	91
6.3	Bargaining Power at Three Levels	95
6.4	Conclusions	100

Chapter 7
The New Faces of International Diplomacy

7.1	Introduction	102
7.2	The New Faces of Diplomacy	105
7.3	The Changing Nature of Diplomacy and Training in Diplomacy	111
7.4	When Attitude toward Sovereignty and Diplomacy remains unchanged in a Changing World	117
7.5	Diplomacy and International Trade	117
7.6	Conclusions	128

Chapter 8
Conferences

8.1	Introduction	130
8.2	Principal Purposes of holding Inter-governmental and International Conferences	131
8.3	Conference Diplomacy	133
8.4	Organisation of Conferences	134
8.5	Conference Procedure	135
8.5.1	The Agenda	135
8.5.2	Delegations	136
8.5.3	Observers	137
8.5.4	Credentials	137

		Page
8.5.5	The Authority to make Proposals and to take Decisions	137
8.5.6	Management of a Conference	138
8.5.7	Rapporteurs	139
8.5.8	Records	140
8.5.9	Languages	140
8.6	Conclusions	140

Chapter 9
Diplomatic Protocol and Procedures

9.1	Introduction	141
9.2	The Use of National Flags	142
9.3	State Ceremonies	142
9.4	Diplomatic List	143
9.5	Communications between Diplomatic Missions and the Government of the Receiving State	144
9.6	Official Mourning	144
9.7	Conclusions	144

Chapter 10
The Ministry of Foreign Affairs

10.1	Introduction	147
10.2	The Composition of the Ministry of Foreign Affairs	153
10.2.1	Political Affairs	154
10.2.2	Treaties and Legal	154
10.2.3	Protocol	155
10.3	Credentials and Letters of Introduction	159
10.4	Arrival and Notification of Arrival of New Heads of Mission in London	160
10.5	Commencement of Functions	161
10.6	Procedure	161
10.7	Calls on FCO Ministers and Officials	161
10.8	Termination of Appointment	162
10.9	General	162
10.10	Relations with Foreign Missions	163

INTERNATIONAL LAW AND DIPLOMACY

		Page
10.11	Relations with its own Missions in Foreign Jurisdictions	164
10.12	Conclusions	165

Chapter 11
The Diplomatic Mission

11.1	Introduction	167
11.2	The Diplomatic Mission and its Principal Officers and Offices	167
11.2.1	The Head of Mission	168
11.2.2	Chancery	170
11.2.3	Local Staff	171
11.2.4	Accountants	171
11.2.5	Consular Section	171
11.2.6	Commercial Section	171
11.2.7	Press and Information Section	171
11.2.8	Attachés	172
11.3	The Diplomatic Mission and the Vienna Convention on Diplomatic Relations, 1961	173
11.4	Conclusions	175

Chapter 12
The Vienna Convention on Diplomatic Relations, 1961

12.1	Introduction	177
12.2	A Brief Historical Background to the Convention	178
12.2.1	An Analysis of the Convention	178
12.2.2	Definitions of Certain Terms and Classifications of Heads of Mission	179
12.3	Methods of establishing Diplomatic Relations between States	181
12.4	The Functions of a Diplomatic Mission	181
12.5	Duties of a Diplomatic Mission	183
12.6	Methods of accrediting Diplomats	185
12.7	General Powers and Duties of a Sending State and a Receiving State (Articles 10–21)	187
12.8	The meaning of Diplomatic Privileges and Immunities	188

		Page
12.9	The Concept of Inviolability	190
12.10	Diplomatic Immunities in regard to Property	191
12.11	Inviolability of a Mission and its Articles and Communications	197
12.12	Treatment to be accorded to a Mission by a Receiving State	210
12.13	Extent of Immunities to be accorded to a Diplomatic Agent and Waiver of Immunity	212
12.14	Extension of Privileges and Immunities to Members of the Family of a Diplomatic Agent, Private Servants, and the Local Staff	215
12.15	The Duration of Privileges and Immunities	215
12.16	Ending of Functions of a Diplomatic Agent	216
12.17	Other Provisions	216
12.18	When Absolute Immunity may not be claimed	217
12.18.1	The State Immunity Act 1978	221
12.18.2	Anatomy of the Act	222
12.18.3	A Brief Analysis of the Act	223
12.19	Diplomatic Asylum	229
12.20	The Law Governing Diplomacy	237
12.20.1	The Representative Character Concept	238
12.20.2	The Functional Necessity Concept	238
12.20.3	The Extraterritoriality Concept	239
12.21	Heads of State	243
12.22	Conclusions	243

Chapter 13

A Brief Analysis of the Vienna Convention on Consular Relations, 1963

Part I – A Brief Analysis of the Historical Evolution of Consular Relations

13.1	Introduction	249
13.2	The History of International Trade and Commerce and Consular Relations	249
13.3	Modern Developments	255
13.4	Comments	258

		Page
13.5	Classification of Consuls and Certain Other Relevant Officers	259
13.6	An Analysis of the Vienna Convention on Consular Relations, 1963	260
13.7	Consular Relations in General	262
13.7.1	Facilities, Privileges and Immunities Relating to Consular Posts, Career Consular Officers and Other Members of a Consular Post	268
13.7.2	Regime relating to Honorary Consular Officers and Consular Posts headed by such Officers	278
13.7.3	General Provisions	281
13.7.4	Final Provisions	282
13.8	Conclusions	282

Chapter 14
The United Nations and International Diplomacy

14.1	Introduction	284
14.2	The UN System Generally	288
14.2.1	Purposes – Article 1	288
14.2.2	Principles – Article 2	288
14.3	The UN System	291
14.3.1	Some Preliminary Information	291
14.3.2	Structure of the United Nations	292
14.3.2.1	The General Assembly	292
14.3.2.2	The Security Council	295
14.3.2.3	Powers and Functions of the Security Council	299
14.3.3.3	Peace-making and Peace-keeping Functions of the Security Council	300
14.3.4	The Secretary-General	301
14.3.5	The Economic and Social Council	308
14.3.6	Secretariat	312
14.3.7	International Court of Justice	312
14.4	Conclusions	313
Conclusions		314
Appendix I	*Vienna Convention on Diplomatic Relations and Optional Protocols*	317

		Page
Appendix II	*Vienna Convention on Consular Relations and Optional Protocols*	336
Table of Statutes		369
Table of International Conventions		370
Other Primary Sources		372
Other Sources		376
Author Index		384
Index		387

LIST OF CASES

Aaland Islands 1920	24
Abdul Rahman Baker v Ashford (1960)	153n
Achille Lauro Affair and Co-operation in Combating International Terrorism	56
Aerial Incidents case	26
Alcoa case	61
Alcom Ltd v Republic of Colombia	193
Al-Fin Corporation's Patent (1969)	152n
Alfred Dunhill of London Inc v Republic of Cuba 1952	218–9
American Banana Co v United Fruit Co 1909	61n
Application of the Convention on the Prevention and Punishment of the Crime of Genocide (Bosnia-Herzegovina v Yugoslavia (Serbia-Montenegro)), Provisional Measures, ICJ Reports	272n
Arab Bank Ltd v Barclays Bank DCO (1954)	152n
Asylum Case (Colombia v Peru)	234ff
Baccus SRL v Servicio Nacional del Trigo (1956)	221n, 223n
Barcelona Traction, Light and Power Company	53n, 54
Beagle Channel Arbitration (Argentina v Chile) (1979)	150n
Belgium v Nicod and Another	198n
Board of Accountancy, The and Ferguson	3n
Bosnia-Herzegovina v Yugoslavia (Serbia and Montenegro) Provisional Measures, ICJ Reports	272n
Briggs v The Lightships (US case)	241
British Nylon Spinners Ltd v Imperial Chemicals Industries Ltd	59
Burkina Faso and Mali Frontier Dispute	27
Carl-Zeiss-Stiftung v Rayner & Keeler (No 2) (1967)	152n
Caroline, The, case	108
Case Concerning America and Other Mexican Nationals (Mexico v US), International Legal Materials	274
Case concerning Rights of Nationals of the United States of America in Morocco (France v United States), ICJ, 1952	254
Certain Expenses of the UN case 1962	110n

List of Cases

Commercial Solvents case (1974)	57n, 63
Compania Naviera Vascongado v SS Cristina (1938)	217
Corfu Channel case	286–7
Czarnikow Ltd v Rolimpex (1978)	219n, 221
Dallal v Bank Mellat 1986	3n
De Haber v The Queen of Portugal	241
Democratic Republic of Congo v Belgium, ICJ Reports 2002	55n
Diplomatic Immunities and Privileges, 1985	207n
Diversion of the waters of the River Meuse (1937)	17n
DPP v Doot (1973)	51n, 57n
DPP v Stonehouse (1978)	51n, 57n
Duff Development Co v Government of Kelantan	153n, 223n
Duke of Brunswick v The King of Hanover	240
Dyestuffs Cartel (1969)	57n, 62
Eichmann trial	55
Ex parte Mwenya (1959)	153n
Fatemi v the US	198n
Foster v Globe Venture Syndicate (1900)	153n
Nuclear Tests case	287
Frontier between Turkey and Iraq (1925)	17
Gagara, The (1919)	152n
Geigy v Commission	63
Genocide case	29n
Germany v United States, Case Concerning the Vienna Convention on Consular Relations	270ff
GUR Corporation v Trust Bank of Africa Ltd	152
Haya de la Torre case *(The Asylum* case*)*	8
Hellenic Lines Ltd v Moore (1965)	204n
Hertford Fire Insurance Co v California	62
ICC v Commission (1972)	62n
Intpro Properties (UK) Ltd v Samuel	194
Iran Hostage case	184
Islamic Republic of Iran v Pahlavi	246n
Island of Dalwas Arbitration (1928)	30n
Island of Palmas Arbitration	46

Jimenez v Aristeguieta	245
Joyce v DPP	54
Jupiter, The	217n
Krajina v Tass Agency (1959)	220n
Kuwait Airways Corporation v Iraqi Airways Co (1995)	219n
Legal Status of Eastern Greenland	150–1
Liangsiriprasert v Government of the United States of America (1991)	57
Lotus, The, case	51–3
Luigi Monta of Genoa v Cechofracht Co Ltd (1956)	152n
Luther v Sagor 1919	36, 152n
Oscar Chinn case	41ff
Mellenger v New Brunswick Development Corporation	220
Mighell v Sultan of Jahore (1894)	153n
Minority Schools in Albania (Permanent Court of International Justice, 1935)	118ff
Murray v Parkes (1942)	152n
Nicaragua v the United States	287
North Atlantic Fisheries Arbitration 1910	24
North Charterland Exploration Co (1910) Ltd v The King (1931)	153n
North Sea Continental Shelf case	26n
Nottebohn case	54
Nuclear Tests (Australia v France) Interim Protection, ICJ Report (1973)	272n, 287
Paraguay v United States of America Provisional Measures, ICJ Reports (1998)	272n
Parlement Belge, The 1860	217, 239–40, 241, 242n
Philippine Embassy Bank Account case	192–3
Philippine Admiral (Owners) v Wallem Shipping (Hong Kong) Ltd	218
Post Office v Estuary Radio Ltd (1968)	153n
R Governor of Pentonville Prison ex parte Teya (1971)	153n
R v Botrill (1947)	153n
Rahimtoola v Nizam of Hyderabad	218
Rani Kunwar v Commission of Income Tax	246

List of Cases

Re (P (GE) (an Infant)	53n
Re Grand Jury Proceedings	246n
Reel v Holder (1981)	152n
Reservations to the Convention on the Prevention and Punishment of the Crime of Genocide (ICJ)	23, 26n
Fagernes case, 1927	152n, 153n
Restrictions to the Death Penalty (ICJ)	23n
Right of Passage over Indian Territory 1963	24, 25
Rights of United States nationals in Morocco (1952)	17n
Rio Tinto Zinc Corporation and Others v. Westinghouse Electric Corporation	59, 60
Schooner Exchange v McFadden (1812) (US)	240, 241
Secretary of State for Foreign and Commonwealth Affairs ex parte Samuel	203
Shearson Lehman v MacLaine Watson Co Ltd and International Tin Council (Intervener)	196
Shoshone Indians v United States	17
South West Africa cases (1961 and 1966)	17n
Taraz Hostage case	209
Tehran Hostage case	200ff
Territorial Jurisdiction of the International Commission of the River Oder	26
Thai-Europe Tapioca Service Ltd v Government of Pakistan	218
Thakore Saheb Khanji Kashari Khanji v Gulam Rosul Chandbhai	245n, 246n
Third Avenue Associates v Permanent Mission of the Republic of Zaire to the United Nations 1993	197n
Timberlane LBR Co v Bank of America	62
Trail Smelter Arbitration, The	47n, 286
Travaux Preparatoires	26–7
Treatment of Polish Nationals in Danzig (1932)	26n
Trendtex Trading Corporation v Central Bank of Nigeria (1977)	219, 220, 221, 228, 244n
Underhill v Hernandez	61
Union Carbide case	50
Union Nationale des Transport Fluviaux (Unatra)	42ff

United States v Iran	190
United States v Pilkington	62
United States Diplomatic and Consular Staff in Tehran Provisional Measures ICJ Reports	272n
US v Aluminium Co of America 1945	61n
US v Aluminium Company of America (Alcoa) (1944)	51n
US v Gonzalez	54
US v Watchmakers of Switzerland Information Center Inc	61
US v Yunis	55n
USA v Wagner	245
Watchmakers of Switzerland case	61
Western Sahara case	27n
Westminster City Council v Government of Islamic Republic of Iran (1986)	204
Westminster City Council v Tomlin	203
Wood Pulp case	63
Zones of Upper Savoy, The, and the District of Gex (1932)	25

INTRODUCTION

It is a daunting task to write a book on diplomacy and international law for two primary reasons: (a) that the perception still exists that diplomacy can be conducted without any heed to the principles of international law; and (b) that to many it is not useful to relate the relevant principles of international law to diplomacy, particularly when diplomacy in the contemporary period is predominantly based on the domination of the strong over the weak.

This author's position is simple; diplomacy must pay attention to the principles of international law and apply them, where necessary. In other words, there is an intricate relationship between diplomacy and the principles of public international law. Thus, a diplomat, in addition to being familiar with the basics of international politics, history, geography, languages, customs etc must be conversant with the principles of public international law.

Diplomacy has a chequered history; most of which is about resolving conflicts. It has been explained in this work that diplomatic interaction between States during its early years took place primarily for two purposes: (a) interaction for economic, including trade relationship; and (b) conflict resolution through third parties.

It is pertinent to mention that the history of diplomacy is paved with the history of warfare; and this has become evident particularly until the days of the League of Nations.

It is unfortunate that during the period of the UN, diplomacy has been operated in some respects in the old-fashioned way – the diplomacy of warfare, which, in fact, defeats the whole objectives of true diplomacy. The series of warfares during the UN period, El Salvador, Grenada, Iraq, Kosovo, Nicaragua and Viet-Nam, and, of course, Arab-Israeli conflict, to name but a few, remind one of the failures of diplomacy or what may be called pro-war diplomacy, which runs counter to the philosophy of the UN.

The matrix of diplomacy of warfare and that of peace are different; diplomacy of peace is more difficult than the diplomacy of warfare; the latter is primarily based on military tactics. Diplomacy of peace requires a comprehensive ingenuity, knowledge and foresightedness on the part of diplomats. Whereas diplomacy of warfare is based on *"might"*, diplomacy of peace requires the power to negotiate, which requires skills, knowledge and a purpose which would lead to lasting friendship.

Economic diplomacy is a major part of diplomacy of peace. Mutual economic benefits form a significant part of foreign policy making. It is economic ties with countries that form real friendship, and minimise the incidence of warfare.

Bearing some such issues in mind, this work, in addition to discussing some general issues of diplomacy, namely, history, a general discussion of the Vienna Convention on Diplomatic Relations, 1961, the Vienna Convention on Consular Relations, 1963, the Foreign Office, etc., attention has been paid to certain controversial issues too, namely, bargaining power, ethics in diplomacy and the kind of training a diplomat in the contemporary world may need.

In writing this work, reliance has been placed upon primary sources of information; secondary sources of information have been referred to where necessary.

For the convenience of the reader the texts of the Vienna Convention on Diplomatic Relations, 1961, and the Vienna Convention on Consular Relations, 1963, together with their Optional Protocols, are reproduced in the Appendices, starting on page 317. For this the author gives due acknowledgement and thanks to the United Nations Publications Board, New York, NY 10017, USA.

CHAPTER 1

Certain Essential Terms

1.1 INTRODUCTION

A diplomat is supposed to be familiar with the essential and common terms which are used in the world of diplomacy. This Chapter attempts to explain some of the most important terms which are commonly used in the world of diplomacy. It is to be emphasised however that the list of such terms can never be complete and perfect. The most common terms used in diplomacy have been explained in the hope that diplomats will find it useful. In discussing these terms references have been made to the most established works and documents on diplomacy.

1.1.1 Belligerency

A particular form of aggression. It must be pointed out in this connection that *"aggression"* or *"belligerency"* is prohibited by Article 2(4) of the UN Charter.

What foreign policy experts and diplomats should consider seriously is whether it is impermissible for the Member States to derogate from the obligations they have undertaken under Article 2(4) of the UN Charter, and be engaged in belligerency. See further the Chapter on the *Use of Force*.

Until 1945, that is, the year in which the UN Charter came into force (24 October 1945) belligerency was permissible in international law. Even the Covenant of the League of Nations did not abolish belligerency. Now that *"belligerency"* is aimed to have been abolished, it is for foreign relations experts and diplomats to restrict the use of *"belligerency"* in modern times.

It is to be emphasised that wars are almost always initiated by states; international organisations, the primary actors of peace-making, may sometimes find themselves in a hopeless position to remove the cause of belligerency.

1.1.2 Buffer State

The meaning of the word *"Buffer"* in the context of diplomacy would be: a state or zone lying between two others, usually owing allegiance to neither, and serving as a means of preventing hostilities between them.

It stands for a lesser state between two stronger states. It largely relies for its security on the position of the powerful neighbouring states; in other words, because of the presence of powerful neighbouring states third states will be deterred from occupying that lesser state.

1.1.3 Calvo Doctrine

This doctrine which is named after Carlos Calvo (1824-1906), an Argentinian diplomat, proclaims that an alien may not seek diplomatic protection of his own country and submit any dispute arising under a contract to local jurisdiction. In order to give effect to this doctrine, the Latin American States insist that contracts with aliens must include a *Calvo clause*, in order to prevent aliens from seeking the diplomatic protection of their countries, and to submit any disputes under the contract to the local jurisdiction / courts.

But effectiveness of a Calvo clause may be questioned on two possible grounds: (a) that by signing a Calvo clause, a state may not necessarily prevent an alien from seeking diplomatic protection if an injury is caused to an alien in performing or not performing the contractual obligations, which issue may have to be resolved by relying on the principle of international responsibility and the international minimum standard; and (b) should an alien be asked to preclude protection of his State by means of or through a commercial contract, to which he is entitled under the general principles of international law.

1.1.4 Casus Belli

The term has its origin in the treatise in international law written by the famous Dutch international law author, Hugo Grotius. It stands for an action justifying a war.

Casus belli should be used sparingly by states, and in particular by the states that are Members of the United Nations. Under Article 2 Paragraph 4 of the UN Charter, the Member States have undertaken not to use force, let alone be engaged in wars, against any other state. Article 2(4) provides that:

> "*All Members shall refrain in their international relations from the threat or use of force against the territorial integrity or political independence of any state or in any other inconsistent ... with the Purposes of the United Nations.*"

However, force used in self-defence is the only exception (Article 51) made to the provisions of Article 2(4). One can only hope that, in national foreign relations, officers and diplomats representing their governments will bear the point in mind about the non-use of *casus belli* in the modern times.

1.1.5 Casus Foederis

The event at the occurrence of which the duty to render the promised service by a member allied to the other must be performed. In other words, the *casus foederis* occurs when a war is declared against a member of an alliance. Ideally, treaties of alliance should precisely define which event(s) might constitute the *casus foederis*; as otherwise, the purpose of military alliances may be defeated. Greece refused to recognise that *casus foederis* had occurred under the Greece – Serbian Treaty of 1913, and hence she had a duty to render any service to Serbia[1].

1.1.6 Cold War

"Cold war" is a misnomer in that all wars whether weapon-based or not should be *"hot wars"* or simply wars. In international relations, this term is used to denote a degree of hostility that exists between states when their foreign policy interests clash. Cold wars can be very protracted. The example in point is the cold war that persisted between the United States and the former Soviet Union. A situation of the so-called cold war may be avoided or effectively dealt with by shrewd diplomacy, otherwise a cold war may lead to a *"hot war"* or a proper weapon-based war.

1.1.7 Comity

This stands for the relationship between States by applying rules of politeness, convenience and goodwill. These rules of international conduct are known as rules of comity. By virtue of these rules, for example, diplomatic envoys were allowed exemptions from customs duty. Many rules of comity have been incorporated in the body of rules of international law. Rules of the comity of nations may form part of the rules of international law, although they themselves are not a source of international law. Comity is something which is more than mere courtesy, but less than a legal obligation[2].

1.1.8 Concordat

It stands for an agreement concluded between the Catholic Church (the Holy See) and a State. In order to distinguish treaties to which the Holy See is a party from other treaties, in international practice, this special term was chosen.

A special term used for such treaties is significant and useful in that by virtue of enjoying a special status in international law, states do not conclude too many standard and commercial or defence treaties with the Holy See. By carrying a special title, treaties with the Holy See became clearly distinguishable.

1.1.9 Condominium

There exists a *condominium* when two or more states jointly exercise sovereignty over a territory. Sudan, for example, was under the condominium of Great Britain and Egypt for the period from 1898 to 1955. The concept of *condominium* is sometimes applied to the use of water of rivers or bays or gulfs; for example, see the Treaty between Brazil and Paraguay of 1973 concerning the hydroelectric use of the Paraná River. Under a *condominium*, the interested states agree to adopt provisional measures for territories in the form of joint

---

[1] See 12 American Journal of International Law, (1918) 312

[2] *Dallal v Bank Mellat* [1986] QB 441; and *The Board of Accountancy and Ferguson*, International Law Reports, 18 (1951) No. 7

sovereignty until their final status is determined, and they do not exercise their individual sovereignty over such territories.

An important example of the administration of *condominium* was the Kuwait-Saudi Arabia neutral zone, established by the Uqair Convention of 2 December 1922. Until their final status was determined, it was decided that the two governments would share equal rights over the zone. Of course, in 1965, this *condominium* came to an end when the neutral zone was partitioned with two sections, one of which was annexed to Kuwait, and the other to Saudi Arabia.

1.1.10 Contadora Group

In order to seek democracy, human rights, peace and related matters and reduction of arms in Central America through negotiations, the Contadora Group was set up. Its original members were Colombia, Mexico, Panama and Venezuela. In 1985, a Support Group consisting of the following countries joined the Contadora Group: Argentina, Brazil, Paraguay and Peru.

1.1.11 Consular Invoice

An invoice certified by the consul of an overseas country pertaining to goods dispatched, whether by air or by ship, to that country.

The use of consular invoices has been in international trade practice for a considerable period of time. Consular invoices serve as a safety valve for business as they confirm the genuineness of invoices sent from overseas countries. Consular invoices are often found necessary in many developing countries for the purpose of seeking foreign exchange to settle the invoice amount. The central bank in a foreign country usually finds it acceptable as these invoices have been certified by its consular office in the country of the seller. Such invoices also offer sellers much psychological satisfaction as the possibility of their being settled becomes high.

Consular invoices are not very common in rich countries. Trade between the European Union countries need not be conditional upon certification of invoices by consuls of buyers' countries, as two of the fundamental principles on which European Union trade is operated are the free movement of capital and the free movement of goods.

1.1.12 Coup d'état

The method whereby a revolutionary group or military unlawfully seizes control of the government in power. It often proves to be difficult for the new government to be recognised *de jure*. Probably most governments will be inclined to recognise a government that has come into power through such a method on a *de facto* basis, or not to recognise it at all, at least for some time. Usually, such regimes prove to be short-lived. Sometimes however military regimes transform themselves into democratic regimes, as it happened in Poland.

1.1.13 Démarche

The meaning of this French word is:

> "*step, proceeding, manner of action, especially a diplomatic initiative, a political step*"[3]

In the world of diplomacy and international relations, it stands for the initiative that a government usually takes to adopt a fresh policy, following an unsatisfactory foreign relations situation. In a way, it stands for a corrective attempt on the part of a government.

1.1.14 Denunciation

To denounce a treaty means to leave or withdraw from the treaty regime. In practice, the term *"denunciation"* is used in the case of bilateral treaties; whereas the term *"withdrawal"* is used in respect of multilateral treaties; however, the legal effect of both the terms remains same. Whereas, denunciation by one party to a bilateral treaty brings the treaty to an end, withdrawal from a multilateral treaty regime by one party does not terminate the treaty. Although many treaties enter provision for withdrawal or denunciation, legally, a sovereign state has the inherent right to withdraw or denounce, as the case may be, from a treaty regime at any time, provided it satisfies the conditions of withdrawal or denunciation embodied in a treaty or implied (usually by serving a notice to all other parties to the treaty and settles its financial liability, if any). Denunciation or withdrawal from treaties of a stated duration is not usually allowed. Article 56 of the Vienna Convention on the Law of Treaties (1969) provides that:

> *(1) "A treaty which contains no provision regarding its termination and which does not provide for denunciation or withdrawal is not subject to denunciation or withdrawal unless:*
>
> > *(a) it is established that the parties intended to admit the possibility of denunciation or withdrawal; or*
> > *(b) a right of denunciation or withdrawal may be implied by the nature of the treaty.*
>
> *(2) A party shall give not less than twelve months' notice of its intention to denounce or withdraw from a treaty under paragraph 1."*

On the other hand, Article 59 provides that:

> *"1. A treaty shall be considered as terminated if all the parties to it conclude a later treaty relating to the same subject-matter and:*
>
> > *(a) it appears from the later treaty or is otherwise established that the parties intended that the matter should be governed by that treaty; or*

---

[3] *The Oxford English Dictionary*, Oxford, Clarendon Press (1986) Vol IV at 432

(b) the provisions of the later treaty are so far incompatible with those of the earlier one that the two treaties are not capable of being applied at the same time.

2. The earlier treaty shall be considered as only suspended in operation if it appears from the later treaty or is otherwise established that such was the intention of the parties."

1.1.15 Depositories

A depository is an institution or a party with which a treaty must be deposited. A treaty becomes effective as from the date of deposit with the depository or the date on which the consent of a state to be bound by a treaty is received. The relevant Articles in the Vienna Convention on the Law of Treaties are 15 and 16.

Article 15

"The consent of a State to be bound by a treaty is expressed by accession when:

(a) the treaty provides that such consent may be expressed by that State by means of accession;
(b) it is otherwise established that the negotiating States were agreed that such consent may be expressed by that State by means of accession; or
(c) all the parties have subsequently agreed that such consent may be expressed by that State by means of accession."

Article 16

"Unless the treaty otherwise provides, instruments of ratification, acceptance, approval or accession establish the consent of a State to be bound by a treaty upon:

(a) their exchange between the contracting States;
(b) their deposit with the depositary; or
(c) their notification to the contracting States or to the depositary, if so agreed."

It is for the parties to a treaty to decide where to deposit the treaty. In the case of a bilateral treaty, with two authentic original texts, each party will retain one; but where a bilateral or even a multilateral treaty of a limited type has only one authentic original text, the parties must decide, who may retain the original or where to deposit it; others will receive certified copies of the treaty. Article 77(1) of the Vienna Convention on the Law of Treaties lists a depository's functions:

"The functions of a depositary, unless otherwise provided in the treaty or agreed by the contracting States, comprise in particular:

(a) *keeping custody of the original text of the treaty and of any full powers delivered to the depositary;*

(b) *preparing certified copies of the original text and preparing any further text of the treaty in such additional languages as may be required by the treaty and transmitting them to the parties and to the States entitled to become parties to the treaty;*

(c) *receiving any signatures to the treaty and receiving and keeping custody of any instruments, notifications and communications relating to it;*

(d) *examining whether the signature or any instrument, notification or communication relating to the treaty is in due and proper form and, if need be, bringing the matter to the attention of the State in question;*

(e) *informing the parties and the States entitled to become parties to the treaty of acts, notifications and communications relating to the treaty;*

(f) *informing the States entitled to become parties to the treaty when the number of signatures or of instruments of ratification, acceptance, approval or accession required for the entry into force of the treaty has been received or deposited;*

(g) *registering the treaty with the Secretariat of the United Nations;*

(h) *performing the functions specified in other provisions of the present Convention."*

It is not obligatory to appoint a single depository; the Nuclear Test Ban Treaty, 1963, for example, was deposited with more than one depository. Where a state party to a treaty becomes its depository, it assumes a dual role, and its role as a party to the treaty and that as a depository are different; the functions of a depository are of an international character. Often, international organisations are appointed as depositories for the functions of a depository[4].

Article 102 of the UN Charter provides that:

"1. Every treaty and every international agreement entered into by any Member of the United Nations after the present Charter comes into force shall as soon as possible be registered with the Secretariat and published by it.

2. No party to any such treaty or international agreement which has not been registered in accordance with the provisions of paragraph 1 of this Article may invoke that treaty or agreement before any organ of the United Nations."

1.1.16 Détente

In foreign and diplomatic relations, it means relaxation of tension between governments. *Détente* became a fashionable term during the 1970s and 1980s. Although the nature of *détente* is a matter for foreign-policy makers

---

[4] See Articles 76(2) and 77(2) of the Vienna Convention on the Law of Treaties, 1969

to determine, it is worth considering its merits in diplomacy. Whether *détente* can lead to a lasting relaxation of tension is one of the vitally important issues that diplomats should seriously consider.

On the other hand, diplomats must have appropriate skills and experience to achieve relaxation of tension; otherwise, conflicts may take place.

1.1.17 Diplomatic Asylum

Asylum granted to an individual in the premises of a diplomatic mission or in other such premises that are entitled to immunity. The famous case of diplomatic asylum is the *Haya de la Torre* case, otherwise known as *The Asylum* case. In this case, the Colombian embassy in Lima (Peru) offered diplomatic asylum to an alleged Peruvian fugitive on the ground that it was customary for the Latin American countries to grant asylum in the circumstances such as those of *Haya de la Torre*. The government of Colombia failed to produce admissible evidence in support of its contention. The International Court of Justice found in favour of the Peruvian Government. Deposed heads of states often seek asylum of this kind.

1.1.18 Diplomatic Relations

The term *"diplomatic relations"* stands for the inter-state relations which are established and developed through diplomats. Historically, it is a very old concept[5], and diplomatic relations between states started because of the need for mutual co-operation, whether in respect of economic or military matters.

Diplomats represent their sovereigns. They are carriers of foreign policies adopted by the foreign policy experts at the national level. A diplomat's training programme should therefore consist of elements which will train him/her as to how to negotiate with and/or present an argument before a foreign governmental authority, and the attendant manners and etiquette. A diplomat's academic background should allow him or her to be able to comprehend most of the complex international issues, in particular, issues relating to international law, international economics and history. Nationalistic attitudes rigidly held, in disregard of international issues and the need for mutual co-operation, may be regarded as an unhelpful strategy for diplomatic relations, particularly in the contemporary period, when the issue of inter-dependence between states has become particularly important. It is because of the growing need for inter-dependence that states often, as a matter of course, establish diplomatic relations with other states. From this standpoint, one should consider whether the old-fashioned diplomacy, which was not troubled with the issue of cold wars of the nature the contemporary international community has been witnessing, or with the economic issues, are to be strictly

---

[5] Although even in antiquity ambassadors enjoyed special protection and certain privileges, it was not until the 13th century that the first permanent legations made their appearance; see further *Oppenheim's International Law*, vol I, Jennings and Watts (eds), Harlow, Longman (1992) Chapter 10

adhered to. It is essential therefore for a diplomat to be able to deal with many economic, military and other important issues, keeping an eye on the obligations that his/her state has undertaken through international conventions.

Although traditionally, diplomacy has been associated with states, it is now extremely important for diplomats to be familiar with diplomacy at an international level, such as participation at UN conferences at which important resolutions or conventions may be adopted. By the same token, diplomats are required to be familiar with diplomacy at regional levels. This means that they are required to protect their national interests, and also develop principles and policies which would be useful for the entire international community or the members of a regional integration as the case may be. The caution must be entered that regional policies do not conflict with international policies.

Diplomats require a special training when representing their states before the United Nations. They are required to be familiar not only with the aims and obligations of the United Nations, but also its work procedure. Unless, highly qualified with broad-based education and training, diplomats may not be able to fully appreciate its aspirations, and the way his/her country could contribute to its cause.

It would be improper to maintain that the United Nations is not necessarily required to respect the wishes of its Member States. There are two issues about it:

(a) that it is not practicable for the United Nations to respect the wishes of all its Members, although it must try to come to their aid in respect of any legitimate interests; and

(b) that the Member States have through the Charter given the United Nations a mandate; legally speaking, unless the Member States abrogate it or amend it, the usual mandate stands, and on the basis of it, the United Nations has the authority to implement the provisions of the Charter. Again, legally speaking, the United Nations Charter obligations are based on the principle of *pacta sunt servanda* (a treaty constitutes a contract between the parties, and that its terms are binding and must be observed).

In recent years, a gross misunderstanding on the part of many States as to the power-base of the United Nations and its status, has become evident. Under the Charter, a Member State has the right to withdraw from the United Nations, but history provides no evidence to that effect.

Member States should not also disregard their treaty obligations with the United Nations. Foreign policy-makers and diplomats perhaps should review this issue, in an attempt to increase the degree of co-operation between themselves and the United Nations.

There can therefore be diplomacy at different levels: national, regional and international. Regional diplomacy, such as that required at the European Union level, again is a type of diplomacy that requires consideration of protection of interest of both parties, the European Union and its Member States. It requires a special attitude and training of diplomats.

In order to maintain appropriate and effective diplomatic relations, whether with states or with international or inter-governmental organisations, the discipline called *Diplomatic Studies* should be broad-based, multi-faceted, allowing future diplomats not only to understand the complexity of the modern-day international relations but also to develop vision. *Diplomatic Studies,* when narrowly based and narrowly gauged, defeats its entire obligations, and create diplomats accordingly.

1.1.19 Domino Theory

This theory is based on the characteristics of a *"house of cards"*, in which a fall of one card will lead to the fall of the other cards in line. Applying this analogy in the world of diplomacy, it means that there may be a set of circumstances in which the fall of a government may lead to the downfall of a neighbouring government, and a chain of downfalls may take place. In practice, however, in modern time, the domino effect may be difficult to come across.

1.1.20 Envoys

Envoys accredited to the Head of State are not considered to be personal representatives of their sovereign. Thus, they do not enjoy the status of ambassadors; nor can they at all times ask for an audience with Heads of State. Envoys may not, by right, but by courtesy only, bear the title of *"Excellency"*. Envoys do nevertheless render important services on behalf of their States.

1.1.21 Estrada Doctrine

This doctrine relates to the policy of recognising or not recognising a government by other governments. The doctrine is named after the then Mexican Foreign Minister, who, in 1930, supported the policy of continuing diplomatic relations irrespective of revolutionary changes in regimes. The Estrada doctrine did not find the need for any formal acts of recognition of governments; the new regime will be regarded as a legitimate authority without any approval of any other government. But the irony of the Estrada doctrine was that Mexico herself refused for thirty years to recognise Franco's regime in Spain. During the 1930s the Estrada doctrine did not attain any popularity; in fact, it lived a very short life.

Ironically, in 1977 and 1980 the governments of the United States and of the United Kingdom respectively decided to avoid the use of formal recognition of regimes.

1.1.22 Exequatur

This term is derived from the term *"exsequor"* which means *"let him perform"*. Under Article 19 of the Vienna Convention on Consular Relations, a sending or receiving state's laws may require the grant of an *exequatur* to consular officers other than the heads of consular posts. In the absence of such laws and/or regulations, the appointment of these officers is merely notified to the receiving state (Article 24), and unless the latter rejects the appointment, its consent is presumed.

Usually, in order to obtain an *exequatur* it is for the diplomatic envoy of the sending state to submit the commission of the appointed consul to the Minister for Foreign Affairs for notification to the Head of the State. A receiving state may issue the *exequatur* either in a special document or by writing the word *exequatur* across the commission. Heads of consular post are admitted to the exercise of their functions through the grant of the *exequatur* by the receiving state. Where delay takes place in receiving head of the consular post, pending delivery of the *exequatur*, is obtained. Bilateral consular conventions may require a receiving state, which has withdrawn an *exequatur*, to state the reasons for doing so[6].

1.1.23 Extradition

Extradition is the delivery of an accused or a convicted individual to the state where he is accused of, or has been convicted of a crime by the state on whose territory he is present. A request for an extradition of a convicted or an accused person may not be complied with by the requested state if the latter believes that the fugitive may not be entitled to a fair trail on his return. Extraditable offences may be committed *in absentia*, that is, while the fugitive was outside the territorial jurisdiction of the requesting state, for example, when an offence was committed on board ships or aircraft, or in a place which is not under the *de jure* control of the requesting state. Extradition of fugitives is facilitated by means of bilateral treaties between states, although multilateral conventions in this regard exist, for example, the Inter-American Convention on Extradition, 1987; or the Council of Europe Convention on Extradition, 1957. It is also possible for states to have special arrangements in this regard between themselves; for example, between Ireland and the United Kingdom, a wanted person may be arrested in one state and sent to the other on the basis of a warrant issued in the latter state.

Provisions for extradition of fugitives may be made in treaties, which are strictly not confined to extradition matters. Informal extradition practices are also prevalent, whereby a wanted individual may be handed over by the requested authorities to the state which wishes to prosecute him.

The principle of *aut dedere aut judicare* has been adopted in certain of the international conventions, namely, the Genocide Convention, 1948, the Tokyo Convention on Offences and Certain Other Acts Committed on Board Aircraft, 1963, and the Convention on Psychotropic Substances, 1971. According to this principle, in order to represent the general condemnation of the international community certain international conventions adopt the

---

[6] See, for example, the Franco-Italian Consular Convention, 1955, Article 4

practice whereby parties to these conventions would be required either to extradite persons found on their territory to the requesting states concerned, or to try such persons themselves.

Many states have enacted special laws detailing the crimes for which extradition shall be granted, for example, the Extradition Act, 1870 (United Kingdom), subsequently replaced by the Extradition Act 1989. Under this Act, however, Commonwealth countries are treated differently from other countries. This is because in 1966, at a meeting of the Commonwealth Law Ministers, it was decided that Commonwealth extradition arrangements should be based upon reciprocity and substantially uniform legislation containing certain common elements. This meeting formulated a Scheme which would form the basis for legislation in each Commonwealth country (Cmnd 3008). Certain revisions were introduced to this Scheme in 1990[7]. In concluding bilateral extradition treaties it should be considered seriously whether such treaties would run counter to the internal law of the state.

It must be pointed out, however, that subject to treaty obligations, a state has its inherent right to refuse extradition for any crime. On the other hand, international law allows a state to grant extradition for any crime it deems appropriate. Where a state has extradition law, it should ensure that extradition treaties are consistent with that domestic law, and the types of extraditable crimes are included in such treaties accordingly.

"Double criminality" has always been regarded as a major criterion for extradition; under this principle, extradition is only granted in respect of an act which is regarded as a crime under the law of the state which is requested to extradite as well as under the law of the state which demands extradition; the designation of the offence need not be identical – there should be substantial similarity between the offences in both the requesting / demanding and requested state.

Political criminals, persons who have committed offences against religion, for example, are not usually subject to extradition; furthermore, where death penalty may be enforced for a crime, many states usually refuse extradition of the offender[8].

In so far as the general procedure is concerned, no extradition is granted unless asked for by the requesting state; and the formalities stipulated in the treaty concerned and under the extradition laws must be completed. Requests for extradition are usually submitted through diplomatic channels, by giving details of the criminal, the crime he/she has committed, and that a warrant for his/her arrest has already been issued, unless by means of a convention or a treaty requests for extradition through diplomatic channels have been dispensed with (see, for example, the Benelux Convention on Extradition and Judicial Assistance in Penal Matters, 1962). The criminal must be handed over

---

[7] See *Commonwealth Law Bulletin* 16 (1990) at 1036–43

[8] See, for example, Article II of the European Convention on Extradition, 1947, and section 12(2)(b) of the UK Extradition Act, 1989

to the police of the requesting state. Under English law, a wanted person may request the courts to have the lawfulness of his proposed extradition examined. States parties to human rights conventions are required to ensure that the grant of extradition by it in a particular case will not be inconsistent.

The issue of non-extradition of political criminals has currently assumed importance; its origin may be traced in the 19th century. Political criminals may be regarded as an unacceptable term because of the connotations attached to it, as in many instances political asylum seekers are effectively described as political criminals by the state which they have abandoned. Indeed, it is a necessary condition for seeking political asylum.

Customary international law is silent on the issue of whether there is any obligation for a state to extradite or not to extradite a political criminal. Furthermore, there exists the difficulty of defining a *"political crime"*. This difficulty arises from the lack of consensus among states as to what constitutes a political crime, and thus what crimes may be designated as political crimes. In view of this difficulty the definition of a political crime has been left principally to the internal law of each state. In the United Kingdom, the Extradition Act 1989 simply adopted the phrase *"offence ... of a political character"* for extradition purposes. (See also the Fugitive Offenders Act 1967 particularly in regard to the circumstances in which a fugitive may not be returned to his home state). Extradition still seems to be treated by a majority of states as a domestic matter.

In order to limit the meaning of *"political offence"*, international attempts have been made since 1934, initially through the Council of the League of Nations, and gradually through the Genocide Convention, 1948 (Article 7 of the Convention provides that the crime of genocide shall not be considered a political crime for the purpose of avoiding extradition); the Council of Europe Convention on Extradition, 1957 (Article 3 of the Convention prohibits extradition of offences if the offence is regarded as a political one); the Inter-American Convention on Extradition, 1982 (Article 4 of this Convention provides that extradition is to be derived in respect of a political offence), but *"political offence"* has not been defined by the Convention); and the Convention on the Status of Refugees, 1951 (Article 31 of this Convention, which is otherwise known as the Asylum Convention prohibits the return of a refugee to a state or territory where his life or freedom would be threatened because of his race, religion, membership of a particular social group or political beliefs). The relevant international Conventions in this regard are: the Convention for the Suppression of Unlawful Seizure of Aircraft, 1970; the Convention for the Suppression of Unlawful Acts against the Safety of Civil Aviation, 1971; and the European Convention for the Suppression of Terrorism, 1977.

1.1.24 Formal Apology

In the diplomatic world, a formal apology must satisfy certain criteria, namely, a salute to the flag or to the coat of arms of the wronged State or by sending a special emissary bearing apologies. This is a serious matter and should be dealt with to the satisfaction of the wronged State, otherwise future rapport between the two States may be in jeopardy.

1.1.25 Franchise du quartier or jus quarteriorum

This maxim is based on the principle of the inviolability of diplomatic premises in its absolute sense. It was developed at a time when the official residences of envoys were considered to be outside the jurisdiction of the receiving states. On the basis of this notion and practice, an envoy could claim the right to grant asylum, within their residences to any individual who took refuge there. The maxim *franchise du quartier* was opposed by most states, and in the eighteenth century it totally disappeared, except in the Latin American practice.

Nowadays, the issue of the inviolability of diplomatic premises has assumed a very complex dimension, which issue has been discussed in this work in various chapters.

1.1.26 Full Powers

This term is relevant to the treaty-making power of States. The treaty-making power of States is usually exercised by Heads of States or by their governments; and treaties are concluded either as between Heads of States or between governments. It is to be pointed out however that under the contemporary State practice agreements between governmental departments are quite common. Treaty-making power is often exercised by representatives of Heads of States on behalf of the States concerned, but the fact that such representatives have been endowed with full powers must be notified[9]. Full powers stand for the fullest extent of authority conferred on one representative of a State to participate in treaty-making procedures.

Article 7(1)(b) of the Vienna Convention provides that:

> *"(1) A person is considered as representing a State for the purpose of adopting or authenticating the text of a treaty or for the purpose of expressing the consent of the State to be bound by a treaty if: ... (b) it appears from the practice of the States concerned or from other circumstances that their intention was to consider that person as representing the State for such purposes and to dispense with full powers."*

Unless full powers have been officially conferred on the representative(s), the room for controversy may always persist that the representative exceeded his/her powers. Intervention by a representative without full powers, may invalidate a treaty, unless his/her act is subsequently confirmed by the State

---

[9] See Article 7(1)(a) of the Vienna Convention on the Law of Treaties, 1969

concerned. Article 8 of the Vienna Convention on the Law of Treaties provides that:

> *"An act relating to the conclusion of a treaty performed by a person who cannot be considered under article 7 as authorized to represent a State for that purpose is without legal effect unless afterwards confirmed by that State."*

For those of the States that have adopted the *"ratification"* policy, participation of representatives on behalf of their States does not commit their States to a treaty. Therefore, more complex legal problems may arise for a State, which do not follow the *"ratification of treaty"* procedure, but its representative has exceeded its power. The same argument may apply to the instruments which may enter into force on signatures of the representatives of States.

1.1.27 Governments in Exile

A government may be required to be in exile for a limited period in a friendly State while his State is temporarily occupied by invaders or usurpers. The circumstances in its State compel the government to flee to a friendly State until the situation returns to normal, that is, when the occupier or usurpers failed to establish their rebel regime in that State. A government in exile remains as a recognised government. On the other hand, it would be premature to recognise a revolutionary government in exile, because by so doing the recognised government will be effectively de-recognised, which act may not be sustainable in international law. The recognition of the provisional government of Algeria, located in Tunisia, by a number of States, prior to Algeria's attaining independence proved to be controversial in the world of diplomacy and international law.

1.1.28 Hot Pursuit

This term is also used to justify similar action in respect of an individual fleeing from one state to another by land.

The right of hot pursuit is an exception to the exclusiveness of jurisdiction of a flag state over ships on the high seas whereby a vessel of a coastal state may pursue a foreign merchant ship on the high seas if that coastal state authorities have sufficient reason to believe that the ship has violated that state's laws and regulations, whilst in its waters, but now on the high seas. The coastal state's jurisdiction is thus temporarily extended onto the high seas; but the pursuit must commence within the jurisdiction. The United Nations Convention on the Law of the Sea, 1982 (UNCLOS III) provides that the right of hot pursuit may be extended to violations in the exclusive economic zone or on the continental shelf, including safety zones around continental shelf installations.

In order for the pursuit to be lawful, it must have been uninterrupted[10], meaning thereby that the pursuit which commenced within the jurisdiction of

---

[10] See Article 111(1) of the 1982 Convention

the coastal state concerned is now necessary to be continued within the high seas. If the pursuit is broken-off, it may not be resumed. Furthermore, with the entry of the vessel into the territorial sea of the coastal state concerned or of a third state, the right of pursuit must cease. Article 111(3) of the 1982 Convention provides that:

"The right of hot pursuit ceases as soon as the ship pursued enters the territorial sea of own state or of a third state."

In other words, the pursuit may be continued into the exclusive economic zone of a foreign state.

The criteria of hot pursuit under the 1982 Convention have been detailed in Article 111, paragraph 4:

"Hot pursuit is not deemed to have begun unless the pursuing ship has satisfied itself by such practicable means as may be available that the ship pursued or one of its boats or other craft working as a team and using the ship pursued as a mother ship is within the limits of the territorial sea, or as the case may be within the continuous zone or the exclusive economic zone or above the continental shelf. The pursuit may only be commenced after a visual or auditory signal to ship has been given at a distance which enables it to be seen or heard by the foreign ship."

The procedure for a pursuit by an aircraft is similar to that allowed by a government authorised ship, except that the pursuit will be carried out in the airspace. Article 111(b) of the 1982 Convention provides, inter alia, that:

"The aircraft giving the order to stop must itself actively pursue the ship until a ship or another aircraft of the coastal state, summoned by the aircraft, arrives to take over the pursuit, unless the aircraft is itself able to arrest the ship. It does not suffice to justify an arrest outside the territorial sea that the ship was merely signalled by the aircraft as an offender or suspected offender, if it was not both ordered to stop and pursued by the aircraft itself or other aircraft or ships which continue the pursuit without interruption."

Article 111(5) provides that:

"The right of hot pursuit may be exercised only by warships or military aircraft, or other ships or aircraft clearly marked and identifiable as being on government service and authorised to that effect."

1.1.29 Incognito Travelling

When the Head of a State travels incognito – without notifying the other State(s) through which he is travelling, he is known to be travelling *incognito stricto sensu*. However, when the Head of a State stays in a country *incognito* but with the official knowledge of the latter, he receives the usual official formalities and privileges and immunities, as if he was travelling non-incognito.

However, in the former situation described above, he travels as any other foreign individual, although he may, at any time, make his presence known, whereupon he will be entitled to the treatment otherwise due to him.

1.1.30 In Dubio Mitius

Under this principle, where the meaning of a term of a treaty is ambiguous, that meaning of the term which would be less onerous to the party undertaking an obligation, or which would subject a party or the parties to less general restrictions, must be preferred. In its Advisory Opinion on the *Frontier between Turkey and Iraq*[11], the Permanent Court of International Justice confirmed that in choosing between several possible interpretations of a term or phrase, the one which involves the minimum obligations for the parties should be adopted[12]. In *Shoshone Indians v United States*, the United States Supreme Court declined to accept that treaties with Indians must be interpreted and construed favourably to the minority in order to remedy injustices.

1.1.31 Internationally Injurious Acts of Diplomatic Envoys

Accredited diplomats, as representatives of their sovereign, are not supposed to commit any internationally injurious act on the territory of the receiving State. Of course, they are not supposed to commit any offence or injurious act whether recognised internationally or according to any domestic law. However, in the event of an accredited diplomat committing an offence, the sending State is usually held responsible, unless a diplomat has at his/her own volition been involved in a serious criminal act, and the diplomat concerned is usually recalled by the sending State, and apologises to the receiving State. A diplomat involved in such an activity will of course be declared *persona non grata* by the receiving State. This is one of the reasons why the sending State will call back such a diplomat.

1.1.32 Inter-temporal Law

It suggests that a treaty is to be interpreted by reference to the general rules of international law in force at the time of its conclusion. By the same token it maintains that a judicial fact must be evaluated in the light of the contemporary law. It is an accepted rule that the terms of a treaty should be interpreted in accordance with their meaning and the circumstances that prevailed at the time the treaty was concluded[13].

It has been the general view however that in interpreting a treaty, the subsequent development in the relevant field of law may not be disregarded.

---

[11] PCIJ (1925), Series B, No. 12 at 25

[12] See also *Diversion of the Waters of River Meuse* case (1937) PCIJ, Series A/B No. 70 at 70

[13] See *Rights of United States Nationals in Morocco*, ICJ Reports (1952) at 76; *South West Africa* cases (ICJ Reports (1966); and *Aerial Incidents* case, ICJ Reports (1989)

1.1.33 Juges Consuls or Consuls Marchands

It was a common practice in the medieval commercial worlds of France, Italy and Spain, in particular, to appoint fellow merchants by merchants as arbitrators of commercial disputes; these merchants or settlers of disputes were known as *juges consuls* or *consuls marchands*.

1.1.34 Jus Cogens

Article 53 of the Vienna Convention on the Law of Treaties, 1969 describes *jus cogens* as norms:

> "... *accepted and recognized by the international community of States as a whole as a norm from which no derogation is permitted and which can be modified only by a subsequent norm of general international law having the same character.*"

There does not exist any consensus in the international community as to which rules may receive the status of peremptory norms. In its Draft Articles on the Law of Treaties, the Law Commission regarded the prohibition of the use of force as an example of a peremptory norm[14]. Examples of other issues about which peremptory norms have been established are: piracy, genocide, trade in slaves, the observance of human rights, and the principle of self-determination[15]. It is for the international community, particularly by means of international treaties to develop and acknowledge more peremptory norms of international law.

1.1.35 Laissez-passer

A permit (a licence) to travel or to enter an area. Persons enjoying diplomatic status, whether of a temporary or permanent basis, should carry this permit so as not to be disallowed entry by legitimate authorities in a foreign state or institution.

1.1.36 Lateran Treaty of 1929

The Lateran Treaty was concluded between the Holy See and Italy in order to settle the international status of the Holy See. It was by this Treaty that Italy recognised the sovereignty of the Holy See in international law, but at the same time she also recognised the State of the Vatican City under the sovereignty of the Supreme Pontiff. Article 24 of the Lateran Treaty made it clear that the Vatican City shall in all circumstances be regarded as neutral and an inviolable

---

[14] Article 50 of the *Year Book of the International Law Commission* (1966)

[15] See also the *Year Book of the International Law Commission* (1966)

territory. Indeed Article 1 of the Concordat of 1984 re-affirmed that *"the State and the Catholic Church are, each in its own order, independent and sovereign."*

1.1.37 Monroe Doctrine

Named after the message of the US President, James Monroe, to the Congress on 2 December 1823. In his message, the President declared, *inter alia*, that the US while it would disclaim any intervention in wars in Europe, could not, on the other hand, allow European States to extend their political systems to any part of America, and in particular, intervene in the independence of the South American States. The Monroe Doctrine therefore suggested that when a conflict might arise between an American State and a European State, having consequences upon the American continent, the United States would be ready to intervene.

In this connection, one should also refer to the Declaration of the Principles of Solidarity of America which was adopted in Lima, on 24 December 1938, according to which the States of the Americas must be protected from all foreign interventions. Similar ideas were also upheld in a declaration of the Ministers of Foreign Affairs of the American Republics adopted at Havana in July 1940. According to this declaration, any attempt on the part of a non-American State against the integrity of an American State, will be regarded as an act of aggression against all the American States, signatories to the declaration. In line with the Monroe Doctrine, and perhaps, going beyond that, various American States, in the Convention on the Provisional Administration of European Colonies and Possessions in America, declared that any transfer or even attempted transfer of the sovereignty or any interest in or control over colonies of non-American States in the Western Hemisphere would be construed as being against American sentiments and rights of American States to maintain their security and political independence. This attitude and policy culminated in the Act of Chapultepec of 3 March 1945, adopted by the Inter-American Conference on Problems of War and Peace. In an attempt to resist any influence by the international communist movement over any American State, which act would be construed as a threat to the sovereignty and political independence of the American States, the Caracas Declaration of Solidarity was adopted in 1954. On the basis of this Declaration, the Government of Cuba was excluded from the Organisation of American States in 1962.

The Brezhnev Doctrine, on the other hand, was in reality adopted as a counterpart of the Monroe Doctrine, in order to consolidate Soviet domination in Eastern Europe; indeed, the Soviet intervention in Czechoslovakia in 1968 was justified by the invocation of the Brezhnev Doctrine.

1.1.38 Nemo Plus Juris Ad Alium Transferre Potest Quam Ipse Habet

According to this privilege, irrespective of the purposes of the cession of a territory, with or without any compensation, the ceded territory is transferred to the new sovereign with all international obligations attached to that territory. This principle is particularly important when a territory, prior to its being ceded, contracted debts, whether from private sources or from international financial institutions, namely, the International Bank for Reconstruction and Development, which is popularly known as the World Bank.

1.1.39 Notarial Act

In the world of diplomats, it stands for an act of an official, usually a consular officer, who attests and/or validates documents. In many states, foreign documents or credentials, unless notorised, are not accepted for official use or purposes.

1.1.40 Plenipotentiary

Delegates of a country involved with full powers, especially as the envoy of a foreign ruler, exercising absolute power or authority.

1.1.41 Plenipotentiary Conference

A conference for the purpose of drawing up or revisiting an international instrument at which delegates have full powers. An international instrument drawn up or revised at such conferences may not automatically come into force in those states that follow national ratification procedures.

1.1.42 Procès-verbal

Procès-verbal often contains statements *ad verbatim* regarding the correction or amendment of an international treaty. In fact, the *procès-verbal* of any instrument is a very important document for the understanding of the provisions of that instrument, and also for ascertaining the intention of contracting parties to that instrument. A *procès-verbal* is regarded as a primary source of information, and *procès-verbal* of all international treaties or conventions are usually available at the UN archives. In the diplomatic world, *procès-verbal* should be examined by diplomats in order to be able to comment responsibly on any international treaty or convention, including the position of his/her own state.

1.1.43 Plurilingual Treaties

Over the recent years plurilingual treaties have become a common practice; but not all need be authentic texts. Article 33(1) of the Vienna Convention on the Law of Treaties provides that:

> *"When a treaty has been authenticated in two or more languages, the text is equally authoritative in each language, unless the treaty provides or the parties agree that, in the case of divergence, a particular text shall prevail."*

Paragraph (2) of the same Article provides that:

> *"A version of the treaty in a language other than one of those in which the text was authenticated shall be considered an authentic text only if the treaty so provides or the parties so agree."*

According to paragraph (2) of the same Article:

"The terms of the treaty are presumed to have the same meaning in each authentic text."

1.1.44 Protocol

This term may be used in two contexts:

(a) It means formal diplomatic behaviour, and

(b) It also stands for a document that supplements or amends a treaty or an instrument.

It has been a common practice in international relations to renew privileges, such as most-favoured nation treatment in trade, by means of Protocols.

1.1.45 Punctationes

Negotiations on the issues of a future treaty without creating any obligations for the participating states to conclude that treaty.

1.1.46 Rapporteur

The literal meaning of the word is: *"A person who prepares an account of the proceedings of a committee."*[16]

In practice, most conferences engage a *rapporteur* from the participating members. He/she is a person, who summarises the proceedings of a conference/seminar/session. But, he/she may participate in discussions, and pay attention to the particular need for which the conference/seminar/session is held. Usually, a person who is knowledgeable and experienced in the subject matter of the discussion is highly acknowledged. It is possible for a conference/seminar/session to appoint more than one rapporteur. A rapporteur must submit his / her Report to the institution that appointed him/her.

1.1.47 Rapproachment

The literal meaning of the word is:

"A comity or bringing together an establishment of harmonious relations."[17]

In the world of diplomacy, it stands for a renewal of improved relations between states. Relations between states often become unpredictable because of many unforeseen factors. Rapproachment therefore becomes necessary between states as a gesture of confirming relations between them.

---

[16] *The Oxford English Dictionary*, Oxford, Clarendon Press (1989) Vol XIII at 191

[17] ibid., Vol XIII at 191

1.1.48 Recognition *de facto*

It means recognition as a matter of fact. Such recognitions are different from *de jure* recognitions.

1.1.49 Recognition *de jure*

It means recognition on a legal basis. It is different from recognition *de facto*. Recognition *de facto* is not a pre-requisite for recognition *de jure*.

1.1.50 Regents

It has been in practice in monarchies that where a monarch is incapable of exercising his powers, whether owing to illness, absence abroad or otherwise, to appoint a regent to exercise the monarch's powers on his behalf. A regent is entitled to all privileges due to a monarch, as he is in effect a replacement of the monarch with a special position. During the regency however the monarch remains the sovereign. A regent is not a sovereign, but in international practice, he will be treated as the sovereign and/or the head of the state. It is a special institution recognised by the international community.

1.1.51 Res Extra Commercium

This is a Roman law concept, according to which the high seas can never be under the sovereignty of any state, nor may any state have the right to acquire any part of the high seas. However, the high seas is regarded as an object of the law of nations, that it is to be regulated by the relevant rules of international law.

1.1.52 Reservations

Article 2(1)(d) of the Vienna Convention on the Law of Treaties, 1969 defines a reservation as:

> *"... a unilateral statement, however phrased or named, made by a State, when signing, ratifying, accepting, approving or acceding to a treaty, whereby it purports to exclude or to modify the legal effect of certain provisions of the treaty in their application to that State..."*

Article 23(1) states that:

> *"A reservation, an express acceptance of a reservation and an objection to a reservation must be formulated in writing and communicated to the contracting States and other States entitled to become parties to the treaty."*

A contracting party (a state) may therefore enter a reservation at any of the following stages: signature, ratification, acceptance, approval or accession to a treaty. Secondly, the words used for a reservation must *"purport to exclude or to modify the legal effect of certain provisions of a treaty in their application to that state."* Reservations after ratification or accession may be possible only with the consent of all other parties to a treaty. An articulate drafting of reservations is important, the use of generic terms often makes reservations subject to legal interpretation. Reservations are interpreted in accordance with international law[18].

Reservations to bilateral treaties are almost meaningless and have proved to be unworkable, as in the event of their not being accepted by the other party the treaty will lose its purpose. Reservations to multilateral treaties are quite common, but again, reservations as to fundamental issues might not receive the consent of many other parties to such a treaty. In fact, in its Advisory Opinion *Reservations to the Convention on the Prevention and Punishment of the Crime of Genocide*[19] the International Court of Justice maintained that under customary rules of international law, reservations are not permissible in all circumstances. In this connection one should refer to Articles 19 and 21 of the Vienna Convention on the Law of Treaties, 1969.

Article 19

"*A State may, when signing, ratifying, accepting, approving or acceding to a treaty, formulate a reservation unless:*

 (a) the reservation is prohibited by the treaty;
 (b) the treaty provides that only specified reservations, which do not include the reservation in question, may be made; or
 (c) in cases not falling under sub-paragraphs (a) and (b), the reservation is incompatible with the object and purpose of the treaty."

Article 21

 (1) "*A reservation established with regard to another party in accordance with articles 19, 20 and 23:*
   (a) modifies for the reserving State in its relations with that other party the provisions of the treaty to which the reservation relates to the extent of the reservation; and
   (b) modifies those provisions to the same extent for that other party in its relations with the reserving State.
 (2) The reservation does not modify the provisions of the treaty for the other parties to the treaty inter se.
 (3) When a State objecting to a reservation has not opposed the entry into force of the treaty between itself and the reserving State, the provisions to which the reservation relates do not apply as between the two States to the extent of the reservation."

Reservations incompatible with the object and purpose of the treaty are impermissible; from a practical standpoint, no other parties would accept such reservations. The legal effect of a reservation is that through a reservation a

---

[18] See the Advisory Opinion of the International Court of Justice in *Restrictions to the Death Penalty* (1983) 70 International Law Reports, 449, 470–471

[19] *ICJ Reports* (1951) at 15

party to a treaty modifies the terms of the treaty unilaterally for itself; whether this practice, which is based on the sovereignty of contracting parties, is tenable or not is a matter for the international community to consider. In the *Genocide Convention* case the International Court of Justice stated that if a party should consider a reservation made by another party incompatible with the object and purposes of the Convention, the former can regard the latter as a non-party to the Convention.

A reservation may be withdrawn at any time but all parties to the treaty must be notified of the withdrawal in writing.

1.1.53 Right of Expatriation

The right of expatriation is the right of an individual who has already acquired or is eligible for acquiring a new nationality, to renounce the nationality of the state of his origin. State practice on this matter is varied. The United Kingdom recognised the right in 1870. Many states still allow the exercise of this right on condition of compliance with various countries, including the fulfilment of the duties of military service. Article 15(2) of the Universal Declaration of Human Rights provides that no one shall be denied the right to change his nationality; but the right of expatriation has not yet formed part of the customary rules of international law.

1.1.54 Servitudes

International law recognises certain rights which are not contractual in their nature, but are valid against the whole world (right *erga omnes*), and these rights which run with the land obligate successors and the rights of beneficiaries may not be taken away. The leading cases on this issue are: *North Atlantic Fisheries Arbitration,* 1910[20]; the *Aaland Islands,* 1920[21]; the *Right of Passage over Indian Territory,* 1960[22]. Although in the *North Atlantic Fisheries Arbitration,* the United States claimed servitude over the territory, the Tribunal confirmed that Britain had given the United States only an *"economic right"*, which would not lead to servitude. In the *Aaland Islands* case, the issue of the servitude was considered by an International Commission of Jurists, which Commission cast some doubt on whether there existed any true international servitudes, although it did recognise that the European Powers had on many occasions attempted to create true objection law, implying that an objective legal regime may produce the same legal effects as servitudes. The Commission did hold that the Treaty of 1856 between Great Britain, France and Russia for permanent demilitarisation of the Aaland Islands created a special international status for the Aaland Islands, which, until it was replaced, every interested state had the legitimate right to insist upon.

---

[20] Scott, *Hague Court Reports,* 141

[21] League of Nations, *Official Journal,* Special Supp. No. 3 at 3

[22] *ICJ Reports,* at 6

In the *Right of Passage over Indian Territory* case, Portugal claimed a right of passage over Indian territory for the purposes of exercising Portuguese sovereignty over its enclaves – Dadra and Nagar Haveli. According to the International Court of Justice, during the British rule in India, a right of passage for the Portuguese authorities was established by constant and uniform practices, and that right could not be affected by the change of regime which occurred after India attained her independence.

Servitudes may be extinguished by agreement between the states concerned or perhaps by renunciation of the privilege, expressly or tacitly. Tacit renunciation of servitude, or renunciation by amalgamation or merger of the two states' territories is possible.[23]

Transit rights are often subject to special agreements; and this issue is particularly important in respect of land-locked states' access to and from the sea[24]. The most relevant article is Article 125 of the Convention, according to which land-locked states *"shall have the right of access to and from the sea for the purpose of exercising the rights provided for in this Convention, including those relating to the freedom of the high seas and the common heritage of mankind"*, but the terms and conditions of these rights will be determined by means of either bilateral or sub-regional or regional agreements.

1.1.55 Territorial Asylum

The term *"asylum"* means: *"A sanctuary or inviolable place of refuge and protection of criminals and debtors, from which they cannot be forcibly removed without sacrilege."*[25]

The *"territorial asylum"* is often misleading in that, political asylum is usually offered by the authorities of another state (territory). The asylee seeks a right to reside in a territory other than his/her own. The more appropriate term seems to be *"political asylum"* as under the Asylum Convention, a person may seek asylum on the ground of political persecution by the state authorities in which he/she currently lives. *"Persecution"* and *"threat to life"* have always been treated as the two main factors in dealing with the application from a prospective asylee. Parties to the Convention are required to deal with an application for asylum bearing in mind their obligations under the Convention.

Apart from political asylum, in international practice, examples of asylum seekers in religious entities such as the Vatican or temples, churches, mosques etc. are available, albeit, rather rarely.

The Asylum Convention does not prohibit a state to give a more liberal interpretation to a term such as *"persecution"*, *"threat to life"* than what was intended by the drafters of the Convention. What must be ensured is that a contracting state does not give a narrower interpretation to a term than was

---

[23] On the issue of tacit renunciation, see *The Zones of Upper Savoy and the District of Gix* (1932) PCIJ, Series A/B No. 46

[24] See further Part X of the UN Convention on the Law of the Sea and Freedom of Transit

[25] *The Oxford English Dictionary*, Vol 1, Clarendon Press, Oxford (1980) at 736

intended. A state has the right to exercise its political and humanitarian discretion in granting political asylum to an asylum seeker.

Problems do however arise when a person, for technical reasons, seeks asylum in a religious institution, instead of seeking political asylum. The case of President Noriega of Panama is in point. Diplomacy comes to its extreme point when a government, on an alleged ground of criminality of that person, brings pressure upon the religious institution to hand over to that government.

It is however doubtful whether in this world of changing diplomacy, asylum offered by a religious institution will necessarily receive the support of the government in which the religious institution is located. In other words, in the final analysis, it is political asylum that matters and legitimises the asylee's legal position. A religious institution is devoid of political and legislative authority (except matters over which ecclesiastical law may apply); therefore, asylum offered by a religious institution, if found sustainable under the political system, satisfying the national criteria of the grant of asylum, must be approved and legitimised by the national authority concerned.

1.1.56 Travaux Préparatoires

These are the records of discussion/negotiation prior to concluding a treaty or minutes of meeting (usually plenary) and of conferences. Information contained in *travaux préparatoires* are extremely useful in the understanding of a treaty or convention provisions, and the historical reasons thereto. The intention of the parties, and the circumstances which led the drafters to draft a document with particular provisions, becomes evident when reading the *travaux préparatoires* preceding the drafting of that document.

These are regarded as primary sources of information, and the World Court (both the Permanent Court of International Justice and the International Court of Justice) have affirmed the usefulness of referring to *travaux préparatoires*[26].

In the *Territorial Jurisdiction of the International Commission of the River Oder*[27] the Permanent Court of International Justice refused to refer to the *travaux préparatoires* on the ground that the states parties to the proceedings did not participate in the negotiations of the relevant treaty, but in the *Aerial Incident* case[28], the International Court of Justice referred to the *travaux préparatoires* of the Statute of the Court even though none of the parties to the proceedings had participated in the negotiations of the Statue.

Despite such anomalies in the practice of the World Court, which seems to be justified in the circumstances of the cases referred to above, it is maintained

---

[26] See, for example, *Treatment of Polish Nationals in Danzig* case, PCIJ (1932), Series A/B, No. 44, pp 33–35; the *Genocide* case, ICJ Reports (1951), p 15; *South West Africa* cases, ICJ Reports (1961) p 43; and *North Sea Continental Shelf* cases (1969) – in the last mentioned case, particularly the preparatory work by the International Law Commission

[27] PCIJ – (1929) Series A, No. 23

[28] ICJ Reports (1959) at 127

that the importance of *travaux préparatoires* in treaty interpretation or interpretation of any document may not be over-emphasised.

1.1.57 Uti Possidetis Juris

In order to avoid boundary disputes between themselves, this doctrine was adopted by the Spanish-American states following their independence respectively in 1810 and 1822 for the former Spanish colonies in South America and Central America. This doctrine maintains that the boundaries must remain as they were at the declaration of independence. This is because in South America and Central America uncertainty persisted as to many of the colonial boundaries. The *uti possidetis* doctrine is based on the idea that there was no land territory at the time of their independence which would be regarded as *terra nullius*[29]; in other words, each parcel of the available land belonged to somebody.

This principle was also adapted to Africa by the Cairo Resolution of the Organisation of African States of 21 July 1964[30].

In *Burkina Faso v Mali*[31] a Chamber of the International Court of Justice, in effect, subordinated the self-determination to the *uti possidetis* principle in that according to it, in order to maintain stability, abstract legal title would be preferred to the right of self-determination or effective possession. Any abstract application of this principle would also mean that a victor who gained a territory by force, would be allowed to retain it, and that acquisition of territories by force would be deemed legal.

1.1.58 Vatican City in International Law

The Vatican City has a territory of about 100 acres and its population is about 1,000 inhabitants, who are almost exclusively employees of the Holy See. Controversy still exists as to whether sovereignty is vested in the Holy See or the Vatican City; in other words, whether they are united or two persons. It is generally believed that the Lateran Treaty created the State of the Vatican City, with the Holy See as its Head; but, in practice, this belief is not shared by all States.

Many States have diplomatic relations with the Vatican City, and the latter participates in major international conferences concerned with matters of international concern. It does not maintain any national interest; thus its approach to matters of international law becomes truly neutral in order to promote the interests of the international community.

---

[29] This concept was discussed by the International Court of Justice in the *Western Sahara* case, ICJ (1975).

[30] *International Organisation* (1967) at 102-127; See also the Report of the International Court of Justice in *Burkina Faso and Meli Frontier* Dispute, ICJ Reports (1986) at 554

[31] (1986)

1.1.59 Veto

The literal meaning of the words is *"I forbid"*. This term is most popularly used at meetings at the point of voting. A veto stands for a *"negative vote"*. Where unanimity rule is the prescribed method of decision-making, a diplomat (representing his/her government) should take prior instruction from his/her foreign office as to how he/she should vote on a particular issue. Usually, a government may decide to cast a veto if in the national interest, an affirmative vote may not be cast. Reasons for casting a veto can be multifarious: protection of the national interest; support for an ally or opposition to a policy if it is a not-so-friendly or enemy country. The right to veto has been given to the Permanent Members of the Security Council of the UN[32].

1.1.60 Volte face

An abrupt or a complete reversal of the previous policy.

1.1.61 Warships in Foreign Waters

A warship has in international law a special status, as it is regarded as a state organ, it benefits from that state's privileges, sovereign immunity from the jurisdiction of other states. Therefore, everybody on board a warship, and their belongings, remain under the jurisdiction of the flag-state, that is the state the flag of which it flies. This is to be even when a warship may be staying in foreign waters. The grant of privileges and immunities to warships became universally recognised during the 19th century. The principle of granting privileges and immunities to warships is so sacrosanct that without the permission of the commander no official of the coastal state would be allowed to board the vessel. As it is regarded as the land territory of the flag state, crimes, if any, committed by any person in the service of the warship will be dealt with by the flag state, although the coastal state authorities may request the surrender of the alleged offender. Unless the alleged offender is surrendered to the coastal state, the latter cannot assume jurisdiction. If a national of the coastal state concerned commits a crime while on board a warship, he/she may be taken to the home country of the ship, but there is no reason why the state of which he is a national may not propose to try the alleged offender.

The commander and crew of a warship, whilst ashore, are under the jurisdiction of the coastal state, but a distinction is made between a stay on land in the service of the warship and that for other purposes. However, even if they commit crimes ashore, they remain under the exclusive jurisdiction of the home state; indeed the coastal state has a duty to surrender them to the warship at once. But, this principle does not apply when they may be ashore for purposes other than the service of the warship. The coastal state will have exclusive jurisdiction over any crime committed by such persons whilst ashore.

---

[32] See Article 27(3)

The distinction between a government vessel engaged in commercial purposes and a warship is important to maintain. The privileges and immunities discussed above are relevant only to warships and not to government vessels engaged in commercial activities. In this connection one may like to consider the relevant provisions of the United Nations Convention on the Law of the Sea, 1982[33].

It should be pointed out however that warships are nevertheless required to comply with the port regulations of coastal states. Failure to comply with these regulations may lead to the expulsion of the vessel by the coastal state[34].

1.2 CONCLUSIONS

As stated in the Introduction to this Chapter, the list of the terms essential for the world of diplomacy can never be complete. Furthermore, the diplomatic world may provide different interpretations to many of these terms. Bearing this in mind, an attempt has been made to provide the most acceptable definitions of the terms based on practice and scholastic opinions.

It is expected however that these definitions would be of some assistance to practising diplomats. Diplomacy should be regarded as a profession, and familiarity with these terms should help them achieve professionalism.

---

[33] As to the right of innocent passage through the territorial sea, Articles 29-32; jurisdictional immunity, Articles 32, 95 and 96; seizure of pirates, Article 107; and hot pursuit, Article 111(5)

[34] See Articles 30 and 31 of the United Nations Convention of the Law of the Sea (1982)

CHAPTER 2

A Brief Account of the Historical Growth and Development of Diplomatic Relations

2.1 INTRODUCTION

"Diplomatic Relations" is another name for State-to-State relations, initiated and conducted by diplomats on behalf of their sovereigns. Of course, in the contemporary world, interaction with international and inter-governmental institutions is also regarded as a diplomatic activity. The concept of territorial sovereignty originated long time ago[1], but the practice of interacting with rulers by rulers primarily for the purpose of developing friendly relations and security of trade between friendly rulers preceded the concept of territorial sovereignty. According to *Oppenheim's International Law* (vol I) legation for the purposes of negotiating between different States is as old as history[2]. Records confirm that diplomatic relations between the Greek city-States even for limited purposes existed. For example, in the *Iliad,* Homer wrote of the embassy of Menelaus and Odysseus to Troy for the purposes of securing the release of Helen[3]. Nicolson's writings suggest that the Romans deserve similar credit in initiating and operating diplomatic relations, but neither Greeks nor the Romans developed an identifiable framework for diplomatic relations[4]. *Oppenheim's International Law* further maintains that the Italian republics, and Venice in particular, stationed representatives at one another's capitals for the better negotiation of their international affairs; but it was not until the 13th century that the first permanent negotiators made their

---

[1] See Article 1 of the Montevideo Convention, 1933; see also *Island of Dalwas Arbitration* (1928), *Reports of International Arbitral Awards,* vol 2 at 829, and J Crawford, "The Criteria for Statehood in International Law", *The British Year Book of International Law (1976–77)* at 99

[2] *Oppenheim's International Law*, Vol. I, Jennings and Watts (eds), Harlow, Longman (1993) at 1053

[3] Homer, The Iliad, ii, 210; see also J C Barker, *The Abuse of Diplomatic Privileges and Immunities: A Necessary Evil?*, Aldershot, Dartmouth (1992) 15

[4] H Nicolson, *Diplomacy*, Oxford, Oxford University Press (1949); see also H Nicolson, *The Evolution of Diplomatic Method*, Constable & Co Ltd (1954); Coleman Phillipson, *The International Law and Custom of Ancient Greece and Rome*, London, Macmillan & Co Ltd (1911); D J Hill, *A History of Diplomacy in the International Development of Europe*, London, Green & Co (1905); and E Young, "The Development of the Law of Diplomatic Relations", 40 *British Year Book of International Law* (1964) 141

appearance[5]. In the 15th century, the Italian republics began to keep permanent representatives in England, France, Germany and Spain, and as from the end of the same century these countries kept permanent legations at one another's courts. However, it was not until the second half of the seventeenth century that permanent legations became a general institution[6]. This chapter provides a brief account of the historical growth and development of diplomatic relations.

2.2 A BRIEF ACCOUNT OF HISTORICAL GROWTH AND DEVELOPMENT OF DIPLOMATIC RELATIONS

History suggests that diplomatic relations during the Roman times were regulated by an institution known as the College of Fetials (whose practice gave rise to the *jus fetiale*). On the issue of the importance of the College of Fetials, two opposable views exist. Whereas Hill saw it as a form of diplomatic activity in Rome, including the task of negotiation of whatever matter on behalf of the Roman people, according to Nicolson, it was simply performing what may be described as external relations activity, which are usually performed by the modern day Foreign Offices. Whatever from an historical perspective might be the status and functions of the College of Fetials, the fact remains that Rome was familiar with diplomacy, albeit without any identifiable framework for it[7].

Most historians attributed professional diplomacy to the Byzantine Empire particularly because in conflict resolution between States it employed diplomacy rather than settling them by warfare[8]. The Byzantines also established embassies in foreign countries. They also set up what is now known as standard Foreign Ministries to deal with external affairs on behalf of a country and dispatch of embassies abroad. It is believed that what is known as the *"art of diplomacy"* originated during the Byzantine period[9]. By the 12th century however the Byzantine Empire was conquered by the Ottoman Empire; but the technique of diplomacy survived, albeit, compared to the modern method, in perhaps a little unsophisticated version.

The Byzantine time seems to have established the qualities and characteristics a diplomat should possess – illustrious men, they must be men of learning; and they must be sagacious[10]. This perspective of the qualities and

---

[5] *Oppenheim's International Law*, vol 1, op. cit., at 1053; for some early developments in India and the East Indies, see C Alexandrowicz, *An Introduction to the History of the Law of Nations in the East Indies* (1967)

[6] This information is drawn from *Oppenheim's International Law*, vol. 1, op. cit., at 1053–1054

[7] See further J C Barker, op. cit. at 16–17; see also Hill, vol. 1 op. cit., and Nicolson, *The Evolution of Diplomatic Method*, op. cit., at 15

[8] F L Ganshoff, *The Middle Ages: A History of International Relations*, London, Harper & Row (English Translation) (1970) at 38

[9] See further H Nicolson, *Diplomacy*, op. cit. at 10

[10] See further D J Hill, op. cit., vol I at 209

characteristics of a diplomat still seems to persist. The Venetians, in particular, pursued the diplomatic techniques developed by the Byzantines, and refined them. It was the Venetians who developed the system of preserving records of inter-State relations, and kept their embassies abroad informed of all local and foreign developments. By the 15th century, all the principal States of Italy had established diplomatic relations with one another[11], but not missions on a permanent basis[12]. It was Hill who pointed out how the perception of diplomatic relations changed when the major European Powers intervened into Italy, but at the same time spread the Italian method of diplomacy.

By the 16th century a huge surge of diplomatic activity within Europe became evident. There grew a realisation that it is not by war but by diplomatic means that friendly relations between States may be achieved. In order to consolidate the diplomatic practice, and to emphasise its importance, many works were published, of which mention should be made of:

(a) Gentili's *De Legationibus Libri Tres* (1585);

(b) Hotman's *L'Ambassadeur* (1603);

(c) Grotius' *De Jure Belli ac Pacis* (1625);

(d) Cornelius van Bynkershoek's *De Foro Legatorum* (1721); and

(e) Vattel's *Le Droit Des Gens* (1758).

History also suggests that it was during the reign of Louis XIV in France that the importance of creating and maintaining friendly foreign relations was realised; indeed, the world of diplomacy during the 17th and 18th centuries was dominated by France. It was Richelieu who advocated that foreign relations must come under the control of a single identifiable governmental body – eventually the diplomatic method of France became the model for all Europe[13]. Indeed, the French language came to be regarded as the language of diplomacy, although the perception seems to have changed later in favour of the English language[14].

Whatever may be the cause of the development of the diplomatic relations during the early days, it may be stated that three issues attained prominence in the early diplomacy: (a) the illustrious character of a diplomat; (b) his power to negotiate based on his knowledge in languages; and (c) the importance of confidentiality in the diplomacy.

One of the most important documents that purported to regulate diplomatic relations was Annex XVIII to the Acts of the Congress of Vienna in 1815. By

---

[11] H Nicolson, *The Evolution of Diplomatic Method*, op. cit., at 33

[12] See further, D J Hill, op. cit., vol II at 309

[13] See further H Nicolson, *The Evolution of Diplomatic Method*, op. cit., at 62

[14] See further *Oppenheim's International Law*, vol I, at 1054–1055

this instrument ambassadors or officers of equitable rank, ministers and chargés d'affaires were established. This instrument aimed at establishing a uniform system of receiving diplomats from sending States, and to avoid bias in appointing diplomats.

The real transformation from the old to the new diplomacy took place in the early 20th century[15]. However, one should not turn a blind eye to the development that took place in the world of diplomacy during the 19th century, which was primarily occasioned by the improvement in the communications system. Of course, the 19th century witnessed the height of colonisation, and the strength of the Concert of Europe which represented a shared goal between the five Great Powers and the domination over the lesser powers and less civilised communities. The Concert also established that dealings between themselves must be based on good faith, standards of dignity and humanity[16]. In fact, these factors are important for an ideal form of diplomacy between States. Thus, it may be concluded that during the colonial period diplomacy stood for diplomacy between the colonial powers and other powerful non-colonial powers. But, the act of diplomacy was not unknown to Asia, in particular China and India.

During the 19th century (1895) the first codification of diplomatic law was attempted by the Institute of International Law when it adopted the Regulation of Cambridge, but was subsequently revised in 1929. It was during the 19th century again that export trade between States necessitated them to establish embassies and consular posts between the political and economic powers. This does not mean however that the tenets of diplomacy developed by writers such as Bynkershoek, Grotius or Vattel were disregarded; only certain practical aspects of diplomacy, namely the duties of protocol departments in Foreign Offices and those of consuls were more consolidated. It could be maintained that whereas by the 19th century the basic rules of inter-State diplomacy were clearly identified, it was during the 20th century that a much more sophisticated version of diplomacy was developed primarily by means of a variety of instruments culminating in the Vienna Convention on Diplomatic Relations, 1961.

The nature of growth and development of diplomacy during the 20th century may be examined with reference to: (a) the pre-UN period; and (b) the post-UN period. The pre-UN period would include both the First World War and the establishment of the League of Nations, which ceased to exist in 1946.

From the standpoint of this work, it may be stated that during the First World War, obviously, there did not occur any progressive development of diplomacy, until the Peace Treaties (otherwise known as the Treaty of

---

[15] See generally, H Nicolson, *Diplomacy*, op. cit., Chapters II and IV, and by the same author, *The Evolution of Diplomatic Method*, op. cit., Chapter IV; and Do Nascimento e Silva, *Diplomacy in International Law*, Leiden, Sijthoff (1972).

[16] See further H Nicolson, *Diplomacy*, op. cit., at 37

Versailles) were concluded in 1919. But that was primarily what may be described as *"a transitional diplomacy"* from war to peace. It contained a large number of issues, whether political, war-related or otherwise. It is worth pointing out that the aim of the League of Nations was not to abolish warfares, but to humanise them.

The only provision that was included in the Covenant of the League representing its activities in non-political issues was paragraph (e) of Article 23 which provided that:

". . . the Members of the League:

. . . will make provision to secure and maintain freedom of communications and of transit and equitable treatment for the commerce of all Members of the League. In this connection, the special necessities of the regions devastated during the war of 1914-1918 shall be borne in mind; . . ."

During the League period inter-State and international diplomacy were of a limited nature, and concentrated mostly on issues of warfare; thus economic diplomacy or diplomacy for international development, for example, was not on the agenda of the League diplomacy. In fact, in a way, the League period reached the height of international war diplomacy. The Treaty of Versailles made an attempt to bring peace, but the League could not prevent the Second World War from taking place. In other words, peace-making diplomacy generally failed during the League period.

The UN era ushered a new vista for international diplomacy. Its objectives are significantly different from those of the League of Nations. It became an institution specifically for peace-making through socio-economic development. Issues such as human rights, de-colonisation, international economic co-operation, among others, received attention. Diplomats are required to have a multi-dimensional knowledge of international issues. Whether the UN has been successful in implementing its objectives should be assessed by referring to the attitudes of its Member States towards a universal organisation, in addition to the nature of diplomacy diplomats play at that forum.

It is to be emphasised that the contemporary diplomacy and techniques of diplomacy are significantly different from those of the 19th and 20th centuries.

Contemporary diplomacy is multi-dimensional, rights-based, and need not be power-based. It is a discipline which must be concerned with national, regional and international interests. A contemporary diplomat is thus required to possess a thorough knowledge in several disciplines, namely, geography, history, economic relations, peace-making, negotiating techniques, international law, international relations and conflict avoidance. By the same token, a contemporary diplomat must be forward-looking, amiable, tolerant, and a person of cross-cultural understanding.

2.3 CONCLUSIONS

It is worth pointing out that during the UN period the two Vienna Conventions, namely, the Vienna Convention on Diplomatic Relations, 1961 and the Vienna Convention on Consular Relations, 1963 were concluded. They do not establish anything new about diplomatic missions or diplomats or consuls etc; they simply codify the practice developed in the world of diplomacy and consular relations over the centuries. These two instruments seem to be adequate enough even to deal with the new situations such that arose in the US-Iran case or Libyan Bureau incident in London. These two instruments have been supplemented by contemporary diplomacy which entails diplomacy at international fora; thus diplomats are required to be familiar with the procedures at international institutions. Finally, modern day diplomacy is diplomacy for peace-making and not for peace-keeping.

CHAPTER 3

Sovereignty

3.1 INTRODUCTION

Sovereignty is a fundamental principle of public international law. International relations are established by and between sovereign States, and yet it is the sovereign States which can terminate such relations. Diplomatic and consular relations are established by means of bilateral treaties, thus, only sovereign States can be parties to such treaties. It is these treaties that form the basis for diplomatic and consular relations as they also determine the scope of their relations. The Vienna Convention on Diplomatic Relations or the Vienna Convention on Consular Relations come into play after diplomatic and/or consular relations have been established between two sovereign States. The diplomatic relationship with The Holy See is somewhat different from the usual relationship that is established between two States in that The Holy See is not engaged in the kind of diplomatic relations which may be developed between two States.

The purpose of this Chapter is not to discuss the principle of sovereignty in detail, but to relate its various dimensions to diplomacy. Thus, the intention is not to enter into controversial academic theories on Sovereignty, but to relate the functions, uses and abuses of sovereignty to diplomacy.

3.2 MEANING AND CHARACTERISTICS OF SOVEREIGNTY

The term *"sovereignty"* means *"omnipotence"* – all powerful. It can do or undo anything it likes within its territorial jurisdiction. It is the law-maker, a democratic sovereign will justify why a particular legislation is necessary, a non-democratic sovereign need not do so. A sovereign's authority extends to include its unchallenging power over domestic matters, including fiscal matters. It controls its territorial waters, and its airspace. It has the discretion to decide with whom it would establish diplomatic relations; or cease these relations. Foreign firms or individuals may be restrained from or encouraged to enter into its territory. It has total control over its foreign policy and trade policy.

A sovereign can do anything within its territorial jurisdiction in the national interest, and the genuineness of it may not be questioned. In *Luther v Sagor*, the Russian Soviet Federative Socialist Republic passed a decree in June 1918, declaring all mechanical sawmills of a certain capital value and all woodworking establishments belonging to private or limited companies to be owned by the Republic. In 1919, the plaintiff's mill or factory in Russia seized by the agents of the Republic, purported to sell a quantity of the stock so seized to the defendants, who imported it into England. His Majesty's Government recognised the Soviet Government as the *de facto* Government of Russia. The plaintiffs brought an action for a declaration that they were entitled to the wood. The Court of Appeal held that:

> "... *the Government of this country had recognised the Soviet Government as the* de facto *Government of Russia ... before the decree of June 1918; that therefore the validity of that decree and the sale of the wood to the defendants could not be impugned, and that the defendants were therefore entitled to judgment.*"[1]

Warrington LJ stated, inter alia, that:

> "*It is well settled that the validity of the acts of an independent sovereign government in relation to property and persons within its jurisdiction cannot be questioned in the Courts of their country.*"[2]

A sovereign is not amenable to any other sovereign; the principle being that all sovereigns are equal. From this standpoint, there is no difference between a small State and a large State. Indeed, in the General Assembly of the United Nations, each sovereign Member has one vote[3]. However, in respect of commercial matters in which a State or its departments may be involved, immunities from a foreign court's jurisdiction will have to be waived in many jurisdictions. Take, for example, the British and US practices in this regard.

§1330, section 4 of the US Federal Sovereign Immunities Act, 1976 provides that:

(a) A Foreign state shall not be immune from the jurisdiction of courts of the United States or of the States in any case

- *(1) in which the foreign state has waived its immunity either explicitly or by implication, notwithstanding any withdrawal of the waiver which the foreign state may purport to effect except in accordance with the terms of the waiver;*

- *(2) in which the action is based upon a commercial activity carried on in the United States by the foreign state; or upon an act performed in the United States in connection with a commercial activity of the foreign state elsewhere; or upon an act outside the territory of the United States in connection with a commercial activity of the foreign state elsewhere and that act causes a direct effect in the United States;*

---

[1] [1921] 3 KB 532

[2] op. cit., at 548

[3] See Article 2(1) of the UN Charter. The principle of Sovereign equality however runs counter to the Monroe doctrine.

>
> (3) in which rights in property taken in violation of international law are in issue and that property or any property exchanged for such property is present in the United States in connection with a commercial activity carried on in the United States by the foreign state; or that property or any property exchanged for such property is owned or operated by an agency or instrumentality of the foreign state and that agency or instrumentality is engaged in a commercial activity in the United States;
>
> (4) in which rights in property in the United States acquired by succession or gift or rights in immovable property situated in the United States are in issue;
>
> (5) not otherwise encompassed in paragraph (2) above, in which money damages are sought against a foreign state for personal injury or death, or damage to or loss of property, occurring in the United States and caused by the tortious act or omission of that foreign state or of any official or employee of that foreign state while acting within the scope of his office or employment; except this paragraph shall not apply to
>
> > (A) any claim based upon the exercise or performance or the failure to exercise or perform a discretionary function regardless of whether the discretion be abused, or
> >
> > (B) any claim arising out of malicious prosecution, abuse of process, libel, slander, misrepresentation, deceit, or interference with contract rights ...
>
> (b) A foreign state shall not be immune from the jurisdiction of the courts of the United States in any case in which a suit in admiralty is brought to enforce a maritime lien against a vessel or cargo of the foreign state, which maritime lien is based upon a commercial activity of the foreign state."

Section 2 of the State Immunity Act, 1978 (England) provides that:

> (1) A State is not immune as respects proceedings in respect of which it has submitted to the jurisdiction of the courts of the United Kingdom.
>
> (2) A State may submit after the dispute giving rise to the proceedings has arisen or by a prior written agreement; but a provision in any agreement that it is to be governed by the law of the United Kingdom is not to be regarded as a submission.
>
> (3) A State is deemed to have submitted
>
> > (a) if it has instituted the proceedings; or
> > (b) subject to subsections (4) and (5) below, if it has intervened or taken any step in the proceedings.

(4) Subsection (3)(b) above does not apply to intervention or any step taken for the purpose only of

(a) claiming immunity; or

(b) asserting an interest in property in circumstances such that the State would have been entitled to immunity if the proceedings had been brought against it.

(5) Subsection (3)(b) above does not apply to any step taken by the State in ignorance of facts entitling it to immunity if those facts could not reasonably have been ascertained and immunity is claimed as soon as reasonably practicable.

(6) A submission in respect of any proceedings extends to any appeal but not to any counterclaim unless it arises out of, the same legal relationship or facts as the claim.

(7) The head of a State's diplomatic mission in the United Kingdom, or the person for the time being performing his functions, shall be deemed to have authority to submit on behalf of the State in respect of any proceedings; and any person who has entered into a contract on behalf of and with the authority of a State shall be deemed to have authority to submit on its behalf in respect of proceedings arising out of the contract.

A sovereign has the discretion to become discriminatory in granting privileges, whether in trade or otherwise, and it is not required to justify its act. Trade privileges are usually granted by means of bilateral treaties; where a multilateral treaty with a most-favoured nation clause has been issued, an ostensible equality is created between the contracting parties[4]. Privileges can be based on historical grounds; in fact neither the Vienna Convention on Diplomatic Relations, 1961 nor the Vienna Convention on Consular Relations, 1963 prohibits states from granting extra privileges. Article 47, paragraph 2(a) and (b) of the Vienna Convention on Diplomatic Relations provides that:

"*2. However, discrimination shall not be regarded as taking place:*

(a) where the receiving State applies any of the provisions of the present Convention restrictively because of a restrictive application of that provision to its mission in the sending State.

(b) where by custom or agreement States extend to each other more favourable treatment than is required by the provisions of the present Convention."

---

[4] See further G Schwarzenberger, "The Most-favoured Nation Standard in British State Practice" 22 *British Year Book of International Law* (1945) 96–121; S K Hornbeck, "The Most-favoured Nation Clause" (Part I) 3 *American Journal of International Law* (1909) 395–422; see also S K Chatterjee, "Forty Years of International Action for Trade Liberalization, 23 *Journal of World Trade* (1989) 45–64

Article 72, paragraphs (a) and (b) of the Convention on Consular Relations made *mutadis mutandis* similar provisions too.

In the name of the national interest, a sovereign State can, for example, impose restrictions on immigration of foreign nationals, including foreign corporations, or imports of foreign products or employment of foreign nationals or ownership of property by foreign nationals. But, of course, where the taking of property of foreign nationals proves to be necessary, international law requires it to pay compensation (prompt, appropriate and effective)[5].

A sovereign has an absolute authority over its jurisdiction and its domestic affairs. Sovereignty cannot be shared with anybody, thus it is indivisible[6]. These two attributes of sovereignty, in particular, absoluteness and indivisibility, often contribute to maintaining a rigid view by a sovereign of its power and manifest its unwillingness to co-operate with others or perceive international or inter-governmental bodies as institutions that might encroach upon their sovereignty. Take, for example, Article 2, paragraph 7 of the UN Charter, which provides that:

> "Nothing contained in the present Charter shall authorize the United Nations to intervene in matters which are essentially within the domestic jurisdiction of any state or shall require the Members to submit such matters to settlement under the present Charter; but this principle shall not prejudice the application of enforcement measures under Chapter VII."

A degree of flexibility in the application of the above provision has become evident particularly as from the mid-1960s, that is, that period by which most of the former colonies joined the United Nations as independent sovereign States. Of course, during the initial period of the United Nations, the meaning of the word *"intervention"* provoked controversy. In fact, two schools of thought developed and each provided its own argument. Whereas one school of thought which was led by Goodrich and Hambro pointed out that the term should not be given *"a narrow technical meaning"*[7], the other school of thought which was led by Sir Hirsch Lauterpacht maintained that the term should be understood in its technical meaning, that is, for example, dictatorial interference by the United Nations should be avoided[8].

The above controversy does evidence the fact that the contemporary society is still divided in its views as to the true use of sovereignty *vis-à-vis* a truly

---

[5] See UN General Assembly Resolution No. 1803 of 1962 entitled *Permanent Sovereignty over Natural Resources*

[6] But in the case of a Condominium, sovereignty may be shared jointly by two or more powers. Sovereignty may also be held in trust for the population of a territory, for example, the League of Nations maintained control over the Saar before its return to Germany in 1935.

[7] Goodrich & Hambro, Charter of the UN, *London, Stevens (1949) 120*

[8] H Lauterpacht, 70 *Hague Recueil* (1947), i at 31, n 2; see also M Rajaz, *The United Nations and Domestic Jurisdiction* (1961); Q Wright, "Is Discussion Intervention?", 50 *American Journal of International Law* (1956) 102; and "Matters of Domestic Jurisdiction", 74 *Hague Recueil* (1949) I, 553; and R Higgins, *The Development of International Law through the Political Organs of the United Nations*, Oxford, Oxford University Press (1963), Part II

international organisation. A high degree of co-operation from sovereign States is needed to develop a framework legislation under the auspices of the United Nations, and also particularly for economic and trade diplomacy. Without reciprocity between States sovereigns would be unable to survive meaningfully.

Interestingly enough, in the *Oscar Chinn* case[9], the Permanent Court's attitude towards sovereignty under an international treaty proved to be rather rigid. The dispute was based on the Convention of Saint-Germain-en-Laye of 10 September 1919, Article 1 of which provides that:

> *"The signatory Powers undertake to maintain between their respective nationals and those of States, Members of the League of Nations, which may adhere to the present Convention a complete commercial equality in the territories under the authority within the area defined by Article 1 of the General Act of Berlin of February 26th, 1885, set out in the Annex hereto, but subject to the reservation specified in the final paragraph of that Article."*

Annex

Article 1 of the General Act of Berlin of February 26, 1885

Final paragraph

> *"Subject to the provisions of the present Chapter, the navigation of the Niger, of its branches and outlets, and of all the rivers, and of their branches and outlets, within the territories specified in Article 1, as well as of the lakes situated within those territories, shall be entirely free for merchant vessels and for the transport of goods and passengers.*
>
> *Craft of every kind belonging to the nationals of the Signatory Powers and of States, Members of the League of Nations, which may adhere to the present Convention, shall be treated in all respects on a footing of perfect equality."*

However, Article 13 of the Convention signed by the two Governments concerned provided that:

> *"Except in so far as the stipulations contained in Article 1 of the present Convention are concerned, the General Act of Berlin of February 26th, 1885, and the Geneva Act of Brussels of July 2nd, 1890, with the accompanying Declaration of equal date, shall be considered as abrogated, in so far as they are binding between the Powers which are Parties to the present Convention."*

At the beginning of 1929, Mr Chinn, a British subject, established a river transport and ship-building and repairing business in Leopoldville. It should be pointed out however that until 1925, transport services in the Congo had been operated by or under the auspices of the Belgian Government, although not to the exclusion of private enterprises. In 1921, the transport services

---

[9] Permanent Court of International Justice (1934) Series A/B

business was transferred to a company known as *"Sonatra"*, but in 1925, that company continued with a private company known as *"Citas"*, and it became the *Union Nationale des transports fluviaux* (Unatra), in which the State owned more than 70,000 shares out of 120,000.

During the early 1930s' commercial depression, on 20 June 1931, the Belgian Minister for the Colonies reduced the net price of a number of commodities, in addition to the expenses of transportation and handling and rates for the carriage to such an extent that Mr Chinn found it difficult to run his business in the Congo, but the Minister confirmed that governmental assistance must be confined to transport undertakings over whose rates the Government had a right of supervision[10]. By 13 May 1931 Mr Chinn's business was laid up, as he was unable to sustain any more losses. Mr Chinn brought an action against the Colony before the Court of First Instance, and thereafter the Court of Appeal, but both courts found against him. However, before the delivery of the Court of Appeal's judgment, he appealed to his Government for protection, and the latter took up his claim.

The following were the primary legal issues as identified and submitted by the Government of Great Britain to the Permanent Court of International Justice:

1. whether the Belgian Government was in breach of the obligation incumbent upon all States in respect of the vested right of foreigners in their territories; alternatively, whether the Belgian Government was not in violation of its obligations under an international treaty;

2. whether by enjoining a reduction of tariffs on Unatra in return for a promise of temporary pecuniary compensation, the Belgian Government did not make it impossible for the other fluvial transporters, including Mr Chinn, to retain their customers, and enabled Unatra to exercise a *de facto* monopoly which was incompatible with the Belgian Government's obligation to maintain commercial freedom and equality, and also with the obligation arising out of Article 5 of the Convention of Saint-Germain, which applies those principles to fluvial navigation; and

3. whether by creating for the advantage of Unatra a regime in the benefits of which Mr Chinn was not entitled to share, the Belgian Government did not practice a discrimination contrary to the equality of treatment stipulated in the Convention of Saint-Germain.

The Belgian Government maintained however that:

"The measures which it adopted became necessary in order to safeguard the interests of the community as a consequence of the position of colonial products in the markets of the world; it never formed part of the intentions of the Belgian

---

[10] op. cit., at 75

> *Government to create a monopoly of any kind for Unatra in order to drive embarrassing competitors out of business. The measures that it took were lawful from the standpoint of international law, whether conventional or customary.*"[11]

The Belgian Government further maintained that:

> "*... a distinction must be drawn between the sphere of navigation and that of the management of national shipping. Whereas in the former sphere, the riparian State is forbidden to encroach on freedom of navigation, its freedom of action in the latter sphere is not subject to restriction.*"[12]

In regard to the British Government's contention based on general international law, the Belgian Government considered that:

> "*... no injury has been caused to already existing vested rights; at the utmost, injury may have been caused to private interests.*"

According to the Court:

> "*... the freedom of navigation referred to by the Convention comprises freedom of movement of vessels, freedom to enter ports, and to make use of plant and docks, to load and unload goods and to transport goods and passengers.*"[13]

The Court further maintained that:

> "*... freedom of navigation implies, as far as the business side of maritime or fluvial transport is concerned, freedom of commerce also. But it does not follow that in all other respects freedom of navigation entails and presupposes freedom of commerce.*"[14]

The Court recognised that freedom of navigation and freedom of commerce are, in principle, separate concepts, and that in the context of this case, there was no need to examine them separately. According to the Court, the Convention of Saint-Germain was based on the idea of commercial freedom, but that idea had not the same import in the Convention as in the Act of Berlin. This Act really meant by free trade the regime of the open door.

The following passage clearly represented the Court's view on competition and trade and commerce:

> "*Freedom of trade, as established by the Convention, consists in the right – in principle unrestricted – to engage in any commercial activity, whether it be concerned with trading properly so-called, that is the purchase and sale of goods,*

---

[11] op. cit., at 82
[12] op. cit., at 82
[13] op. cit., at 83
[14] ibid.

or whether it be concerned with industry, and in particular the transport business; or finally, whether it is carried on inside the country or by the exchange of imports and exports, with other countries. Freedom of trade does not mean the abolition of commercial competition; it presupposes the existence of such competition. Every undertaking freely carrying on its commercial activities may find itself confronted with obstacles placed in its way by rival concerns which are perhaps its superiors in capital or organisation. It may also find itself in competition with concerns in which States participate, and which have occupied a special position even since their formation, as is the case of Unatra. Mr Chinn, a British subject, when, in 1929, he entered the river transport business, could not have been ignorant of the existence of the competition which he would encounter on the part of Unatra, which had been established since 1925, of the magnitude of the capital invested in that Company, of the connection it had with the Colonial and Belgian Governments, and of the predominant role reserved to the latter with regard to the fixing and application of transport rates."[15]

The Court rejected the British Government's argument that a monopoly of any nature was established by the Belgian Government. On the contrary, the Court maintained that if a monopoly was established others were bound to respect it[16].

By six votes to five, the Court decided that the measures taken and applied in the month of June 1931 by the Belgian Government in connection with Unatra and in relation to fluvial transport on the waterways the Belgian Congo were not in conflict with the international obligations of the Belgian Government towards the Government of the United Kingdom.

It is worth pointing out that whereas Judge Altamira and Judge Hurst gave Dissenting Opinions, Judge Anzilotti and Judge van Eysinga gave Separate Opinions in this case. Briefly, Judge Altamira emphasised the issue of *"a complete equality"* under Article 1 of the Convention of Saint-Germain by pointing out that:

"Nevertheless, this freedom, though very wide, cannot be exercised beyond the point where it would entail infringement of the equality accorded to such nationals in their commercial activities."[17]

He further pointed out that the term *"navigation"* in the context of the Treaty should be interpreted in conjunction with the term *"freedom" "since the latter may apply equally well to the ship itself as to the economic function which it serves and which is the chief reason why freedom of movement is associated to it."*[18]

---

[15] op. cit., at 84
[16] op. cit., at 85
[17] op. cit., at 92
[18] op. cit., at 94

Judge Sir Cecil Hurst, on the other hand, referred to the intention of the Belgian Government in adopting the measures of 1931 to concentrate the river transport in the hands of Unatra, and maintained that the British Government failed to establish, by evidence, that there became manifest any intention on the part of the Belgian Government.

As to the question whether the Belgian measures of 1931 were inconsistent with the international obligations of Belgium, Sir Cecil pointed out that:

> "*Chinn possessed no right, either under the Treaty of Saint-Germain or under general international law, which entitled him to find customers in the Congo, i.e., people who were desirous of contracting with him*
>
> ...
>
> *the fact that these other individuals found it to their advantage not to contract with Chinn, involved no violation by them of a right belonging to him.*"

According to him, the Belgian Government was under no obligation to the Government of the United Kingdom to see that the trade of all nations enjoyed complete freedom[19].

In his Separate Opinion, Judge van Eysinga maintained however that:

> "*... whereas the General Act of Berlin covers the nationals of any country whatever, Article 3 of the Convention of Saint-Germain only applies to the nationals of certain States. But there is nothing to show that, within this restricted group, individual equality does not continue to be the law. This individual equality, which is such a characteristic feature of the work accomplished at Berlin – the result of which was to internationalize the legal regime of the Congo Basin in so many respects – was not modified by the Convention of Saint-Germain.*
>
> ...
>
> *that in inequality of treatment created by the Belgian Government's measure of June 20th, 1931, in favour of Unatra and to the detriment of the only other enterprise in the Congo which exclusively transported the goods of others, Mr Chinn's business is in conflict with the international obligations of the Belgian Government towards the United Kingdom.*"[20]

Judge van Eysinga also contested the decision of the Court that *"freedom of navigation"* and *"freedom of commerce"* are in principle two different concepts. He stated that:

---

[19] op. cit., at 124
[20] op. cit., at 139

> "If the Belgian Government's argument is that freedom of fluvial navigation merely signified freedom of movement for ships, leaving the commercial aspect out of account, the judgment, in the present case, adopts a diametrically opposite standpoint, and interprets freedom of fluvial navigation by the provisions relating to the liberty of commerce. The truth lies mid-way between the two standpoints: freedom of navigation certainly possesses a commercial aspect; but it is an independent notion, and is not determined by the provisions relating to freedom of trade."[21]

On the basis of what Judge van Eysinga stated, one may perhaps infer that the Belgian Government maintained a rigid notion towards sovereignty to protect the position of Unatra, a national commercial entity, in disregard of its international obligations towards the Government of the United Kingdom under the Treaty of Saint-Germain.

In the *Island of Palmas* Arbitration, Max Huber, the Arbitrator, described territorial sovereignty in the following terms:

> "Sovereignty in the relation between States signifies independence. Independence in regard to a portion of the globe is the right to exercise therein, to the exclusion of any other State, the function of a State."[22]

Sovereignty may form the psychological basis for power which may manifest in a variety of ways. A dictator's sense of authority or power has a psychological basis – omnipotence. This psychological power-base leads to the notion of bargaining power in international relations, which need not necessarily be based on logic or rationality. In justification of this comment, one may reflect on the involvement of a number of States in Afghanistan, Iraq, Kosovo and Yugoslavia, which did not receive the full support from the United Nations. Sovereignty may lead to megalomania; diplomats should be pro-active in mellowing the aggressive aspect of sovereignty.

The aggressive dimension to sovereignty of certain states can motivate others to form their own alliance. This can be confirmed by the activities of the Allied Powers in Iraq when Iraq invaded Kuwait in 1990; secondly, when NATO was deployed in Kosovo in response to aggression towards the ethnic Albanian population by the Yugoslavian regime of President Slobodan Milošević. The intervention of these Powers was not on the grounds of self-defence[23]. Humanitarian intervention is a concept which provokes controversy[24].

---

[21] op. cit., at 144

[22] 22 *American Journal of International Law* (1928) 875

[23] See further Chapter 4 Ethics in Diplomacy

[24] See further R B Lillich and F C Newman, *International Human Rights: Problems of Law and Policy* (1979), 493–495; I Brownlie, "Humanitarian Intervention" in *Law and Civil War in the Modern World*, J Moore (ed), (1974) 217–228; and S K Chatterjee, "Some Legal Problems of Support Role in International Law: Tanzania and Uganda", 30 *International and Comparative Law Quarterly* (1981) 755–768

The perception of the superiority of a sovereign with all its attendant powers should be applied to the domestic affairs and in the exclusive domain of a sovereign, which is the narrower aspect of sovereignty.

Sovereignty in the contemporary period must be related to three areas: domestic affairs; State-to-State relations; and relations with international organisations. A Sovereign's supremacy over its domestic affairs has already been explained. State-to-State relations between sovereign States is based on bilateral treaties which are governed by the Vienna Convention on the Law of Treaties, 1969. Necessarily, therefore, the contracting parties to a bilateral treaty are bound by the principles of the Law of Treaties, which clearly suggests that sovereigns, as parties to such treaties, are required to abide by or surrender to the law of treaties. This is an instance of sovereign States being governed by the rules of law which are not created by themselves. Furthermore, limits to sovereignty are imposed by customary rules of international law[25].

Diplomacy is at its most necessary when it comes to inter-State relations and relations with international and inter-governmental organisations. State-to-State relations on a bilateral basis needs very high diplomatic skills in order to develop trade relationship mostly on a reciprocal basis. This is where a sovereign may be required to accept the other sovereign's terms, or mutually agreed terms. In other words, in the case of State-to-State relations, a sovereign represented by its diplomats is required to accept that it cannot maintain its utmost superiority which it does within its domestic jurisdiction; however, the issue of the mutual gains requires such reciprocal arrangements.

In explaining the *River Oder Commission* case, it was pointed out that by appointing an external body with the objectives of maintaining the operational efficacy and up-keep of the river the riparian States should not have the perception that they would thus surrender their sovereignty to that body. The common interest of States may be well protected by international organisations. Thus, sovereign States are required to adopt a flexible attitude towards sovereignty which forms the basis for international co-operation. It may be described as *"co-operative sovereignty"*. This is the essence of relations with international organisations. The question of surrendering or losing sovereignty does not arise; it is only the sovereign States that can give international organisations mandates, and both sovereign States and diplomats need a proper understanding of the functions of these organisations, and that without the co-operation of the sovereign States international organisations cannot work. It is for sovereign States through their diplomats that they should direct international organisations as to what rules of international law or rules of conduct for States would be needed to be developed. Sovereign States

---

[25] For example, in relation to transboundary-pollution of the environment (see *The Trail Smelter Arbitration* between the US and Canada (1938 and 1941), 3 RIAA (1905) or, the Convention on the Prevention and Punishment of the Crime of Genocide, 1948 or, transit right through territorial waters or over the airspace of a country)

should disregard the notion of absolute sovereignty in accepting resolutions adopted by international organisations and implement them in their local circumstances. Resolutions of international organisations should not be treated as national legislation in nature; they are primarily broad-based directives to States in the latter's interest.

When the concept of the modern sovereignty was developed by Machiavelli (1469 – 1527) and Bodin (1530 – 1596) in the 16th century, and Hobbes (1588 – 1679) in the 17th century, it was essential to use it in its rigid form to shake the foundation of medieval Christendom. Bodin rightly suggested that in the then chaotic French political situation, an identifiable all-powerful entity was needed from whom commands must flow. Bodin's sovereign thus was represented as a dictatorial person whose command would be the law. It is to be borne in mind that the concept of parliament came into being only as late as the 18th century. Thus, with the establishment of parliaments, which are supposed to be based on democratic principles, Bodin's idea of a dictatorial sovereign proved to be unpopular, particularly in the West. Ironically, many sovereigns still seem to maintain Bodin's precept of sovereignty – indivisible, omnipotent and unamenable to anybody.

The modern system of international law grew, to some extent, out of the usages and practices of States, writers and jurists of the 15th–18th centuries, who also formulated some of its most important tenets, namely national and territorial sovereignty, equality of States and independence of States. In fact, these tenets have also been accepted not only by the old States but also by the newly-born ones. It is to be borne in mind however that many of the newly-born States were sovereign States prior to their being colonised. Thus, privileges and immunities to ambassadors, laws and usages of war or treaty-relationship between older States may be found many centuries before the dawn of Christianity, for example, in ancient Egypt and India[26].

During the period of antiquity therefore sovereigns appreciated the importance of inter-State relationship and sent out their ambassadors, plenipotentiaries or envoys to other sovereigns. In the context of this work, it may be stated that the theories developed by authors, in general, sought the rules of international law mainly in custom and treaties. This can be found in the writings of: Francisco de Vitoria (1480 – 1546), a Professor of Theology at the University of Salamanca, Spain; Belli (1502 – 1575), an Italian soldier and jurist; Suárez (1548 – 1617), a Spanish Jesuit; Gentili (1552 – 1608), an Italian lawyer, who became Professor of Civil Law at Oxford; Pufendorf (1632 – 1694), a Professor at the University of Heidelberg, Germany; Bynkershoek (1673 – 1743), a Dutch jurist; Wolff (1679 – 1754), a German jurist and philosopher; von Martens (1756 – 1821), a German Professor of law; and Vattel (1714 – 1767), a Swiss jurist and diplomat. Of course, there were jurists who placed emphasis upon the law of nature, *jus civile* or divine law

---

[26] See A Nussbaum, *A Concise History of the Law of Nations* (1954), H Chatterjee, *International Law and Inter-State Relations in Ancient India* (1958)

(for example, Grotius, a Dutch scholar and jurist (1583 – 1645)). Incidentally, Grotius' *De Jure Belli ac Pacis* (The Law of War and Peace, 1625) is more respected as a work that included principally the rules and usages of warfare, but he will remain known as the creator of a comprehensive work on international law.

It was Grotius who propounded the *"the law of nature"* as an independent source of the law of nations, in addition to custom and treaties. Grotius' *Mare Liberum* (1609) is, of course, regarded as the historic work on the doctrine of the freedom of the seas.

Returning to the issue of sovereignty and diplomacy, it may be pointed out that diplomats represent their sovereigns; they act on behalf of their sovereigns on the basis of the mandates they receive from the latter. Thus, it is the attitude of a sovereign towards sovereignty that dictates a diplomat to act on behalf of his sovereign.

If the primary objective of diplomacy is to establish inter-state relationship, then it is difficult to see how sovereignty in its absolute form may be exercised. In fact, as stated earlier, in developing inter-State relations, reciprocity between the States concerned becomes inevitable; thus, sovereignty loses its absolute form. In fact, in tracing the history of diplomacy, since the Middle Ages, it becomes apparent that Emperors or Kings appreciated the need for reciprocity, particularly in relation to economic matters. Economic diplomacy is a forerunner / precursor of the so-called political diplomacy. It has been emphasised in this work that without an active and effective economic diplomacy on a bilateral basis, the foundation of political diplomacy will remain feeble.

3.3 TYPES OF JURISDICTION

Sovereignty is territorial; thus, within its territorial boundaries, its jurisdiction – authority, remains unchallengeable. According to Oppenheim, jurisdiction *"concerns essentially the extent of each State's right to regulate conduct or the consequences of events"*, but always within its territorial boundaries. States have the authority over all persons, property and events occurring within its territorial boundaries[27], this authority is of an absolute nature. This aspect of sovereignty can also lead a sovereign to abuse its powers. It is true that no external authority, sovereign or otherwise, may encroach upon the domestic jurisdiction of a State, but if abuse of sovereignty takes place, for example, in respect of human rights or illegal taking of an alien's assets within the territorial jurisdiction of a sovereign, then it may form the subject matter of an international claim. This absolute aspect of territorial jurisdiction can be modified either by general principles of international law or by specific obligation which may have been undertaken by a sovereign state, whether, by means of a

---

[27] *Oppenheim's International Law*, Sir R Jennings and Sir A Watts (eds), Harlow, Longman (1992) at 456

bilateral treaty or an international convention. For example, by virtue of ratifying / accepting the Vienna Convention on Diplomatic Relations, 1961, many States have agreed to allow diplomats immunity from their local jurisdiction. In this context, the two basic sub-principles of sovereignty should be pointed out: (a) sovereignty is territorial; and (b) all sovereigns are equal. As to the first sub-principle, it should be borne in mind that under special arrangements or agreements, a sovereign may extend its authority extra-territorially. Take, for example, the US military base in Cuba. A State's authority to execute its power within its territorial jurisdiction over its nationals, properties and actions, whether friendly or unfriendly, may not be questioned, and that power or authority even if apparently abused, may not be judged by any foreign court. A sovereign may exercise its power extra-territorially only under certain arrangements between itself and another sovereign concerned. The issue of extra-territoriality provokes controversy however in public international law. Enforcement of jurisdiction can take place only within a State's own territory, unless it allows enforcements beyond its territorial boundaries under certain special arrangements or the principles of international law allow this power.

Territoriality of jurisdiction stands for the genuine connection of the matter within the territory concerned. This issue may be discussed with reference to both civil and criminal matters. In so far as the civil jurisdiction is concerned, municipal courts concerned must assume jurisdiction and apply private international law where appropriate in cases containing a foreign element, but these courts are often reluctant to assume jurisdiction concerning a foreign element and rely on the territoriality principle – a principle establishing connection with the territory, unless, of course, the accused volunteers to submit to the jurisdiction.

Over the years a number of principles have been developed to justify assumption of jurisdiction by States over civil and criminal matters. Civil matters in this context will also include acts coming under the purview of *"negligence"*. These principles are: territoriality principle; nationality principle; passive personality principle; and the universality principle. These are now briefly explained.

3.3.1 The Territoriality Principle

Under this principle, the territory in which an act, civil or criminal, takes place, will assume jurisdiction. *"Territory"* in this context includes its territorial sea (12 nautical miles from the coast), the airspace above and its land and sea territory. Thus, the UK assumed jurisdiction to prosecute the Libyan nationals accused of blowing up a US aircraft in the skies above Lockerbie, Scotland in 1988. In the *Union Carbide* case, courts in India were allowed to assume jurisdiction as the disaster took place in India; the US corporation claimed that by virtue of its being incorporated in the US, relevant courts in the US should be allowed to assume jurisdiction. Of course, legal problems may arise when an act is committed in parts in a number of jurisdictions. Each State concerned may claim jurisdiction on the basis of the territoriality principle, but that would create a *"legal mess"*; in practice, all aspects of the investigation, and prosecution are allowed to be conducted by a single State, usually, the State that has suffered most, or where the act was consummated. Again, the Lockerbie incident confirms this practice – the bomb is said to have been loaded aboard the US aircraft in Malta, but the aircraft was blown up in the UK airspace.

However, the territoriality principle has sometimes been given extensive application; both the United Kingdom and the United States have extended the application of this principle to assume jurisdiction over their nationals wherever the act was committed. This principle has two variants: subjective territorial jurisdiction and objective territorial jurisdiction. The subjective territorial jurisdiction creates jurisdiction over crimes connected with the State but completed or consummated abroad. If one applies this principle, then in the Lockerbie incident, Malta could have assumed jurisdiction as the bomb is said to have been loaded aboard the aircraft in Malta. The objective territoriality principle is applied to assume jurisdiction when an essential constituent element of a crime or act is consummated on the territory of a State even though it was initiated outside its territory.

A State can rely, and indeed, in practice does so, on both subjective and objective territoriality principles to assume jurisdiction. The objective territoriality principle is applied to assume jurisdiction in respect of violation of anti-trust[28] laws, or in cases of conspiracy[29].

The objective territoriality principle was largely applied by the Permanent Court of International Justice in *The Lotus* case[30], but the judgment of the Court has never been short of controversy. The case concerned a collision on the high seas between the French steamer, the Lotus, and the Turkish steamer, the Boz-Kourt which resulted in the death of eight people. M Demons, the officer of the watch on the Lotus was prosecuted by the Turkish authorities when the steamer entered Constantinople (now Istanbul). Proceedings were also instituted against the captain of the Turkish steamer. France objected to the proceedings against M Demons on the grounds that it is impermissible for a State to extend its laws to foreign vessels on the high seas. The Court held that Turkey was entitled to prosecute M Demons. According to the Court:

> *"... the first and foremost restriction imposed by international law upon a State is that – failing the existence of a permissive rule to the contrary – it may not exercise its power in any form in the territory of another State. In this sense jurisdiction is certainly territorial: it cannot be exercised by a State outside its*

---

[28] *US v Aluminium Company of America* 148F.2d. 416 (1944)

[29] See, for example, *DPP v Doot* [1973] AC 807; or *DPP v Stonehouse* [1978] AC 55

[30] Judgment No 9 (1927), PCIJ, Series A, No 10

territory except by virtue of a permissive rule derived from international custom or from a convention."

In this case, the Turkish authorities arrested M Demons after the steamer entered a Turkish port – part of the Turkish territory, and thus, within Turkish enforcement jurisdiction. But, the question remains whether M Demons should have been prosecuted by the Turkish authorities for an act which was committed outside the Turkish territory. The Court's reaction to this issue may appear to be unclear. In this context, it would be apt to quote the following passage:

> "It does not, however, follow that international law prohibits a State from exercising of jurisdiction in its own territory, in respect of any case which relates to acts which have taken place abroad, and in which it cannot rely on some permissive rule of international law. Such a view would only be tenable if international law contained a general prohibition to States to extend the application of their laws and the jurisdiction of their courts to persons, property and acts outside their territory, and if, as an exception to this general prohibition, it allowed States to do so in certain specific cases. But this is certainly not the case under international law as it stands at present. Far from laying down a general prohibition to that effect that States may not extend the application of their laws and the jurisdiction of their courts to persons, property and acts outside their territory, it leaves them in this respect a wide measure of discretion which is only limited in certain cases by prohibitive rules ..."[31]

Put it simply, the Court maintained that it is permissible for a State to exercise its jurisdiction extraterritorially over persons, property and acts outside its territory, although it qualified this right of a State by saying that *"it leaves them in this respect a wide measure of discretion which is only limited in certain cases by prohibitive rules ..."* The legal consequences of such a view are far-reaching.

The Court again argued that:

> "International law governs relations between independent States. The rules of laws binding upon States therefore emanate from their own free will as expressed in Conventions or by usages generally accepted as expressing principles of law and established in order to regulate the relations between these co-existing independent communities or with a view to the achievement of common aims. Restrictions upon the independence of States cannot therefore be presumed."[32]

It is not true that a sovereign State is free to do what it wishes; if it does so, then it can encroach upon the jurisdiction of another sovereign State which act would be in breach of the principle of sovereign equality.

The protective principle does not seem to have been applied by the Court in the *Lotus* case. The Article in the Turkish Penal Code which provided for

---

[31] op. cit., at 19

[32] op. cit., at 18

punishment of acts abroad by foreigners against Turkish nationals and involved the protective principle of jurisdiction was not dealt with by the Court – the issue of compatibility of the relevant provision of the Turkish Penal Code with international law.

Apparently, in the *Lotus* case, the Court applied the objective territoriality principle in a rather subtle way. The Court assimilated the Turkish vessel to Turkish national territory; thus it established that it affected Turkish territory. This assimilation, of course, allowed Turkey to discharge her burden of responsibility for criminal acts on her territory.

The Court's view in the *Lotus* case in regard to extraterritorial jurisdiction provokes controversy, particularly when such attempts made by certain States have received opposition from various quarters. A State cannot take measures on the territory of another State by way of enforcement of national laws without the consent of the latter. This applies to civil, criminal or financial matters.

3.3.2 The Nationality Principle

Allegiance with a State especially as nationals forms the basis for exercising jurisdiction over extra-territorial acts[33]. However, this principle may be extended to attempt to provide protection to aliens on the grounds of residence or by virtue of other connections as evidence of allegiance[34]. Where however an individual has the benefit of *"dual nationality"*, he/she will be requested to sacrifice one nationality – to seek protection on the grounds of this principle; and diplomatic intervention between the States concerned will be necessary to settle the person's real allegiance with a State.

It must be pointed out however that the method of acquiring by or conferring nationality on an individual is not an issue; the usual methods of having nationality are (a) by birth (unless there exist restrictions for aliens)[35] or (b) by descent (*Jus Sanguinis*) or (c) by naturalisation.

In the case of companies, protection under this principle is not as straightforward; State practices differ on this issue[36]. States following the common law system, in general, seem to accord nationality to companies on the basis of their incorporation in a State, regardless of the location of the actual business or management of the company. States governed by civil law system, in general, do not seem to place most emphasis on the place of incorporation, but rather the place where the company has the seat of its management.

---

[33] R Y Jennings, "Extraterritorial Jurisdiction and the United States' Antitrust Laws", 33 *British Year Book of International Law* (1957) 146

[34] *Re P (GE) (an infant)* [1964] 3 ALL ER 977

[35] In the UK, for example, a child born by alien parents, who are not nationals or residents in the UK, may not be a British national by birth in the UK. Thus, the UK does not follow the *jus soli* principle.

[36] See further *Barcelona Traction, Light and Power Company*, Second Phase, Judgment, *ICJ Reports* (1970) at 3

Whatever may be the requirements and characteristics of a legal system, the fact remains that a State can always apply the nationality principle if it should decide to provide protection to its nationals. This discretion is apparently based on the notion of the genuine factual link of the individual / corporation with the State[37].

It must be emphasised however that in neither *Nottebohm* nor *Barcelona Traction* case was the Court concerned with the issue of the effectiveness of nationality of an individual or a corporation. However, in the final analysis, it is the discretion of a State whether or not to apply the nationality principle to protect its nationals abroad for whatever reason.

3.3.3 The Passive Personality Principle

According to this principle, aliens may be punished for acts abroad which have proved to be harmful to nationals of the forum[38]. In the *Cutting* case, a Mexican Court exercised jurisdiction in respect of a publication of a defamatory nature by a US citizen in a Texas newspaper. As the defamation was of a Mexican national, the Court applied the passive personality principle among others. The outcome of the dispute remained inconclusive. *Cutting* provoked controversy; it was an example of an excessive jurisdictional claim. The passive personality principle has not formed part of customary international law.

3.3.4 The Protective Principle

This is really a principle which is meant to be applied for national security reasons. Under this principle, States assume jurisdiction over aliens for acts done abroad but which affected or may affect the security of the State. Again, this principle is not founded necessarily on legal justification but on political considerations. The classic example of the application of this principle in England is the *Joyce v DPP* case[39]. During the Second World War William Joyce, a British subject, worked as a radio broadcaster, but he started working against Britain, and co-operated with the Germans; he was eventually issued with a German passport. Shortly after the Second World War in Europe ended, Joyce was arrested in Germany and prosecuted by His Majesty's Government on the grounds of treason, as he broadcast propaganda for an enemy during the War.

The US also asserted jurisdiction under this principle[40]; and under the Maritime Drug Law Enforcement Act, 1986. Many other States would prefer to exercise jurisdiction over aliens on the basis of treaties. The application of the protective principle is discretionary, and has a political bias.

---

[37] See *Nottebohm*, Second Phase, Judgment, *ICJ Reports* (1955)

[38] See further R Y Jennings, "Extraterritorial Jurisdiction and the United States' Antitrust Laws", 33 *British Year Book of International Law* (1957) 146

[39] [1946] AC 347

[40] *US v Gonzalez* 776 F.2d. 931 (1985)

3.3.5 The Universality Principle

According to this principle, jurisdiction over acts of non-nationals may be assumed by courts in any country. This is a controversial principle in that jurisdiction may not be justified by the *"connection theory"*. The classic example of exercising jurisdiction on the basis of universality principle was the *Eichmann* trial[41]. Eichmann did not commit crimes in Israel; he killed people of Jewish faith in Germany and Poland. The Israeli courts assumed jurisdiction on the grounds that Israel, being the land of Jewish people, would be the most appropriate jurisdiction to prosecute Eichmann.

The universality principle is justified on the grounds that certain crimes are so condemnable that every State may have a legitimate interest in their repression[42]. Piracy, hijacking, international terrorism, crimes against humanity, war crimes are examples of crimes which may come under the universality principle. An assertion of jurisdiction under the universality principle must be justified by the State concerned. In the United Kingdom universal jurisdiction is asserted in sections 47 and 51 of the Anti-Terrorism, Crime and Security Act, 2001 if the offence of knowingly causing a nuclear explosion without authorisation is committed.

3.4 EXTENSION OF JURISDICTION BY MEANS OF TREATIES

Extension of jurisdiction by means of treaties has become common in recent years. This is a permissible act under international law, as all treaties are based on consent of the parties to a treaty. In fact, it facilitates resolution of inter-state disputes. Treaties, in this context, would also include international Conventions.

Article 5 of the International Convention Against the Taking of Hostages, 1979 provides that:

> *"1. Each State Party shall take such measures as may be necessary to establish its jurisdiction over any of the offences set forth in article 1 which are committed:*
>
> *(a) in its territory or on board a ship or aircraft registered in that State;*
>
> *(b) by any of its nationals or, if that State considers it appropriate, by those stateless persons who have their habitual residence in its territory;*
>
> *(c) in order to compel that State to do or abstain from doing any act; or*
>
> *(d) with respect to a hostage who is a national of that State, if that State considers it appropriate.*

---

[41] See further W E Beckett, "The Exercise of Criminal Jurisdiction over Foreigners", 6 *British Year Book of International Law* (1925) 44

[42] See *US v Yunis* 681 F. Supp 896; Arrest warrant of 11 April 2000 (*Democratic Republic of Congo v Belgium*) *ICJ Reports* 2002 at 3; 41 *International Legal Materials* (2002) 563

> 2. *Each State Party shall likewise take such measures as may be necessary to establish its jurisdiction over the offences set forth in article 1 in cases where the alleged offender is present in its territory and it does not extradite him to any of the States mentioned in paragraph 1 of this article.*
> 3. *This Convention does not exclude any criminal jurisdiction exercised in accordance with internal law."*

Section 51 of the Anti-Terrorism, Crime and Security Act, 2001 provides that:

> *"(1) Proceedings for an offence committed under section 47 or 50 outside the United Kingdom may be taken, and the offence may for incidental purposes be treated as having been committed, in any part of the United Kingdom.*
>
> *(2) Her Majesty may by Order in Council extend the application of section 47 or 50, so far as it applies to acts done outside the United Kingdom, to bodies incorporated under the law of any of the Channel Islands, the Isle of Man or any colony."*

The 1983 Extradition Treaty between the United States and Italy, which came into force on 24 September 1984, did not list extraditable crimes but provided for extradition for any crime punishable under the laws of both States. Article 3 allows extradition for extraterritorial crimes so long as the offence meets the requirement of double criminality. But Article 7 specified that extradition may be refused if the persons being sought are being proceeded against by the requested State for the same offence. Extradition may also be refused if the offence is punishable by death in the requesting State but not in the requested State unless the requesting State gave assurances that capital punishment will not be imposed or carried out (Article 9)[43].

In such treaties, the general principle of where the alleged offender has been *"found"* seems to have been followed, and the courts in that location will assume jurisdiction. From this standpoint, it may be maintained that a treaty based jurisdiction loses its importance or application. International law accepts that the location of the crime determines jurisdiction, unless it extradites the alleged offender. Treaty based jurisdiction may however facilitate extradition of the alleged offender.

Apart from the nationality principle or the universality principle, the other principles on the basis of which jurisdiction is usually assumed relate to the territoriality or location concept. However, neither of these latter principles foresees any difficulties in determining the location of an offence. A crime or its various facets may be a *"continuing crime"*, that is, it may be committed in more than one jurisdiction.

---

[43] See further documents concerning *The Achille Lauro Affair and Co-operation in Combating International Terrorism*, 24 *International Legal Materials* (1985) 1509

English courts have distinguished between *"conduct crimes"* and *"result crimes"*, whereas the former is concerned with what act has been committed, and the latter the results emanating therefrom. In fact, this distinction is also based on the subjective and objective aspects of territorial jurisdiction[44].

International law pays attention to both the issues: what has actually been done, and the consequences thereof. In the case of probable overlapping jurisdictions, each of the competing jurisdictions is required to justify why it should be allowed to assume jurisdiction over the matter.

In regard to enforcement jurisdiction, international law maintains that it may not be exercised in the territory of another State without the consent of the latter. The territoriality principle thus forms the primary basis for enforcement jurisdiction. Furthermore, there are certain matters over which no State should encroach upon the jurisdiction of another State – tax, matrimonial, criminal law etc. These issues are not dealt with by the principles of international law. A sovereign has an exclusive jurisdiction / power over such matters; however, this power should be exercised in a legitimate manner. Examples do exist to confirm that States attempt to obtain custody of alleged offenders without going through the foundations of extradition procedures[45]. States also seized wanted individuals from the territory of another State. Such acts are blatantly violative of the territorial sovereignty of the State from which an individual is extracted.

Thus, in so far as subject-matter jurisdiction is concerned, it is generally accepted that a State has the power to make laws regarding conduct within its territory (the territoriality principle) and to regulate the behaviour of its citizens abroad, including corporate bodies registered / incorporated under its law (the nationality principle). An extension of the territoriality principle takes place when a State is recognised as having jurisdiction not only where an act originates but also where the objectionable conduct originates abroad but is completed within its territory (the objective territoriality principle). In such a situation, of course, more than one State may assert jurisdiction over the same matter. Of course, the dilemma remains whether an act which is committed by a subsidiary company in a foreign jurisdiction may be attributed to its parent, and thus the parent company's courts may assume jurisdiction, unless it is clearly established that the subsidiary alone is to be held responsible for the act and not its parent. The *"entity doctrine"* maintains that all subsidiaries and branches of a transnational corporation constitute one economic unit[46].

---

[44] See *DPP v Doot* [1973] AC 807; *DPP v Stonehouse* [1978] AC 55; and *Liangsiriprasert v Government of the United States of America* [1991] 1 AC 225

[45] See further Vaughan Lowe, "Jurisdiction" in *International Law*, M Evans (ed), Cambridge, Cambridge University Press (2003) 329

[46] See also Decision of the EEC Commission in the *Dyestuffs Cartel* case, Jo No L 195, 7 August 1969; and the Decision of EEC Commission in the *Commercial Solvents* case (1974) CMLR 309

According to Mann, a State has enforcement jurisdiction abroad only to the extent necessary to enforce its legislative jurisdiction[47]. Jennings maintained that extraterritorial jurisdiction may not be exercised in such a way which would contradict the law of the place where the alleged offence was committed[48].

There does not exist any consensus as to what extent enforcement jurisdiction may be applied by a foreign authority. The British view seems to be that a State acts in excess of its own jurisdiction when it purports to regulate acts which have been done outside its territorial jurisdiction by persons who are not its nationals, and which have no substantial effect within its territorial jurisdiction. Thus, substantial connection, and/or substantial effect within its own territory may justify enforcement of its orders.

3.5 ABUSE OF SOVEREIGNTY

Sovereignty may be abused within the internal spheres of the sovereign by becoming despotic, indifferent to the needs and wishes of its people, suppressor of human rights and freedoms and an oppressor of the citizens who may oppose his despotic rule. In the world of diplomacy, such a sovereign will have limited diplomatic relations with other democratic States and may be isolated. Prior to transforming the regime in South Africa, the minority regime which lasted for many years satisfied many of the criteria of a despotic sovereign. Through pro-active diplomacy coupled with the international community's abhorrence to such despotic sovereigns the regime can be changed. This is an instance where, sacrificing national interests, concerted diplomacy of all countries is necessary to hasten the process of transformation. Thus, internal abuse of sovereignty may be stopped by a coherent and pro-active policy adopted by diplomats representing the international community. Again, this is where the platform of the United Nations should be effectively used. Thus, the regime of a despotic sovereign is not unassailable; the international community can be instrumental to changing it.

Abuse of sovereignty can take place when a sovereign extends its power across its national boundaries. Here, the issue of extra-territoriality becomes important. Extra-territoriality stands for extending the power, judicial orders, and laws of a sovereign to the territory of another sovereign. In the context of this work, only the basic issues relating to extra-territoriality have been explained.

Extra-territorial application of sovereignty in any form takes place when a sovereign extends its laws, regulations or judicial orders across its national boundaries. An extra-territorial act runs counter to the principle of equality of

---

[47] See further F A Mann, "The Dyestuffs case in the Court of Justice of the European Communities," 22 *International and Comparative Law Quarterly* (1973) 35

[48] ibid.

sovereign States. Unless there exists a treaty arrangement between the two States concerned, there is no reason why a sovereign State should be amenable to the orders of another sovereign. Furthermore, sovereignty is territorial, meaning thereby that a sovereign may not exercise its sovereignty beyond its territorial limits. If a sovereign's acts, including its judicial orders are extended to include another sovereign's jurisdiction, then the latter becomes subservient to the former.

International law abhors extraterritorial application of sovereignty, but it has been the practice of certain States to use their sovereignty extra-territorially. An extraterritorial act may also be regarded as an expression of power, political or economic or even judicial. An extraterritorial act, if not based on a treaty, hits the root of international diplomacy. The only legitimate way to stretch sovereignty extra-territorially would be for national courts to discourage application of sovereignty in this manner or that there should be a truly international convention prohibiting it; or that all States adopt legislation against it. It can also be potentially an issue for diplomacy. The classic cases decided in the English jurisdiction on the issue of the extraterritorial application of judicial orders are:

(a) *British Nylon Spinners Ltd v Imperial Chemicals Industries Ltd*[49]; and
(b) *Rio Tinto Zinc Corporation and Others v. Westinghouse Electric Corporation*[50].

In the first case, the defendants, an English corporation, were ordered, inter alia, by a foreign court whilst within the jurisdiction, to cancel an existing agreement with a foreign company and to reassign to that company certain patents and rights previously assigned to the defendants for registration in the United Kingdom. Prior to the making of the order by the foreign court, the defendants had entered into a contract in England with the plaintiffs, an English corporation, to grant them licences to exercise and practise all the inventions covered by the assigned patents within defined territories. At the date of the order the patents were not registered nor was any licence granted under the English contract.

The plaintiffs issued a writ against the defendants requiring specific performance of their contract, and asked for an injunction to restrain the defendants from reassigning the patents in compliance with the foreign court order.

The Court of Appeal held that:

"... *in so far as the foreign court order asserted an extraterritorial jurisdiction, the effect and intention of which was to destroy or qualify statutory rights under an English contract vested in an English national who was not subject to the jurisdiction of the foreign court, the courts would not, despite the comity of*

---

[49] [1953] 1 Ch 19
[50] [1978] 2 WLR 87

nations, recognise such extraterritorial jurisdiction and would intervene to restrain the defendants from obeying the order."[51]

In the second case, in connection with an alleged uranium cartel, the US Department of Justice applied to the judge of a court in Virginia for an order to compel testimony under USC Section 6002/3 applicable when a witness claimed privilege (which the English witnesses did) on the grounds of self-incrimination but under which no testimony might be used against the witness in a criminal case. The judge of the Virginia Court made the order. RTZ and the persons concerned appealed the decision. The House of Lords held, inter alia:

"That the intervention of the Department of Justice converting the letters rogatory into a request for evidence for the purposes of a grand jury investigation, changed their character, seeking to use the Act of 1975[52] for purposes for which it was not intended by extending the grand jury's investigations internationally in a manner which was impermissible as being an infringement of the United Kingdom sovereignty, a context to which the Courts were entitled to take into account the declared policy of Her Majesty's Government."[53]

In 1980 the British Government passed the Protection of Trading Interests Act, the purpose of which is to:

"... provide protection from requirements, prohibitions and judgments imposed or given under the laws of countries outside the United Kingdom and affecting the trading or other interests of persons in the United Kingdom."

Section 1(3) of the Act provides that:

"The Secretary of State may give to any person in the United Kingdom who carries on business there such directions for prohibiting compliance with any such requirement or prohibition ... as he considers appropriate for avoiding damage to the trading interests of the United Kingdom."

Section 2(1) of the same Act provides that:

"If it appears to the Secretary of State:

(a) *that a requirement has been or may be imposed on a person or persons in the United Kingdom or produce to any court, tribunal or authority of an overseas country any commercial document which is not within the territorial jurisdiction of that country or to furnish any commercial information to any such court, tribunal or authority; or*

---

[51] ibid
[52] Evidence (Proceedings in Other Jurisdictions) Act 1975
[53] op. cit., at 83

Sovereignty

> *(b) that any such authority has imposed or may impose a requirement on a person or persons in the United Kingdom to publish any such document or information; the Secretary of State may, if it appears to him that the requirement is inadmissible ... give directions for prohibiting compliance with the requirement."*

The US judicial practice in exercising jurisdiction extraterritorially has provoked controversy[54].

In *Alcoa*[55] and *Watchmakers of Switzerland*[56] the US courts took the view that whenever an activity abroad has consequences or effects within the United States (and which are contrary to the local legislation) then the US courts may make orders requiring, inter alia, the disposition of property of foreign corporations or the production of documents. In the *Alcoa* case the US courts asserted jurisdiction over the conduct of a non-US company that was a member of an aluminium cartel, and whose activities would have affected imports to or exports from the United States, and in fact, it did so. This is popularly known as the *"effects"* doctrine. These decisions do not depend upon whether any physical acts have been committed within the US territory. These court orders may be enforced in the United States against the individuals or property present within the territorial jurisdiction of the United States, but the point remains whether an assumption of jurisdiction by the US courts in the circumstances stated above may be justified from a legal standpoint particularly when it asserts jurisdiction over nationals of other sovereign States. Furthermore, such enforcement action is not conditional upon actual injury caused to the US business world. An intention to cause an injury, if proved by admissible evidence, would be enough. This is like taking action on the basis of an anticipatory breach in the law of contract, which often provokes legal controversy. The US judicial acts on the basis of *"effects"* doctrine have provoked controversy not only outside of the United States but also within the United States. This practice is based on the Sherman Act 1889. It is also questionable whether a municipal legislation should provide for its effects outside of the United States. The classic case on the issue of act of State doctrine is *Underhill v Hernandez*[57] in which the US courts stated that:

> *"Every sovereign State is bound to respect the independence of every other sovereign State, and that courts of one country will not sit in judgment on the acts of the government of another one within its own territory."*[58]

---

[54] See the Joint Department of Justice and Federal Trade Commission *Antitrust Enforcement Guidelines for International Operations* (April 1995) para 3.31; see also A V Lowe, *Extraterritorial Jurisdiction* (1983); Olmstead, *Extraterritorial Application of Laws and Responses Thereto* (1984)

[55] *US v Aluminium Co of America* 148 F 2d 416 (1945)

[56] *US v Watchmakers of Switzerland Information Center Inc* 133 F. Supp. 40 (1955); 134 F. Supp. 710 (1955)

[57] 168 US 250 252 18 S ct. 83, 84, 42 L. Ed 456 (1897)

[58] See also *American Banana Co v United Fruit Co* 213 US 347, 29 S Ct. 511, 53 L Ed. 826 (1909)

How on the basis of a domestic legislation (Sherman Act) US judicial orders may be applied extraterritorially has remained unresolved. Even among American courts and commentators there is no consensus on how far the jurisdiction should extend[59]. In *Timberlane LBR Co v Bank of America*, NT and SA[60] the US court stated, inter alia, that:

> "There is no doubt that American antitrust laws extend over some conduct in other nations..."[61]

US antitrust law embraced the *"effects"* doctrine, that is, when a conduct outside her borders may have consequences within her borders which the State reprehends. In *Hertford Fire Insurance Co v California*[62], substantial effect in the United States was referred to. In 1994, the International Antitrust Enforcement Assistance Act was passed with a view to improving the ability of the US enforcement agencies to obtain evidence from abroad on the basis of reciprocal agreements between the US and specific countries, including confidential information. US antitrust laws are applied not only to extraterritorial behaviour that affects imports into the US, but also jurisdiction may be asserted where US companies are obstructed by anti-competitive behaviour in their attempts to gain access to foreign markets[63]. The first case in which the US challenged conduct abroad that denied foreign access was the case of *United States v Pilkington*[64]. This case was decided by a consent decree.

3.6 THE EXTRATERRITORIAL APPLICATION OF EC COMPETITION LAW

This issue may also be discussed with reference to both subject-matter jurisdiction and enforcement jurisdiction. In so far as the *subject-matter jurisdiction* is concerned, attention should be paid to both the economic entity doctrine and the effects doctrine.

The European Court of Justice developed the economic entity doctrine in the *Dyestuffs* case[65]. The court was satisfied that three non-EC undertakings, Geigy, Sandoz and ICI had participated in illegal price fixing within the EC through the subsidiary companies located in the EC but under the control of non-EC parents. In this case, both the issues of *"one-economic entity"* and *"independent legal personalities"* of the companies concerned arose; but the

---

[59] See, for example, W Fugate, *Foreign Commerce and Antitrust Laws* (1973); J Vine Lise, *Understanding the Antitrust Laws* (1973) Miller, "Extraterritorial Effects of Trade Regulation" 111 *University of Pennsylvania Law Review* (1963) 1092

[60] 549 F 2d 597 (1976)

[61] op. cit., at 608

[62] 509 US 764 (1993)

[63] See further R Whish, *Competition Law*, London, Butterworths (2001) 397

[64] (1994 – 2) Trade Cases (CCH) 70, 482 (1994)

[65] *ICC v Commission* [1972] CMLR 557; see also F A Mann, "The Dyestuffs case in the Court of Justice of the European Communities", 22 *International and Comparative Law Quarterly* (1973) 35

evidence that the parent controlled its subsidiary was of a limited nature. The doctrine of one *"economic entity"* was certainly confirmed by the *Commercial Solvents* case[66].

The effects doctrine has also been recognised by the Commission[67]. In the *Wood Pulp* case, the Commission, in finding that there was a concerted practice between undertakings in several non-EC countries, held that jurisdiction could be founded on the effects doctrine; the court, on the other hand, relied on the territoriality principle of public international law pointing out that it was irrelevant to consider whether the implementation was effected by subsidiaries or agents or any other entity; the territory in which the event took place outweighed other arguments.

The enforcement jurisdiction entails enforcement of one State's law in the territory of another sovereign State, which is, in reality, impermissible under international law. In *Geigy v Commission*[68] the Commission sent its grounds of objections to Geigy's Swiss offices, but the latter maintained that the service was unlawful both under internal and public international law. The ECJ confirmed that it was in order for the Commission to send a letter to the non-EC undertaking.

The UK government does not support the *"effects doctrine"*; it prefers the application of either the territoriality principle or the nationality principle[69]. Section 2(1) of the Competition Act 1998 provides that an agreement will be deemed void if it may affect trade and competition within the UK. The jurisdictional problem has been dealt with by section 2(3) which provides that:

> *"Subsection (1) applies only if the agreement, decision or practice is, or is intended to be, implemented in the UK."*

Section 18 of the Act does not refer to extraterritorial application; furthermore, s 18(3) requires that the dominant position must have taken place within the UK. It may thus be inferred that the UK practice and legislation are still opposed to the *"effects doctrine"*. Abuse of sovereignty may take place in respect of economic matters too.

3.7 CONCLUSIONS

The relationship between diplomacy and sovereignty may apparently seem to be remote, but diplomacy at both bilateral and multilateral levels is very much based on the perception of sovereignty held by diplomats. Diplomats are, in the

---

[66] op. cit.

[67] See the Eleventh Report on Competition Policy [1987] points 24–42; the Commission's decisions in the *Wood Pulp* case [1985] 3 CMLR 474

[68] Case 52/69 [1972] ECR 787

[69] See further the Protection of the Trading Interests Act, 1980; see also the *Aide Memoire* submitted by the UK government to the ECJ following the Commission's decision in the *Dyestuffs* case. The text of the *Aide Memoire* has been produced in Lowe at 144-147; see also the UK's objections to the effects doctrine in the *Wood Pulp* case.

first instance, representatives of their sovereigns. A diplomat is required to function at three levels: (a) national; (b) regional; and (c) international. As a diplomat he/she is required to protect his/her national interest; thus, in concluding any bilateral treaty or arrangement this issue assumes paramountcy, but often such treaties establish reciprocal benefit, be they investment treaties or treaties for exchange of scientific information or research.

Regional diplomacy is primarily aimed at developing the interests of the region, in addition to protecting the interests of each member State of the region, where necessary. Currently, the best example of regional diplomacy would be that aimed at the European Union. Within this Union, agriculture has always received particular attention of the Member States, and indeed, the Agricultural Policy of the European Union has been protective of the national interests of its Member States. However, in the pursuit of regional diplomacy, diplomats should bear in mind that such diplomacy does not run counter to the interest of the international community. In fact, regional organisations can adversely affect the trading interests of non-members of such arrangements. Diplomacy at the international level has an entirely different and unique purpose. At this level; diplomats are required to work in the interests of the entire international community, although of course, in certain circumstances, in developing framework rules, national interests of specific countries may have to be specifically protected, as it was done in respect of the law-locked States at the time of drafting the UN Convention on the Law of the Sea (UNCLOS III). In such cases, the issue of the national sovereignty may not be allowed to assume much importance. International fora, in particular the UN, should be allowed to be involved in matters which generally affect the international community, and in such instances, any attempt to rigidly guard a State's sovereignty would defeat the entire purpose of establishing these organisations. Diplomats and their sovereigns are required to appreciate that disinterested technical assistance from these organisations may help improve the socio-economic conditions in many States.

Abuse of sovereignty, particularly on the basis of a superior military or economic power, should be avoided. Diplomacy at an international level is concerned with ideology and purpose which are so different from national or regional diplomacy. Diplomacy at an international level has become particularly important since the days of de-colonisation. As the nature of world politics becomes increasingly complex, and as the North-South divide becomes wider, the need for diplomacy at an international level becomes even more pressing. It is to be emphasised that what used to be regarded as matters of exclusive domestic jurisdiction of States are no longer necessarily so. Take, for example, international terrorism, money laundering, drugs-related problems; child labour; poverty or environmental issues. These issues may not be resolved single-handedly by any State, rich or poor. Hence, the need for international co-operation, the framework of which may only be determined by diplomats.

In order to resolve such problems, sovereigns and their diplomats should adopt a flexible approach towards sovereignty, and accept participation by international organisations. In fact, the distinction between *"Sovereign right"* and *"sovereignty"* is important to bear in mind in this context. Where necessary, sovereigns may find it useful to share their sovereign rights with other sovereigns, which does not amount to surrendering their sovereignty to anybody, but which forms the basis for international co-operation.

The days of power-based diplomacy should be over; such diplomacy defeats the essence of negotiation-based diplomacy, and indeed, creates coercive diplomacy which act counter to the principle of sovereign equality. Coercive diplomacy runs counter to what may be described as *"participatory diplomacy"*. Coercive diplomacy often proves to be counterproductive in that it gives rise to conflicts, and strains international relations between States. Take, for example, the case of Iraq; the issue is not whether intervention in Iraq by some of the Western Powers was legal or illegal; it has not fully produced the anticipated results, and even if it does so eventually, one should weigh the benefits against the losses of human lives, and the damage to the economy for which Iraqis will suffer. Regime change, if found appropriate, should be approached by multilateral diplomacy, and through the intervention of the UN. By pursuing this route, no Member State of the UN will be in breach of Article 2, paragraph (4) of the UN Charter. This is where much work is needed by diplomats. Coercive diplomacy by a few has undermined the UN. Again, take for example, the case of North Viet-Nam – nobody won the war, but, the loss of human lives was unduly high. It was a prolonged war. In the final analysis, the people in North Viet-Nam suffered for a long time both from social and economic standpoints.

Aid-based diplomacy is no diplomacy. Aid or loan to a country by another country has an effect of subserviency. From a psychological standpoint, a receiver of aid or loan loses its bargaining power, and effectively becomes a supporter of the aid giver. Diplomats should consider whether loans should be provided exclusively by institutions, international or otherwise, in order to avoid the situation of subserviency. If necessary, diplomats may take the initiative to change the terms and conditions of institutional loans. One of the advantages of institutional loans is the technical assistance that may be attached to them.

Respect for each other's sovereignty is fundamental to international diplomacy; thus abuse of sovereignty in any form invites disrespect from the abused to the abuser. So long as misconceived bargaining power remains the basis for diplomacy, particularly between the economically strong and the economically poor States, there will be no diplomacy *stricto sensu*.

CHAPTER 4

Ethics in Diplomacy

4.1 INTRODUCTION

Ideally, diplomacy should be clear and ethical; its principal function being development of friendly relations between States. Diplomatic relations aimed at developing or strengthening economic relations on a bilateral basis must be ethical, mutually beneficial and clear. The objectives of bilateral diplomacy primarily are: (a) to create and maintain economic relations; (b) to create and maintain relationships in other areas which would be mutually beneficial, namely, exchange of scientific ideas and knowledge; exchange of other facilities deemed to be mutually useful for the countries concerned; and thus (c) to be engaged in cultural and educational exchanges. It is maintained that cultural and educational exchanges have their benefits but these may be described as the spill over effect of bilateral diplomacy.

In the case of multilateral diplomacy however the nature of interest is different from that of bilateral diplomacy in that it is primarily an attempt to achieve something on a multilateral basis for the benefit of everybody unless special exceptions are made for certain States which deserve preferential treatment. Take, for example, the multilateral Trade Negotiations Rounds in relation to GATT and thereafter WTO/GATT.

What is ethics in diplomacy? It simply suggests that diplomacy must be carried out in an ethical manner. But, whose ethics? This is where the problem arises. There does not exist any internationally recognised standards of ethics for diplomats. In other words, it is individualistic; furthermore, there seems to exist an assumption that diplomacy will be done in an ethical fashion. Thus, the entire issue of ethics in diplomacy remains vague. Diplomats are often required to compromise between personal moral convictions and official obligations. It is often maintained that the principal goal of a foreign policy is national survival. Standards of ethics are developed by societies; thus it varies from society to society, but it is again a vague concept; furthermore, unlike societal ethics which is governed by the moral standards maintained by a society, which is a cohesive unit, ethics in diplomacy is non-cohesive, fragmented, as its constituents (diplomats) come from a variety of societies governed by different standards of morality. However, the tradition of idealism in leadership was provided by Jean-Jacques Rousseau and Immanuel Kant. But not all leaders may be persuaded by any idealism. Given the objectives of diplomacy the role of ethics may not be denied[1].

The next question that arises is whether ethics in diplomacy and ethics in a society should be comparable; do they carry similar attributes and objectives. Societal ethics is concerned with a society's moral standards – that is, the standards of morality that a society determines to uphold in order to ensure that the moral fibre of a society is not disturbed; on the contrary, it should be upgraded. Ethics in diplomacy, on the other hand, is individualistic, particularly in relation to bilateral diplomacy. Here again, standards of ethics may vary from one geographic region to another or broadly the Christian States and non-Christian States. Niccolò Machiavelli maintained that where a State's security is in danger, the issue of *"just"* or *"unjust"* is important. According to Dean Acheson, a former US Secretary of State, ethics and aesthetics are not suitable tools in relation between countries[2].

In the case of multilateral diplomacy however the scenario becomes quite different in that multilateral ethics is supposedly based on the common standards of ethics, which in fact, is difficult to determine because of the varying demands and problems with which a large number of States are concerned. Thus, in such a case, what would be *"just"* becomes the principal issue. In a way, ethics in multilateral diplomacy is primarily concerned with and synonymously used with *"just diplomacy"*. *"Just"* is not entirely concerned with *"ethics"*, although ethics plays a role in achieving a *"just solution"*. Diplomacy is not primarily concerned with legal rules; its main objective is to reach a *"just"* solution in the circumstances of a case. Bilateral diplomacy, be it between two Christian States or between a Christian and a non-Christian State, is also concerned with *"just diplomacy"*. In fact, a recognition of *"just diplomacy"* will give rise to controversy surrounding *"ethics in diplomacy"* or *"ethical diplomacy"*. Bilateral diplomacy creates a preferential treatment between the two States concerned, which form of diplomacy is unethical, when considered in relation to the entire world; this is another reason why *"just diplomacy"* seems to be more appropriate; two sovereign States have the right to strike any deal they like between themselves, as long as it is not illegal.

Ethics in diplomacy is often motivated by emotion or by particular States' policies; the examples of Yugoslavia and Iraq are relevant. National interest is another factor which often shapes ethics in diplomacy, but may sometimes prove to be unethical when considered from the perspective of the entire international community.

Given some of the dilemmas with which the so-called *"ethics in diplomacy"* is concerned, this chapter attempts to explain what ethics in diplomacy really means, and how it operates in the real world.

---

[1] See further T Donaldson, "Kant's Global Rationalism", in *Traditions of International Ethics*, T Nardin and D R Mapel (eds), Cambridge, Cambridge University Press (1992)

[2] D Acheson, "Morality, Moralism and Diplomacy", *The Yale Review*, Yale University Press (1959) at 488

4.2 IS THERE ANYTHING CALLED *"INTERNATIONAL MORALITY"*?

"International morality" should stand for morality of the community of States. But is that identifiable? Furthermore, as explained before, the standards of morality under different cultures being different any reference to an international morality is ill-conceived. Nevertheless, the perception of *"international morality"* exists. Generally, outrageous immoral acts, such as manslaughter or killings on the grounds of religion, are unethical and impermissible. But then, history clearly suggests that when warfare was a common phenomenon, irrespective of whether it involved the killing of human beings, the morality or immorality of the act was not seriously considered. It is interesting to note that the Convention on the Prevention and Punishment of the Crime of Genocide, 1948 contained many reservations.

If diplomacy is all about balance of power or domination over the weak by the strong, then there is no room for ethics or justice. On the other hand, in his *Prince*, Niccolò Machiavelli (1469–1527) stated that the principal foundations of all States are good laws and good armies, and that good laws cannot exist without good armies; conversely, where there are good armies there must be goods laws[3]. In fact, contrary to the popular belief, Machiavelli was not all that unrealistic. The majority of States in the contemporary period seem to operate on the basis of what Machiavelli said about six hundred years ago. Diplomacy is often military-based, and national interest, whether in the form of security of State or otherwise, still remains an important factor in international diplomacy.

Leaving Machiavelli aside, any discussion of ethics in diplomacy is irrelevant when diplomacy is power-orientated, because power has a blinding effect. Thus, diplomacy may be of two types: (a) power-based; and (b) non-power-based. Power-based diplomacy need not be ethical, although it often seeks justification from the international community. Non-power-based diplomacy is non-coercive, concerned with negotiated results, and is not involved in any outrageous international immorality. Whether diplomacy is outrageous or not depends upon how just it is.

In diplomacy, sovereignty matters, but regrettably it is often abused in that it is applied in disregard of the interests of peoples or sometimes States. Thus, *"might"* rather than legitimate authority as an expression of sovereignty is used. Over-use of sovereignty is unethical. Sovereignty is the fountain of power, it is also the source of discretionary and/or discriminatory judgments, which are based on bias for or against a State or people, but in the final analysis, the act is unethical. Examples of such use of power in diplomacy are available: free movement of people (immigration) has always been a discriminatory and discretionary policy between States; ownership of property by foreigners; or the right to set up businesses by foreigners (other than regional economic integrations) are other examples of it. By referring to the Vienna

---

[3] N Machiavelli, *The Prince*, Oxford, Oxford University Press (1998) at 41

Convention on Diplomatic Relations, States believe that the principle of the sovereign equality should be maintained in promoting international diplomacy[4]. During the UN era certain issues having an ethical dimension have been made part of the principle of State responsibility: observance of human rights by regimes, protection of the environment, minority rights to mention but a few. Ironically, the aspirations of the UN still largely remain unfulfilled. The concept of *"international justice"* based on international ethics still remains at a theoretical level[5]. By contrast, the inherent power of a sovereign may also be exercised on the grounds of the national interest, which may not be questioned by any other authority, political or judicial.

It is an act of international immorality to build weaponries for the purpose of attacking others; it is also so to intervene in the regimes of other States in the name of humanitarian intervention[6], particularly when the meaning of this latter term remains unclear. Is it an act of international morality to allow drug production and drug trafficking to perpetuate with knowledge of its consequences? The income from drugs and the availability of markets keep the trade live.

Again, is it an act of international morality to provide financial and military assistance by a State to another in order to strengthen any oppressive and undemocratic regime? Is it an act of international morality to offer preferential trading arrangements to different States in a discretionary and discriminatory fashion? The list of such questions may indeed be very long. In many cases, the answers are obvious, but in many others more than one answer may be available evidencing the fact that there does not exist any identifiable common standards of international morality. Often, an act of morality is supported from the standpoint of self-interest, whether in the form of foreign investment or to gain control over a particular regime or even for image-building purposes. A bi-lateral interest may not thus be equated to international morality.

Although the concept of *"international morality"* seems to be vague, it nevertheless seems to be perceived in Locke's idea of a state of nature which stands for a moral world into which the concepts of right and wrong, ultimately founded upon God, applies, and according to him it would be the duty of a political government to ensure that these moral laws are reflected in legislation. But, if one follows Hobbes, the advocate of *"realism"*, then one would maintain that the concepts of moral right and wrong do not apply, and that international relations, including international co-operation, are to be conducted on the basis of national self-interest. Realism rejects moralism with respect to international affairs; thus, according to it, there is no room for ethics in international relations and diplomacy.

---

[4] M Stearns, *Talking to Strangers: Improving American Diplomacy at Home and Abroad*, New Jersey, Princeton University Press (1996) at 165

[5] On the issue of international justice, see further M R Amstutz, *International Ethics: Concepts, Theories and Cases in Global Politics*, Rowman & Littlefield (1999)

[6] See section 3 of this Chapter

The other issue which ought to be considered in this connection is whether the moral framework appropriate to relations between individual human beings is relevant to relations between States[7]. Although a State is composed of individuals, the latter's interests and scope of morality are different from those of the former. Whereas an individual's scope of morality is individualistic in nature and is predominantly concerned with his / her own interests and welfare, it is the State's duty to preserve the standards of morality of its individuals. A State's morality in respect of international relations, as stated earlier, is usually based on self-interest, that is, the benefit that it will derive from a bi-lateral deal; in other words, there may not be any morality in that deal; it may be a deal for a bilateral defence treaty, or a treaty for a preferential trading arrangement which is discriminatory, and yet, serves the best interests of the State. Interestingly enough, bilateral treaties, which may not satisfy the conditions of morality, may serve the interests of the State and its peoples. In the circumstances, how should one judge what is moral or immoral, although an act may be totally unethical? A State's interests in international diplomacy and those of individuals may not coincide, although the latter may benefit from the former's acts. This is the nature of ethics in the context of international diplomacy.

Although the scope of international morality should be broad, it is not so as yet, as the issues which are so far concerned with international morality are limited in number, namely, mass killing of people, pollution of the environment or oppressive regimes. But, these have been made issues of international morality by international conventions, which have formed part of customary international law.

There does not exist any definition of international morality because there seems to exist a belief that everybody understands what it should stand for, although this may not necessarily be the case.

A few nations' morality, when summed up together, may not necessarily constitute an international morality.

4.3 ETHICS IN DIPLOMACY AND POLITICS OF DIPLOMACY

To many, a discussion of politics of diplomacy would be unacceptable, as diplomacy is generally perceived to be a profession of the accomplished whose task it is to develop friendly relations between States. But the issue remains for what purposes diplomacy or friendly relations should be developed. One of the principal objectives of diplomacy / friendly relations is economic security, that is, trade between two States. Diplomats negotiate bilateral trade and investment treaties based on the relevant principles of public international law. It has been stated earlier that cultural exchanges between the States concerned may be an aspect of such treaties.

---

[7] See further Gordon Graham, *Ethics and International Relations*, Oxford, Blackwell (1997) at 19

Included in the politics of diplomacy are economic and military interests among other interests. The choice of countries with which to conclude such treaties is based on the foreign policy of the country concerned. Foreign policy formulation by States is often subject to the preferential choices made by countries, whereby friendship will be maintained with those of the countries which have traditionally been regarded as friends and allies; or new countries may be included in the fold of the foreign policy, and by the same token, certain countries will be rejected as they may no longer be treated as friends or allies. In fact, selfish interests of countries often motivate them to formulate their foreign policies. Investment opportunities in countries, be they developed or developing, prove to be a deciding factor for interacting with such countries. This practice of States need not be criticised; this is the reality. It is emphasised that diplomacy at a national level is mostly concerned with economic prosperity, and of course, to maintain peace and security within the country by avoiding conflicts with other States. The protection of the national interests is at the heart of bilateral diplomacy. In fact, in order to consolidate their position the system of exchange of diplomats and setting up of missions of sending States in receiving States originated. The Vienna Convention on Diplomatic Relations, 1961 and the Vienna Convention on Consular Relations, 1963 thus provide the framework for conducting relations, diplomatic and consular, based on State practice and a common ethical framework. It is to be borne in mind that any dispute as to the interpretation of these Conventions will be governed by the Vienna Convention on the Law of Treaties, 1969, but any dispute between a receiving State and a sending State as to diplomatic or consular relations between them should be resolved by diplomatic negotiation[8], and if that dispute cannot be settled by such method, then of course, the diplomatic or consular relations as the case may be between those two States will come to an end. This is where training of diplomats becomes necessary; their expertise lies in settling disputes amicably and continuing to strengthen friendly relations between States.

Protection of the national interest plays a dominant role in carrying out diplomacy at a regional level. Take, for example, the Agricultural Policy of the European Union, the national interest of the Member States was so dominant to protect their farmers that the EU allowed high subsidies to be provided by each Member State, and almost 50% of the budget of the EU is allocated to agriculture.

The issue of the national interest became evident, for example, in regard to the common currency; national interest is also associated with the issue of national sovereignty. Diplomacy in this context, particularly on the part of those Member States which decided not to accept the common currency (Euro) was also based on foreign economic policy of the States concerned, which is part of the foreign policies of those States. Similar issues arose in

---

[8] This will include good office, conciliation and negotiation

regard to the constitution of the European Union. A regional integration is based on the assumption that all Member States would join the integration in every possible way, and yet, national interest intervenes, whether for right or wrong reasons. This is what is meant by politics of diplomacy.

In so far as the EU is concerned, the other aspect of politics of diplomacy is rather disturbing. An economic integration has its first obligation towards its Member States; thus, the Union or the economic area is required to allow its Member States to take advantage of the market by selling their goods to it; there is almost a guaranteed market. This puts the outsiders, particularly developing countries, in a difficult situation in that hardly any market is available for their goods, unless market access has been allowed on a bilateral basis. The duration of these treaties may be short, thus denying any permanent access to the market. Furthermore, in view of the fact that each of the Member States is strong in the agricultural sector, developing countries are not in a position to sell their agricultural products, their principal produce, unless there exist special bilateral treaties to that effect.

Interventionist diplomacy is another example of unethical diplomacy; it is also an aspect of politics of diplomacy. When diplomacy is directed at a particular direction by an external power to change a regime in another country, it is an interventionist diplomacy. In fact, it is no diplomacy, because it does not entail any negotiation between the two parties. It is the domination of one by the other. It is also interventionist because usually the wish of the peoples in a country is not taken into account. There is no need to provide examples of this type of diplomacy; suffice to say that it creates opportunities for private foreign investment and makes the changed regime dependent upon the intervening power. This may also be called diplomacy of dependency; the sovereign will or the sovereign authority of one party is not allowed to exercise in a democratic way. Unless external help is sought by the majority of the people in a country, any external power's involvement in overthrowing an existing regime, directly or indirectly, even by providing finance and / or weapons, amounts to intervention.

Interventionist diplomacy often leads to human sufferings, killings and other inevitable consequences. Intervention even on the grounds of humanitarian act (humanitarian intervention) is also unsustainable in law. In recent years, support for humanitarian intervention came from Lillich and Newman. They suggested that it is only in quite exceptional circumstances that unilateral action by a State may be considered as legally justified on the basis of the doctrine of humanitarian intervention, particularly if that action involves the use of force on a scale of some magnitude[9]. They also supported such intervention on certain other grounds[10]. Brownlie contested this argument

---

[9] R B Lillich and F C Newman, *International Human Rights: Problems of Law and Policy*, Syracuse University Press (1979) at 495

[10] ibid., at 493

by saying that it was not based on practice of States or that the view should be offered *tout court* as a proposal to change the existing law[11]. Brownlie also pointed out that no customary law existed in regard to humanitarian intervention, and that this concept militates against its legality, and many of the eminent jurists, namely, Brierly, Briggs, Friedmann, Goodrich, Hambro, Jessup and Schwarzenberger opposed it[12].

In the event of a conflict arising between ethics in diplomacy and politics of diplomacy, the question arises which should prevail. Although, in theory, there may be an answer to the question, in the real world, reaction to this issue can be very different. Power politics forms the foundation of politics of diplomacy.

4.4 WHAT ROLE MAY ETHICS IN DIPLOMACY PLAY IN RESTRAINING POLITICS OF DIPLOMACY?

Not much. This is because ethics in diplomacy is a vague concept, although there exists a perception that it is identifiable. Politics of diplomacy cannot be restrained for a variety of reasons: (a) ethics in diplomacy has not set any universally acceptable standards; (b) moral constraints in interventionist diplomacy are relatively rare[13]; and (c) the default in developing a framework of ethics allows politics of diplomacy to reign supreme.

Indifference of States to the miseries of other States or to the coming to the rescue of an aggressed State are but a few examples of tolerating injustice to other States or peoples therein.

The role of ethics in international diplomacy is almost like the role of religion in a nation's life. Religion does play a role in a nation's life in that it tends to inculcate in some people religious beliefs, but there is no compulsion for people to be subject to any inculcation even though in certain countries the mainstream religion is financially supported by the State (in the form of providing salary to priests and other appointed religious incumbents). Furthermore, the propagation of religious beliefs has a long history in the world particularly when churches in Christendom ruled nations; it is difficult to do away altogether with the religious fibre in a society. It is the function of a State to uphold and spread the dicta of ethics and morality to keep the *"evil"* separate from the *"good"*.

Religion in the context of a State thus serves a national interest, international diplomacy, on the other hand, deals with and protects national interest, irrespective of whether it proves to be ethical or not; as stated earlier, under the current international diplomatic practice, it is not considered to be

---

[11] I Brownlie, "Humanitarian Intervention" in *Law and Civil War in the Modern World*, J Moore (ed) Baltimore, Johns Hopkins University Press (1974), 217–219

[12] ibid., see further S K Chatterjee, "Some Legal Problems of Support Role in International Law: Tanzania and Uganda", 30 *International and Comparative Law Quarterly* (1981) 755

[13] See further Gordon Graham, op. cit., at 35

unethical to remain indifferent to issues of international importance. Perhaps no analogies should be drawn between the notion of ethics at a national level and that at an international level. Furthermore, the ethical issues for a State at a domestic level and those at the international level may be different.

In fact, the perception of ethics at a national level and that at an international level may also be different. Take, for example, the issue of death penalty – whereas certain States still do not consider it to be unethical to carry out death penalty on human beings, the international community, as a whole, abhors it. Again, whereas by not promulgating and implementing legislation against child labour certain States directly maintain that it is not illegal, the international community, as a whole, considers it unethical and expects States to prohibit it by law[14].

The international community's notions of what is *"just"* or *"unjust"* are still not uniform. Whereas Article 2(4) of the UN Charter prohibits the use of force by one Member State against another as a peremptory norm, many States do not consider it to be unethical to be involved in warfares even though their consequences are foreseeable. Is it not unethical for a UN Member State to conclude a defence treaty with another of its Members in derogation of the provisions of Article 2(4) of the UN Charter[15]? Is it not unethical for a State to intervene in the domestic affairs of another State and then compel the UN to provide humanitarian assistance to the affected people?

The issue of ethics in international diplomacy becomes complex when it comes to providing assistance by the rich to the poor. To transfer surplus agricultural products in the West (particularly in the EU) to poor States looks ethical but by so doing the sources of income and employment for people in the poor countries will be jeopardised, thus it would be grossly unethical for rich countries to do so.

The standards of bilateral diplomacy vary from State to State depending upon the standards of ethics a State maintains. For many States, it is not unethical to supply weapons to other States knowing full well the consequences of supply of weapons on its people. By the same token, sending of troops to other countries when a war is waged on a limited consensus of the international community as a whole, knowing its consequences, is unethical, but not considered so.

In the final analysis, the principle of sovereignty is at the root of all problems. The international community is almost in every sphere still dominated by the principle of sovereignty in its absolute form; thus ethics or notions towards ethics are determined by reference to a sovereign's intention. Furthermore, the issue of popularity of a sovereign in the eyes of its subjects attains prominence;

---

[14] See the ILO Convention entitled "Elimination of the Worst Forms of Child Labour" the text of which has been reproduced in 38 *International Legal Materials* (1949) 1207

[15] Article 2(4) states: "All Members shall refrain in their international relations from the threat or use of force against the territorial integrity or political independence of any state, or in any other manner inconsistent with the Purposes of the United Nations."

going into a war and winning it or at least not being defeated in it, is a major source of popularity for the sovereign, and in that situation, the battle for ethics is relegated to a secondary position.

The dichotomy between the principle of sovereignty in its absolute form and the issue of the national interest and ethics in diplomacy need not be over-emphasised. Bilateral diplomacy is predominantly concerned with the issue of the national interest, ethics in international diplomacy is predominantly concerned with developing ethical standards about issues with which the international community, as a whole, may be concerned. In multilateral diplomacy, ethics may be relevant to issues which are matters of international concern, that is, those matters which may, unless appropriately regulated, adversely affect the international community. The so-called standards of international ethics may not thus play any significant role in restraining politics of diplomacy.

4.5 IS MULTILATERAL DIPLOMACY TOTALLY SHORT OF ETHICS?

It would be inappropriate to say that multilateral diplomacy is entirely short of ethics; the crucial question remains how does one develop the standards of ethics in multilateral diplomacy. Ethics in multilateral diplomacy represents the minimum and common standards of ethics that the international community, as a whole, has reached over matters of international concern. Two factors are therefore extremely important in developing any framework for ethics in multilateral diplomacy: (a) to identify areas of *"international concern"* and (b) to identify the willingness and consensus that ethical standards should be developed over specific issues. Matters of the international interest may not necessarily be matters of domestic interest; but there exist matters which are apparently domestic in nature but of international concern. For example, production or manufacture of drugs beyond the permissible limits set for scientific and medicinal uses by a State which finds illicit markets in the various foreign jurisdictions, or how the lack of control of money laundering at a national level or the development of nuclear warfares or weapons of mass destruction discreetly by a State will have repercussions on the international community, and these being matters of international concern, they need international co-operation for their resolution. These are matters which, without any international co-operation, may not be settled even at a national level. Ethical standards about such matters may be set by concluding international conventions, and / or by adopting resolutions at the UN General Assembly level.

Ethics in diplomacy becomes relevant to multilateral diplomacy when it relates to matters of multilateral concern, and requires negotiation and consensus at a multilateral level. Take, for example, the prohibition of nuclear tests even for peaceful purposes. In 1974, France carried out nuclear tests in the Pacific, and the affected countries, Australia, Fiji and New Zealand brought an action[16] before the International Court of Justice against France on the grounds that such tests were contrary to the Partial Test Ban Treaty of 1963. France was not a party to the Nuclear Test Ban Treaty; thus, she relied on the *res inter alios acta* doctrine, according to which a third party may not be sued against under a treaty. The court did not accept that plea as the said Treaty developed and established a peremptory norm[17]. The conclusion of the Nuclear Test Ban Treaty was an act of multilateral diplomacy.

On the other hand, where a high degree of national interest prevails in respect of particular matters, multilateral treaty negotiation may fail. Such was the case with the WTO negotiation at Cancún in 2003. Neither the rich countries nor the developing countries could afford to lose their respective interests in their agricultural sector. In fact, although apparently unethical for rich countries not to allow the developing countries access to the former's markets, from a pragmatic standpoint, rich countries cannot afford to sacrifice their agricultural sector to the developing countries. Thus, where national interests reign supreme, multilateral treaties may not be concluded as there will be no consensus among the States having national interest in the subject matter of the treaty or resolution.

Again, in so far as UN General Assembly Resolutions are concerned, take for example, the resolution entitled *the Charter of Economic Rights and Duties of States, 1974*[18]. The contents of the resolution were excellent, except for a limited number of articles in it; in fact, the vast majority of the articles were based on State-practice. This resolution predominantly recorded the aspirations of developing countries, although most of the provisions related to both rich and poor countries. However, the provisions for cartelisation of commodities including their price determination, and a non-obligatory provision as regards the payment of compensation in the event of the taking of private foreign assets predominantly prompted developed States to reject the resolution. In fact, except Australia, none of the rich States accepted this resolution. It was an example of an ill-thought out diplomacy, because cartelisation of commodities is impermissible in a free market, and it would also provoke rich countries to do the same about transfer of technology or skills; furthermore, there was no reason for developing countries to decide to derogate from the customary rule of international law about paying compensation in the event of the taking of private foreign assets. This would be contrary to the principle of state responsibility and ethics. To include such provisions in a resolution of an international importance is also an unethical act.

On the other hand, in concluding the UN Law of the Sea Convention III, 1982, it was only ethical for rich countries to allow the land-locked State to

---

[16] In the actual proceedings Fiji was absent

[17] A peremptory norm is a binding norm from which no derogation even by a third party is permissible

[18] UNGA Res 2631 of 1974

share the common heritage of mankind (which was achieved by means of diplomatic negotiations)[19].

Again, take for example, the case of the Universal Declaration of Human Rights, 1948. Nobody can say that this instrument which is a product of multilateral diplomacy is not based on ethics, and yet, many countries have failed to implement its provisions, either because they do not have the resources required for its implementation or that many governments have not accorded any priority to the implementation of these provisions or that some of the provisions of this instrument run counter to their societal culture.

This is where one of the difficulties in identifying and implementing international ethics arises. The remit of ethics in diplomacy is thus narrow, and perhaps shall remain so for the foreseeable future, unless radical changes in societal attitudes and practice of sovereign States take place.

4.6 CONCLUSIONS

As stated earlier, it is difficult to articulate ethics in diplomacy. Its importance is appreciated, but its dimensions let alone its definition is difficult to achieve. The concept of ethics in diplomacy is wrapped up with the concept of the national interest. Ethics in bilateral diplomacy between two sovereign States may not necessarily form the basis for ethics in multilateral diplomacy. The problems giving rise to such an unsatisfactory situation are manifold: (a) the particular national interest of sovereign States; (b) socio-cultural reasons; and (c) the lack of prioritisation of ethics in international diplomacy by many States.

Ethics in diplomacy is also torn with the history of States, which has had a long tradition of warfares. The history of peoples and nations, including their origins and statehood, are associated with warfares. This was followed by the period of colonisation particularly as from the 18th century. Neither warfares, nor colonisation, nor subjugation of peoples was considered to be unethical by the mighty. The League of Nations, which was the first international organisation for the maintenance of international peace and security, did not abolish warfare. Article 15 paragraph 7 of the Covenant of the League provided that:

> *"If the Council fails to reach a report which is unanimously agreed to by the members thereof, other than the Representatives of one or more of the parties to the dispute, the Members of the League reserve to themselves the right to take such action as they shall consider for the maintenance of right and justice."*

The setting up of the United Nations in 1945 seemed to be a great step forward to reverse the history of mankind and the world, but it was not to be. Article 2(4) of the UN Charter provides that:

---
[19] Article 125(1)

INTERNATIONAL LAW AND DIPLOMACY

> *"All Members shall refrain in their international relations from the threat or use of force against the territorial integrity or political independence of any State, or in any other manner inconsistent with the Purposes of the United Nations."*[20]

But, if one takes a look at the history since 1945, one can easily confirm how many warfares have taken place without the consent of the United Nations (Viet-Nam, El Salvador, Grenada, Nicaragua and then the controversial intervention by the Allied Powers in Iraq in 2003).

During the early days of the United Nations, de-colonisation of the countries by the colonial powers was acknowledged by the international community as an obligatory act[21]; however, the technique or method of de-colonising them was never an issue of ethics. In most cases, political independence of the former colonies made them economically dependent upon the former colonial powers and international organisations, in particular, the International Monetary Fund and the World Bank. The debt situation of the majority of the former colonies is so hopeless that in 1996 the World Bank found it necessary to set up a new fund entitled the *Heavily Indebted Poor Countries' Trust Fund* in order to alleviate their position, but there also the progress will be slow.

On the other hand, in so far as transfer / acquisition of technology is concerned, the United Nations adopted guidelines so as to ensure that the home countries would advise their transnational corporations to transfer their technology which would satisfy the acquiring country's needs. In most cases, that has not happened. Furthermore, the guidelines provided, inter alia, that emphasis should be placed on providing assistance to developing countries whereby they would be able to develop their indigenous technology.

Implementation of these guidelines has proved to be slow, and multilateral diplomacy in this regard has remained rather inactive. Where proactive action is necessary, complacency or inaction is unethical.

Ethics in bilateral diplomacy is individualistic; the choice of relationship between two countries, whether reciprocal or otherwise, may not affect the entire world; multilateral diplomacy cannot be so. The latter has a broader purpose; it must set standards of behaviour for the international community whether by means of international Conventions or Declarations or Resolutions adopted by and through international organisations, such as the United Nations. In recent years, through the untiring efforts of the United Nations, ethical standards have been established in respect of the protection of human rights, prohibition of genocide or the protection of the environment[22].

Standard of ethics in multilateral diplomacy must not be allowed to be set aside by a limited number of States, be they powerful or less powerful States;

---

[20] Emphasis added

[21] See UNGA Resolution entitled The Declaration on the Granting of Independence to Colonial Countries and Peoples, (1960) Resolution No 1514 (XV)

[22] See further the Stockholm Declaration on Human Environment of 1972 and the Rio Declaration of 1992 on Environment and Development

Ethics in Diplomacy

they must be based on the common will and aspirations, and if a member of the international community derogates from these standards, that unacceptable conduct must be dealt with by the international forum, that is, the United Nations. If the forum of the United Nations is considered to be ineffective, then it is unethical for the members of the international community not to reform it.

> Ethics in multilateral diplomacy is concerned with those issues which are for the general good of the international community. There may not thus be any progression between ethics in bilateral diplomacy and that in multilateral diplomacy.

| Good bilateral diplomatic practice may give rise to good and ethical multilateral diplomacy culminating in multilateral conventions eg right of innocent passage through the territorial waters – Law of the Sea Convention | Non-hierarchical  | National interest – based on multilateral diplomacy is unethical and can be rejected. See the Charter of Economic Rights and Duties of States, 1974 or the Cancún Round of WTO. |

Bilateral diplomacy can be narrow, reciprocal or non-reciprocal; may be based on historical relationship; may also be culture-based and national interest-based.

CHAPTER 5

Diplomacy and Diplomats

5.1 INTRODUCTION

There exists a perception that the meaning of *"diplomacy"* is well-understood by everybody, which does not seem to be the case. By the same token, functions of a diplomat are thought to be clear, but when it comes to defining them, difficulties seem to begin. In this chapter attempts are made to explain, in particular, the meaning of diplomacy, the attributes of a diplomat and the functions of a diplomat.

The author wishes to make it clear that the discussion in this chapter is not meant to be exhaustive or complete; in fact, as the world of diplomacy continually becomes complex, so do his / her functions and demands on his / her capacity.

5.2 WHAT IS DIPLOMACY?

The Oxford English Dictionary defines *"diplomacy"* as:

> *"The management of international relations by negotiations; the method by which these relations are adjusted and managed by ambassadors and envoys; the business or art of the diplomatist, skill or address in the conduct of international intercourse and negotiations."*[1]

Thus, diplomacy stands for the management of international relations, that is, primarily state-to-state relations. *"Management"* in this context would mean settlement of differences, which should be achieved by negotiation. This definition also suggests that international relations are adjusted and managed by means of a method. Learning of that method by diplomats is thus essential.

Differences between two or more States may arise in respect of any matter: boundaries between two States; demarcation of continental shelves; environmental issues, trade-related matters; or general breakdown of friendly relations between two States; or threats posed by one to the national security of the other.

It is clearly evident that a diplomat is required to be an informed individual of the issues in a dispute or difference. Effective diplomatic solution can avoid court proceedings. Interestingly enough, unfortunate though, the need for training in war diplomacy has returned. These wars are, in most cases, based

---

[1] *The Oxford English Dictionary*, vol IV, Clarendon Press, Oxford (1989) at 696

on some kind of ideology, and this has become evident as from the Viet-Nam war. It is also interesting to note that in all cases of war, since the Viet-Nam war, the parties who have been involved are all Members of the United Nations, the Charter (Article 2(4)) of which prohibits the use of force of any kind, unless resort to it is taken on the grounds of self-defence. It is thought apposite to quote the provisions of Article 2, paragraph 4 and Article 51 of the UN Charter in this context:

Article 2(4)

> *"All Members shall refrain in their international relations from the threat or use of force against the territorial integrity or political independence of any state, or in any other manner inconsistent with the Purposes of the United Nations."*

Article 51

> *"Nothing in the present Charter shall impair the inherent right of individual or collective self-defence if an armed attack occurs against a Member of the United Nations, until the Security Council has taken measures necessary to maintain international peace and security. Measures taken by Members in the exercise of this right of self-defence shall be immediately reported to the Security Council and shall not in any way affect the authority and responsibility of the Security Council under the present Charter to take at any time such action as it deems necessary in order to maintain or restore international peace and security."*

An analysis of these Articles appears in Chapter 7.

The need for diplomacy between States can hardly be over-emphasised. Economic interdependence is, in reality, at the root of bilateral diplomacy. Historical evidence is clear to suggest that in the olden days, tracing as far back at the Middle Ages, rulers interacted with each other for trade; this proved to be the basis for establishing consular relations between States. Indeed, the need for bilateral diplomacy becomes stronger whenever the need for trade (import or export) arises.

Acquisition of territory by force was a norm until the end of the Second World War. Warfares needed diplomatic solutions. The sovereigns or their envoys were engaged in such activities. Skills to negotiate were essential for diplomats to settle such disputes.

After the Second World War and with the establishment of the United Nations, the entire gamut of diplomacy has changed. Article 2, paragraph 4 of the UN Charter prohibits its Member States from using force in any form or manner. Furthermore, the UN Charter emphasises the importance of international co-operation in respect of socio-economic, monetary (including trade) and welfare matters. Thus, modern day diplomats are required to have even more skills to participate in complex bilateral and multilateral international co-operation processes than ever before.

5.3 WHAT ARE THE ATTRIBUTES OF AN IDEAL DIPLOMAT?

Some might say that an *"ideal diplomat"* is a misconception. There seems to exist an assumption that diplomats are aware of the attributes they should possess. However, it is opportune to point out nevertheless what attributes diplomats should generally possess. An ideal diplomat is one who uses all the attributes to their utmost in the light of the circumstances of each situation.

The qualities of a diplomat should be derived from the purpose for which diplomacy stands. It stands for *"skill of managing international relations"*[2]; or *"skill and tact in dealing with people"*[3]. To *"manage"* means to maintain control or influence over a person[4]. *"Skill"* means *"ability to do something well; expertise or dexterity"*[5]. All these qualifications, when combined, should provide the attributes of a diplomat.

None of these attributes may be appropriately utilised unless a diplomat has fundamental knowledge and expertise in matters which he / she may be required to deal with. Skill and tact in dealing with people, in particular, requires certain additional attributes, namely, high threshold of tolerance; willingness to understand and consider other party's point of view; not to mar the environment of negotiation; and the language of the other party should not prove to be a barrier. *"International relations"* in this context would include relations on both bilateral and multilateral levels. Again, negotiation of issues, and development of ideas for creating policies at a multilateral level requires special skills and expertise.

"Tact" means sensitivity in dealing with others. A diplomat should not be devoid of tact; flexibility, command of the language, and the skills to strike a balance in order to protect the interests of the parties concerned.

Historically, diplomats and diplomacy have been associated with aristocrats and aristocracy. Indeed, diplomacy, until recently, was maintained as a reserved domain for aristocrats for the reason of the necessary attributes of aristocrats, namely, manners, etiquettes, politeness, command of the language. These attributes are still considered to be necessary for diplomats in the contemporary world. But the complexity of modern diplomacy and international relations requires diplomats to possess a thorough knowledge of power politics, and economic issues.

Furthermore, contemporary diplomacy is primarily about the maintenance of peace and developing economic relations between States, in addition to creating policies at the international level to regulate the conduct of States.

---

[2] See *The Concise Oxford English Dictionary*, Oxford, Oxford University Press (2002) at 405

[3] ibid

[4] ibid at 864

[5] ibid at 1344

Thus, the scope and purpose of contemporary diplomacy have proved to be significantly different from those of the olden days.

Ethics in diplomacy is an important issue in that an ethical approach to any issue or problem simply commands respect from the other party. *"Tactics"* and *"ethics"* are two different elements in diplomacy; whereas the former relates to strategies and their application at the most appropriate moment, an honest approach to the factual causes of conflict or differences is at the heart of the ethics. Manipulation of facts or to conceal facts to win over the other side is an example of unethical diplomacy. Diplomacy is about developing and maintaining relationship with other States, and avoiding conflicts. Aristocracy is no longer a necessary attribute of diplomacy; it is now an entirely skill-based profession.

The following may be identified as the most important attributes of a diplomat:

- *professionalism;*
- *skills and tactics in dealing with people;*
- *expertise in negotiation;*
- *ability to comprehend the issues and problems for both sides, where relevant, from an international perspective;*
- *flexibility in respect of strategies;*
- *comprehension of problems for which international diplomacy is needed;*
- *ethical;*
- *vision;*
- *leadership, including management of situations / crisis.*

The Member States should not also disregard their treaty obligations with the United Nations. Foreign policy-makers and diplomats perhaps should review this issue, in an attempt to increase their degree of co-operation between themselves and the United Nations.

There can therefore be diplomacy at different levels: national, regional and international. Regional diplomacy, such as that required at the European Union level, again is a type of diplomacy that requires consideration of protection of interest of the European Union and its Member States.

In order to maintain appropriate and effective diplomatic relations, whether with states or with international or inter-governmental organisations, the discipline called *Diplomatic Studies* should be broad-based, multi-faceted, allowing future diplomats not only to understand the complexity of the modern-day international relations but also to develop vision. *Diplomatic Studies*, when narrowly based and narrowly gauged defeat its entire purposes, and create diplomats accordingly.

5.4 DIPLOMATIC STUDIES AND INTERNATIONAL LAW

Many universities offering academic programmes in Diplomatic Studies and International Relations do not seem to place sufficient emphasis on the importance of learning the basic principles of public international law, without appreciating that a lack of knowledge in these principles may prompt a diplomat to violate them or deal with an issue solely from a diplomatic point of view. Certain principles of international law in relation to topics such as, sovereignty, jurisdiction, recognition of governments, international responsibility are vitally important for a diplomat to be familiar with in order to enable himself/herself to perform his/her diplomatic role effectively.

The notion that diplomacy can be validly and legitimately carried out in disregard of the established principles of international law is not only unfounded but also unsafe and misconceived. Should diplomats negotiate treaties, whether of a commercial or military nature, in disregard of the established principles of international law? Shouldn't diplomats keep developing new principles of international law through state practice? Diplomacy, in disregard of legal principles may be regarded as *"politics"*, and for politics, no special principles or studies seem to be necessary.

A diplomat representing its government before the United Nations will not be allowed by his/her fellow members to disregard the principles of international law, including the jurisprudence developed by the International Court of Justice. It is also necessary for a diplomat to justify its state's acts, if condemned by other states, with reference to the established principles of international law, otherwise the state to which the diplomat belongs may be subject to sanctions.

There are certain specific issues in the contemporary world with which all diplomats should be familiar: human rights, the limits of sovereign power, the protection of the environment, natural resources law, and treaty law to name but a few. Even the legal rules embodied in the Vienna Convention on Diplomatic Relations, 1961 and the Vienna Convention on Consular Relations, 1963 are essential for diplomats to learn in order to know the extent of their privileges and immunities, and their duties under these Conventions.

Diplomats need not be lawyers; nor are they expected to be politicians. Diplomats are primarily negotiators and are required to negotiate with other states; the outcome of their negotiations may take the form of a treaty or a memorandum of understanding or an agreement.

Misconception seems to persist that diplomats need not know the principles of public international law. It is inconceivable that diplomacy may be effectively and judiciously carried out without any knowledge of the fundamental principles of public international law, namely, sovereignty, state responsibility in addition to knowing the organisational and fundamental purposes of the UN. Unlike the practice in the olden days, not all conflicts in the contemporary period may be resolved by bilateral means. The use of the UN machinery may prove to be useful in settling disputes.

5.5 FUNCTIONS OF A DIPLOMAT

The Vienna Convention on Diplomatic Relations does not directly refer to the functions of a diplomat; but instead, in Article 3, it details the principal functions of a diplomatic mission, which consist in:

> *"(a) representing the sending State in the receiving State;*
> *(b) protecting in the receiving State the interests of the sending State and of its nationals, within the limits permitted by international law;*
> *(c) negotiating with the Government of the receiving State;*
> *(d) ascertaining by all lawful means conditions and developments in the receiving State, and reporting thereon to the Government of the sending State;*
> *(e) promoting friendly relations between the sending State and the receiving State, and developing their economic, cultural and scientific relations."*

When analysing these provisions, one should be able to catalogue the functions of a diplomat.

In order to discharge any of these functions, a diplomat requires appropriate training and skills. The functions of a mission detailed in Article 3 refer, however, to what a diplomat as a representative of the sending sovereign should do with and in the receiving State. The functions of a mission and a diplomat under Article 3 are purely of a bilateral nature. It does not refer to a diplomat's function in a wider world, that is, truly international diplomacy. As explained in the Chapter on the Vienna Convention on Diplomatic Relations[6], the Convention simply embodied the state practice developed by the older states over the years. In the olden days diplomatic relations between States were primarily of a bilateral nature; diplomacy with international organisations or regional institutions, in the main, was not in existence until the 20th century, and in particular, until the League of Nations was set up. Thus, diplomatic relations under the Vienna Convention stood for state-to-state relations. In fact, one should not look for the international functions of a diplomat in the Vienna Convention on Diplomatic Relations, 1961.

The primary function of a diplomat is to negotiate on behalf of his / her government in accordance with the mandate given to him / her. Depending upon the status of a diplomat, the scope and extent of his / her functions vary. A national diplomat is to comply with the instruction of his / her government. From this standpoint, a diplomat's remit of authority is limited. This is an issue which should receive the attention of sovereigns: should the scope of training of diplomats be broad-based in order to enable them to voice

---

[6] Chapter 12

their views in respect of matters in which both national and international interests become prominent?

The size of a country often becomes a factor for determining the scope of a diplomat's function. Larger countries with considerable commercial and other interests in foreign jurisdictions require more diplomats with more extensive nature of duties than a small and economically weak country. Of course, rich countries, irrespective of their size, can afford to employ more diplomats than the poor countries. The military and commercial divisions in many such embassies or high commissions are considerably larger; naturally, the scope and extent of diplomatic activities in such missions will also be extensive.

A diplomat must be able to present a case on behalf of his/her country before other diplomats in a concise and articulate fashion so that the instruction of his/her government is conveyed correctly. He/she must be polite, courteous, understanding and tolerant. The training programmes for diplomats should contain elements which will allow them to develop these qualities. Often simulation of situations help in learning such qualities.

In addition to discharging his/her functions according to his/her country's instruction and policy, a diplomat will profit much by learning the issues from the other party's point of view. Diplomacy must not stand for obstinacy. Mutuality and co-operative attitudes are the two most important bases of successful diplomacy. A comprehensive knowledge of the socio-economic and political structure and culture of the other party often stands in a diplomat's good stead in negotiating with the other party, be it a commercial matter or otherwise.

There should not be any feeling of superiority-inferiority between diplomats. Such pre-conceived ideas will destroy the very basis of negotiations and belie his/her training. From a legal standpoint, it is to be maintained that all sovereigns are equal, and that diplomats are representatives of sovereigns of an equal status. Furthermore, in a competitive diplomatic world, that is, where through negotiations a variety of choices are available, there is hardly any justification for maintaining any superiority of any diplomat over another. What matters most is the negotiation skills of the diplomat, the status of his / her country in the league of powerful countries is immaterial.

In a starkly divided world between the rich and the poor, functions and attitudes of diplomats need to be even more direct, honest, co-operative than ever before. Diplomats from the developing world often suffer from an unfounded perception that they lack bargaining power. It is an art to know when to use one's own bargaining power. The sources of bargaining power are not exclusively financial, military or technological might; the real sources are the understanding of one's own strategies and one's demands. Subordination of one by the other often takes place, particularly when the strategies and the nature of demand and alternative strategies and alternative demands have not been identified. Diplomats must not aggravate a situation by attempting to deflect from the principal issues or by denying his/her country's liability by virtue of doing something unacceptable to another country. The symptom of good diplomacy is to admit the truth, and when necessary send an apology, in order to ensure that the rapport between the two countries is not jeopardised. The use of bargaining power has received attention in a separate chapter of this work.

Diplomats are required to be alert and prompt in replying; they must ensure that by their inaction other parties do not gain. Cooling-off time often proves to be useful in avoiding stalemates. A diplomat's function is not to worsen a situation, but to improve it. Personality and knowledge of a diplomat often seem to help in handling difficult diplomatic negotiations. Although a diplomat's remit of functions is determined by his / her employer, their inner qualities are their own. A diplomat must be able to tackle a situation with wit and sagacity which qualities can never be taught by any external sources or means.

The functions of the UN diplomats are significantly different from those of national diplomats. United Nations diplomats represent the United Nations; they perform their functions to promote the cause of the United Nations, as such the issue of the national interest does not take precedence over the international interest, although they remain mindful of the particular national interests. They must be familiar with the United Nations strategies, its purposes and objectives. They are often required to consider particular national interests in relation to the United Nations policy and objectives pertaining to particular issues. They are required to negotiate in order to work out a compromise programme, and it requires good skill and understanding of the issues and problems from an international standpoint, and it often requires a balancing act between the interests of developed and developing countries.

Whereas a national diplomat's work, in the main, centres on his / her national interest, a UN diplomat must be concerned with the interests of the international community. A UN diplomat has also an advisory role which requires him/her to guide a state in respect of a programme for which it may seek assistance from the United Nations. Such a diplomat must be neutral; must possess an understanding of the needs of the international community, both rich and poor states, and be forward-looking. A UN diplomat's plans and strategies for any programme must be much more broad-based than those of a national diplomat.

In terms of their mandate they must work for the United Nations; they do not serve any particular government. The UN diplomats' perspective of work thus becomes significantly different from that of national diplomats. A much larger and complex task is therefore mandated to a UN diplomat, for which a broader and deeper understanding of an issue from the United Nations point of view is required of these diplomats.

5.6 CONCLUSIONS

Diplomacy is a very old discipline; certain characteristics of this discipline, which have their origins in the old-fashioned world, still seem to be associated with it. In the olden days, diplomacy had rather narrow confines. Bilateral relationship on a reciprocal basis was its principal aims. In other words, reciprocal use of sovereignty was a prime concern of bilateral diplomacy which primarily centred on the doctrine of sovereignty in its absolute form.

Although *"reciprocity"* is still the basic foundation of inter-state diplomacy, modern day international relations require sovereign states to carry out diplomacy beyond the bounds of strict reciprocity. The reciprocity rule generally applies to establish bilateral diplomatic relations, in the form of exchange of diplomats, grant of visa rights, tax exemptions, grant of diplomatic privileges and immunities.

Grant of concessions, whether in respect of trade, or in the form of exemptions of duties or quantitative restrictions, may be accorded unilaterally by one state to another. Prior to the abolition of Commonwealth preferences many of the Commonwealth countries were granted such concessions by the government of Great Britain/United Kingdom.

Training in diplomacy should be multi-faceted, as total indifference to international matters may not be possible for any country. Furthermore, new areas requiring international diplomacy are constantly emerging; a national diplomat must, by training, be capable of dealing with them. Areas such as the law of the sea, the protection of the environment, human rights, cold wars constantly demand an efficient treatment for which a diplomat's training must be broad-based. In other words, a diplomat should be trained not only in relation to matters of national interest but also in respect of international matters in which his/her country's meaningful participation becomes necessary.

Command of the most-used languages at international fora, namely, English, French and perhaps Spanish, is essential for any diplomat. Although traditionally, from a nationalistic point of view, many diplomats use their national language (other than those mentioned above) and their statements/speeches are in many instances instantaneously interpreted, it is thought appropriate for all diplomats to understand and make statements/speeches in any of the above-mentioned languages without having to rely upon interpreters. This is particularly important when a national diplomat is required to participate at an international forum. Furthermore, an expression in a language may lose its special meaning and connotation, when interpreted. Command of the most-used languages proves to be extremely useful in drafting documents, and understanding them.

In modern times, diplomacy cannot be kept confined to any narrow parameters. A so-called national issue may arouse international concern. The days of diplomacy based on pure nationalism are over. International standards and norms developed by international conventions may require a State to adopt and implement them, and it is for diplomats again to consider and develop the norms that will raise the international standards of conduct.

In many countries, the Ministry of Foreign Affairs holds training programmes for diplomats, and such training programmes may be reviewed in the light of the changing nature of international diplomacy and international affairs. Efficient diplomacy requires a thorough knowledge and understanding of national and international issues, the power politics and the interests of both large and small states.

Diplomats are required to learn the technique of peace-making, as they are also required to be familiar with the United Nations System[7] in this regard. The parameters of diplomacy may no longer be kept confined to political issues. Economic and politico-economic issues, matters of international concern, are now to be treated as an integral part of diplomacy. In sum, diplomatic relations must be maintained through diplomacy, but the latter must be able to strike a balance between the national interests and international interests. Training programmes for diplomats should be developed accordingly.

---

[7] The United Nations System has been discussed in Chapter 14 of this work

CHAPTER 6

Bargaining Power

6.1 INTRODUCTION

The issue of bargaining power has dominated international relations and international diplomacy in the presumed belief that the stronger or mightier has a prerogative to dominate the weak. This perception of the bargaining power seems to be deeply rooted in the history of the international community.

A state's bargaining power has traditionally been based on military, and economic strength. The question remains whether possession of such power should necessarily give a stronger state the prerogative to dominate the other party in negotiating any matter. From a legal standpoint, it is difficult to sustain any agreement or contract which is not based on the *ad idem* (two minds have met) principle. The basis for developing the perception of bargaining power is therefore not in law, but in psychology, which disregards the fact that any domineering conduct whether during a negotiation process or otherwise, may deprive the other party of an opportunity to exercise its rights.

Traditionally, there has also existed the perception that the weak and the poor lack bargaining power; consequently, their position in international relations and international law are deemed to be weaker than the stronger states. In fact, it is not difficult to find examples to justify that power has often been exercised by the stronger to achieve their objectives, but this must not be regarded as the exercise of bargaining power. International relations seem to have been proceeding in the belief that only the stronger has a bargaining power and that it must be allowed to exercise it, as a privilege, which may not be true when one rationalises the meaning and nature of bargaining power.

In this chapter an attempt is made to explain the true meaning of *"bargaining power"* and its constituents, and whether weaker states may have any bargaining power at all. The effect of bargaining power on international law has also received attention. It is worth considering whether developing states, by default, have lost their bargaining power, or whether *"bargaining power"* exclusively stands for a stronger economic, financial and military power. This chapter also attempts to establish that a power-orientated bargaining runs counter to the formation of peremptory rules of international law, and that the current practice of international diplomacy needs a re-appraisal of its techniques.

6.2 WHAT IS BARGAINING POWER?

According to the Oxford English Dictionary to *"bargain"* means: *"discussion between two parties of the terms on which one is to give or do something to or for the other"*. It also stands for an *"agreement between two parties setting how much each gives and takes, or what each performs and receives in a transaction between them"*[1]. Therefore, *"bargaining power"* stands for a discussion for doing or giving something to the other; or mutual giving and taking. In this process, the idea of dominating one party over the other should not enter, although in practice, it seems to do so. It would be interesting to examine the basis for exercising bargaining power by states in their efforts to conduct international relations.

Bargaining power is not an inherent power; it must be acquired; it is not necessarily concerned with the acquisition of power relating to economic, financial or military matters. It simply stands for the negotiating position of a party, irrespective of whether it is poor or rich, strong or weak. Bargaining power is concerned with placing oneself at a negotiating situation after having determined its strategies. Lack of strategies and the failure to identify alternative strategies and requirements weakens the bargaining position of a party. A clear understanding of one's own demands, supported by rationale, is essential for being involved in bargaining. Precise and articulate presentation of demands and identification of alternative strategies and requirements are two very important conditions of exercising bargaining power.

The concept of *"bargaining power"* seems to have been abused by many states in developing international relations in that it is based on the perception of a stronger position of a state in several respects. It also seems to have influenced the psychology of states in the international community. Bargaining power, in the sense of superiority over the other party, becomes relevant when a state is capable of asserting its position by virtue of being exclusive or near exclusive; for example, as one of the few producers of a particular commodity or mineral resources. Even in that situation it may be possible to dismantle the monopoly or near-monopoly position of that state. Take, for example, the oil crisis of 1973; the particular conflicts between the West generally and most of the countries in the Middle East which were the primary cause of this conflict allowed the oil producing countries in the Middle East along with the other OPEC Member countries, albeit for a relatively short period of time, to control the supply and pricing of oil; but through international pressures, that situation was not allowed to persist for a long period. In this case, the consumer countries lacked the so-called bargaining power over the OPEC Member countries; but, in reality, international co-operation between States brought the issue to an end. In other words, any short-sighted use of the so-called bargaining power may prove to be counter-productive. Again, take for example, the UN resolution entitled the Charter of Economic Rights and Duties of States

---

[1] Oxford English Dictionary, Vol 7, Clarendon Press (1989) at 953

1974[2] in which the developing countries demonstrated their bargaining power particularly in their attempt to cartelise commodities[3], which attempt also failed, as polarisation of powers of any kind cannot be approved.

Real bargaining power represents the determination of a party to obtain something through negotiation. A true negotiation technique does not admit of an encounter of opposable ideas and terms; it entails the technique of obtaining benefit by both parties protecting mutual interest. When international relations are conducted ruthlessly on perceived superior bargaining power then the process exceeds the limits of international relations. Protection of mutual interest, and respect for each party's position as a sovereign state, are the purpose of a negotiation. To take advantage of a party's weakness, based on its weak position, is to dominate but not to negotiate. It is difficult to justify the sources of bargaining power in international relations; true international relations stands for interaction between States to develop friendly relations.

In international relations, domination by one state over another particularly in respect of military affairs has a long history. Any attempt to settle an issue affecting the interest of two or more States by warfare, is nothing but a demonstration of sheer military power in the process of which the initiators of military warfares do not seem to place much importance on the sufferings that the ordinary people may experience. Nationalism is kindled, although it is often short-lived. The validity of the pre-1945 techniques of international relations which accepted warfare as part of the efforts to maintain international peace and security was rejected by the founders of the United Nations. Sadly, the pre-1945 attitudes of states in carrying out international relations during the post-1945 period still persist. At this point, it would be interesting to reflect on the pre-1945 technique of carrying out international relations, as such an exercise should prove their relevance or irrelevance to the post-1945 techniques of fostering international relations.

The need for interaction between states need not be over-emphasised. This process has a long history, but the question remains whether the old-fashioned techniques of developing international relations are still valid. The pre-1945 international relations system was primarily dominated by the national interest. Development of international norms for international peace and security was almost totally absent, although certain customary rules of international law developed particularly in respect of international trade or economic relations[4]. Two issues deserve a particular mention. The pre-1945 period was primarily the colonial period; the domain of international relations was predominantly limited to the colonial powers; the US did not play any major role in international relations until about the time the First World War broke out. Colonialism was predominantly the platform for international relations.

---

[2] UN GA Res. 3218

[3] Article 5. This Charter was not accepted by any developed states, except Australia

[4] See Article 23(e) of the Covenant of the League of Nations

In this process, the colonies did not have any legitimacy to become actors in international relations.

This issue gives rise to two sub-issues: first, that after being independent states, they were required to participate in international relations, without any experience; and second, that the psychological perception that the older states have a prerogative over bargaining power seemed to have provided legitimacy to bargaining power.

The matrix of international relations during the pre-1945 period and that during the post-1945 period has significantly changed; indeed, the ethos of international relations of the contemporary period seems to have been missed out by most states, powerful or otherwise. This issue has been developed in a latter section of this work. It is to be emphasised however at this stage that in the absence of an appropriate ethos of international relations, international diplomacy becomes sham.

The pre-1945 international relations and diplomacy was primarily power-based; use of military force was a common phenomenon. In fact, the Covenant of the League of Nations did not abolish wars; article 15 of the Covenant provides that:

> *"If there should arise between Members of the League any dispute likely to lead to a rupture, which is not submitted to arbitration or judicial settlement in accordance with Article 13, the Members of the League agree that they will submit the matter to the Council. Any party to the dispute may effect such submission by giving notice of the existence of the dispute to the Secretary General, who will make all necessary arrangements for a full investigation and consideration thereof.*
>
> *For this purpose the parties to the dispute will communicate to the Secretary General, as promptly as possible, statements of their case with all the relevant facts and papers, and the Council may forthwith direct the publication thereof.*
>
> *The Council shall endeavour to effect a settlement of the dispute, and if such efforts are successful, a statement shall be made public giving such facts and explanations regarding the dispute and the terms of settlement thereof as the Council may deem appropriate.*
>
> *If the dispute is not thus settled, the Council either unanimously or by a majority vote shall make and publish a report containing a statement of the facts of the dispute and the recommendations which are deemed just and proper in regard thereto.*
>
> *Any Member of the League represented on the Council may make public a statement of the facts of the dispute and of its conclusions regarding the same.*
>
> *If a report by the Council is unanimously agreed to by the members thereof other than the Representatives of one or more of the parties to the dispute, the*

Members of the League agree that they will not go to war with any party to the dispute which complies with the recommendations of the report.

If the Council fails to reach a report which is unanimously agreed to by the members thereof, other than the Representatives of one or more of the parties to the dispute, the Members of the League reserve to themselves the right to take such action as they shall consider necessary for the maintenance of right and justice.

If the dispute between the parties is claimed by one of them, and is found by the Council, to arise out of a matter which by international law is solely within the domestic jurisdiction of that party, the Council shall so report, and shall make no recommendation as to its settlement.

The Council may in any case under this Article refer the dispute to the Assembly. The dispute shall be so referred at the request of either party to the dispute, provided that such request be made within fourteen days after the submission of the dispute to the Council.

In any case referred to the Assembly, all the provisions of this Article and of Article 12 *relating to the action and powers of the Council shall apply to the action and powers of the Assembly, provided that a report made by the Assembly, if concurred in by the Representatives of those Members of the League represented on the Council and of a majority of the other Members of the League, exclusive in each case of the Representatives of the parties to the dispute, shall have the same force as a report by the Council concurred in by all the members thereof other than the Representatives of one or more of the parties to the dispute."*

Acquisition of territory by force was permissible; in other words, the principle of territorial integrity, which is a fundamental attribute of sovereignty was not regarded as a peremptory norm of international relations and international law. Exploration and exploitation of natural resources by transnational corporations in developing countries was a common phenomenon, the colonies and the owners of natural resources, where appropriate, concluded agreements (licences) against royalty, giving foreign corporations almost total authority over exploitation of their natural resources. The colonisation system almost naturally provided the colonial power with domineering position, and the real owners of the natural resources were relegated to a subordinate position, the consequential effect of which was that the newly-born states lacked experience in management techniques, administration of economic and political affairs, training to cope with new situations. The opportunity to enjoy a stronger position over the centuries turned into a habit for colonial powers and transnational corporations. In this process, the weak felt weaker, and even if it wanted to be strong, the foundations or a minimal platform for strength, training, education, experience were in most cases unavailable.

Furthermore, the incorporation of the colonial powers' laws, particularly in respect of international trade had a profound effect on the position of the newly-born states. The network of the international trading system (including the documentary credits mechanism or trade terms) is so complex and pervasive that it is virtually impossible to "undo" it. In many cases, the law of the developed supplier's country has been the governing law of contracts, on the assumption that the legal system in a newly-born country is not to be trusted. Submission by a poor country to the rich country's laws became a common phenomenon. This is not the occasion to evaluate the colonial system, but it is to identify its consequential effect on the position of developing states in international relations.

Although, in most cases, developing countries did not have any plans as to how to handle their newly-acquired independence, the rich and/or colonial powers lacked plans as to how to interact with the new sovereign States, and prepare them for a different type of international relations which required skills in many issues, economic, political or otherwise. In other words, in the maze of international relations, the newly-born states became novice players and the older states retained their dominant position. In such a situation, the question of reciprocity became irrelevant, and consequently, appropriate interaction between the rich and the poor became distant. Psychologically, the newly-born states, in general, seem to have accepted a subservient role in international relations; this subserviency seems to have been developed by the help, financial or otherwise, provided by rich countries. This had a profoundly negative effect on confidence-building in the newly-born states. The lack of planning and strategies, combined with their failure to improve their primary economic sector, simply precipitated their dependence on outside assistance. It was not a question of not having any bargaining power, but a lack of appreciation of one's own potentials. Of course, financial indebtedness and the lack of confidence maintain a concomitant relationship between themselves.

The bases for the so-called bargaining power, which in fact is negotiation power, are the following: knowing one's own strategies; awareness of what one requires and on what terms; confidence in getting through negotiation amicably and no sense of inferiority or superiority complex. It is against these bases that one should consider whether the newly-born states lack the so-called bargaining power or whether they help to allow rich States to dominate them.

6.3 BARGAINING POWER AT THREE LEVELS

At the *first level of bargaining power* is the internal power of states, rich or poor alike, to enact legislation, to promote and restrict private foreign investment within the territory in accordance with the priorities set by the sovereign authority. At the root of it is the *"sectorisation"* of the economy, which is a common phenomenon in almost all countries. Sectorisation is often done on the basis of the economic policy of a country in consideration of the priorities set by the governmental authorities. Often, the natural resources sector, which is in most cases under governmental control, is opened to private foreign investors on licence-basis allowing them contractual rights to explore and exploit these resources under some conditions, namely: supply of materials from the local sources as much as possible; supply of labour force from that local labour market; utilisation / development of distribution network, participation in management and control etc. Of course, in order to develop a particular sector of the economy, a government may allow the entry of a private foreign investor without much restriction but with incentives, usually for a specified period of time. On the other hand, in state practice, it has become evident that the agricultural sector and domestic industries sector are to be kept reserved for the indigenous people and companies. In Norway, fishery and travel industries are closed to private foreign investors; in Australia, the uranium sector is almost exclusively under state control; and in Indonesia, the petroleum sector is very much under the state control. These examples clearly suggest that, by domestic legislation, the access of private foreign investors to the closed sectors may not be allowed. This practice also suggests that the protection of basic sectors of the economy requires countries to deny opportunities to private foreign investors. In this situation, the question of being involved in any bargaining process with a private foreign investor would not arise; what is needed is business negotiation.

Economic self-sufficiency in sectors, namely, agriculture and small and medium scale industries, strengthens the position of a country, and improvement in these sectors, and in particular, in the agricultural sector, may not require much technological expertise or technology. The available local resources often prove to be sufficient to develop the agricultural sector, or even when external help becomes necessary, it does not entail much financial investment. This point may be confirmed by historical examples: the vast majority of rich countries in the world are self-sufficient in their agricultural sectors; the spill-over effect in this sector helped them develop the other sectors of their economy, although in this latter situation, some external help and interaction may be necessary. Some of the developing countries are self-sufficient in their agricultural sectors in consequence of which the incidence of dependence on foreign sources becomes minimally essential.

Where however development in the agricultural sectors may not be achieved owing to the lack of natural resources or otherwise, then the position, of course, becomes difficult.

However, in general, self-sufficiency in the agricultural sectors is much quicker to achieve than in any other sector; thus, at least, the need for importing food products is minimised. Self-sufficiency in the agricultural sector forms the basis for strengthening a country's other economic sectors.

The bargaining power of a country may be demonstrated at a *bilateral level* in concluding treaties, whether commercial, economic or otherwise. The investment treaties that have been concluded between states seem to be based on the general assumption that the investor's position is stronger than that of the host country in disregard of the fact that an investor enters into a foreign jurisdiction for earning profits. Furthermore, a host country has opportunities to choose the most appropriate investor on most profitable terms. But, a host country can exercise this choice provided that she has determined her needs. In other words, a host country must know what technology she should acquire rather than shifting the task to a transferor of technology. The emphasis must be on acquisition rather than transfer of technology; and the acquirer of a technology will also be determined not to accept any package preferred by a transferor. Prior to acquiring any foreign technology, a country should consider whether indigenous technology and capability have been correctly determined. It is also worth considering whether the industrial base of a country should be strengthened necessarily with the employment of any foreign technology. This point becomes important for two reasons: (a) that the habit of acquiring foreign technology gives rise to dependence; and (b) that the initial capital cost for acquiring and installing foreign technology requires a country to remain as a debtor for a long period of time. Furthermore, with the advancement of science and technology, the process of turning technology obsolete is rather rapid. The issue of replacement of parts and servicing of technology which will entail extra expenditures should not be disregarded.

At the bilateral level, therefore, an acquirer of resources or technology who has an opportunity to exercise its choice, is to be regarded as its bargaining power. In fact, the better the understanding of the requirement for technology, the stronger the bargaining power. The understanding of requirements of technology or any other material emanates from the study of a country's requirement from a realistic point of view. In other words, the ability to utilise a technology, including the ability to service and repair it, and the capacity of a country should be the other important criteria for determining the nature and type of foreign technology that a country may lack. It should be emphasised that technological dependence is much easier to attain than emancipation from it; package deals in technology transfer make the position of the transferor inviolable. Again, it is by means of policy-making motivated by a sense of national self-sufficiency that the platform for bargaining power may be strengthened. The study developed by the UN Centre on Transnational Corporations concerning the role of transnational corporations in world development, pointed out how developing countries may use their bargaining power in acquiring foreign technology:

"... *developing countries have generally shown pragmatism and flexibility, recognising that the world technology market is imperfect, that it is difficult to determine the reasonableness of the price for technology and that in the final analysis, the price is the outcome of the crude bargaining power of the technology supplier and the recipient. Even so, the purpose of regulation has been, first, to strengthen the bargaining position of the national recipient entities; secondly, to reduce the overall level of technology payments; and thirdly, to take an integrated view of foreign participation for evaluating the implications instead of looking only at foreign equity investment. To a certain extent, governments have also been motivated by the need to minimise unjustified transfers through transactions between parent companies and affiliated enterprises."*[5]

Bargaining power at the *international level* (the third level) requires certain pre-requisites which are in many ways different from those that are required at the other two levels already discussed. International level in this context stands for truly international platforms such as the United Nations, including its specialised agencies. Here, *"bargaining power"* usually represents a *"collective bargaining power"* between the rich and poor countries. The aim is to formulate principles and policies by united ideas on these *fora*. Unity of ideas, policies, strategies and preparation for answering back are some of the most important pre-requisites for collective bargaining power at the UN level. Take, for example, the tariff negotiation efforts made by UNCTAD (the UN Conference on Trade and Development) through various Rounds, in particular, the Tokyo and Uruguay Rounds. The untiring efforts made by UNCTAD for the recognition of the Generalised System of Preferences (GSP) is another example of the strength of collective bargaining power of developing states. The proposal for GSP did not originally meet with the approval for a waiver under Article XXIV of the General Agreement on Tariffs and Trade (GATT), nor was there any possibility of gaining the recognition by GATT as it became obvious that a unanimous vote from the GATT contracting parties which was required for the approval of such proposals under Article XXX of the Agreement was remote, and yet, through a novel process of an *"enabling clause"*, GSP was recognised.

The concept of the *"exclusive economic zone"* embodied in the UN Convention on the Law of the Sea (UNCLOS III) which was proposed by Kenya, and supported by the developing countries and many developed countries, is another example to demonstrate that poor countries do have bargaining power. In his study of UNCTAD in world trade, Dr Koul maintained that the *"group"* method of negotiations has been recognised in the decision-making machinery of UNCTAD and contributes increasingly to achieve its objectives, although he maintains that the results have been minimal[6].

Any aspiration for over-using bargaining power may meet with failure. Examples in support of this point are available; but the danger of exercising excessive bargaining power may be demonstrated by the inappropriate

---

[5] UN Centre on Transnational Corporations, *Transnational Corporations in World Development*, New York (1985) at 51

[6] A K Koul, *The Legal Framework of UNCTAD in World Trade*, Leyden, Sijthoff (1977) at 66–67

initiative taken by the developing states in certain respects in preparing the Charter of Economic Rights and Duties of States, 1974[7].

Nowhere in economic relations did the exercise of the bargaining power of developing states become more evident than in determining the primary commodity trade policies, the major suppliers of commodities, particularly, minerals and other natural resources in developing countries. They are in a position to manipulate the market forces, but of course, excessive use of this proved to be counterproductive and the rich countries did not accept the proposal embodied in the Charter of Economic Rights and Duties of States, 1974. The over-exercise of bargaining power through the Organisation of the Petroleum Exporting Countries (OPEC) during the post-1973 period did not last long.

The UN Resolution entitled the Charter of Economic Rights and Duties of States, 1974 was initiated by developing countries with the idea of affirming/developing norms in relation to economic issues. In fact, most of the rights and duties included in this Resolution are non-controversial; they simply reiterate the international practice in relation to many of the matters included in the resolution. However, the provisions that particularly defeated the objectives of the resolution related to cartelisation of primary commodities or denial of the obligation under customary international law to pay compensation in the event of their taking of private foreign assets / investment in the national interest. Of course, the issue of apartheid in the resolution provoked controversy; the developing countries perceived *"apartheid"* as an integral issue of an economic development programme, but there was resistance for accepting it as an issue which should be included in this resolution. Although, in theory, this proved to be a laudable attempt by developing countries to register their aspirations, the fact remains that the inclusion of the issue of apartheid in that resolution had an adverse effect upon it which was otherwise a comprehensive resolution evidencing what should be the economic rights and duties of a state. What was to be the culmination of bargaining powers of developing countries in promoting the concept of a new international economic order failed to materialise.

Perhaps nowhere in international economic law has the issue of the lack of bargaining power of developing countries received more attention than in respect of the position of these countries vis-à-vis the International Monetary Fund and the International Bank for Reconstruction and Development (IBRD). The controversy about the lack of bargaining power of developing countries or the stronger bargaining power of the rich member states of these two institutions has drawn the attention of authors[8] and the international community.

---

[7] See also S K Chatterjee, "The Charter of Economic Rights and Duties of States: An Evaluation After 15 Years", 40 *International and Comparative Law Quarterly* (1991) 669

[8] See further, M Williams, *International Economic Organisations and the Third World*, New York, Harvester Wheatsheaf (1994) at 83

One should seriously consider whether the plight of the Member States from the developing world in seeking funds from the IMF or the IBRD should be regarded as an issue of bargaining power. In this connection it would be appropriate to briefly examine the procedure for assessing loan applications made by the Member States, and the voting structure thereto. Before going into the details of the voting structure operational within the International Monetary Fund in relation to loan applications made by the Member States, it is opportune to point out that the information provided by a Member State plays a crucial role in considering the viability of an application. *"Information"* in this context includes information on all aspects of the economy, society, overall progress of the economy over a period of time to be reflected on employment, import / export trade, domestic market, health, education etc. The onus is on the applicant to establish its case on how it plans to utilise the borrowed fund, what are its chances of repaying the loan by the stipulated date and, furthermore, whether the proposed programme for which the loan is sought is consistent with its current economic programme. Simply, the sustainability of the plan must be established from a socio-economic perspective.

The voting system which is operational within the IMF is known as the *"weighted"* voting system under which system, the voting power depends on a country's contribution to the Fund. The membership of the Fund is imbalanced in that developing states outnumber the rich states. In the unlikely event of all rich states voting against a loan application, the developing member states' votes will outnumber the votes cast by the developed states. The fact of the matter is that often applications for loans are ill-drafted or inadequate information is provided by the applicant member state. IMF or IBRD often reconsider loan applications. It is to be emphasised however that both the IMF and IBRD are required to justify approval of each loan; in the final analysis, they are accountable to their member states, as the latters' contributions may form part of the loan too.

6.4 CONCLUSIONS

The notion of bargaining power seems to have been based on the concept of *"might"*. This notion also seems to have been justified by reference to military and technological strength of a country. As explained in this chapter, *"bargaining power"* stands for negotiating the terms of an agreement in which the essence of *"reciprocity"* is fundamental. An inappropriate perception of *"bargaining power"* may be responsible for slipping away from one's own strength and unconsciously giving in to the demands and choices of the other party.

In international diplomacy, bargaining power is often misconceived and abused. In the name of bargaining power, parties use force or coercion, belying the objectives of bargaining. In fact, overuse of the misconceived bargaining power may prove to be counterproductive, whereby, international relations between states will deteriorate. On the contrary, bargaining power should be utilised for a better co-operation between and among states, at all levels, national, regional or international.

Diplomacy is primarily meant for developing inter-state, regional and international co-operation; not for promoting relations with states on the basis of brute muscle force. Diplomacy is a matter of intellectual interaction, not of force. It is unfortunate that the concept of *"bargaining power"* has been misinterpreted for such a long time in the history of international relations and international diplomacy.

CHAPTER 7

The New Faces of International Diplomacy

7.1 INTRODUCTION

Traditional diplomacy has always been concerned with developing and establishing friendly relations with States, initially interacting with trade, including investment, and eventually extending to include full diplomatic relations and cultural exchanges. Trade relations have always formed the basis for diplomatic relations between sovereign States. The need for buying and selling products and services and to increase investment flow between countries becomes inevitable irrespective of the economic strength of a country. The nature of economic relations between countries also determines allies and unfriendly countries for a State. Thus, a sovereign State's allies and not-so-friendly States may vary over a period of time. By the same token, a sovereign State wishing to develop diplomatic relations with another sovereign State with which it had no diplomatic relations in the past may do so because of trading or economic needs. But, of course, if diplomatic relations from a sovereign State are withdrawn, trade relations will automatically be withdrawn. For example, for many years neither the United Kingdom nor the United States maintained any diplomatic relations with Libya; thus, trade relations with this country were also withdrawn. On the other hand, it is possible for a sovereign State to establish economic relations (trade and investment) with an unrecognised government of another State. Thus, it may be maintained that economic relations may precede diplomatic relations. The more pervasive the economic relations, the larger is the presence of the country in a receiving State. Economic relations between States often diffuse tensions between States. For example, in order to ensure that crude oil supply remains secure and predictable from Saudi Arabia and Kuwait, the States in the West often try to avoid dissensions between themselves and these two States, and if differences of opinion occur, these are often settled by amicable means.

Over the past five decades or so however international diplomacy has been changing its faces. The question remains whether these changes have proved to be necessary because of the changing world scenarios or have diplomacy's faces been changed forcibly? These questions may be answered only by referring to examples. Prior to the Second World War, international diplomacy was predominantly a diplomacy of managing colonisation for the colonial powers, and searching for peace (The Peace Treaties of 1919). During Hitler's regime not all types of war diplomacy proved to be the main strength, although eventually the Allied Powers crushed Hitler's regime; but the crushing of the regime was not primarily an outcome of diplomacy, but of sheer warfare. Experiences in that diplomacy do not seem to be relevant to the contemporary period because not only has the nature of warfare changed but also the rules of conducting wars are very different from those which existed at that time. The United States entered into the arena in a significant way since her rise as from 1935 as a direct result of the New Deal. This proved to be the beginning of military diplomacy or power politics or power diplomacy. Power diplomacy or military diplomacy has a blinding effect; it becomes conscious of its power and indeed becomes prone to using it whenever opportunities may arise. Power diplomacy / military diplomacy is at its worst when it is coupled with financial power.

During the concluding period of de-colonisation, diplomacy at the international level was primarily concerned with implementing the de-colonisation policy advocated by the UN[1], which was originally initiated by Woodrow Wilson's Fourteen Points. The diplomacy operated during the first two decades of the UN (1945 – 65) may be described as a diplomacy of economic domination of the newly-born States by some of the economically strong States. This became evident in the form of financial aid and technology transfer. De-colonisation, in most cases, did not liberate the former colonies economically, rather it proved to be another form of economic colonisation. The diplomacy during this period was predominantly a diplomacy of dependency. In fact, the effect of diplomacy of dependency is a continuing one in that the States that received most financial aid from certain States are grateful to them, and are naturally hesitant in protesting against the diplomacy of the donor countries. In other words, this is not diplomacy; it may be described only as a case of domination-diplomacy.

During the first two decades of the United Nations another form of power politics became evident: to suppress or deal with the rise of communism. The conflict between the Soviet Union and the United States is an example of the point. The Viet-Nam war clearly proved that military domination may not achieve the objectives of the militarily powerful State. In the US, the Viet-Nam experience received mixed recognition of the effect of the military powers of the United States.

Military and/or power diplomacy is necessarily limited in nature for two reasons: (a) it creates or increases rivalry between the powers or the opponents; and (b) its objectives are to conquer the enemy, with no other ethical objectives. In the contemporary world, polarisation of opinion takes place on the use of military power by States. Take, for example, the use of power in Iraq in 2003.

The apparent reasons for overthrowing President Saddam Hussain were the unacceptable regime he was operating particularly by suppressing the basic

---

[1] See further UN General Assembly Resolution entitled *Declaration on the Granting of Independence to Colonial Countries and Peoples*, 1960

human rights of the Iraqi people and, in many instances, by making them subject to inhuman torture; and the presumed belief that he had weapons of mass destruction (WMD). But the motive to secure the supply of crude oil could not be entirely overruled. The new faces of diplomacy should take into consideration the view of others over the acts of some others. Use of power without any justification in the eyes of the world would be condemned.

Overthrowing of regimes by military means entailing deaths of the local people and foreign military personnel does no longer, in general, attract appreciation of the international community. Modern diplomacy is a diplomacy of a balancing act. In other words, part of the international community is moving from war to peace, whilst others are not. Thus, diplomats are required to transform the entire international community from the notion of warfare to that of peace-making. The contemporary diplomacy cannot disregard the issues of the North-South relationship, otherwise the world will remain divided as it is now. If diplomacy is to remain as power-based, then any discussion of the North-South dialogue becomes a theoretical and also a hypocritical gesture. One is required to return to the basic issue: what is the purpose of diplomacy: the protection of the national interest; and the development of friendly relations between States. Diplomats are required to develop a framework of international diplomacy, preferably at an international forum (such as the United Nations) whereby the North-South division is narrowed and eventually eliminated.

Modern diplomacy seems to be concerned with the polarisation of the world; regionalism is evidentiary of this fact; absence of any constructive policy, rather than ad hoc policies, for the South, is a matter for international concern. The North's superiority may not be maintained if the South is not developed. This is a facet of diplomacy which seems to have remained neglected.

Modern diplomacy should also be concerned with the means of changing rigid attitudes towards sovereignty maintained by many States. When a regime proves to be unacceptable, there should be a concerted effort through an international organisation (namely, the United Nations) to change the regime and allow the peoples under that regime to enjoy their basic rights. This should be done by peaceful means, whether by good offices or by negotiation.

In fact, the recognition policy in international law is, in many ways, responsible for having unacceptable regimes. Many authoritarian regimes are recognised regimes; thus the recognition policy is flawed. Diplomats should consider whether the policy of de-recognition is a panacea or whether the policy of *de facto* recognition should be operated in its strictest sense. But, of course, the proponents of human rights will reject this notion[2].

---

[2] See H Lauterpacht, *Recognition in International Law*, Cambridge, Cambridge University Press (1947); see further, H Kelsen, "Recognition in International Law", 25 *American Journal of International Law* (1941) 605; J Kunz, "Critical Remarks on Lauterpacht's Recognition in International Law", 44 *American Journal of International Law* (1950) 713

How to tackle the rather unacceptable regimes is a new issue with which diplomats should be concerned; perhaps time has arrived to determine whether criteria for unacceptable regimes should be established, and whether a central body should be set up to monitor the activities of these regimes rather than relying on the concept of intervention by external entities.

7.2 THE NEW FACES OF DIPLOMACY

International relations based on religious faith or for promoting religion(s) has a long history; the creation of Papal States or the Vatican in the Christendom is a manifestation of this form of diplomacy. In fact, religion being one of the vehicles of promoting socio-economic policies, it was inevitable for it to find its own space in the political firmament. But, then, the nature of international relations was simpler, narrower and less interactive compared to what the contemporary international community experiences. International relations totally based on religious faiths may be unworkable for diplomatic relations, as the latter embraces interactions at various levels of the international community. Differences in religious philosophies seem to precipitate conflicts and widen the gulf between actors. International relations based on religious philosophies may have a polarising effect in that they may give rise to *"preferential diplomacy"*, that is, intense diplomatic relations between certain States. *"Polarised diplomacy"* may lead to diplomacy based on powers, military, economic or otherwise; which defeats the primary objectives of democratic diplomacy. Democratic diplomacy may develop confidence in the minds of all as to the conduct of States; create certainty as to their mutual co-operation in times of both prosperity and adversity; and command respect for each other. If diplomacy is primarily conducted on the basis of historical relations, then any effective interaction between old and new States will take an unpredictably long time to take place. A host of the newly-born States are looked at as States which deserve the sympathy and assistance of the former colonial powers; in consequence of which the newly-born States feel subordinated to the former colonial powers, and, in the majority of instances, simply tend to subscribe to the views held by them.

"Predictable diplomacy" is different from *"democratic diplomacy"*; whereas the former represents the predictable conduct of States whether by virtue of being traditionally tamed by the powerful or because of historical relations, the latter abhors both and aims at developing inter-State relationships without any pre-conceived ideas or ties. One should remind oneself of the circumstances in which the Group of 77 or UNCTAD were set up; these institutions are primarily looked at by the developing States as *fora* for solidarity. The answer is not that such institutions are more effective in opposing, where necessary, the conduct of the powerful States; on the

contrary, polarisation of States must be avoided to allow more direct and friendly interactions between States on a democratic basis.

Since the days of de-colonisation, diplomacy seems to have been promoted in three main directions: between the developed and developed; between developing and developing; and nominally, between developing and developed States, the last primarily with a degree of sympathy. Diplomacy for this last category presents challenges which States do not seem to be prepared to accept or alternatively are incapable of accepting. This is where a new kind of training of diplomats, with vision, proves to be essential, which training will consist, inter alia, of the rules for developing international diplomacy in order to create international diplomacy for each other's needs in the international community, avoidance of bias, and development of realistic rules of conduct for the benefit of all. As stated earlier, the issue of inter-dependency, particularly in the field of economic issues, including import – export trade, and policies regarding common heritage of mankind, in addition to certain common issues, namely, protection of the environment, development of infrastructure in the developing world, and understanding and protection of human rights, to name but a few.

The quality of a government and the quality of diplomacy maintain a concomitant relationship between them. *"Quality"* in this context stands for a government's attitude towards developing and maintaining international relations, whether in a polarised fashion or on a democratic basis; its records of respect for the rules of international law; its records of observance of human rights; its commitment to resolving matters of international concern; its policy of non-adherence to warfares; and its policy of adherence to the maintenance of international peace and security. As diplomats are representatives of their sovereigns, it is the latter on whom the onus lies to brief their diplomats bearing in mind that the days of old-fashioned, national interest-based diplomacy are over. The growing and efficient network of communications seems to be winning time and distance, making the world even closer; diplomacy thus requires to be instant, comprehensive and dynamic. These qualities of modern-day diplomacy must be developed by national authorities in their diplomats.

Diplomacy is meant for developing international co-operation, and resolving differences, political, economic, attitudinal or otherwise between States. Diplomacy is required to use two platforms: national (bilateral) and non-national (regional or universal). As more and more national issues are becoming non-national issues, be they relating to economic, health, the environment or commerce, common consensus among States pioneered by diplomats becomes essential.

Over the past four decades or so, diplomacy has predominantly been diverted to conflicts and wars or its other permutations, based on the might of powers. In this process, real diplomacy becomes unnecessary, as *"might"* represents a low level diplomacy; when diplomacy is represented by might, the very essence of diplomacy becomes absent, cultivating the idea that the domination of the powerful over the less powerful or weak States is an important aspect of diplomacy. Legally speaking, diplomacy of this nature disregards the doctrine of sovereign equality, and violates the principle enshrined in Article 2(4)[3] of the UN Charter.

The transformation of international diplomacy into what may be described as a *"polarised"* diplomacy is an unfortunate development in the diplomatic world. In the process of polarised diplomacy, the lesser powers, or even the powers, who are wealthy, but cannot conform to the policies of the polarised diplomacy, remain indifferent. Take, for example, the Iraq episode in 1990. The purpose is not to determine who was right or who was wrong, but to discuss briefly the legal implications of the episode.

Was there any legally sustainable basis for forming the Allied Powers? Should the other States which joined the Allied Powers have done so in violation of their obligations under the UN Charter? Is the concept of *"collective self-defence"* a legally viable concept? What action did Kuwait take to justify her position vis-à-vis the United Nations? Can one form an allied power first, take action and then have it legitimised by the Security Council of the United Nations? What was Iraq's position in international law in regard to the incident? One may raise a host of other questions, but an attempt to ascertain the answers to these questions should reveal the precise position and the nature of the event that incapacitated the United Nations and thus the application of the relevant rules of international law.

All the States that were involved in the Iraq episode, including Iraq, were Members of the UN and therefore necessarily bound by the obligations arising from the UN Charter, which is a multilateral treaty. Article 2 obligations are binding. Paragraph 4 of this Article should be read with Article 51 which provides that:

> *"Nothing in the present Charter shall impair the inherent right of individual or collective self-defence if an armed attack occurs against a Member of the United Nations, until the Security Council has taken measures necessary to maintain international peace and security. Measures taken by Members in the exercise of this right of self-defence shall be immediately reported to the Security Council and shall not in any way affect the authority and responsibility of the Security Council under the present Charter to take at any time such action as it deems necessary in order to maintain or restore international peace and security."*

Upon an analysis of this Article, it will appear that a Member State of the United Nations which has been attacked or against whom force of an appreciable nature has been used (e.g., Kuwait) by another Member State (e.g., Iraq)

---

[3] *"All Members shall refrain in their international relations from the threat or use of force against the territorial integrity or political independence of any state, or in any other manner inconsistent with the Purposes of the United Nations."*

can take action in self-defence, and that the aggressor State must notify the Security Council immediately. It is for the Security Council then to take appropriate measures/action. Did Kuwait notify the Security Council and did Kuwait take any action in self-defence? These questions are required to be considered with another question, that is, whether the US-Kuwait defence treaty should have been activated, and whether States should be allowed to conclude such treaties.

Currently, sovereign States' right to conclude defence treaties between themselves is not prohibited by international law, but the consequences of implementing such treaties are obvious; indeed by allowing States to implement such treaties, a new war-regime is created outside the peace-making regimes of the United Nations. International diplomacy should be concerned with such issues, instead of allowing certain States to demonstrate their excellence in warfare rather than peace-making, the consequences of which are manifold, and in particular: (a) the socio-economic effect of warfare not only on the affected States, but also generally on the international community; and (b) whether their action is in conformity with their obligations under the UN Charter. In the event of international diplomacy being allowed to develop outside the UN system, even when matters fall squarely within the system, then one should wonder the purpose of setting up such an organisation. It is for the Member States to re-organise the organisation, if necessary. Proper international diplomacy does not encourage violation of treaty law.

It should also be considered what was the source of legitimacy of the Allied Powers? The concept of the *"collective self-defence"* is unsustainable. Unless States or a few of them constituting the Allied Powers were attacked how may the argument of collective self-defence be applied? Higgins rightly pointed out that the defence of the self cannot be collective[4]. Therefore, the attack by the Allied Powers was not in self-defence. From a strict legal standpoint, the *"Allied Powers"* did not have a *locus standi*. Iraq also violated article 2(4).

The issue when an action in self-defence is permissible and the extent to which force may be used in self-defence is settled in international law. The case in point is *The Caroline*.[5]

There must be a *"necessity of self-defence, instant, overwhelming, leaving no choice of means, and no moment for deliberation"* and the action taken must not *"be unreasonable or excessive"*, and *"limited by the necessity and kept clearly within it."*[6]

---

[4] R Higgins, *The Development of International Law through the Political Organs of the United Nations*, Oxford, Oxford University Press (1963) at 208

[5] 29 Brit & For, St Papers 1137

[6] Moore, J B, *Digest of International Law*, vol VII p 919, see also Jennings "The Caroline and MacLeod Cases", 32 *American Journal of International Law* (1938)

Relying on Bowett's argument, Higgins further maintains that the right of collective self-defence in Article 51 exists only when the interests of the attacked State are so intrinsically bound up with the territorial integrity and political independence of another State[7].

One is also required to consider the proportion to which force in the Iraqi war was used. The laws of war require a party to justify the intensity of a warfare that it may launch, and the consequences, including human miseries that follow it. Parties engaged in a warfare are required to abide by the provisions of the Geneva Conventions of 1949 dealing with wounded and sick on land, wounded, sick and shipwrecked at sea, prisoners of war, and civilians, and the two Additional Protocols to these Conventions, and the plea of *res inter alios acta* (third parties are not bound by a treaty provision to which they do not adhere) is not sustainable. It is to be appreciated that the primary reasons for concluding humanitarian conventions such as the Geneva Conventions is to develop deterrence and humanitarian awareness among States. The post-1945 aspirations expressed by the founding members of the UN through the organisation were to establish the foundation of peace and not warfare, and diplomats carry a heavy burden to discharge if they decide to depart from these aspirations. This applies to the newly born States too.

In so far as the defence treaties are concerned the conclusion of which is not prohibited by the UN Charter (but see Article 102) one is required to consider the circumstances in which the prohibition was not imposed. Historically, immediately after the conclusion of the Second World War, the contemporary world could not place a total confidence in the United Nations as an organisation that might not have the same fate as the League of Nations. The superior powers therefore retained their right to regulate the conduct of the violators of peace. It is for diplomats to consider whether a new understanding of peace-making is not necessary, bearing in mind that every war requires the countries concerned to take a backward step consequential upon the adverse effects of war, and then be involved in socio-economic development work for which dependency grows.

The Congo and the Middle East Situations

The Congo and the Middle East situations in the 1950s and 1960s presented a remarkable example of how the UN machinery may be employed in difficult situations in which countries may be involved. During the material period, the Congo experienced deep-rooted civil strifes making the country's political situation uncertain. Each of the two rival groups, one led by Dr Lumumba and the other by Dr Kasavubu, claimed control over the country. In an attempt to resolve the problem in June 1960 both Lumumba and Kasavubu telegraphically requested the then Secretary-General of the

---

[7] ibid, at 29; see also D W Bowett, 32 *British Year Book of International Law* (1955–56) 130

United Nations (Dag Hammarskjöld) to send an emergency force to the Congo for a ceasefire. This request presented a problem in that in discussing the Congo situation in the General Assembly it became clear that in respect of any proposal for an emergency force for the Congo, two of the permanent Members of the Security Council, France and the USSR, would exercise their veto power. The Secretary-General referred the matter to the General Assembly which organ is competent to consider issues relating to the maintenance of international peace and security under Articles 10 and 11 of the UN Charter. On the basis of the General Assembly Resolution, entitled *Uniting for Peace*[8], UN Emergency Forces were sent to the Congo[9], as they had been to the Middle East in 1956. When France and the USSR objected to contributing to the expenses incurred on the Emergency Forces on the grounds that the resolution of the General Assembly was not valid as being *ultra vires*, the General Assembly sought an Advisory Opinion from the International Court of Justice to confirm whether or not such expenses might be regarded as the ordinary expenses of the organisation, and therefore all Member States were required to contribute to these expenses in accordance with their individual subscriptions to the United Nations, and that the General Assembly had full authority to recommend or not to recommend any expenses under its budgetary powers. These expenses were regarded as *"ordinary expenses"* of the organisation by the International Court of Justice.

Both the Congo and the Middle East situations were effectively dealt with by the United Nations, and it is to be re-iterated that the request for assistance came to the United Nations from the country concerned. In other words, prompt action by and co-operation from the Member State concerned is an essential element of making the UN machinery a success.

Unfortunately, modern diplomacy seems to be returning towards a power-based diplomacy. Power in this context stands for both economic and military powers of certain States. Take for example, the cases of North Viet-Nam, Iraq and Kosovo. The North Viet-Nam situation represented a conflict of political issues – capitalism *versus* non-capitalism. The fear of the spread of the latter prompted the United States to attack Viet-Nam, a war which had no conclusion, but of course, caused immeasurable human miseries for both the United States and North Viet-Nam. Under the UN Charter, no Member can indulge in any warfare, and the use of force is permissible only in self-defence. There was no effective diplomacy in settling the North Viet-Nam situation; it ended in a long-drawn war, and the Government of the country remained unrecognised for a prolonged period of time, which also adversely affected its

---

[8] Dated 3 November 1950, Res 377(v)

[9] See Security Council Resolutions of 14 July 1960 and 9 August 1960. See also the Advisory Opinion of the International Court of Justice in *Certain Expenses of the UN* Case (1962) ICJ Rep 151.

membership of the United Nations; which requires the recommendation of the Security Council.

In the case of Iraq, the Allied Powers tended to justify the attacking of Iraq on the grounds of *"collective self-defence"*, an expression which has found a place in Article 51 of the UN Charter but which provokes controversy. How can the defence of the self-defence be collective?[10] Furthermore, if a few Members of the United Nations wish to attack another Member of it, under the UN Charter, the proposal for attack must receive the support from the Security Council; otherwise, they will be in breach of Article 2(4) of the UN Charter.

Article 51 only provides exceptions to Article 2(4). The expression *"collective self-defence"* is a misnomer; unless the expression is amended to state *"collective defence"*, under the UN Charter, there are no legal grounds for a few Members of the UN to attack another Member of it. But, even though the expression *"collective defence"* appears in Article 51, it cannot be justified against the provision of Article 2(4), which is a binding provision of the UN Charter[11]. The concept of *"collective self-defence"* is controversial.

7.3 THE CHANGING NATURE OF DIPLOMACY AND TRAINING IN DIPLOMACY

Traditionally, *"diplomacy"* has been treated as an art of managing relations between States, and with institutions – non-governmental, inter-governmental or international. In fact, prior to the existence of any such institutions, diplomacy was primarily of a bilateral nature. In the olden days, diplomacy was predominantly used for establishing political and cultural relations between sovereigns, and in fact, it may be maintained that the Vienna Convention on Diplomatic Relations, 1961 is very much based on this traditional notion towards diplomacy. Diplomats are to be treated with dignity as representatives of their sovereigns, and they are to promote friendly relations between States, and institutions.

Conflicts between States is an historical phenomenon. Breakdown of friendly relations between States, whether for cultural, religious or for reasons of acquisition or loss of territory etc gives rise to conflicts. Diplomacy is at its most crucial test when it is to be employed to resolve them; often assistance is sought from third parties as mediators to resolve conflicts. In other words, in the world of diplomacy, attempts should be made to resolve conflicts amicably, and there should not be any limit to this method of settling inter-States disputes. In the early history of international diplomacy, conflict resolution primarily stood for resolution of wars, and wars were not forbidden.

---

[10] R Higgins, op. cit.

[11] *Nicaragua v US* [1984] ICJ Reports

Interestingly enough, in the vast majority of cases, the causes of inter-State conflicts in the contemporary period and those in the olden days have in the main remained the same, only the characteristics of conflicts and warfares have changed due to the advancement of science and technology. This latter point requires diplomats to have a special kind of training to deal with the modern day diplomacy. At this point, it is worth asking what is the remit of diplomacy?

A modern-day diplomat must not only protect and promote his / her national interest while negotiating with other countries; this may become evident particularly in relation to trade and commerce or exchange of scientific ideas, or invitation to private investors with a view to strengthening the country's economy and industry. However, he / she must also promote the interest of his / her country vis-à-vis a regional economic arrangement, whether by means of association agreements or where advisable, to negotiate membership with such arrangements. But, most of all, a diplomat has also the function to develop new ideas in the form of resolutions or conventions at the UN level, the beneficiary of which would be the entire international community. This is where a diplomat is required to be person of multidimensional expertise. The faculty to negotiate, conciliate and settle disputes and issues must be developed by all diplomats.

In the final analysis, diplomacy stands for an art or a technique employed to develop and maintain friendly relations with States. It has two aspects: creative and preventative. Whereas its creative aspects are to be employed to develop and maintain friendly relations with States, avoidance, and if necessary settlement, of conflicts is created by what may be described as *"negative diplomacy"*. Knowledge of power politics, the politics of international economic relations, and of historic ties with States is essential for a successful interaction with foreign governments. The ever-increasing dimension of international relations, and issues affecting the interest of various States, require diplomats to be familiar with new developments be they economic or political or military or environmental or politico-economic. It is precisely for this reason that a diplomat is required to have a comprehensive knowledge of matters and issues with which contemporary international and inter-State relations are concerned.

Multilateral diplomacy, developed since the end of the First World War, and in particular, since the days of the United Nations, is a complex form of diplomacy. Matters of international concern or interests will come within the remit of multilateral diplomacy, eg international trade and investment, international monetary system, the issue of protection of the environment, human rights, etc. These issues require national diplomats to participate for the purpose of developing policies and principles. Diplomats are thus required to be familiar with such issues in order to be able to effectively participate in discourses at an international level.

Many of the so-called domestic matters are no longer to be treated as such. Take for example, the issue of illicit drug-trafficking. Without international co-operation and understanding of the international community, illicit drug-trafficking may not be eradicated. A concerted action of the international community through diplomatic policies seems to be essential for dealing with this problem. In other words, diplomats are required to be familiar with the issues pertaining to this issue and suggest remedies.

Again, take for example, the Kosovo episode. Originally, it was a Serbian issue, but when the *"ethnic cleansing"* became pronounced, the situation became a matter of international concern, although the manner in which this issue has been dealt with through the intervention of NATO has provoked controversy. But, here was a case of multilateral diplomacy for the resolution of the problem. Diplomats are now required to learn even more specialised knowledge in dealing with such situations, instead of leading them to warfares. If resolution of international issues by warfares remains as an alternative, then diplomacy takes a secondary role; there are no alternatives to diplomacy. This is why training of diplomats should entail a thorough understanding of negotiating techniques and rules of international law.

A diplomat is not a politician. He or she should be a person of vision with creative intellectual faculty. At an international level, in particular, a diplomat is required to master the techniques of managing and applying multilateral diplomacy for the cause of the international community, although in special circumstances, exceptions or reservations may have to be sought and achieved in order to protect the national interests; however, in general, national interests should not reign supreme – it simply defeats the purpose of developing international norms or rules of international co-operation. Generally speaking, a diplomat is often required to take the role of a conciliator, an adviser, a friend to the parties afflicted by a conflict. A diplomat may also be required to take the role of an *amiable compositeur*.

The changing nature of diplomacy is attributable to many factors, notably, the advanced communication system; technology-based international relations; the current state of power politics; internationalisation of issues; the changing nature of international trade and commerce; the common concern for human rights; the return of the use of force mostly in the name of humanitarian interventions, and the domination of transnational corporations. Given the complex nature of the issues and the world of international relations, the training package for diplomats should match the demands of diplomacy. Any distinct division of diplomacy between *"national"* and *"international"* is no longer possible nor is it tenable, unless certain matters may be regarded as uniquely national in nature.

The changing nature of international interaction requires diplomats to have the expertise to deal with them; it requires a special type of understanding of the world affairs, and the aspirations of the States. Diplomacy should not be used as a tool to dominate a State, and impose the choice of the strong upon the weak. It would be appropriate to maintain that *"power politics"* of the modern day and the nature of classical diplomacy are significantly different in that modern day power politics is not supposed to be power-orientated; it should be understanding-orientated; it is not by power that a country may be motivated to accepting a solution to a problem; it must be a *"disinterested"* solution, which will not entail any *"interest"* overt or covert of the negotiators (diplomats).

War-diplomacy should be replaced by peace-diplomacy; and such replacement of the former by the latter will be in conformity with the Purposes and Principles of the UN Charter.

Training of diplomats should therefore include a package whereby a multi-dimensional knowledge will be earned otherwise one is required to return to the pre-UN period, during which period warfares were common phenomena. It is essential for diplomats to consider whether they should place emphasis on peace-making rather than peace-keeping. Failure to resolve political problems between countries should not prompt diplomats to resort to warfare; if diplomacy should fail then the causes of the failure should be ascertained and alternative peaceful strategies adopted. To initiate wars would certainly mean that diplomacy has failed; but warfare is no alternative to diplomacy.

Diplomacy should not be power-based, that is, it must not be used as a tool to use powers. A decision to use power, military or otherwise, does not require any diplomacy. Thus diplomacy should not be used as a ploy to use military power. This is why it is emphasised that diplomacy should not be power-based. One should not derogate oneself from the basic functions of diplomacy – development of friendly relations between States.

Where States are not friendly, diplomacy, should be initiated by a third party, be it the UN or a friendly country, and it should be initiated to diffuse the strained relationship between the two countries as a step towards re-establishing diplomatic relationship between those States.

Diplomacy is required to be seriously directed to intentional economic issues, namely, development of equitable rules of international trade; improving the means of developing economic infrastructure; means of exploiting human resources in the most effective way; issues of common heritage of mankind; international environmental issues; and the prospects of improving the means of export trade. The plans and strategies of development at a forum such as the UN should be implemented at domestic levels, and where necessary, means of providing technical assistance to those of the countries which lack the capacity to implement them should be developed.

Knowledge of the use of technology has in recent years proved to be essential to operate international diplomacy, but the caution should be entered to ensure that the application of technology is not abused, whether for collecting information from the other party surreptitiously to use them to its advantage[12]. On the other hand, knowledge of the use of technology makes diplomacy speedier, and thereby resolves problems urgently, or pays urgent attention to them. Advanced countries with high technology are in a position to dominate the less advanced countries in this regard, and a code of conduct in relation to such matters should prove to be useful. This is another issue which deserves the urgent attention of the world of national diplomats. It is not by sagacious conduct of diplomats that friendly relations between States may be enhanced, the effect of such conduct is soon revealed.

The remit of training of diplomats is almost unlimited. In addition to acquiring the basic training required for bilateral diplomacy, diplomats should be trained in public international law; negotiating techniques; rules of various international organisations; treaty law; and particular knowledge of various important issues, namely, protection of the environment, human rights, conciliation, the techniques of how international organisations work, and above all, a thorough understanding of the North-South issues.

Knowledge in International Relations may not necessarily improve knowledge in diplomacy – the latter stands for a special technique in resolving problems and conflicts. This function may not be successfully performed unless a thorough understanding of the issues at an international level, that is, how the interest of the international community may be best protected, has been attained. This is usually attained by means of international conventions, which should not contain any elements of narrow national interests. In other words, diplomacy at a bilateral level and at an international level are different in contents, characteristics and purposes.

Diplomacy should be learned at three levels: bilateral, multilateral and international. Whereas bilateral diplomacy stands for diplomatic intervention between two States, multilateral obviously requires interaction between many States. But diplomacy or diplomatic interaction between two developed States and between a developed and a developing State require different kind of demands and requirements. Diplomacy between a developed and a developing State requires more acumen than that between two developed States. The former requires an understanding on the part of a developed State of the requirements and demands of developing States. In interacting, a diplomat belonging to a developed State must not display or demonstrate any *"pity"* or *"sense of favour"* showing to the diplomat belonging to a developing State. Diplomats belonging to developed States require a thorough understanding of the history, geography, economic and political structure of the country in

---

[12] See L D Baker, "Tolerance of International Espionage: A Functional Approval", *American University International Law Review* (2004) 1091–1113 in which the author identifies the reasons why espionage for seeking information may be legitimate activity; see also G B Demarest, "Espionage in International Law", 24 *Denver Journal of International Law and Policy* (1996) 321; and K W Abbott, "Trust but Verify": The Production of Information in Arms Control Treaties and Other International Agreements", 26 *Current International Journal* (1993) 1

addition to appreciating their demands. A sense of superiority or inferiority will take away the basis for an international and effective diplomacy.

Diplomacy or diplomatic interaction between two developing States is often based on historical and cultural basis, economic gains derivable from each other may be minimal. Take for example, the cases of the nature of diplomatic relations developed between any two developing States: such interaction strengthens their friendly mutual exchanges. Free movement of goods between such countries often proves to be a secondary matter as from a technological advancement point of view one cannot claim superiority over the other. This form of diplomacy may be described as *"neighbourly diplomacy"* to signify solidarity between themselves. Economic or military gains from such interaction is minimal. This was, incidentally, the principle of diplomacy in the olden days, extending up to the time of the Second World War.

Diplomacy or diplomatic interaction between two rich States is often based on commercial and military considerations. The alliance between the United Kingdom and the United States confirms this Western form of diplomacy. Furthermore, the comparable strengths of countries of this standing in respect of scientific advancement, defence and finance, prompt them to initiate and continue diplomacy with a commercial and military orientation, although this statement may not be true in respect of States that have a policy of maintaining military neutrality.

International diplomacy is that diplomacy which is to be carried out at a truly international platform, such as the United Nations. As stated earlier, diplomacy at this level is significantly different from diplomacy at any other level. In this form of diplomacy, a diplomat must have a thorough understanding of what the international community through the UN would like to achieve. The achievement usually takes the form of resolutions of international organisations or adoption of international conventions. Knowledge of treaty law, public international law, in addition to the Principles and Purposes by the UN and its specialised agencies becomes absolutely essential. Any perception that UN resolutions do not become effective is not only unfounded but also misconceived; it is for diplomats to ensure that the minimum level of acceptability by the Member States of the UN becomes evident at the time of adopting a resolution or convention.

Not all resolutions of the UN General Assembly are supposed to be legally binding; many of them simply demonstrate the aspirations of the majority of the Member States of the UN. On the other hand, when the contents of these resolutions directly concern the interest of the Member States often UN GA resolutions are accepted by them[13]. Diplomats have therefore a duty to ensure that resolutions will contain elements which may prompt their States to accept them; thus acceptable norms and principles are to be developed through the UN.

---

[13] Resolution 1803 of 1962 entitled *Permanent Sovereignty over Natural Resources*

Regional diplomacy is a diplomacy of a limited type in that it tends to predominantly concern itself with the regional interests. In fact, diplomacy of such a nature may give rise to conflicts, particularly in respect of economic issues when they adversely affect the interests of non-Member States. Take, for example, the chicken war between the EU and the United States. It is crucial to ensure that regional diplomacy is not promoted at the cost of the interests of the international community. Regional military diplomacy certainly runs counter to the UN obligations of the Members, unless the UN has authorised the regional body to operate its military diplomacy, by means of a dispensation from Article 2(4) of the UN Charter.

7.4 WHEN ATTITUDE TOWARD SOVEREIGNTY AND DIPLOMACY REMAINS UNCHANGED IN A CHANGING WORLD

It has been stated earlier that diplomacy stands for an art which diplomats, on behalf of their sovereigns, must use to interact with other States. This type of art requires skills where interaction / negotiation must be initiated with a view to settling differences or developing friendly relations between States. Diplomacy must be friendly and conciliatory, non-aggressive and non-retaliatory. A negotiating process must be continuous until the common grounds have been identified and the differences settled.

It has also been explained that although, in particular, the post-Second World War diplomacy has often been dominated by power politics, based on false perception of bargaining power, true diplomacy abhors power politics; bargaining power stands for negotiating skills. If power politics is to dominate, then there is no room for diplomacy; the international community will be governed by sheer power of the mighty, which unfortunately has unwarrantedly taken place.

One of the purposes of diplomacy is to establish reciprocity, which stands for a process whereby mutuality, whether in respect of commercial matters or pure diplomatic matters will be exchanged by and between sovereigns. The size and military powers of the sovereign are immaterial in developing a reciprocal arrangement.

7.5 DIPLOMACY AND INTERNATIONAL TRADE

What does diplomacy in international trade stand for? It is a technique of negotiating principles and policies of international trade which would cater for the interests of all members of the international community. In this process the impact of various regional trading arrangements must be taken into consideration, in order to ascertain whether the trading principles and policies adopted by the international community under the auspices of the United Nations, in particular WTO/GATT, are being pursued by them.

The general platform for negotiating and adopting rules of international trade is currently the WTO/GATT. Diplomats are therefore required to be familiar not only with primary issues and problems of international trade and, in particular, the issue of commercial equality, which stands for equality in fact rather than equality in law. This issue is illustrated by means of an established rule of public international law. The case in which this issue was considered by the Permanent Court of International Justice was *Minority Schools in Albania*[14]. In December 1920, the Assembly of the League of Nations recommended that in the event of Albania becoming a Member of the League, she would be required to enforce the principles of the Minorities Treaties, and in October 1921 Albania signed a Declaration, Article 5, paragraph 4 which provided, inter alia, that:

> *"Albanian nationals who belong to racial, religious or linguistic minorities will enjoy the same treatment and security in law and in fact as other Albanian nationals. In particular they shall have an equal right to maintain, manage and control at their own expense or to establish in the future, charitable, religious and social institutions, with the right to use their own language and to exercise their religion freely therein."*

But, in 1933, the Albanian National Assembly modified Articles 206 and 207 of the Constitution of 1928 in the following way:

> *"The instruction and education of Albanian subjects are reserved to the State and will be given in the State's schools. Primary education is compulsory for all Albanian nationals and will be given free of charge. Private schools of all categories at present in operation will be closed."*

This meant that all private schools for the minorities, including the Greek minority, would be closed. At the request of the Spanish representative, the League Council decided to ask the Permanent Court of International Justice for an Advisory Opinion on whether, regard being had to the Declaration of 2 October, 1921, as a whole, the Albanian Government was justified in its plea that as the abolition of the private schools in Albania constituted a general measure applicable to the majority as well as to the minority, it was in conformity with the letter and the spirit of the stipulations laid down in Article 5, paragraph 1 of that Declaration.

According to the explanations submitted to the Court by the Greek Government, *"the fundamental idea of Article 5 of the Declaration was on the contrary to guarantee freedom of education to the minorities by guaranteeing them the right to retain their existing schools and to establish others, if they desired . . ."*[15]

---

[14] PCIJ (1935), Series A/B NO 64

[15] op. cit., at 15

The Court provided the meaning of the phrase *"the same treatment and security in law and in fact"* embodied in the League Council's Resolution of 18 January, 1935.

According to the Court:

> *"... the same treatment and security in law and in fact implies a notion of equality which is peculiar to the relations between the majority and minorities."*[16]

The Court maintained that it is perhaps not easy to define the distinction between the notions of equality in fact and equality in law, but according to the Court:

> *"... nevertheless, it may be said that the former notion excludes the idea of a mere form of equality"*;[17]

and referred to what was said by the Court in its Advisory Opinion on this issue in the case of German Settlers in Poland (Opinion No. 6):

> *"There must be equality in fact as well as ostensible legal equality in the sense of the absence of discrimination in the words of the law."*[18]

The Court's interpretation of the distribution between *"equality in law"* and *"equality in fact"* came out very clearly in the following passage:

> *"Equality in law precludes discrimination of any kind; whereas equality in fact may involve the necessity of different treatment in order to attain a result which establishes an equilibrium between different situations."*[19]

The abolition of the private schools, which alone could satisfy the special requirements of the minority groups, and their replacement by government institutions, would destroy the equality of treatment; thus, it would deprive the minority of the institutions appropriate to their needs, whereas the majority would continue to have them supplied in the institutions created by the State.[20]

The Court further stated that:

> *"... but if the members of the majority should be granted a right more extensive than that which is provided, the principle of equality of treatment would come*

---

[16] op. cit., at 19

[17] ibid

[18] ibid

[19] ibid

[20] op. cit., at 20

into play and would require that the more extensive right should also be granted to the members of the minority."[21]

In their Dissenting Opinions, Sir Cecil Hurst, Count Rostworowski and M Negulesco maintained, *inter alia*, that:

> "The word 'equal' implies that the right so enjoyed must be equal in measure to the right enjoyed by somebody else. 'They shall have an equal right' means that the right to be enjoyed by the people in question is to be equal in measure to that enjoyed by some other group ...
>
> Equality necessarily implies the existence of some extraneous criterion by references to which the content is to be determined."[22]

The Dissenting Opinions also summarised the interpretation of the phrase "*they shall take an equal right*" in the following way:

> "Equality in law and fact not merely excludes all discrimination between the majority and the minority, but may necessitate different treatment of the majority and the minority so as to produce an equilibrium between their respective situations."[23]

In addition to providing guidelines as to what "*equality*" would mean, the *Minority Schools in Albania* case indicated that sovereignty should not be exercised by a State to the detriment of the interest of an identifiable people. This amounts to abuse of sovereignty.

The decision of the Permanent Court of International Justice is still valid and relevant to this day in that the basic tenets of commercial equality are not being observed by many States or regional arrangements. In this context one may find it instructive to examine the nature of international action taken to achieve commercial equality; diplomats are supposed to be familiar with it. Prior to the days of the League of Nations no formal attempt was made to achieve commercial equality; in fact, there was no reason for achieving it. The concept was not taken seriously, if considered at all, by the contemporary international community. Trade in the contemporary world between the few sovereign States used to be carried out on a bilateral basis. The major part of the world remained colonised.

Politicisation of the concept of commercial equality was necessary; but there was no need to do that until the concept of commercial equality was, in reality, revived under the auspices of the United Nations. Article 23(e) of the Covenant of the League of Nations was the only provision which referred

---

[21] ibid., According to the Court "*Far from creating a privilege in favour of the minority, as the Albanian Government avers, this stipulation (Paragraph 5(1)) answers that the majority shall not be given a privileged situation as compared with the minority.*" at 20

[22] op. cit., at 25

[23] op. cit., 26

to certain provisions of international commerce. The text of the relevant provision is:

> "... *the Members of the League ... will make provision to secure and maintain freedom of communications and of transit and equitable treatment for the commerce of all Members of the League. In this connection, the special necessities of the regions devastated during the war of 1914–1918 shall be borne in mind.*"

International action in this regard seems to have commenced with the setting up of the United Nations in 1945. The Charter of the United Nations contains two chapters, IX and X, entitled respectively *International Economic and Social Co-operation* and *The Economic and Social Council* in order to promote international economic co-operation, including co-operation in regard to international investment and trade. WTO/GATT aim at liberalising international trade. It is appreciated that many of the WTO/GATT provisions deserve reviewing, namely whether most-favoured nation treatment, which WTO/GATT believe to be the basis for attaining commercial equality, the issue of subsidy-giving by governments, and the contribution that the TRIPS provisions may make to developing countries etc. The recommendations of UNCTAD and its indomitable efforts to liberalise international trade for developing countries, whether through the introduction of the Generalised System of Preferences (GSP), or through various rounds of tariff negotiations, predominantly the Kennedy, Nixon, Tokyo and Uruguay Rounds, must be acknowledged. But, the terms of international trade, particularly for developing countries are far from perfect. This is where diplomats are required to negotiate terms and principles at an international *fora*. In the process of negotiation a balance must be maintained between the interests of both rich and poor countries. This certainly requires a special training in the techniques of negotiating terms.

At the heart of the so-called international diplomacy is a country's interest in private foreign investment and trade. Realistically, it is for the protection of these interests, in the main, that the relations between States on a friendly basis, become necessary. Often concessions in investment and trade terms are allowed as a gesture of consolidating friendly relations.

It is to be considered whether foreign policy of a State forms the basis for economic relations between States or *vice versa*. In other words, economic realities have a significant role to contribute to formulating the foreign policy of a country. In this context, one should consider the contents and purposes of a foreign policy. It is a policy aimed at maintaining friendly relations with other States. Unfortunately, military assistance by a superior power to a lesser power often takes over the primary ethos of a foreign policy. From an ideological standpoint, a military policy should not form part of an ideal foreign policy especially when peace-making and international co-operation, in the true sense of the terms, are to be the basis for and functions of a foreign policy.

From a practical standpoint however, in view of their obligations under Article 2, paragraph 4 of the UN Charter, Members of the UN are not supposed to provide military assistance to any other Member without the approval of the UN authorities. Furthermore, excessive military policy can unsettle political situation not only inside a country, but also the outside world.

However, relating to the international trade and diplomacy, Barnston rightly pointed out that the political uses of trade involve diplomacy to develop goodwill, promote regional co-operation[24], and initiatives in this regard do have a spill-over effect in other areas too, including political and military.

Diplomacy in regard to international trade takes place at three levels: (a) bilateral; (b) regional-multilateral; and (c) truly multilateral or international. The current trade policies of the States, regional trading arrangements in certain cases, and the international trade policies adopted by WTO/GATT are not only complex but also in certain cases unsatisfactory. Diplomats are required to be extremely familiar with the current trade issues, and keep formulating rules which would be fair and workable for the international community.

Sovereign authorities have the privilege to conclude trade contracts with their counterparts on any basis they like. The current international practice also allows States to set up their regional trading arrangements, namely, European Union (EU), North American Free Trade Area (NAFTA) or Association of South East Asian Nations (ASEAN); the truly international organisation, namely WTO/GATT, and regional trading arrangements might run counter to the rules to be developed and applied by the international community (WTO/GATT).

Certain other issues which require the urgent attention of the international community, namely, pricing of commodities, breach of competition policy, centralisation of commodities; or the impact of placing undue emphasis on environmental issues upon international trade. In this connection one may like to refer to the Kyoto Protocol[25].

Furthermore, one is required to examine whether the treaties governing these institutions and the mechanics of their decision-making process is helpful for developing countries. Take, for example, the Section on TRIPS in the WTO Agreement; it is worth considering whether the provisions pertaining to TRIPS are favourable to the developing countries. Diplomacy should be directed towards the issue of North-South dialogue. Again, it is to be considered whether the position of the UN Conference on Trade and Development (UNCTAD) should be re-inforced in order to properly present the case of the developing countries before WTO.

It is elementary to state that foreign trade should be treated as one of the important pillars of a country's economy, and it is primarily by diplomacy of an

---

[24] R P Barnston, op. cit., at 158
[25] 11 December 1997

economic nature that the basis for it should be developed. In this context diplomacy should concentrate on whether the developing countries may have appreciable market access in the developed world. This is where much work is required to be done by diplomats.

In this connection one may reflect on the reasons for creating the World Trade Organisation (WTO): to adopt principles and rules of international trade for all participants; but WTO is based on the controversial MFN Standard, which may not create the foundation of equality[26]. Furthermore, there are certain fundamental issues, such as subsidies, including the subsidy code, environmental issues, State aid, which deserve serious consideration. If developing countries wish to strengthen their position in the international trade arena, then it is for them to put forward their ideas; the efforts made by UNCTAD in the form of various Rounds, Kennedy, Nixon, Tokyo and Uruguay, were laudable, but they did not achieve what they had been expected to achieve. It is not by tariff concessions alone that access to markets for developing countries may be secured. Without guaranteed markets, developing countries may not increase their export trade flow.

On the other hand, rich countries should be encouraged to increase their investment flow, towards poor countries, and trade with them, in order that the latter's trading position improves, and the spill-over effect may prompt them to invite private foreign investors from the rich world. This is one aspect of the North-South Dialogue which was initiated by the Brandt Commission in 1977.

One of the commercial issues in international trade is trade liberalisation. Diplomatic efforts should be directed at examining whether the current institutional arrangements made and adopted by institutions such as WTO/ GATT may contribute to achieving this goal. In this context, one may like to see the programmes advocated by the United Nations through Chapters IX *International Economic and Social Co-operation* and X *The Economic and Social Council* in conjunction with the increasing efforts made by the UN Conference on Trade and Development (UNCTAD). Restrictions to market access by protectionism, particularly by developed countries, re-inforced by subsidies and safeguard clauses hinder international trade, and they distort competition too. Unilateral import restrictions on goods and services and bilaterally agreed price-fixing, and the creation of exclusive bilateral markets, which is a manifestation of absolute sovereignty, needs serious attention of the international community. Governmental support in the form of export credits has now became a common phenomenon, and in this game, only the rich can participate. Furthermore, quantitative restrictions coupled with high tariff barriers place obstacles to liberalisation of international markets. Managed

---

[26] See further S K Hornbeck, "The Most-favoured National Clause (Part 1), 3 *American Journal of International Law* (1909) 395; G Schwarzenberger, "The Most-favoured National Standard in British Practice", 22 *British Year Book of International Law* (1945) 96; S K Chatterjee, "Forty Years of International Action for Trade Liberalisation" 23 *Journal of World Trade* (1989) 45

trade certainly runs counter to liberalisation of international markets; but management of international trade and trade policies must be balanced and fair to all.

The effect of regional trading arrangements (otherwise known as regional economic integrations) on international trade should be seriously considered. The proactive policy pursued by the European Union (EU) Member States by giving subsidies under the EU Agriculture Policy, whereby the inefficient agricultural farms may stay on the market with guaranteed prices does not usually allow third countries to enter the EU's agricultural market. The term *"agriculture"* in this context includes direct agricultural products; and by-products too. Secured price for farm products combined with the financial support from governments and various funds hinder market access for non-European farmers. Of course, the Agricultural policy of the EEC/EU has always been exclusively addressed to and meant for protecting the EU farmers. Under its Industrial policy, trade enterprises are given funds to participate in the industrial sector; in other words, third countries' small trade enterprises may not have market access to the EU unless they manufacture unique products. Market access to the EU area may be eventually available primarily to the developed countries. The recent *"textile war"* between China and the European Union evidences this fact. All non-EU countries might be allowed to trade with the EU on a quota basis; this is primarily for two reasons: the EU markets are near-saturated in respect of most products; second, that the EU has an obligation first to leave its markets open to its Members. There is, of course, the other issue that not all products from the developing world may meet the EU standards. Thus, eventually, the gap between the North and the South will widen unless active measures are taken by the international community to reverse this process.

The issue is not whether sovereign States have their right to set up regional arrangements; what is more important to consider is whether the trading activities of such arrangements may cause economic harm to others. Strictly speaking, from an international law point of view, this is a matter of international responsibility. By the same token the viability of regional arrangements among developing countries, for example the Association of South East Asian Nations (ASEAN) or Andean Pact, should be seriously considered[27].

The recent Doha Declaration[28] and the Cancún conference highlighted certain interesting issues which deserve further economic diplomacy. In fact, it is the Doha Declaration which identified the principal issues which should be considered for liberalisation of international trade:

---

[27] Members of the ASEAN are: Brunei-Darussalam, Cambodia, Indonesia, Laos, Malaysia, Myanmar, the Philippines, Singapore, Thailand and Viet-Nam. The following are the members of the Andean Pact: Bolivia, Colombia, Ecuador and Peru

[28] For the text of the Declaration see 41 *International Legal Materials* (2002) 746

- *agriculture*
- *services*
- *market access for non-agricultural products*
- *trade-related aspects of intellectual property rights*
- *relationship between trade and investment*
- *interaction between trade and competition policy*
- *transparency in government procurement*
- *trade facilitation*
- *dispute settlement understanding*
- *trade and environmental*
- *electronic commerce*
- *trade economics*
- *trade, debt and finance*
- *trade and transfer of technology*
- *technical co-operation and capacity building*
- *least developed countries and special and differential treatment.*

The Doha Declaration aimed at establishing:

"a fair and market-orientated trading system through a programme of fundamental reform encompassing strengthened rules and specific commitments on support and protection in order to correct and prevent restrictions and distortions in world agricultural markets."

Market access for non-agricultural products from developing countries by lowering or eliminating tariff was recommended by the Declaration. *"Capacity building"* of developing and least developed countries received attention of the Declaration too. It also provided for a *"trade facilitation"* which would include reduction or elimination of administrative formalities, expediting release and clearance of goods, including goods in transit, customs formalities, and other business which prevent an easy access to overseas markets. It planned to initiate action for reviewing the Agreement on Subsidies taking into account the needs of developing and least developed countries.

One of the remarkable features of this Declaration is that it identified the co-relationship between trade, debt and finance, which is so obvious. This is where much diplomatic negotiations or efforts are necessary. If capacity building is taken seriously, countries should not really seek so much funds from foreign sources, be they states or institutions; instead, they should seek technical assistance with the help of which they would be able to build the capacity leading to development of indigenous technology. Thus, there is no need to incur debts occasioned by the aquisition of high technology from the developed world.

The Doha Ministerial Declaration advocated the idea of transferring technology from developed to developing countries. But developing countries should particularly consider the benefits of acquiring technology from developed countries. The issue of *"adaptability"* is crucially important. Acquisition of technology must be appropriate to the needs of the country. Given the current debt situation in many of the developing countries, is it worth joining the technology race with rich countries? Developing countries, in general, lack the capacity to compete with developed countries in respect of invention or innovation.

If, on the other hand, developing countries acquire second hand technology, they at the same time acquire attendant problems:

(a) the productivity of any used technology would be lower than that of any new technology;

(b) the effective life cycle of any used technology would be short;

(c) the quality of products it may manufacture would not match the quality of products manufactured by new technology;

(d) no guarantee may be given as to the level of performance of such technology;

(e) being of inferior quality products may not find profitable markets; and

(f) used technology may significantly contribute to the pollution process in a developing country.

Upon a cost-benefit analysis it would appear that the disadvantages of acquiring such technology outweigh its advantages. Furthermore, in terms of price, the technology market is imperfect; thus an acquirer is required to bargain with transferors, and shop around.

The Doha Declaration also very appropriately places emphasis on *"capacity building"* which includes the capacity to build indigenous technology too[29]. It has two advantages: (a) that people will learn by doing; and (b) that there cannot be a substitute for indigenous technology in that without doubts it must be most appropriate to the country's needs, and that it lessens dependency on foreign providers of technology. What is needed is technical assistance rather than technology. High technology may however be needed for specific sectors of an economy: for example, communication, aircraft industry, ship building etc, but the propriety of acquiring foreign technology for manufacturing industries should be seriously reviewed by developing countries. This is where diplomats are required to adopt a policy, to minimise developing countries' dependence on foreign transferors of technology – transnational corporations.

The Doha Declaration also acknowledged the seriousness of the concerns expressed by the least developed countries in the Zanzibar Declaration adopted by their ministers in July 2001, and recognised that the integration of the least developed countries into the multilateral trading system acquired meaningful market access, trade-related technical assistance, in addition to capacity building. Special and differential treatment in favour of developing

---

[29] In this connection, please see the recommendation of the UN, published in the Report entitled: *Transnational Corporations in World Development*, New York (1985)

and least-developed countries were also advocated by the Declaration and to make them an integral part of the WTO Agreements.

The Doha Declaration was a comprehensive, albeit over-ambitious, framework for allowing developing countries to participate as meaningful actors on the international trade market[30]. But, the point remains whether developed countries would agree to the demands of developing countries. Again, this is where much diplomacy is needed. The Doha Declaration was also concerned with market access for developing countries' products to markets of developed countries. But, not sufficient time was allowed to implement the Doha principles; in the meantime, the Cancún Conference was held. The deadlock on the Singapore issues, particularly in respect of agriculture and trade distorting subsidies and the fundamental differences on trade issues between the North and the South which became manifest at Geneva meetings gave an early signal of the predictable failure at Cancún. The journey to Cancún was premature.

The journey from Doha to Cancún may be described as a journey from the South to the North; it was an uncertain journey; it lacked preparation on the part of developing countries in that they failed to appreciate the strategies of rich countries in trade and agriculture. Doha's aspirations, among others, capacity building by developing countries and technical co-operation, should have been prioritised at Cancún.

The Cancún Conference (September 2003) ended abruptly because it failed to reach a consensus among the members of the WTO on the contents of the Draft Declaration. A degree of bi-polarisation took place at Cancún between the developing countries which refused to allow concessions on issues such as competition policy, trade facilitation, investment and a greater transparency in regard to procurement of goods and materials by governments[31]. The issue of agriculture became the central issue at Cancún, but for obvious reasons, the rich countries did not clearly respond to it; greater market access for agricultural products from developing countries will hurt a very important and basic source of income and create unemployment in developed countries.

Whereas developing countries wanted to see *"development"* as a result of trade, developed countries were predominantly concerned with trade. There was a deadlock; diplomatic strategies should have been clearly identified appreciating that developed countries are also required to protect their interest in both agriculture and trade sectors. Diplomacy on reciprocity, whether by allowing developed countries' products privileges and concessions or more investment incentives, should have received priority. Consensus-based diplomacy on which WTO/GATT operates, requires both parties to think of competing interests of the other party. The interests and ideas of the ACP

---

[30] C Chatterjee, "From Doha to Cancún: A Multilateral Trading System?" 54 *Amicus Curiae*, 2004 22–28 at 24–25

[31] For comments on Doha and Cancún Conferences see C Chatterjee, "From Doha to Cancún: A Multilateral Trading Sytem?", 54 *Amicus Curiae*, op. cit.

Group, the African Union and the least developed countries in regard to agriculture, non-agricultural products, transfer of technology, technical assistance etc were not viewed by many at the Cancún Conference from the standpoint of developing countries.

Briefly, it is not a question of whether rich countries are allowing developing countries adequate preferences or privileges for securing the position of the latter on the world trade markets. Developing countries should not primarily rely on privileges and preferences; diplomats must make efforts to develop an acceptable framework through the instrumentality of an international forum whereby an access-to-all market will be created. Thus, much diplomatic negotiations are needed on issues such as subsidies, government procurement, obstacles to trade created by regional trading blocs, freeing the world trade markets by means of bilateral trade treaties. Above all, however, the issue of capacity building with technical assistance from developed countries should receive the highest priority for developing countries.

7.6 CONCLUSIONS

Diplomacy has two faces: old and new. Its old face represents the traditional methods of diplomacy, which are still valid. In fact, all the provisions of the Vienna Convention on Diplomatic Relations, 1961 are based on the traditional methods of diplomacy, and stand for the minimum standards of conduct which should govern the world of diplomacy. Over the past three decades, in particular, some new faces of diplomacy became the framework of international relations. The perspective of the newly-born States as to how diplomacy should be conducted may not be disregarded.

The politico-economic uncertainties in a number of countries seem to have crated a diplomacy of dependency; on the other hand, evidence of natural resources-based diplomacy exists, for example, the oil crisis of 1973–74 based on the Arab–Israeli conflict, whereby the crude oil market was largely controlled by the OPEC (Organisation for Petroleum Exporting Countries), countries including the determination of supply and price of oil and the payment of royalty[32]. Such conflict should be avoided.

Diplomacy based on religion and culture has had its existence for a very long period[33]. Interventionist diplomacy has proved to be another very identifiable form of diplomacy: North Viet-Nam; dismantling of the Soviet Union; Afghanistan, El Salvador, Iraq, Nicaragua, Panama, to name but a few. Unfortunately, the success record of this type of diplomacy is not good; in fact, it divides the world opinion, but the common factor prevailing in each of these cases has been the questionable conduct of dictatorial governments. Of

---

[32] See, for example, the Geneva Agreement and Teheran Agreement respectively of 1971 and 1972

[33] F S Lyons, *Internationalism in Europe, 1815–1914*, Leiden, A W Sijthoff (1963)

course, the legitimacy of interventionist diplomacy has always been questioned by many.

Over the recent years, in particular, diplomacy in certain quarters has been power-based or on the assumed higher bargaining power. Such diplomacy does not command respect from all; it is a form of self-adorned diplomacy; it runs counter to the very ethos of diplomacy *stricto sensu*. Its objective is not to create relationship between States by negotiation to protect mutual interests or to create international co-operation, but to create what may be described as a diplomacy of dependency.

CHAPTER 8

Conferences

8.1 INTRODUCTION

Multilateral diplomacy often requires negotiation of issues at conferences for the protection of mutual interests. Whereas bilateral diplomacy requires negotiation between two parties (States) with a view to reaching a solution, presentation and discussion of issues and matters by a number of States having interests in those issues and matters for the purpose of reaching agreements becomes the objective of conferences. A conference provides a *forum* at which all interested parties may meet and discuss issues and matters for their solution. A conference may lead to the drafting of international documents / instruments (Conventions or Treaties) or adopting of resolutions.

The old-fashioned diplomacy based on the perception of crude bargaining power is no longer valid in that many small States may jointly hold the key to many issues, particularly, in regard to the supply of natural resources or commodities, as of course, big powers can do the same in respect of many matters such as financial loans, or grants, supply of technology or equipment etc. But, it is worth mentioning that in the world market there is hardly any exclusive supplier, except of course, in respect of certain very unique or rare commodities. In other words, where suppliers are available from various sources and under various terms and conditions, buyers have choices; it is no longer a question of exercising the so-called bargaining power by any of the parties.

Diplomacy is not exclusively concerned with political issues. Economic and socio-economic issues are also matters of diplomacy. Diplomats are therefore required to be familiar with such issues which often become the subject-matter of conferences. Furthermore, economic issues and economic relations often shape political issues; and diplomats are required to resolve such issues at conferences. Contemporary diplomacy is multi-dimensional; training of diplomats must therefore cater for these requirements. Take for example, the apartheid issue in South Africa, which was a multi-dimensional – economic, socio-economic, political and human rights-related. Without sufficient grasp of all these issues diplomats would have been unable to resolve the principal problem relating to the majority rule in South Africa.

Conferences may be classified in the following manner: (a) bilateral or multilateral; (b) ad hoc; and (c) those that are held under the auspices of international and inter-governmental organisations. Diplomatic interventions or dealing with issues at international or inter-governmental conferences, otherwise known as *'conference diplomacy'* (which is rather an odd expression) require diplomats to promote ideas which would be implemented at national levels. Regrettably, over the years, a dilemma has been allowed to be developed in that whereas often at international or inter-governmental conference *fora* commendable resolutions are adopted, they are hardly implemented at national levels. The question is not just whether they are legally binding; if they are adopted only for their non-implementation, then one should question the genuineness of the intention of the international community in making such efforts. Such practice also gives rise to doubts as to the effectiveness of international diplomacy. It is to be seriously considered whether diplomats should adopt resolutions only after a consensus as to their acceptance and implementation has been identified, or otherwise the gestures become a mockery. The issue is not that every sovereign State has the right to accept or reject a resolution adopted by the United Nations. If sovereignty is maintained too rigidly by States then there hardly remains any point in adopting resolutions at the UN level. This is where extensive diplomatic negotiations are necessary for changing the current State practice.

At international conferences, diplomats are entitled to identify and highlight their respective country's interests and position, but they should also see whether valid compromises may be made for a greater cause / interest; otherwise, international diplomacy will virtually stand for diplomacy at a national level.

This chapter explains the procedure which is usually maintained at inter-governmental and international conferences, and the significance of holding these conferences.

8.2 THE PRINCIPAL PURPOSES OF HOLDING INTER-GOVERNMENTAL AND INTERNATIONAL CONFERENCES

The term *'conference'* means consultation, or discussion, or a meeting for discussion. The principal purpose of holding a conference therefore is to discuss or consult with each other on a chosen topic in order to reach a solution. Policies are also developed at conferences which would cater for the international community. Adherence to narrow nationalistic attitude defeats the purposes of holding international or inter-governmental conferences. Where, however, a special case for a State or a type of States (e.g., archipelagic or land-locked etc) exists, inter-governmental or international conferences often pay attention to such issues and incorporate special provisions, by way of exceptions, in favour of such States. Take, for example, the Law of the Sea Convention, 1982 which included special provisions for the land-locked States.

Diplomats representing such States should therefore be properly briefed by their governments and prepared to present their cases in a cogent fashion before inter-governmental and international conferences. They should also anticipate opposition from certain other States, and be prepared to answer them. The caution should be entered that any emotional and biased proposal and answer thereto may meet with challenges and defeat.

Conferences are usually initiated by the administrative bodies (in the case of the UN, usually the Secretariat) of inter-governmental and international organisations, whenever they may consider an issue of an international dimension deserves the attention of governments. A thorough knowledge of the nature of the issues and suggestions as to an effective preventive and/or curative measures for such issues are required of diplomats. Usually, a preliminary report on a chosen topic is prepared by the Secretariat of the UN, an individual or more with thorough expertise in the subject-matter of the topic. Upon receipt of that study sufficient notice of the conference is given to the governments by the Secretariat. It is expected that the delegates (diplomats) will be fully prepared with their comments on the draft proposal already sent to them by the Secretariat.

Depending upon the nature of the topic, the particular office or specialised agency of the United Nations takes the initiative to undertake studies with the approval of the Office of the Secretary-General. The Economic and Social Council (ECOSOC) being the most pervasive office of the United Nations, many such studies are initiated by that office. It must be pointed out however that under Article 13 of the UN Charter, the General Assembly may initiate studies that may come under the purview of the United Nations. The International Law Commission is often requested by the Office of the Secretary-General to study specific legal issues of international importance. This Commission often prepares draft international Conventions for consideration by governments and academics.

The differences between bilateral or multilateral or truly international conferences must be borne in mind. Whereas the scope of proposals discussed at conferences other than that discussed at a truly international and inter-governmental conference is narrow, much wider parameters and policies become the base for inter-governmental and international conferences.

The following are the principal objectives of holding conferences:

(a) to adopt binding resolutions for implementation at a national level (this is primarily done at bilateral and ad hoc conferences);

(b) to adopt recommendatory resolutions (this is done particularly at inter-governmental or multinational conferences); and

(c) to adopt resolutions of a recommendatory nature in the hope that they would be implemented by the participating States in accordance with their respective national system and procedure (this is done particularly at international conferences).

However, in many cases a UN resolution, despite its being of a recommendary nature, may receive widespread recognition in consequence of which it is implemented by a majority of the States, rich or poor alike, and thus eventually forms part of customary rules of international law. Such is the status of the UN General Assembly Resolution entitled *Permanent Sovereignty over Natural Resources, 1962*[1].

Under the European Union system, resolutions adopted by the Council of Ministers are binding for the Member States of the EU, as are the resolutions of the Commission of the European Union on the Competition Policy.

8.3 CONFERENCE DIPLOMACY

Conference diplomacy stands for the diplomacy that is conducted at conferences the principal objectives of which is to attain a consensus after ironing out the differences between differing ideas. Owing to the complex nature of international issues affecting national policies and issues, multilateral conference diplomacy has in recent years assumed an unprecedented importance. Diplomats are therefore required to be trained as to how to participate in such conferences which may be held under the auspices of a State or an international organisation such as the United Nations or one of its specialised agencies.

In order to participate effectively, diplomats are required to familiarise themselves not only with their national policies, but also with the important international Conventions and resolutions which may have an impact upon their national policies. Nuclear proliferation, human rights, sea resources are but only a few examples of such issues. Depending upon the special situations of a particular country, provisions may be made for that country to be exempted from certain general provisions. On the other hand, although under the current practice groups of States press for their own interests being recognised and vote accordingly, the caution should be entered to ensure that extreme ideas of any particular group of States do not prove to be counterproductive resulting in the non-acceptance of a resolution or Convention by certain other groups of States[2]. In drafting the UN General Assembly Resolution entitled *Charter of Economic Rights and Duties of States, 1974,* the developing countries, in general, supported the idea that in the event of the taking (nationalisation) of foreign assets, there would be no obligation for them to pay compensation to the owners of assets, or that cartelisation of commodities should be allowed. Such ideas simply provoke undue controversy leading to the determination by other States not to accept the resolution. It must be pointed out however that the 1974 Resolution was otherwise perfectly acceptable as it simply collated the most important principles from various other generally recognised resolutions or State practices. This is an important aspect

---

[1] UNGA Res. 1803

[2] See S K Chatterjee, "The Charter of Economic Rights and Duties of States", op. cit.

of international diplomacy which signifies that no particular group of States should promote their own narrow or extreme ideas, as it will not eventually be recognised by the general international community.

International diplomacy should not encourage conflicts; on the contrary, it should find out the base for conflict resolution by understanding the root cause of the conflict, rather than following any academic dogma or principles. Rigid adherence to one bloc's interest, which is often opposed by other blocs, does not in the final analysis produce any lasting result. This is where one of the distinctions between the old-fashioned diplomacy and new diplomacy lies. Conference diplomacy at all levels, national, regional or international, must be carried out in conformity with the Purposes and Principles of the UN Charter as most of the States in the world are Members of the United Nations. Derogations from the UN Charter obligations, if they take place, must be justified by the derogator. However, conference diplomacy is to be carried out according to the established procedure, which has received attention in the following Section of this work.

8.4 ORGANISATION OF CONFERENCES

Conferences, whether initiated by a government or an international organisation, are usually organised by an administrative office, which assumes the name of the Conference Secretariat. The administrative functions relating to conferences may also be performed by permanent secretaries. In fact, the organiser's name and address usually appear in the first notification of a conference.

In addition to determining the venue of a conference, the secretariat is predominantly concerned with all related and administrative back-up work, namely, invitations, receptions, hospitality, protocol, technology, transport and even liaison with the local authorities (police, parking facility, airport(s) etc). It is for the secretariat to provide translators or interpreters, where necessary, and to maintain records of proceedings. Where specific documents are necessary for the delegates to respond to issues, they must be provided by the secretariat, as it must also be able to provide copies of specific documents, if called for by any delegate.

The minutes of a conference (*procès-verbal*) must be prepared by the secretariat, both in their draft and final versions, and distributed by it. At the beginning of a conference the Rapporteur(s) is/are appointed and the secretariat must provide officials for the preparation of the minutes. In fact, in preparing his/her report, the Rapporteur often refers to the minutes of the proceedings.

It is for the secretariat to determine with the department(s) concerned which of the sessions of a conference would be open to the public and media, and which would be private and special, and not open to the public and media. The summary proceedings of the private and special sessions may eventually be made available to the delegates.

The secretariat is required to respond to all correspondence that may be addressed to it by prospective participants before they decide to participate in the conference. It may also be required to consider suggestions received for agenda items. In the case of a conference held under the auspices of an international or inter-governmental or a non-governmental institution, it is common for governments or groups of governments or pressure groups to provide suggestions for agendas. Where however similar but not identical suggestions are received, it is for the secretariat to consolidate them.

8.5 CONFERENCE PROCEDURE

All conferences must be conducted according to certain set procedures, which are written rules and which must be observed at all stages and in respect of every conference-related matter. Any departures from the rules of procedure make a conference null and void, and indeed, its proceedings may be challenged by any delegate. International or inter-governmental or non-governmental organisations usually have their established rules of procedure; *ad hoc* conferences may be required to adopt them, and in that event, each delegate must be provided with an opportunity to be familiar with the rules of procedure that would be applied.

The rules of procedure of a conference have a legal status in that breach of its provisions will make a conference null and void. On the other hand, in order to avoid any procedure-related problems, rules of procedure should be as clear and comprehensive as possible. The following Sections detail some of the important issues or items pertaining to conference procedures.

8.5.1 The Agenda

The agenda of a conference provides the list of issues that will be considered at the conference. Selection of issues depends upon the main theme of the conference. Prospective delegates, be they representing governments, international, inter-governmental or non-governmental organisations or a combination of all these types of organisation, and pressure groups, often send their suggestions to the Secretariat, in advance, which are consolidated by the conference secretariat. In fact, in the first circular (notification) of the conference, the final date by which requests for agenda items must be sent to the conference secretariat is stipulated. The agenda items of a conference which would be concerned with matters of international concern, should maintain a balance with matters of national concern. In selecting agenda items attention must be focussed on the primary theme of the conference. It is to be emphasised that most international conferences aim at developing ideas and principles which would cater for the international community.

In order to make a conference concerned with matters of international concern, governments and diplomats are required to comprehend the increasingly complex international issues by which the contemporary international community is often affected, and be prepared to make effective contribution to such conferences. Choice of agenda items is therefore an extremely important matter.

It is for the conference secretariat however to determine the order in which the chosen agenda items will be considered by the conference. Agendas should be distributed in advance in order to allow the participants to prepare their statements in sufficient time. In the case of annual conferences, the minutes of the previous year's conference are approved, or approved with amendment(s), and this is usually the first item on the agenda for the current year. Amended minutes must also be distributed among the participants who took part in the last annual conference.

8.5.2 Delegations

In the case of a conference being held by States, the composition of delegates is indicated by the host State, but in that of conferences held under the auspices of the United Nations or one of its specialised agencies, the composition of delegates is usually provided for by the Rules of Procedure of the organisation concerned. According to the UN practice, a maximum of five representatives and a maximum of five alternates are allowed; of course, experts and advisers are not included in this number. Governments should notify the host of the number of representatives (delegates) and their names in advance. Seating arrangements are usually made in accordance with the size of the delegations.

Participant governments should select those of their diplomats who are familiar with the subject matter(s) of the conference, including special issues, if any. Where a State's national interest is required to be highlighted, the participant government concerned should ensure that its delegates, and its chief representative (the leader) are familiar with the complexity of the issue, and are able to present its case cogently and in an articulate fashion. They should also be experienced in drafting special motions and opinions.

Delegates should be familiar with the UN procedure, particularly when a conference is held under the auspices of the UN or one of its specialised agencies, and the relevant rules of international law, in addition to their being familiar with the latest international Convention(s) and resolution(s) adopted by the UN itself, or any of its specialised agencies, on the subject matter of the conference. Furthermore, delegates are not supposed to make any emotionally-loaded statements; they must be prepared to pursue their case and cause on logical grounds, and where necessary, identify the legal issues and interest accurately. Articulate presentation of issues and opinions matters; they draw the attention of the other delegates at the conference, and the Rapporteur(s) should minute them. It is an art to be able to get the message over to others over a short period of time and clearly register a State's point of view in relation to a particular matter or issue.

8.5.3 Observers

"Observers" at an international or inter-governmental conference are those who are only supposed to *'observe'*, that is, listen to the discussions at the conferences, except at special sessions of the Security Council of the United Nations. They cannot express their opinions, nor can they vote. Depending upon the subject matter of the conference, various interest groups seek permission to attend such conferences. Observers are allowed to attend conferences only with the permission of the conference authorities. Observers expenses are not borne by any conference.

8.5.4 Credentials

Credentials are important to establish one's own identity; they are issued by the proper authority and usually verified by a Credentials Committee, which reports to the plenary meeting for approval. Credentials must necessarily be issued in compliance with the rules and procedures of the conference. In the absence of credentials, delegates may not be heard, and if heard, their statements will not be regarded as ones made by any official delegate. Issuing authorities should verify whether credentials have been issued correctly or not.

8.5.5 The Authority to make Proposals and to take Decisions

Delegates have the right to make proposals at conferences in the form of draft resolutions. They may be amended and even withdrawn, before voting takes place. Making of proposals and taking of decisions are usually governed by the Rules of Procedure of the institution / organisation concerned under the auspices of which a conference is held. In the case of a conference held under the auspices of the UN the governing provision is the General Assembly Rule 92. At UN conferences, it is often possible for delegates to vote on separate sections or articles of a proposed resolution. Delegates often vote in this manner either to protest against a proposal / provision or to protect their national interest.

Delegates should be familiar with the voting system that may be followed by a conference. In the case of institutional conferences, such as those convened by the UN General Assembly or the Security Council, voting procedures appear in their respective Rules of Procedure, although under the current practice, resolutions of the General Assembly are adopted by consensus. Where rules of procedure do not exist, for example, ad hoc conferences held under the auspices of any organisation, the voting procedure is explained to the participants by the chairperson of the conference.

Although, usually, at most conferences, including those held under the auspices of the UN General Assembly, each country has one vote, a weighted voting system operates within certain institutions, namely, the International Monetary Fund. Under the weighted voting system, voting right of a participant depends upon the shares held by it by means of financial contribution.

Quorum in voting is a very important issue in that if a meeting or conference is not quorate, that is the minimum number of members are not present, then the conference or the meeting cannot adopt any resolution.

Delegates are supposed to know how voting may be conducted at a meeting or conference, that is, whether by secret ballot or by postal ballot or by a show of hands or by a roll call or by pressing a button. Delegates should take prior instruction from their respective governments as to how they should vote, and they should prepare their position upon receipt of the agenda of the conference or meeting. Often, delegates consult other delegates of governments having similar interest in regard to the items on an agenda. At UN conferences, bloc voting representing the interests of groups of States has become a common practice[3]. Abstentions are also quite common in voting, although abstentions seem to have attained a different meaning from that traditionally attached to the term. For example, although Article 27, paragraph 3 of the UN Charter does not provide for any abstention in the voting procedure applicable to the substantive issues in which votes are sought, since November 1965 (when the resolution for imposing sanctions on Rhodesia was adopted) an unofficial practice seems to have developed whereby two permanent Members of the Security Council abstained and yet a resolution was adopted by the Security Council and implemented by it. In the Rhodesian situation, both France and the Soviet Union abstained, and the resolution was enforced and renewed several times. The legal effect of an abstention at the Security Council level may thus be interpreted in the following way – either abstentions are to be treated as affirmative votes, or abstentions may be disregarded. Until Article 27, paragraph 3 is amended, this inevitable interpretation of abstention may have to be accepted.

Where special issues deserve considered views of experts, sub-committees and working parties are set up. While a conference is in progress, such sub-committees and working groups carry on with their studies, and eventually report to the main conference of their findings at plenary sessions.

In respect of controversial or complex legal issues initiated by a UN organ, in particular, by the UN General Assembly or the Economic and Social Council (ECOSOC), it is common practice for the Secretary-General to request the International Law Commission to study such issues and submit their report to the Commission's Special Services, which, in due course, is submitted to the General Assembly for adoption. Opinions and votings are also recorded in such reports.

8.5.6 Management of a Conference

Management of a conference requires skills on the part of the chairperson or president. He/she must not only have sufficient knowledge in the subject

---

[3] Bloc voting has become a common practice among groups of States, such as the African group, the Asian group, the Latin American group or the Nordic group, or the Group of 77 or the European Union

matter of the conference but also the skills to control it. He/she must conduct the conference according to the Rules of Procedure. Fairness, firmness, impartiality and patience are some of the essential virtues that a chairperson or president must possess. The agenda of a conference / meeting is the other document which the chairperson / president of a conference / meeting must adhere to, although the agenda items are not set by him / her[4]. The chairperson / president of a conference enjoys a degree of flexibility over the arrangement of the agenda items in that the order of the items, with the consent of the conference / meeting may be changed if circumstances so require.

Management of a conference has two main aspects: (a) management by virtue of the knowledge of the subject matter of the conference; and (b) management from a procedural point of view, that is, according to the Rules of Procedure. The procedural aspect of a conference is important in that absence or lack of observance of the written procedures will invalidate any resolution that may be adopted by the conference.

The conduct of a conference, that is, its smooth progress in an orderly fashion, is another aspect of the management of a conference. The chairperson / president must call on the principal speakers on each item, and allow certain participants to make brief comments. Usually, those of the participants who would wish to contribute must submit their names to the chairperson / president in time. The chairperson / president has the prerogative to limit the duration of any speech or contribution, or even advise a participant not to prolong his / her speech. He / she must have the knowledge to clarify certain issues, when necessary. He / she should command the respect of the other participants.

The chairperson / president must be able to deal with acrimonious conduct, if any, on the part of participants, when necessary. However, he / she must always ensure that representations from all principal groups have been allowed. The chairperson / president also enjoys the prerogative to adjourn a conference for promoting informal discussion among delegates so that the proceedings may be carried out meaningfully, but he / she must also ensure that the time for the conference is not exceeded.

Where minutes of the previous conference are to be approved, that must be done; this procedure, of course, would not arise where conferences are not held annually by the same institution among its members.

8.5.7 Rapporteurs

The position of rapporteurs at international conferences is unique. They are chosen on the strength of their expertise in specific issues. It is the function of a rapporteur to produce a consolidated report on the basis of the reports on specific sub-issues studied by each of the members of committees or sub-committees. A conference chairperson / president must allow a rapporteur to

---

[4] In the case of conference held by institutions, agendas are drafted by the Secretariat of the institution concerned

submit his / her report, which must be recorded, and which is often published by international organisations, when a conference is held under the auspices of such an organisation. A chairperson / president of a conference should invite comments from the participants on the report of a rapporteur before he / she finalises his / her report.

8.5.8 Records

Minutes of all conferences / meetings must be correctly produced and retained. They are to be agreed as correct records by the participants. They serve as primary sources of information. Records may take different forms: (a) verbatim records; (b) summary records; and (c) the texts of resolutions only. Of course, the verbatim records give the full account of the proceedings. With the help of technology it is much easier now to prepare verbatim records. As speeches can usually be recorded mechanically, delegates should be well-prepared in making their statements, as they may be quoted in subsequent conferences or documents.

8.5.9 Languages

International conferences are usually conducted in more than one language, and the languages that will be used in a conference are announced. The language(s) in which a conference is conducted is / are called the working language(s) of the conference. Participants are given the choice of a few languages in which they can speak or discuss and their speeches or discussions will be simultaneously interpreted in the other chosen languages. Official languages, on the other hand, stand for those languages in which the reports and resolutions are published.

8.6 CONCLUSIONS

Conferences provide diplomats opportunities to discuss matters of mutual interest or matters having international importance, and to formulate policies or adopt resolutions in the hope that they will be implemented by the participants. It is to be emphasised that the basic objective of a conference is not to encounter confrontations but to identify common grounds on which diplomats and their governments can work in the future. Such conferences also provide opportunities for preparing international Conventions for regulating their conduct in relation to specific matters. On the other hand, where national interests deserve special attention, it is for the delegates of the country concerned to draw the attention of a conference to that effect, but always within legitimate bounds. It is essential for diplomats to familiarise themselves with the skills of participating in conferences meaningfully.

CHAPTER 9

Diplomatic Protocol and Procedures

9.1 INTRODUCTION

In the diplomatic world, the precedence of a head of a mission is taken seriously, and is based on classification of diplomats: ambassadors, high commissioners, apostolic nuncio, pro-nuncio[1], envoy extraordinary, minister plenipotentiary, and *chargé d'affaires*[2]. It also depends upon the seniority in diplomatic practice; seniority is determined in two ways: (a) the date on which credentials are presented to the Head of the State by the Head of a Mission; or (b) the date on which he/she notified the Ministry of Foreign Affairs of his/her arrival and sent a copy of his/her credentials to them. It is therefore important for diplomats and the Ministries of Foreign Affairs to know the state practice in this regard. In the United Kingdom, the date of determining seniority is the date on which copies of credentials are handed over to the Head of State. In certain States, diplomats representing the Holy See are accorded precedence over all other heads of mission of the same category.

In the event of two Heads of Mission presenting their credentials on the same day usually the hours of commencing their function becomes the determining factor; alternatively, certain States decide seniority by reference to the title of the State in the alphabetical order.

A *chargé d'affaires en titre* follows the head of mission of an ambassadorial rank, and *chargé d'affaires ad interim* will follow the *chargé d'affaires en titre*. The date of assumption of duty becomes the date of determining the precedence within his / her class.

The following order is followed in respect of precedence of members of the political staff:

Ministerial Plenipotentiary
Minister Counsellor
Counsellor
First Secretary
Second Secretary
Third Secretary

---

[1] The rank of Inter-Nuncio is rarely used in the contemporary period

[2] Chargé d'Affaires may be of two categories: titular or en pied

The place of specialist attachés is determined by individual missions, although in terms of rank, they usually come before a First Secretary. At diplomatic functions, individual precedence is based on rank:

> Doyen (the longest-serving ambassadorial level diplomat, or, in some Catholic countries, the Apostolic Nuncio)
> Ambassador, High Commissioner, Apostolic Nuncio or Pro-Nuncio
> Envoy Extraordinary and Minister Plenipotentiary
> Chargé d'Affaires (*en titre*)
> Chargé d'Affaires (*ad interim*)
> Minister Plenipotentiary
> Minister Counsellor
> First Secretary
> Second Secretary
> Third Secretary

State practice varies in respect of specialist attachés.

The Diplomatic List published by each receiving State shows the order of precedence of members of the political staff; and it is the duty of the Head of a Mission to notify the Ministry of Foreign Affairs of the receiving State of the precedence of the members of his/her Mission.

9.2 THE USE OF NATIONAL FLAGS

Diplomatic missions are entitled to fly their national flags, although in many countries for security reasons, by choice, they may decide not to fly them all the time. The same is true of the residence of the Heads of Missions. However, diplomatic missions do fly their national flags on their national days, including national days of mourning, and on special occasions. National flags are certainly flown (half-mast) to mourn the death of a sovereign from the day of the death until the day of the funeral. They are also flown on their official cars when making official visits to officials of receiving States or in taking part in ceremonies in the receiving State.

Whereas the use of the national flags on the Mission is in the total discretion of the Mission guided by the sending State, but as a matter of diplomatic practice of each State, the use of the flag of the receiving State along with the national flag of the sending State is a matter of diplomatic protocol.

Where multiple national flags are required to be flown, the national flag must be placed in the centre, signifying the highest honour to it, and others must be placed alternately to the right and left of the central point (where the national flag is) in the alphabetical order of the countries.

9.3 STATE CEREMONIES

State ceremonies stand for those ceremonies which are of national significance, and in which the State must take part, e.g. celebration of the independence day, anniversaries of national significance, visits by foreign sovereigns and even funerals. In the preparation of State ceremonies, the Chief of the Department of Protocol is usually involved, and he/she often consults the Dean of the Diplomatic Corps, but consultation with the Dean is very usual when the Diplomatic Corps as a whole would be involved. State ceremonies must be ceremonious, and appropriate provision of security must be made. The following are usually involved in making State ceremonies a success: the police for security, a rank usually extracted from the Forces, the press, civic authorities, security officials at all strategic locations, including airports and seaports, and further police for the regulation of traffic.

Visits by foreign dignitaries, including heads of States, also require the receiving State to observe them ceremoniously. When a foreign dignitary visits a country, the national anthem of the dignitary's country is played by the receiving State, and in addition to the guard of honour inspected, respect is paid to the guest's national flag. In diplomatic practice, motor cycle or horse escort is arranged to take the dignitary to the official place (whether it is the President's House or a Royal palace). Cars or carriages in a procession are arranged in descending order of precedence of diplomats.

When a foreign dignitary pays a visit, the sovereign/Foreign Minister (in the UK, the Secretary of State for Foreign and Commonwealth Affairs) of the receiving State invites the head of the Mission of the State concerned; it is customary for the foreign dignitary to offer hospitality at his/her head of Mission's residence or the Mission for the corresponding dignitary (the counterpart) in the receiving State. Such reciprocal acts are taken seriously in the diplomatic world; by the same token it may be stated that the State ceremonies should be performed meticulously so that the foreign sovereign reciprocates on a similar basis. Foreign dignitaries, as a matter of practice, extend invitation to the counterpart in the receiving State to visit his/her country at a mutually convenient time.

9.4 DIPLOMATIC LIST

As the title suggests, a Diplomatic List simply lists the names of diplomatic missions with their locations, and the diplomats accredited to a receiving State. The rank of each named diplomatic staff, including the Ambassador or the High Commissioner is shown on the List. A Diplomatic List also contains the names of staff of international organisations received in a diplomatic capacity (e.g. the UN or its specialised agencies). Diplomatic privileges and immunities are also extended to the holder of certain special positions, such as the Secretary-General of the Commonwealth Secretariat in London. It is the Foreign Office in every receiving State that prepares the Diplomatic List, and the staff of the Missions of the States recognised by the receiving State are included in the List. The names of diplomatic staff in the List appear in the order of their precedence. Diplomats are listed under the names of their respective States, and States are listed in alphabetical order, in the language of the receiving State.

Certain States issue a separate Consular List, whereas certain others produce a combined Diplomatic and Consular List. Keeping of the Diplomatic and Consular Lists up to date is very much a shared responsibility between the Missions and the authorities of the receiving State.

9.5 COMMUNICATIONS BETWEEN DIPLOMATIC MISSIONS AND THE GOVERNMENT OF THE RECEIVING STATE

Communications between diplomatic missions and the government of the receiving State is an important factor in developing good rapport between the two parties. Communications are only made by or on behalf of the Head of Missions or to the Ministry of Foreign Affairs or any other Ministry to which powers in this regard may have been delegated by the government of the receiving State. Often, communications are made through personal interviews with the appropriate Minister in the receiving State. This method of communication, which is less formal, has become a common practice in the diplomatic world. Diplomatic missions often nominate diplomatic staff to see their counterparts in the receiving State. Such communication system requires articulation and understanding of the issue on the part of both parties. Furthermore, diplomatic activities of a complex nature may be performed more speedily by direct face-to-face interviews and communications, although in many cases, the outcome of such communications is formalised by written communications.

Exchange of Notes between the two parties has always been the traditional means of communication. Most communications follow the standard forms adopted by the diplomatic world. Communications are usually formalised by note *verbale*.

Often diplomats are required to visit the relevant Ministry in the receiving State in order to present the case on behalf of the sending State, and in order to signify his visit as official, an *aide memoire* is prepared to explain the sending State's proposed action or point of view in relation to a particular matter. This document does not bear any signature, nor does it contain any stamp of the embassy or Mission. An *aide memoire* must be precise and unambiguous.

Where a diplomat is not certain of his/her government's position in regard to a controversial or difficult matter, he/she may decide to place a *non-paper* in which the position of the government is stated in a non-committal fashion. Of course, the government may be required to clarify its position on the matter in due course.

9.6 OFFICIAL MOURNING

Official mournings stand for those mournings which a Mission observes when a national personality's death, be it the head of the country or a prime minister or any dignitary in the sending State or of the receiving State, must be mourned. Official mournings may be declared by the head of a foreign mission in which case it is for him/her to complete the formalities, one of which is to hoist the national flag on the Mission building half mast. The number of days for which the national flag will remain in a half mast position is chosen by the sending State; where an official mourning is declared by a receiving State, it applies to the entire Diplomatic Corps, and it is for the receiving State to state how it will observe the official mourning.

There are however certain essential formalities that Missions and Diplomatic Corps, the latter in the receiving State, must observe. They must wear black ties or other national form of dress signifying a state of mourning; female staff must also wear appropriate dress. During the period of an official mourning some of the previously arranged interviews / appointments may have to be cancelled, but they must be re-arranged stating the grounds for so doing.

A photograph of the deceased dignitary surrounded by black ribbon is usually displayed, and official correspondence bears a black edge for a limited period of time to mourn the death. A condolence book is kept at the embassy and at the residence of the Head of the Mission to allow dignitaries and officials of other Missions to sign the book to express their sympathy. Although all State functions are to be observed during the period of mourning, they must be done so (observed) in an unostentatious and solemn fashion. The Head of the Mission notifies the Ministry of Foreign Affairs of the receiving State of the official mourning due to the death of the person named, and of the fact that a book of condolence has been kept at the Mission.

When official mourning is declared by a receiving State, the Diplomatic Corps acts as a body on the instruction of the Chief of the Protocol Department. The members of the Diplomatic Corps would be required to fly their flags half-mast for the designated period of time, and attend the official ceremonies with the solemnity appropriate to the occasion. It is customary for the Heads of Missions to send letters of sympathy to the Minister for Foreign Affairs. They or their representatives usually sign the Condolence book, and leave their cards marked *"p.c."* (*pour condoléances*).

It is very important for foreign Missions in a receiving State to show their sympathy at the death of a dignitary after his/her death has been announced, and a book of Condolence opened. Such issues matter in diplomatic relations. Most of the Missions maintain standard letters in marking such occasions, whether for themselves or for the receiving State. Where possible, the Heads of Missions should pay a personal visit to the residence of the Head of the Mission of the country that goes through an official mourning. Similar types of formality and duty should be performed by Heads of Missions when an official mourning is announced by the authorities of the receiving State.

As to the dress that diplomats should wear to attend State ceremonies or an official mourning, most of the Missions maintain guidelines. In the case of

State ceremonies the invitee indicates in the invitation card whether decorations and medals may be worn for the occasion.

9.7 CONCLUSIONS

In diplomatic practice, most Missions are aware of how diplomatic protocol and procedures should be used. Nevertheless, it is worth pointing out that the observance of formalities and procedures at official ceremonies and State mournings create impressions on the receiving country's Ministry of Foreign Affairs. An appropriate use of diplomatic protocol and procedures simply becomes a point of appreciation, which has a bearing upon the diplomatic relations between the two countries. States setting up Missions in a receiving State for the first time, or during the initial period of their setting up of their Missions, should take particular notice of the diplomatic protocol and procedures. Where a foreign Mission is not familiar with the particular procedure of another foreign Mission, or of a receiving State, it should indirectly ascertain the procedure. Seeking of information is better than creating an adverse impression by mistakes in a receiving State.

CHAPTER 10

The Ministry of Foreign Affairs

10.1 INTRODUCTION

In view of the inevitability of developing and maintaining foreign relations with other States, every government sets up a Ministry of Foreign Affairs. The titles of the Ministry may vary from State to State, although the term *'Foreign'* almost inevitably appears in the name of the Ministry, unless one refers to exceptional cases such as that of the United States, where the ministry of foreign affairs is known as the State Department, the head of which is known as the Secretary of State. In the United Kingdom however, all Heads of Ministries are usually known as Secretaries of State[1].

Foreign relations in the current political climate are often established between recognised governments, between recognised and unrecognised governments and between unrecognised and unrecognised governments. Most of the works on international diplomacy have developed matrics on foreign relations between recognised States, often emphasising that a powerful government dominates a less powerful one. This aspect of foreign relations or diplomacy has been discussed in a separate Section of this work.

However, it must be emphasised that the domain of inter-State or international diplomacy is often required to consider the issue of developing foreign relations with unrecognised governments.

It would be inappropriate to delve into the controversy of the policy of recognition of governments in international relations in this context[2]. Suffice to say that certain governments have no declared policy as to initiating foreign relations with unrecognised governments; nevertheless, they often establish trade, including investment relations; alternatively, they adopt an implied recognition policy. Both the alternatives provoke controversy, political, legal or otherwise.

---

[1] The Head of the ministry of finance (The Treasury) is however known as the Chancellor of the Exchequer

[2] For a comprehensive discussion of the problems of recognition, see H Lauterpacht, *Recognition in International Law*, Cambridge, Cambridge University Press (1947); J Crawford, *The Creation of States in International Law*, Oxford, Clarendon Press (1979); I Brownlie, "Recognition in Theory and Practice", 53 *British Book of International Law* (1982) 197; S Talmon, "Recognition of Governments: An Analysis of the New British Policy and Practice, 63 *British Year Book of International Law* (1982) 231; C Warbrick, "The New British Policy on Recognition of Governments", 30 *International and Comparative Law Quarterly* (1981) 23

As from the early 1980s, both the governments of the United Kingdom and the United States have been following an implied recognition policy, in general, and both of them established trade, including foreign direct investment, relations with unrecognised governments, namely, Taiwan. International diplomacy is thus developing a new dimension, based on politico-economic and legal issues, such as the legal status of commercial treaties with unrecognised governments and also whether by effluxion of time, the implied recognition may attain the status of *de facto*, and eventually, by conduct, a *de jure* recognition. From a theoretical standpoint, it may be described as a form of *'covert diplomacy'*. Again, the denial of an express recognition has a direct adverse impact on the possibility of membership of these States of the United Nations. Although every sovereign government has the inherent discretion to recognise or not to recognise another government, the question remains whether that inherent discretion or prerogative is abused. In this respect, Lauterpacht's idea of recognition of all governments, expressed in the Declaratory theory, is worth considering. According to this theory, statehood or the authority of a government exists independently of recognition. In fact, it refers to the principle of international responsibility, according to which the members of the international community have a responsibility to ensure the participation of all governments in international affairs, and derive benefits from the legitimate membership of the international community and the international organisations therein. Furthermore, the Declaratory theory is based on the concept of the sovereign equality of States; if a government requires the recognition of other governments, then the other governments are superior to the would-be recognised government. Of course, those of the governments which believe in the Constitutive theory maintain that it is an aspect of international responsibility to ensure that undemocratic governments (which decision may be based on value judgments) are not recognised, as their recognition might jeopardise the maintenance of international peace and security. According to this theory, it is the act of recognition alone which creates statehood or which allows a government to attain a legal status in the international community[3]. But, the fact remains that a government may be de-recognised. Denial of recognition may be treated as a breach of human rights on the part of those who refuse to recognise an applicant government. Perhaps, future diplomats should seriously consider this issue.

Foreign relations between States may take various forms: direct bilateral relations between the preferred allies; new bilateral relations between the new States or lesser States; and of course, where appropriate, relations with regional institutions. What one is required to bear in mind is whether trading interests form the basis for foreign relations or the converse. The popular perception has been that the military interests of certain powers prompt them to develop foreign relations with certain specific States; but it is to be

---

[3] See further, *Starke's International Law*, I A Shearer (ed), London, Butterworths

emphasised that military interests entail trading interests too; securing of the supply of certain commodities, including natural resources, also forms the basis for interacting with the supplier States by means of bilateral treaties. Indeed, the need for securing the supply of crude oil from Kuwait was to some commentators the principal reason for the Allied Powers being involved in the Iraq-Kuwait war. The economic interdependence of States often necessitate developing and maintaining workable foreign relations; whereas the economically rich countries must look for more markets whether in the rich or poor world, developing countries usually tend to ensure that they are able to secure markets for their products at affordable terms from various rich countries.

Foreign relations between countries of similar cultures and religious beliefs have historically been a noticeable phenomenon. It is possible to categorise foreign policies of the contemporary world into the following heads: *hot* active military interaction to save a country's national integrity. In this case, the aggressor State is directly in breach of its obligations under Article 2, paragraph 4 of the UN Charter. Such foreign policies seem to attract the attention of the international community, and the conviction towards crude military powers, as an important element of a successful foreign policy consolidates / becomes permanent. *Tepid*, when no active action is taken for proper diplomatic relations for the purpose of promoting non-military, economic, commercial and cultural intercourse between countries; and *flat*, when foreign relations between States are almost on the verge of being strained, but not totally ceased. These latter two categories of foreign relations develop when States tend to disregard the importance of enhancing relations between themselves on the basis of economic and cultural interactions. The politico-military aspects of international diplomacy should be a temporary phenomenon only when prompted by emergency situations, which unfortunately does not seem to be the case in the current practice of the diplomatic world. If peaceful and friendly relations between States are regarded as the primary objectives of international diplomacy, then one is bound to deduce the conclusion that foreign relations between States which are to be promoted by diplomats have developed certain important dimensions.

An aggressive foreign policy is a foreign policy which should be employed only during an emergency situation, and if such a policy is initiated or is caused to be initiated by others, then it is for diplomats to take up the issue at an international forum for disciplining the conduct of the recalcitrant States by peaceful means. It is only then that the need for peace-keeping will be minimised.

A foreign policy conducted by a Ministry of Foreign Affairs should have three dimensions: bilateral, multilateral (regional) and international (interaction with the UN, including its various specialised agencies). On the other hand, it should be directed at three directions: North-South, North-North, and South-South, as the demands and aspirations of each group of States may be different, but always providing opportunities for interactions between the North and the South.

Oppenheim maintains that since the days of the Treaty of Westphalia 1648, the Ministry of Foreign Affairs has, in one form or another, been in existence in every State[4]. The foreign affairs of a country are usually conducted by the Minister for Foreign Affairs, on behalf of the State concerned. Article 41, paragraph 2 of the Vienna Convention provides however that:

> *"All official business with the receiving State entrusted to the mission of the sending State shall be conducted with or through the Ministry of Foreign Affairs of the receiving State or such other ministry as may be agreed."*

If the Head of State deals with foreign affairs himself or herself, it is through the Minister for Foreign Affairs that all international transactions pass. It is rare however in the current State practice for a Head of State to deal with foreign affairs[5]. In regard to foreign affairs, all relevant internal departments, ambassadors and consuls posted in a receiving State are under the direction of the Minister for Foreign Affairs. The Royal Danish Government brought before the Permanent Court of International Justice a suit against the Royal Norwegian Government on the grounds that the latter government head, on 10 July 1931, published a proclamation declaring that it had proceeded to occupy certain territories in Eastern Greenland which, in the contention of the Danish Government, were subject to the sovereignty of the Crown of Denmark. In the case concerning the *Legal Status of Eastern Greenland*[6], the Permanent Court of International Justice indicated that the statements made by a Foreign Minister can be binding on his State.

In the context of the point discussed herein, it may be pointed out that of the correspondence made between the two Governments, the Court heavily relied on the reply given by Mr Ihlen, the Norwegian Minister for Foreign Affairs to the Danish Minister on 22 July 1919.

The Danish Minister made the following statement:

> *"The Danish Government has for some years been anxious to obtain the recognition of all the interested Powers of Denmark's sovereignty over the whole of Greenland, . . . During the negotiations with the USA over the cession of the*

---

[4] *Oppenheim's International Law*, vol 1, op. cit., at 1045

[5] On the functions of Foreign Office, see generally, Sir William Malkin, "International Law in Practice" 49 *Law Quarterly Review* (1933) 489; R B Bilder, "The Office of the Legal Adviser: The State Department Lawyer and Foreign Affairs", 56 *American Journal of International Law* (1962) 633, and G Fitzmaurice and F A Vallat, "Sir (William) Eric Beckett: An Appreciation", 17 *International and Comparative Law Quarterly* (1968) 267

[6] PCIJ, Series A/B, No. 53 at 71; see also *Beagle Channel Arbitration (Argentina v Chile)* 52 *International Law Reports* (1979) 93

Danish West Indies, the Danish Government raised this question in so far as concerns recognition by the Government of the USA, and it succeeded in inducing the latter to agree that, concurrently with the conclusion of a convention regarding the cession of the said islands, it would make a declaration to the effect that the Government of the USA would not object to the Danish Government extending their political and economic interests to the whole of Greenland.

The Danish Government is confident (he added) that the Norwegian Government will not make any difficulties in the settlement of this question."[7]

On 22 July 1919 the Norwegian Foreign Minister replied that:

"*Today I informed the Danish Minister that the Norwegian Government would not make any difficulties in the settlement of this question.*"[8]

The Court considered it beyond all dispute that:

"*... a reply of this nature given by the Minister for Foreign Affairs on behalf of his Government in response to a request of the diplomatic representative of a foreign Power, in regard to a question falling within his province, is binding upon the country to which the Minister belongs.*"[9]

The Minister for Foreign Affairs signs all documents regarding foreign matters. He is usually present when ambassadors present their credentials to the Head of State. He also represents his State at international *fora* for the purpose of performing all acts relating to the conclusion of treaties[10, 11].

A Minister for Foreign Affairs, when he is in a foreign State, is regarded as an internationally protected person under the Convention on the Prevention and Punishment of Crimes Against Internationally Protected Persons, including Diplomatic Agents, 1973. This privilege is also allowed to members of his family when they accompany him.

The following represents the status of statements made by the Secretary of State for Foreign Affairs before the English Courts[12]. It has been the practice of English Courts to accept statements made by or on behalf of the Secretary of State for Foreign and Commonwealth Affairs in the form of certificates

---

[7] op. cit., at 70

[8] ibid

[9] op. cit., at 71

[10] PCIJ

[11] See Article 7, paragraph 2 of the Vienna Convention on the Law of Treaties, 1969

[12] On this issue, see H Lauterpacht, "Recognition of Insurgents as a *de facto* Government", 3 *Modern Law Review* (1939) 1; A B Lyons, "The Conclusiveness of the Foreign Office Certificates", 23 *British Year Book of International Law* (1946) 240; C Warbrick, "Kampuchea: Representation and Recognition", 30 *International and Comparative Law Quarterly* (1981) 234; E Wilmshurst, "Executive Certificate in Foreign Affairs: The United Kingdom", 35 *International and Comparative Law Quarterly* (1986) 157; and C Warbrick "Executive Certificates in Foreign Affairs: Prospects for Review and Control", 35 *International and Comparative Law Quarterly* (1986) 138

relating to certain categories of facts as conclusive[13], unless the Court is required to interpret a term in a commercial document[14] or a statute[15]. English Courts are not obliged however to seek a statement from the Foreign and Commonwealth Office on a matter; on the other hand, the latter may not be drawn on a question put to it by English Courts. In *GUR Corporation v Trust Bank of Africa Ltd*[16] the Court was required to deal with the international status of the Republic of Ciskei which was granted independence by the Republic of South Africa. The Court of Appeal held that:

> "... the Foreign Office certificates were conclusive that the Republic of Ciskei was not recognised as an independent State ..."

The Foreign and Commonwealth Office further maintained that:

> "... it would appear to the Foreign and Commonwealth Office that the capacity to contract and to sue and be sued is a matter for the court to determine having regard to the answer given to the first question, and therefore, that it would not be appropriate for the Foreign and Commonwealth Office to answer the second question."[17]

English Courts exercise their discretion whether or not to accept a statement made by the Foreign and Commonwealth Office as conclusive, and may establish facts in some other way[18]. However, according to Oppenheim's *International Law*, the following are some of the categories of cases in which English Courts have treated the statements made by the Foreign and Commonwealth Office as conclusive:

(a) whether a foreign State or government has been recognised *de facto* or *de jure* by Her Majesty's Government[19];

---

[13] *The Fagernes* [1927] P 311; the confirmation whether the British Channel was part of the realm of England was provided by the Attorney-General

[14] See *Luigi Monta of Genoa v Cechofracht Co Ltd* [1956] 2 ALL ER 769; *Reel v Holder* [1981] 1 WLR 1226

[15] See *Al-Fin Corporation's Patent* [1969] 3 ALL ER 396; see also J Merrills, "Recognition and Construction", 20 *International and Comparative Law Quarterly* (1971) 476; *Murray v Parkes* [1942] 2 KB 123

[16] [1987] 1 QB 599

[17] op. cit., at 618

[18] *Murray v Parkes* [1942] 2 KB 123. The principal issue in this case was whether an individual who was born in Eire, but resided in England since 1934 was liable to be called up for service in the armed forces of the Crown. The Court maintained that the Appellant's case would be governed by s 1(1) of the British Nationality and Status of Aliens Act 1914. The appeal was dismissed. See also, *Arab Bank Ltd v Barclays Bank DCO* [1954] AC 495.

[19] *The Gagara* [1919] P 35; *Luther v Sagor* [1921] 1 KB 456; *Carl-Zeiss-Stiftung v Rayner & Keeler (No 2)* [1967] 1 AC 853; see also J Crawford "Decisions of British Courts during 1985 involving questions of Public International Law", 56 *British Year Book of International Law* (1985) 311

(b) whether certain territory is under the sovereignty of one State or another[20];

(c) the status of a foreign State or its monarch[21];

(d) whether a state of war exists with a foreign country[22];

(e) whether an individual is entitled to diplomatic status[23]; and

(f) the extent of British jurisdiction in a foreign country, if at all[24].

The relationship between a Foreign Ministry and the judicial authorities in a country may vary from country to country. *Oppenheim's International Law* maintains however that many States have adopted the UK model[25].

10.2 THE COMPOSITION OF THE MINISTRY OF FOREIGN AFFAIRS

The composition of the Ministry of Foreign Affairs varies considerably from country to country, but certain sections or departments commonly exist in all Ministries of Foreign Affairs: Political Affairs, Treaties, Legal, Protocol, Trade and Economic Relations, Press and Information, Scientific, Consular Relations, Cultural Relations, Personnel, Administration, Communications and Security, and Archives and Library. The titles of these Sections or departments are self-explanatory as to the activities in which each of them is involved.

In most countries the Ministry of Foreign Affairs delegates its functions in respect of international trade and commerce, cross-border education, cross-border health issues etc. to the respective domestic Ministry, which contains a Section on international issues in relation to such matters, but the

---

[20] *Foster v Globe Venture Syndicate* [1900] 1 Ch.D 811; *The Fagernes* [1927] P 311; and *Post Office v Estuary Radio Ltd* [1968] 2 QB 740 at 753

[21] *Mighell v Sultan of Jahore* [1894] 1 QB 149; *Duff Development Co v Government of Kelantan* [1924] AC 797

[22] *R v Bottrill* [1947] KB 41

[23] *R v Governor of Pentonville Prison ex parte Teja* [1971] 2 QB 274 at 287; or *Engelke v Musmann* [1928] AC 433

[24] *North Charterland Exploration Co (1910) Ltd v The King* [1931] 1 Ch 169; *Abdul Rahman Baker v Ashford* [1960] 3 WLR 121; but see *Ex parte Mwenya* [1959] 3 WLR 767. In this latter case Mwenya, a native of Northern Rhodesia was unlawfully detained by the Governor of Northern Rhodesia, and he applied for a writ of *habeas corpus* issued to the Governor of Northern Rhodesia and the Secretary of State for Colonies. The question arose whether English Courts had jurisdiction to issue writ in the circumstances bearing in mind that Mwenya was a British subject. The Court of Appeal held, inter alia, that: the English writ of *habeas corpus* could be extended to territories which, having regard to the extent of the dominion in fact exercised, could be said to be 'under the subjection of the Crown.'

[25] *Oppenheim's International Law*, vol I, op. cit. at 1051; see further A B Lyons, "Conclusiveness of the Statements of the Executive: Continental and Latin American Practices", 25 *British Year Book of International Law* (1948) 180

Ministry of Foreign Affairs must be kept notified of all information and activities by these domestic Ministries, and the Ministry of Foreign Affairs retains its right to intervene to offer advice and recommendations, when necessary.

In many countries, the Ministry of Foreign Affairs takes a keen interest in the activities of the United Nations, makes their position known at the UN and actively participates in the preparation, including drafting of various international instruments, although most of the important legal issues which require considered opinions of experts are referred to the International Law Commission. Incidentally, it is for the Ministry of Foreign Affairs to choose experts and send its nominations to be placed on the various panels maintained by the UN, including the nominations for judges to the International Court of Justice. The Ministry of Foreign Affairs also recommends to the General Assembly of the UN who would be the country's representative(s) before it or other offices of the United Nations.

It is the Ministry of Foreign Affairs which prepares and implements the country's foreign policy, which is developed by reference to the country's relations, current or future, with other countries. It also develops the foreign policy with regional arrangements, where relevant, and its policy *vis-à-vis* the United Nations.

The other important departments in relation to the subject matter of this work are the following, and their functions are briefly discussed.

10.2.1 Political Affairs

This Section / department deals with the political relations of the countries, when necessary, with which a government maintains relations or with which its relations have been strained. Depending upon the influence and size of the government, this Section / department may be sub-divided into regional departments, e.g. Africa, Asia, Europe, Latin America, North America, Pacific, etc.

10.2.2 Treaties and Legal

Again, depending upon the position of the country in the international community, certain governments set up separate sub-divisions for treaty-related issues and general legal issues; whereas many others may not do so. Where however separate sub-divisions exist, they work closely and indeed close co-ordination between these two sub-divisions is essential. Whereas the treaty division usually negotiates and concludes treaties with other governments, the legal division, where separated from the treaty division, predominantly deals with all international instruments, in addition to considering questions and issues of international law. Unless a separate sub-division on international law is established by a country within its Ministry of Foreign Affairs, the legal department will also deal with any inter-state issue.

10.2.3 Protocol

This is the department which deals with heads of Missions in regard to arrivals and departures of diplomats, their privileges and immunities, reception of visitor and dignitaries from other States. It is through the Protocol department that the Ministries of Foreign Affairs usually deal with matters relating to the personal status of diplomats and other related matters, such as precedence of post, credentials or the Audience of The Queen. The most important functions of the Protocol Divisions are now discussed.

In practice, during the absence of the Head of Mission, the diplomatic staff is usually designated to take charge of the Mission. Where there are two or more staff in the same grade, the Head of the Mission shall decide who may be appointed as the Acting Head of Mission having regard to the local conditions, the efficient performance of the Mission and protection of the Mission's interest. In the event of the Head of Mission seeking leave to be absent from his / her post, he / she should nominate a deputy, obviously, with the consent of the sending State, but the deputised staff may not be entitled to precedence at other times, as procedure is determined by the grade of the member of staff. Precedence is usually based on time in post. In order to meet the local conditions Heads of Mission may vary this rule.

It is for the Protocol Department in the Foreign Office or any other designated office in the receiving State to prepare diplomatic lists, and rule of precedence, almost, exclusively applies to designated staff with diplomatic status who are entitled to privileges and immunities. A host State has the discretion to include the names of non-diplomatic staff in it with sufficient reason therefor.

In the practice of many States, such as the UK, the Defence Adviser takes precedence over other Service Attachés / Advisers; otherwise, Service Attachés / Advisers and the subordinate officers operate according to military rank. Under the British practice, the precedence of non-resident Defence / Service Attaché is for the Head of Mission to determine. Staff assigned to diplomatic service from other departments take the precedence of their equivalent grade in the diplomatic service. If they are employed in a grade that is higher than their substantive grade, precedence is allowed according to what the higher grade may attract, and as from the date of their appointment to the assigned post.

The procedure for appointing a Head of Mission may vary from country to country, but there seems to exist certain common State practices in this regard: the Personnel Division's nomination for the incumbent must be approved by the Head of the State; the Head of Mission is requested to seek, in confidence, agreement from the relevant receiving State, and in so doing, the nominee's career details must be submitted. After receipt of the agreement, the Head of the Mission notifies the relevant authorities. The Personnel Division then notifies the relevant Mission in its own country. Every country has its own journal or medium through which public announcements must be made. The

Protocol Department must be notified, in advance, when the new incumbent may arrive in the receiving State. Within the British Commonwealth, only approval, and not agreement, is sought.

The Personnel Department usually prepares a letter of credence and a letter of recall for the processor, which would be sent to the President's Office (or the Head of State's Office); however, in the British practice, for the High Commissions to Commonwealth countries of which The Queen is not the Head of State, The Queen signs a letter of commission and a letter of recall; these letters are returned to the Foreign and Commonwealth Office (FCO), after signature, and, in turn, to the Mission. The originals of these letters are expected to be handed over at the formal presentation ceremony, and the *copie d'usage*, the working copies, are given to the Protocol Department as soon as possible after the arrival of the new Head of Commission.

High Commissions appointed to Commonwealth countries of which The Queen is Head of State are not given formal credentials; instead, they carry an informal letter of introduction from the Prime Minister to their counterpart in the receiving country. These letters are signed by the Prime Minister.

The Queen usually receives Heads of Mission to overseas countries in Audience before they take up their appointment. Where it proves to be impracticable before he / she leaves for abroad, the Audience is deferred until he / she returns to London on leave or duty.

In the UK, the briefing of Heads of Missions prior to their taking up their appointments is done by the geographical department of the FCO. It is worth pointing out that Heads of Missions are encouraged to share information of their new appointments with their spouses; thus spouses are allowed to attend some of these briefing sessions. Country assessment papers are made available to the Heads of Missions and their spouses.

According to Article 19 of the Vienna Convention on Diplomatic Relations, *chargés d'affaires ad interim* may be appointed only by a fully accredited Head of Mission or a Ministry of Foreign Affairs. In making such an appointment by the Head of a Mission, the Ministry of Foreign Affairs of the receiving country must be notified of it. Where a Ministry of Foreign Affairs makes such an appointment, notification to the Ministry is made either through the Mission of the country in the receiving State or to the Ministry of Foreign Affairs of the country concerned direct. The Head of Mission is required to justify the appointments of a *chargé d'affaires ad interim*, and each such appointment must be approved by the Ministry of Foreign Affairs. But, of course, when a permanent Head of Mission will be absent, appointment of a *chargé d'affaires ad interim* becomes necessary. Where more than one *chargés d'affaires* are appointed in succession to one another, the respective dates of appointment must be clearly stated in the Note by the Head of Mission.

In the United Kingdom, similar practice is followed in respect of Acting High Commissioners of the Commonwealth countries. The position of a Deputy

High Commissioner is recognised by the Foreign and Commonwealth Office (FCO).

General Full Powers which are required for Permanent Representatives to the UN are signed by the Heads of State. General Full Powers for Deputy Permanent Representatives are usually signed by the Minister concerned (in the UK, by the Secretary of State).

In the UK, the Diplomatic Corps in London are responsible for making arrangements for the reception of the new Heads of Mission in London and for its participation in certain functions, State or otherwise. The Officers of the London Diplomatic Corps are:

- The Marshal of the Diplomatic Corps who is a full-time Court Official and whose office is located in the St James's Palace;

- The Vice-Marshal of the Diplomatic Corps which is a part-time Court appointment is held by the Head of Protocol Division;

- The Assistant Marshal of the Diplomatic Corps which is also a part-time Court appointment is held by the Deputy Head of the Protocol Division.

Before sending a new Head of Mission to London, all governments, except those of Her Majesty's Realms[26], must seek The Queen's approval (agrément) through the Foreign and Commonwealth Office. Governments of Realms must notify the FCO of the appointment of a new Head of Mission. Requests for agréments are processed within 2–3 weeks. It is through its Mission in London that the government concerned is required to request The Queen's agrément that the person chosen be received as a High Commissioner or an Ambassador to the Court of St James's. In processing a request for an agrément, the Geographical department of the FCO obtains the view of the British Mission to the country concerned, and where appropriate, of the British Mission to the country where the nominee was last posted. After completion of this stage, the Geographical department advises the Secretary of State whether or not an agrément should be granted, and submits to the Private Secretary:

- a formal submission to The Queen giving the exact name and style of the nominee;

- a draft covering letter from the Private Secretary to The Queen's Private Secretary proving notable details of the nominee's career and personality, and confirming that the Secretary of State considers the nominee as suitable for accepting as a High Commissioner or an Ambassador; and

- a brief biographical note.

---

[26] These are the Commonwealth countries

The Protocol Division and the News Department are also kept informed of this submission to the Private Secretary. The Queen's approval is returned to the Geographical Department by the Private Secretary, which Department then:

- sends two date-stamped copies of the page bearing The Queen's approval to the Ceremonial Section of the Protocol Division, and the latter forwards one copy to the Marshal of the Diplomatic Corps; and

- informs the government concerned of The Queen's approval to the appointment via the channel through which the sending State sought the agrément. The government of the sending State should notify the Geographical Department of the date of announcement of the appointment.

Here is a standard draft Agrément which is submitted to The Queen for the appointment of foreign and non-Realm Commonwealth Heads of Mission.

[Name of the Secretary of State], with his humble duty to Your Majesty, has the honour respectfully to submit for Your Majesty's approval that [name of the nominee], a ... subject/citizen, be received as Ambassador Extraordinary and Plenipotentiary of [or High Commissioner for] the Kingdom/Republic of [country] at Your Majesty's Court.

[Signature of Secretary of State]
Foreign and Commonwealth Office

Date:

As regards the procedure for appointment of Heads of Mission of Realm Commonwealth countries, notification of appointments are processed by the Geographical Department of the FCO within 2–3 weeks.

The Geographical Department thereafter advises the Secretary of State whether or not the appointment would be appropriate. In the event of not having any reason to question it, the Department sends a draft letter from the Private Secretary to the Prime Minister's Private Secretary. The Queen's Private Secretary, the Protocol Division and the News Department are kept informed, by sending copies of the letter, of the proposed appointment. In respect of such appointments no formal agrément is needed, only the Prime Minister's consent to the FCO is necessary notifying the sending State that the British Government will be glad to welcome the High Commissioner-designate. The notification is issued by the Geographical Department of the Diplomatic Corps in London. Two copies of the reply (notification) are sent to the Ceremonial Section of the Protocol Division who forwards one to the Marshall of the Diplomatic Corps.

It is for the sending State to arrange publicity of the appointment of a new Head of Mission in London. Whereas the maintenance of up-to-date and accurate biographical notes on Heads of Mission in London is the responsibility of the Geographical Department, photographs of most Heads of Mission in London are held by the Protocol Division.

Below is a standard draft letter from the Private Secretary to the Secretary of State to the Private Secretary to the Secretary to the Prime Minister.

> We have been informed that ... Government proposes to appoint [name of the nominee] at present ... to be ... the High Commissioner in London in succession to Mr ... I enclose a brief curriculum vitae.
>
> The Foreign and Commonwealth Secretary welcomes this appointment. As you will be aware, it is not the practice between Commonwealth countries of which Her Majesty is Queen to seek formal agrément to the appointment of a High Commissioner. The Foreign and Commonwealth Secretary would be grateful, however, if the Prime Minister would agree to our informing the ... Government that the British Government will be glad to welcome [name of nominee] in London and look forward to continue with him the happy association which they enjoyed with his predecessor.

10.3 CREDENTIALS AND LETTERS OF INTRODUCTION

If an agrément is granted, credentials will be required to accredit the representative of another Head of State to The Queen. Ambassadors present to Her Majesty a Letter of Credence signed by the Head of State. High Commissioners from countries of which The Queen is not the Head of State present to The Queen a Letter of Commission signed by their own Head of State. Usually, a Letter of Recall should be provided by the predecessor of the current incumbent which is to be accompanied by a Letter of Credence or a Letter of Commission. A Letter of Recall may not be available where the Bearer's (not incumbent's) predecessor has died or that a change of regime has taken place or that the current incumbent is arriving for the first time after a break in diplomatic relations. The Queen does not reply to Letters of Credence or Letters of Commission.

High Commissioners from Commonwealth countries of which The Queen is Head represent their governments, but not The Queen; thus, they bring a letter of introduction for the Prime Minister from their own Prime Minister. High Commissioners hand over these letters at the first meeting with the Vice-Marshal (initial call). These letters of introduction are not credentials, and they are not accompanied by Letters of Recall. The Prime Minister does not reply to these letters. Letters of Credence or Letters of Commission, and the Letters of Recall which Heads of Mission are provided by their governments (otherwise known as the working copies of their credentials) are either transmitted before their arrival in London through their Mission to the Protocol Division or delivered during their initial call on the Vice-Marshal. Incidentally, in the case of a *Chargé d'Affaires ad interim*, no accreditation is required, appointment by the Head of Mission or the Ministry of Foreign Affairs of the sending State will suffice. Only a *Chargé d'Affaires en titre* as a permanent Head of Mission in his own right is accredited, in writing, by the Ministry of Foreign Affairs of the sending State to the Secretary of State.

10.4 ARRIVAL AND NOTIFICATION OF ARRIVAL OF NEW HEADS OF MISSION IN LONDON

The Protocol Division and the Ceremonial Section must be informed by the Geographical Department of the travel plans of Heads of Mission without delay. The Protocol Division is required to:

- inform the Marshal of the Diplomatic Corps;

- arrange for the Head of Mission to be met on arrival by a Representative of the Secretary of State (but only during social hours, and not during the weekend or public holiday). Incidentally, the same practice is followed when an Ambassador or a High Commissioner departs from his / her position in London;

- arrange for the Head of Mission to call on the Vice-Marshal.

A newly-arrived Head of Mission must announce his / her readiness to assume his / her duties. This is done by Ambassadors and High Commissioners from non-Realm Commonwealth countries by means of a formal letter addressed to the Secretary of State, and it is sent to the Protocol Division immediately after arrival. In these letters a request is made to be received in Audience by The Queen to present the original of their credentials and also to arrange calls on the appropriate Ministers and senior officials in the FCO. These letters are acknowledged by the Vice-Marshal on behalf of the Secretary of State.

Credentials are not required from High Commissioners from Realm Commonwealth countries; they send a formal letter to the Secretary of State announcing their readiness to assume their functions.

Audience by The Queen is not requested by a *Chargé d'Affaires ad interim* or Acting High Commissioner. Audience of The Queen is arranged by the Marshal of the Diplomatic Corps for all Ambassadors and High Commissioners as soon as possible after their arrival in London, and it is during this ceremony that all those with credentials present them to The Queen. The Audience for Realm Heads of Mission is informal and not ceremonial. It is for the Protocol Division to advise the Geographical Department of the briefing required for the Audience. In the event of The Queen being absent from London, the Audience is granted by Counsellors of State.

10.5 COMMENCEMENT OF FUNCTIONS

The Vice-Marshal of the Diplomatic Corps in London invites the non-Realm Heads of Mission as soon as possible after their arrival in London. Where working copies of their Credentials have not been supplied in advance, the Heads of Mission are required to hand them to the Vice-Marshal at their first meeting with them. If the working copies are in order, the Heads of Mission are advised by the Vice-Marshal that they may immediately start their full functions even though they have not yet presented their Credentials to The Queen. The Vice-Marshal also sees the Realm Heads of Mission as soon as possible after their arrival and it is during their meeting (call) that they present their letter of introduction from their Prime Minister. These Heads of Mission do not present their letters of introduction to the Prime Minister direct, but in practice, Her Majesty's Government encourages Realm Prime Ministers to receive British Heads of Mission upon arrival at post.

10.6 PROCEDURE

In accordance with the provisions of Articles 13 and 16 of the Vienna Convention on Diplomatic Relations, 1961, the List of the Representatives in London of Foreign States and Commonwealth countries in Order of Precedence, otherwise known as the *"Precedence List"* is prepared which involves the names of the Heads of Mission in order of precedence. Ambassadors and High Commissioners are included in the same list, as they must be treated as equals. However, Ambassadors take precedence from the date of start of function, whereas the High Commissioners, by tradition, take precedence as from the date of their arrival in London.

10.7 CALLS ON FCO MINISTERS AND OFFICIALS

Soon after Heads of Mission have called on the Vice-Marshal, the Geographical department arranges their first calls within a week after their arrival on FCO Ministers and senior officials. It is seldom possible for the Secretary of state to receive Heads of Mission on their first courtesy call at the FCO; thus, the Minister with appropriate geographical responsibility receives them. A call on the Secretary of State, if desirable, takes place at a later date. Calls are also made on the Permanent Under Secretary, the Director-General and the Director concerned, and the Head of the Geographical Department. The call on the Permanent Under Secretary should always precede the Audience of The Queen.

10.8. TERMINATION OF APPOINTMENT

When an Ambassador or a High Commissioner will have the knowledge of termination of his/her appointment, he/she should immediately inform the Vice-Marshal of the Diplomatic Corps by means of a letter which should also ask for a farewell Audience of The Queen.

Such audience is not normally granted unless a Head of Mission has been in London for several years[27]. In the same letter, the Head of a Mission may appoint a *Chargé d'Affaires ad interim* or an Acting High Commissioner as from the date of his / her departure. The Vice-Marshal immediately notifies the Marshal of Diplomatic Corps, the Private Office and the Geographical Department concerned. In reality, in general, Ambassadors or the High Commissioners take leave of the FCO. Usually a farewell hospitality takes place for a departing Ambassador or High Commissioner, which is hosted by the Secretary of State or the relevant FCO Minister. It is for the Geographical Department concerned to compile the guest-list.

10.9 GENERAL

In the event of a Head of Mission being absent temporarily, he / she informs the FCO, notifying also whether he / she has appointed a *Chargé d'Affaires ad interim* or an Acting High Commissioner during his / her absence, and if so, it must be done under their own signature[28]. Where no such appointment is made, the FCO deals with the Mission officers in their individual capacity. Where however a Deputy High Commissioner is already in post, the FCO may accept him / her as the Acting High Commissioner during the temporary absence of the High Commissioner without the latter's signature. A copy of the notification of the temporary absence of the Head of Mission must be sent to the Protocol Division and the Geographical Department concerned. Where no *Chargé d'Affaires ad interim* or an Acting High Commissioner has been appointed, or where notification to the FCO has not been made in compliance with Article 19 of the Vienna Convention on Diplomatic Relations, the Protocol Division invites the sending government to notify the appointment either through the British Mission in the sending State or by means of direct communication between the two governments.

---

[27] This is a matter of discretion for the Diplomatic Corps in London

[28] See Article 19 of the Vienna Convention on Diplomatic Relations

Non-resident Heads of Mission are treated like the resident Heads of Mission as far as possible. Upon receipt of their agreement non-resident Heads of Mission should send copies of their credentials to the British Mission in the country of their residence or to the Honorary Consul in London, who forwards them to the Protocol Division for checking. They are received by The Queen in Audience. The Geographical Department makes arrangements for programmes for them in London, whereas the Protocol Division arranges essential transport and provisional hotel bookings.

In the event of the death of a Head of Mission and upon receipt of the news, the Vice-Marshal or the Assistant Marshal informs the Marshal of the Diplomatic Corps and the Geographical Department. The Acting Head of Mission is contacted to offer condolences on behalf of Her Majesty's Government and to offer help. The Private Secretary's office at Buckingham Palace is informed of the news of the death by the Marshal of the Diplomatic Corps, who calls on the Acting Head of Mission to carry The Queen's sympathy. The Marshal thereafter notifies the Lord Chamberlain's Office for information of The Queen.

It is for the Protocol Division to ascertain where the funeral services would take place, and co-ordinates with the Mission, the Geographical department concerned and the Lord Chamberlain's Office for representation at the funeral. With the help of the Protocol Division, the Mission concerned in London organises a funeral in the UK. In the event of the funeral taking place in the country of the Head of Mission, arrangements for transport are to be made by the Mission, and the Protocol Division is notified of the time and place of departure of the body. In accordance with the advice of the Protocol Division, the Mission makes arrangements for the body to be taken from the mortuary to the place of departure. The Marshal of the Diplomatic Corps, members of the Protocol Division and the Geographical Department concerned attend the departure of the body at a London airport or station.

A condolence book is opened at the Mission or the residence of the deceased Head of Mission. The Mission concerned notifies the Protocol Division of the place where the condolence book will be open and for what hours. The Geographical Department, in consultation with the Protocol Division, recommends who should sign the book. The Mission concerned makes arrangements for a memorial service in the UK, and the Protocol Division by means of an Office Circular provides details of the service and makes arrangements for Ministers and Senior Officials to attend the service.

10.10 RELATIONS WITH FOREIGN MISSIONS

The primary objective of exchanging diplomats between countries is to develop good and effective rapport with them through the diplomatic Missions located in a receiving State.

This is where the Ministry of Foreign Affairs in a receiving State is required to take an active and progressive role. It should ensure that all Missions are treated with equal dignity, and treated equally in respect of all matters.

As the initial enquiry by a foreign Mission in a receiving State will be raised with the appropriate Section / department of the Ministry of Foreign Affairs, it must be informed enough to be able to deal with the enquiries satisfactorily or be able to direct the enquiries to the appropriate Ministry of the receiving State, which will also correspond with the Ministry of Foreign Affairs. Such interactions offer opportunities to the Ministry of Foreign Affairs to establish good rapport with the foreign Missions.

The relations with foreign Missions are maintained by a Ministry of Foreign Affairs in various ways: by maintaining friendly relations with the Missions; by trying to negotiate differences, if any, with the foreign Missions in the most amicable fashion and with understanding; receive invitations and reciprocate them; facilitate access to the Minister for Foreign Affairs, when so requested, by a foreign Mission, for discussion of matters of mutual interests and / or concern.

On the other hand, the Ministry of Foreign Affairs is required to deal with different issues that may be presented by a foreign Mission, whether in breach of custom in the diplomatic world or any provision of the Vienna Convention on Diplomatic Relations, 1961 or any persistent breach of any local legislation by a Mission, e.g. traffic-related regulations. By the same token, when the relations between a sending State and a receiving State deteriorate, it is for the Ministry of Foreign Affairs to deal with the issues, including closure of the Mission, where necessary. In other words, it is the Ministry of Foreign Affairs that welcomes a foreign Mission, and it is for the same Ministry to ask the Mission to leave the jurisdiction of the receiving State.

The Ministry of Foreign Affairs is therefore an office which is required to have multi-faceted functions and objectives; indeed, its officials must be trained accordingly to meet with all probable circumstances.

10.11 RELATIONS WITH ITS OWN MISSIONS IN FOREIGN JURISDICTIONS

This is where a Ministry of Foreign Affairs is required to act in the reverse in that it must also perform the other part of its activities with its own Missions in various foreign jurisdictions. A Ministry of Foreign Affairs gives its Mandate to its head of the Mission, and the Head is, in turn, required to report back to its Ministry. Here, the Head of the Mission, who is required to be a dynamic person, should take the initiative to develop very friendly relations with the receiving State, within the remit allowed to him/her, and should recommend the policy that he/she considers his/her government should adopt. In this process, there does not exist any rivalry between the two parties: both the Head of a Mission and the Ministry of Foreign Affairs should work in union; the Head of the Mission being in the local jurisdiction is in a better position to familiarise the Ministry of Foreign Affairs with the current situations in the receiving State, based on his/her knowledge and analysis of the situations.

There are advantages to according such a role to Heads of Missions: he/she can represent his/her country's interests directly, which after all, a Ministry of Foreign Affairs aims to achieve. If the policies of a receiving country change, the Head of a Mission should notify his own government of such changes to allow it to interact with the receiving State accordingly.

It is through the Mission in a foreign jurisdiction that the prospects of trade, commerce, cultural exchange are enhanced. It is a delicate task, and the Heads of Missions should be capable of performing such a task. It is common knowledge in the diplomatic world that certain diplomats and Heads of Missions have left a mark in the world of diplomacy, whereas most others are mere representatives of their governments. The selection of diplomats by the sending States should therefore be a careful process whereby creative diplomats are allowed to be engaged in ever changing complex international diplomacy. As stated earlier, such a diplomat must be shrewd, tactful, a person with good sense of strategies, and a high degree of neutrality. He/she must be a person of good judgment. He/she must not derogate from his/her mandate, but he/she must at the same time deal with his/her duties in a dynamic fashion, although where static position needs to be maintained, he/she must do so.

10.12 CONCLUSIONS

The Ministry of Foreign Affairs is the key Ministry for a country's foreign policy, including policies as to trade and commerce, and diplomacy. The world of diplomacy is an ever-changing world; the Ministries of Foreign Affairs should be likewise, and their staff must be adapted to it through knowledge and experience. Dynamism is essential for a Ministry of Foreign Affairs. Traditionalism should be kept confined to a narrow limit.

A Ministry of Foreign Affairs is the home of diplomacy; it depends upon this Ministry how its diplomacy is perceived. But, if one takes the true meaning of it, diplomacy is not to be polluted; it is a means to develop friendly relations between States. It is an instrument which should be used for constructive purposes; it is a tool which is creative and implicit in it are strategic planning, dynamism and understanding not only of the purposes of the State but also of the other States.

Friendly and unfriendly countries are inevitable to exist in the world; a Ministry of Foreign Affairs should not contribute to the cause of unfriendliness. This latter issue often clouds the world of diplomacy particularly when the essence of power motivates a Ministry to adopt non-constructive policies.

The membership of the United Nations directly or indirectly puts a limit to an offensive foreign policy. The interdependence of States, whether for economic or trade purposes may not be over-emphasised. The UN forum offers opportunities to its Members to create a climate of unity and friendship and States should seize these opportunities.

It is by peaceful means, and not by non-peaceful means, that creative diplomacy can be implemented. However philosophical it might sound, this is the way forward, and Ministries of Foreign Affairs are at the forefront of taking the initiative to develop friendly relations among States. It is again for the Ministries of Foreign Affairs that diplomats are trained accordingly. In this connection, the UN Resolution entitled Declaration on Principles of International Law Concerning Friendly Relations and Co-operation among States in accordance with the Charter of United Nations, 1970[29] is worth looking into. This Declaration evidenced the consensus among the Members of the United Nations on the meaning and elaboration of the principles of the UN Charter[30]. The 1970 Declaration must not be construed as enlarging or diminishing in any way the scope of the UN Charter; it simply elaborates the principles of it. Without going into the details of the Principles, it would suffice to list some of the most relevant principles that the Declaration embodied:

1. The principle that States shall settle their international disputes by peaceful means in such a manner that international peace and security and justice are not endangered.

2. The principle concerning the duty not to intervene in matters within the domestic jurisdiction of any State, in accordance with the Charter.

3. The duty of States to co-operate with one another in accordance with the Charter.

4. The principle of equal rights and self-determination of peoples.

5. The principle of sovereign equality of States.

6. The principle that States shall fulfil in good faith the obligations assumed by them in accordance with the Charter.

These principles are very significant for contemporary diplomacy.

A Ministry of Foreign Affairs without a vision may contribute to creating diplomats likewise. The training and briefing courses conducted by a Ministry of Foreign Affairs must prepare diplomats to perceive the need for a type of diplomacy which will meet the challenges of the world. The importance of socio-economic issues should not be excluded from the domain of foreign affairs. Diplomacy is not only meant for political relations with States; economic relations is an important component of an effective foreign policy.

A foreign policy must not be perceived and implemented as an interventionist policy. Corrections of a foreign policy or a domestic policy of another State can be achieved by a united policy based on the ingredients of peace. Thus, abuse of sovereignty expressed through an interventionist policy must be avoided. A constructive foreign policy offers the platform for a constructive diplomacy.

---

[29] See the Annex to UNGA Res. 2625 (XXV)

[30] See further I Brownlie, *Basic Documents in International Law*, Oxford, Clarendon Press (1984) at 35

CHAPTER 11

The Diplomatic Mission

11.1 INTRODUCTION

The term *"diplomatic mission"* is significant in that it is an institution which is more than an office; it is an institution to which delegates are sent by the sending State to be stationed in a receiving State for the purpose of achieving its objectives, namely, promoting relationship between the sending and receiving States: cultural, economic, political or otherwise. Where however the relationship is not so friendly, it is the function of the existing Mission to make the relationship friendlier, primarily through trade and investment incentives, or by conciliating the causes responsible for straining the relationship between the two States. The purposes for which diplomatic Missions are set up are at the heart of diplomatic relations. The clearer the mission, the clearer are the functions of diplomats and diplomatic Missions. In fact, the success of a Mission may very much depend upon the mandates given by the home State to the Mission, and the creative initiatives that diplomats may take.

From a diplomatic and legal point of view, a Mission in a host State must be operated to achieve its objectives in the true sense of the term, and not for carrying out any activity of a subversive nature. The success and failure of a diplomatic Mission thus depends upon the principles and policies a Mission maintains and implements.

In this chapter an attempt is made to discuss, generally, the offices and functions of a mission in the sense the concept of a Mission has been developed in the diplomatic world.

11.2 THE DIPLOMATIC MISSION AND ITS PRINCIPAL OFFICERS AND OFFICES

A diplomatic mission is led by a head of the Mission. The Vienna Convention on Diplomatic Relations defined the *'head of the mission'* as the person *" ... charged by the sending State with the duty of acting in that capacity."*[1] Article 1 of the Convention also defines certain other important expressions which are relevant to a mission, namely, *"members of the staff of the mission"*, *"members of the diplomatic staff"*, *"diplomatic agent"*, *"members of the administrative and technical staff"*, *"members of the service staff"*, and *"premises of the*

---

[1] Article 1 of the Vienna Convention on Diplomatic Relations, 1961

mission". In other words, these posts are common to almost all diplomatic Missions.

Article 3 of the Vienna Convention on Diplomatic Relations details the functions of a Mission as:

"*(a) representing the sending State in the receiving State;*

(b) protecting in the receiving State the interests of the sending State and of its nationals, within the limits permitted by international law;

(c) negotiating with the Government of the receiving State;

(d) ascertaining by all lawful means conditions and developments in the receiving State, and reporting thereon to the Government of the sending State;

(e) promoting friendly relations between the sending State and the receiving State, and developing their economic, cultural and scientific relations."

Under the Convention, a diplomatic Mission has the authority to perform consular functions (Article 3(2)).

There are two terms, *'diplomatic agent'* and *'diplomatic rank'* which need a brief comment. Traditionally, the term *'diplomatic agent'* meant the head of a Mission, but the current diplomatic practice has extended its meaning to include members of the diplomatic staff of a Mission, and this latter expression includes any staff holding a diplomatic rank. The term *'diplomatic agent'* seems to be the traditional term in the diplomatic world, although it is often interchangeably used with the term *'diplomat'*.

The term *'diplomatic rank'* stands for the rank which not only recognises the person as a diplomat, but also attaches full diplomatic privileges and immunities.

Although the size of a diplomatic mission often dictates the issue of the setting up of various departments in it, most diplomatic Missions maintain the following sections / divisions: chancery, commercial, consular, information and military, the latter including naval and air.

11.2.1 The Head of Mission

As the title suggests, the Head of a Mission is the overall in-charge of the mission, although he/she delegates his/her powers and functions to his/her staff. The Head's functions emanate from the purposes for which he is appointed. He is responsible to his own government and he must promote the cause of the government in the receiving State, and strengthen the rapport between the receiving State and his own State. In this sense, the Head of a Mission has a dual responsibility. Although the Head of a Mission is governed by the mandate he receives from his own government, often the personality of a Head and the respect he commands in the diplomatic world by virtue of his knowledge and diplomatic acumen enables him to perform his functions more effectively. The functions of the Head of a mission are not formalised by the Vienna Convention on Diplomatic Relations, 1961; these functions have broadly been developed by State practice. It must be pointed out however that the Convention does not catalogue the functions of the Head of a mission; nevertheless, they may be identified from the various provisions of it. The following is a list of functions that the Head of a mission usually performs:

(a) *The formulation of the diplomatic policy of the Mission*

Although the Head of a Mission is usually assisted by his principal advisers, the senior staff of the mission (usually the heads of various sections) can take special initiatives to develop friendly relations with a receiving State, provided in doing so, he does not exceed his mandate and the traditional duties as a Head. This is where the personality and his intimate knowledge and understanding of the peoples and governments of the two States (the sending and the receiving States) become essential[2].

The Head of a Mission should have a broad knowledge not only about the two States but also in regard to the contemporary nature of international relations so as to be able to demonstrate whether his country conforms to it or not and if not, why not. He must also understand his country's position *vis-à-vis* the United Nations and other international organisations. The creativity in the Head of a Mission makes all the difference. In addition to his depth of knowledge in and contribution to his chosen discipline, Professor Galbraith of the United States, is remembered as a creative Ambassador; this creativity comes from within, and is based on his knowledge, experience, ideology etc. Authorities of sending States should take special care in choosing their Ambassadors / High Commissioners, as the case may be. Feltham maintains that the diplomatic policy of a mission is the *"product of political judgment, political sense and political wisdom,"*[3] but perhaps one should add to this – based on the understanding for the need for peaceful international co-operation, instead of international polarisation.

(b) Communicate his government's views to the receiving State's government, and act as a channel of communication between the two governments. This is where a thorough training and experience becomes necessary; the Head of a mission must know the technique of conveying messages to the receiving State in order to avoid any unnecessary rift between the two governments.

---

[2] See also R G Feltham, *Diplomatic Handbook*, Harlow, Longman (1993) at 18

[3] R G Feltham, ibid.

(c) To report to the sending State matters of significance, which might directly or indirectly affect the national interest, and also comments made by third parties, journalists, other diplomats or local politicians on his country's policies.

(d) To establish rapport with the diplomatic community, in general, and people of political influence in the receiving State.

The Head of a Mission is also a conciliator and a negotiator. Again, this is where the personal qualities and acumen of the person become relevant. A successful diplomat must cultivate the qualities of being a successful conciliator and negotiator: a balanced view of the problem(s), the capacity to conciliate or negotiate in order to protect the interests of all parties concerned. This quality is even more important for negotiating and conciliating matters of international concern.

11.2.2 Chancery

The Chancery forms an integral part of a diplomatic Mission. This office is usually involved in the following types of work: political, administrative, co-ordination with other offices of the Mission, security, secretarial, accounts, local personnel and other technical services. This may be described as the central office of a Mission headed by a chief executive. Co-ordination between departments of the Mission, the security of the Mission and the welfare of staff, both at the diplomatic and non-diplomatic levels and compilation of the local information are its most onerous functions. This last item requires obtaining information from the relevant government departments, including the department of foreign affairs, with which the Mission deals, and this information is provided to the staff of the Mission, when necessary. The Chancery also collects information on the local facilities that the Mission members may require: schools, universities, medical, housing, domestic help, accommodation etc. This information is obviously sent to the sending State for the briefing of the future members of the Mission. The Chancery also maintains a list of influential persons in various fields, namely, military, commercial, academic and industrial.

Security of the premises of the Mission is an extremely important function that the Chancery is required to perform. Security of the premises is required not only for the protection of documents and information in connection with the operation of the Mission, but also for the protection of the staff of the Mission. This particular function of the Chancery requires even more efficiency now than ever before because of the unprecedented advancement of information technology and a Chancery must be able to match its capacity to absorb and disseminate information with the Chanceries of other Missions. A Chancery must also remain alert that no abuse of information takes place.

It is for the Head of the Mission to notify the Foreign Office of the receiving State and seek extra protection from it if the security of the premises of a Mission is feared to be jeopardised.

11.2.3 Local Staff

Almost all missions employ a percentage of staff from the local community in the receiving State in the commercial, consular and information sections. They are not usually entrusted with those positions that require dealing with information of a confidential nature, which would jeopardise the security of the mission and also of the sending State. Most of the secretarial and manual staff are taken from the local community by foreign missions.

11.2.4 Accountants

Accountants are also usually taken from the local community; this is because the locally qualified accountants are supposed to be more knowledgeable and familiar with local tax and other relevant legislation than foreign accountants.

11.2.5 Consular Section

The Consular Section of Mission works under the control of the Head of the Mission. The consular activities of a Mission are governed by the instructions issued to it by the sending State and of course by the relevant provisions of the Vienna Convention on Consular Relations, 1963. This issue has been discussed in the chapter on Consular Relations.

11.2.6 Commercial Section

This is one of the most important Sections of a Mission, as through this Section the commercial and trading interests of a sending State are promoted and/or developed. To this end, the Commercial section of a Mission provides information, on behalf of the Mission, on commercial issues, including opportunities for business and investment, and invites businessmen from the local community. Of course, a Mission can liaise with other Missions in the same country for this purpose. A good and forward-looking commercial section of a Mission will hold information on the country's infrastructure, legislation, facilities, tax credits, import-export restrictions etc., preferably in writing so that this information may readily be made available to a prospective business or investment entity. The service that the Commercial Section of a Mission renders in the form of information-giving is different from that rendered by the Press and Information Section of a Mission. Depending upon how the connotation of the term *'commercial'* is extended, the activities of a Commercial Section expand.

11.2.7 Press and Information Section

This Section is usually concerned with providing information on political and social issues; it also notifies the sending State of any news about the receiving

State, whether of a political nature or otherwise. When a news or an incident in the sending State is considered to be sensational, the Press and Information Section may be required to provide that information or news in such a way which would not jeopardise the country's interest, nor the rapport between the sending State and the receiving State; however, news and information must be provided accurately. The Press and Information Section of a Mission is also often required to liaise with the local media and newspapers. In fact, one of the most important aspects of the functions of this Section is to do what is known as *'briefing'*. This Section works closely with the Head of the Mission, as in the final analysis, it is the Head of the Mission who may be interviewed by the media or may be required to justify any information that may have been provided by the Mission. This Section of the Mission must be thoroughly familiar with the policies, in particular the foreign policy, of the sending State.

11.2.8 Attachés

Attachés are those officers who are required to serve a particular specialist department; in traditional diplomacy, the position of Attachés was curious in that they were not usually career diplomats. They were appointed in view of their specialist knowledge and experience in a particular field of activity. In the contemporary practice, most of the large Missions engage Attachés with diplomatic status, namely, cultural, commercial, educational etc. Most of the Missions however engage commercial, cultural and military Attachés. Often, smaller Missions with complex military strategies open a department for military Attachés. Each Attaché is required to promote the activities of its department. For example, whereas a military Attaché may be involved in promoting military relationship with the authorities in the receiving State, and purchase and sale of military equipment or war materials, it is the primary function of a cultural Attaché to promote cultural exchange between the sending State and the receiving State by arranging, for example, cultural visits to each other. Such activities also produce favourable effect on other fields, namely, business and education. Much of the promotional activities of a Mission depends upon the Attachés. It is therefore important for governments to choose their Attachés carefully, as they are very much involved in giving a lead to the sending State in respect of many important matters.

Again, depending upon the position and status of a country in the world, in particular fields of activity, a Mission may appoint other Attachés, namely, scientific, agricultural, fisheries etc. In order to promote tourism, many Missions set up Tourism departments with Attachés as their heads. On the other hand, in many cases, a particular department, for instance, cultural and education, may be required to perform many other duties, which are not traditionally allocated to such departments by larger Missions. An effective participation of an Attaché can be extremely useful for commercial States.

11.3 THE DIPLOMATIC MISSION AND THE VIENNA CONVENTION ON DIPLOMATIC RELATIONS, 1961

A Mission has many functions to perform; the Vienna Convention on Diplomatic Relations describes the traditional functions of a Mission, which are of a broad nature. A Mission is often required to perform its functions in accordance with the practice developed and established by the contemporary diplomatic world; it is therefore necessary that a Mission is familiar with the current acknowledged procedures and formalities in relation to the matter they deal with. Whereas certain of its functions are to be performed in accordance with its national criteria, others, such as, reporting to the authorities in the receiving State of the appointments, arrivals and departures of diplomatic staff, are required to be done in compliance with the criteria set by a receiving State.

Appointments of the Heads of Missions, military, naval and air Attachés require the formal approval of the receiving State in advance, but the Protocol Department of the Ministry of Foreign Affairs must be notified of all other appointments as soon as possible, including the intended date, time and place of their arrival. The same practice is applicable when a member of the diplomatic staff leaves a receiving State. The formalities in regard to arrivals and departures also apply to the families of diplomatic staff.

As to arrival of Heads of Missions in a receiving State, the usual practice has been to call on the Head of the State to present his/her credentials. Where the Head of a State is unable to receive the Head of a Mission immediately upon his/her arrival because of his/her other engagements, the Head of the Mission must notify the Minister of Foreign Affairs of the receiving State as soon as possible, and present him with a copy of his/her credentials. The urgency in this regard is maintained in the interest of the Head of a Mission too; it is the responsibility of the receiving State to provide him/her with diplomatic privileges and immunities. The actual visit to the Head of the receiving State may be arranged at a mutually convenient later date. The receipt of the credentials of the Head of a Mission by the Minister of Foreign Affairs together with the letter notifying his/her arrival (in addition to his/her predecessor's letter of recall, in certain cases) would be enough for the Head of a Mission to formally assume his/her duties. But, a uniformity of procedure as to a particular class of Head of a Mission must be maintained by a receiving State; this is because of the principle of sovereign equality in public international law.

When the Head of a Mission holds the rank of a *Chargé d'Affaires*, the formalities in regard to his/her appointment are somewhat different. He/she will be accredited to the Minister for Foreign Affairs and will deliver his/her credentials to the Minister. Where however a *Chargé d'Affaires* holds the rank of an ambassador, he/she will call on the Head of State to present his/her credentials, and all the formalities attached to the accreditation of an ambassador will be completed in respect of that ambassador too. Like all other Heads of Mission, he/she will also, after assuming his/her duties as such, advise the Dean of the Diplomatic Corps (Doyen) and other Heads of Mission in the receiving State, and call on them. Obviously, arrangements for meeting are made at a mutually convenient time and date. In order to make arrangements for calling on the Minister for Foreign Affairs, the Protocol Department should be contacted.

There are certain cities in which a considerable number of foreign Missions exist, and indeed, over the years, the number of foreign Missions seems to be increasing rapidly. Examples of such cities are: London, New Delhi, Paris and Washington, DC. In such cities, the traditional diplomatic formalities in their fullest form may not be initially observed. The foreign Head of a Mission contacts the offices of the Minister for Foreign Affairs for presenting his/her credentials to the Minister, and thereafter notifies the other officers, namely, the Head of the Diplomatic Corps, local dignitaries, the Head of the State in due course. But, if the Head of a Mission delivers a speech on the occasion, the Minister for Foreign Affairs must be provided with a copy of it in advance.

The Head of a Mission is required to complete certain formalities in relation to his/her departure from the receiving State. The departure of the Head of a Mission is initiated by what is known as a *"letter of recall"* (i.e., a notification of his/her recall by the sending State). Shortly before he/she relinquishes his/her post, he/she must notify the Minister for Foreign Affairs in the receiving State of his/her recall and ask for an audience with the Head of the State. Formalities are an integral part of diplomacy; this is because representatives of sovereign States must be treated with respect. Therefore, it is only natural that the representative of a sovereign State must be seen by a receiving State at his/her departure. Of course, such farewells are not usually ceremoniously held; they are usually private ones, but then, such formalities often depend upon the relations between a receiving State and a sending State.

If the letter of recall is not presented to the Head of the State at the farewell, then in current diplomatic practice, it is usually combined with the successor's letter of credence. As upon his/her arrival, the Head of a Mission writes to the Dean of Diplomatic Corps, the other Heads of Missions, and chosen prominent figures in the receiving State, prior to his/her departure, he/she is required to notify them of his/her departure.

The requirements of notification of arrival and departure of the Head of a Mission have certain legal aspects. The receiving State must be notified of the arrival of a new Head of a Mission in advance so that sufficient measures for his/her protection and security of his/her residence may be taken, in addition to making arrangements for conferring privileges and immunities on him/her; similarly, upon notification of his/her departure the receiving State authorities must ensure that diplomatic privileges and immunities are allowed until the date of his/her departure, and that proper protection to his/her person, his/her family and security to his/her residence is offered until he/she actually leaves the receiving State. If the Head of a Mission is required to delay his/her departure, the authorities in the receiving State must be notified accordingly, and it is customary for him/her, including the members of his/her family, to be allowed privileges and immunities until their departure; but he/she, including his/her family is required to leave the receiving State within a reasonable period of time.

Where however a recall of the Head of a Mission is requested by the authorities in a receiving State, no formal audience with the Head of the State is found necessary. Most often, the Head of a Mission will be a *persona non grata*; hence the need for a formal audience with the Head of the receiving State would not arise; nevertheless, on a *de facto* basis, the Head of a Mission is given protection until he/she leaves the receiving State, but for obvious reasons, he/she must leave the receiving State at the earliest possible opportunity.

In a normal situation, however, a representative of the Department of Protocol in the receiving State sends off the Head of a Mission at his/her point of departure. Again, the issue of showing respect to the representative of a foreign sovereign justifies the observance of such formalities.

11.4 CONCLUSIONS

The success of a diplomatic Mission very much depends upon the Head of a Mission. Although he/she is primarily governed by the mandate issued to him/her by his/her sovereign, as stated earlier, the Head of a Mission should be a dynamic person who would promote the cause of his/her State within the parameters of the mandate given to him/her. He/she must be a person who should have a clear understanding of his/her mission (aims and objectives), culture, political and socio-economic system of his/her country, and the position of his/her State in the world, whether from a political, economic or military standpoint. A thorough knowledge of the history of his/her country is essential for conducting business. He/she is an ambassador of his/her country, and must perform his/her duties maintaining the dignity of his/her country, and he/she must project his/her country in the appropriate perspective. In order for him/her to do so, he/she must possess a thorough knowledge of the history, culture, economy, political structure, geography and the position of the country in the world, and in particular, the demographic structure, institutions, resources – human or otherwise, the trading position, financial, industrial and agricultural information. The position of his/her State vis-à-vis other States must be understood by him/her, as must the position of his/her State in relation to inter-governmental, regional and truly international organisations.

Furthermore, a successful Head of a Mission must possess negotiation skills, and the skills in analysing and examining events in both sending and receiving States, and report on them in an articulate fashion, when necessary. It goes without saying that he/she must also possess a good communication skill.

INTERNATIONAL LAW AND DIPLOMACY

These skills may not necessarily be taught in their entirety; they must be natural, and the intellectual ability of the Head of a Mission should help him/her apply these skills. It is primarily these skills that make the Head of a Mission and the Mission successful.

CHAPTER 12

The Vienna Convention on Diplomatic Relations, 1961

12.1 INTRODUCTION

The Vienna Convention on Diplomatic Relations, 1961 primarily consolidated the practice of diplomats, which receiving States and sending States developed over the centuries. From this standpoint, the Convention does not provide any new information to the reader. The customary rules of diplomatic practice have always provided guidance to States about issues relating to the subject matters of the Convention. Indeed, the Preamble to the Convention affirmed that:

> "... the rules of customary international law should continue to govern questions not expressly regulated by the provisions of the present Convention."

The purpose of concluding this Convention has been clearly stated in its Preamble:

> "... that an international Convention on diplomatic intercourse, privileges and immunities would contribute to the development of friendly relations among nations, irrespective of their differing constitutional and social systems."

In view of its consolidating function, the newly born States, which did not participate in the drafting sessions, are required to accept this Convention; furthermore, the framework of the Convention is such that no State should find it unacceptable; this represents the essential issues with which diplomats and the activities of sending and receiving States have been concerned over the centuries. Of course, the Contracting parties' freedom has been presumed by allowing them to enter reservations in respect of certain of the provisions of the Convention. It is to be emphasised that the Convention simply codified the state practice, which was primarily the practice of the States, that existed as non-colonised States, although the Convention was concluded during the decolonisation period. The newly-born States, if they accept this Convention, must comply with its provisions although they have the right to enter reasonable reservations.

It is the purpose of this Chapter to analyse the Convention, and to examine the extent to which its provisions are, in general, implemented by the Contracting States.

12.2 A BRIEF HISTORICAL BACKGROUND TO THE CONVENTION

12.2.1 An Analysis of the Convention

It is possible to analyse the Convention roughly under various sub-headings:

1.	Definitions of certain terms and classification of heads of mission	–	Articles 1, 14, 15 and 16
2.	Methods of establishing diplomatic relations between States	–	Article 2
3.	The functions of a diplomatic mission	–	Article 3
4.	Duties of a diplomatic mission	–	Articles 41 and 46
5.	Methods of accrediting diplomats	–	Articles 4 - 9
6.	General powers and duties of a sending State and a receiving State	–	Articles 10 - 21
7.	Inviolability of a mission and its articles and communications	–	Articles 22, 24, 27, 29 and 30
8.	Treatment to be accorded to a mission of a receiving State	–	Articles 23 – 26, 28, 44 and 45
9.	Extent of immunities to be accorded to a diplomatic agent, and waiver of immunities	–	Articles 31 – 36, 38, 40 and 42
10.	Extension of privileges and immunities to members of the family of a diplomatic agent, private servants, and the local staff	–	Articles 37 and 38
11.	The duration of privileges and immunities	–	Article 39
12.	Ending of the functions of a diplomatic agent	–	Article 43
13.	Others	–	Articles 47 – 53

These sub-headings are now discussed.

12.2.2 Definitions of Certain Terms and Classifications of Heads of Mission

Heads of the Mission	The head of the Mission is the individual who is chosen by the sending State to act in that capacity.
	It is expected that the sending State will choose or select that individual as the head of its mission bearing in mind the capacity and quality of the individual who will be able to develop and protect the sending State's interest in the receiving State. Where the commercial interest of the sending State is significant in the receiving State, the sending State should ensure that the Mission is really capable of matching the interests of the receiving State and the sending State.
	On the other hand, where a sending State wishes to strengthen its diplomatic and commercial relations with the receiving State in a dynamic way, it should choose or select its head of the Mission accordingly.
Diplomatic Agent	A diplomatic agent is the head of the Mission or a member of the diplomatic staff of the Mission.
	In the absence of the head of the Mission, a member of the staff of the Mission holding diplomatic rank may be promoted to the status of a *"diplomatic agent."* Thus, whoever may be officiating as the head of the Mission, for whatever reason, is designated as a diplomatic agent.
Members of the Mission	The following constitute the members of the mission: the head of the Mission and members of the staff of the Mission.
Members of the Staff of the Mission	These include the following: – *members of the diplomatic staff;* – *members of the administrative staff;* – *members of the technical staff; and* – *the service staff of the Mission.* *Diplomatic Staff* are those officers of the mission who hold diplomatic ranks. *Administrative Staff* are the officers who are employed in the administration of the Mission, that is, the work needed to be done for the running of the mission, including issuance of passports and visas.

INTERNATIONAL LAW AND DIPLOMACY

	Technical Staff represents the staff who are employed in the technical services of the Mission.
	Service Staff are engaged in the domestic service of the Mission, that is, the staff who perform non-diplomatic functions.
Private Servant	A private servant is an individual who is engaged in the domestic service of a member of the Mission; he/she may not be an employee of the sending State. He/she may be engaged by the head of the Mission or by any diplomatic or administrative or technical staff of the Mission.
	Legal problems do arise however when a private servant is brought over from the sending State on the grounds of familiarity with the social culture of the sending State.
Diplomatic Agent	A diplomatic agent is the head of the Mission or a member of the diplomatic staff of the Mission.
	In the absence of the head of the Mission, a member of the staff of the Mission holding diplomatic rank may be promoted to the status of a *"diplomatic agent."* Thus, whoever may be officially the head of the Mission, for whatsoever reason, is designated as a diplomatic agent.
Premises of the Mission	These constitute the premises of the Mission, and the land appurtenant thereto, and the residence of the head of the Mission. Premises are to be used for the purposes of the Mission. This latter condition is very important when the premises are not owned by the Mission. However, if a Mission has several premises, all of them will be considered to be one for the purposes of defining the premises of the Mission.
	The size of the premises of a Mission is determined by the receiving state. Indeed, this is usually determined by reference to the commercial and military interests of both receiving State and sending State[1]

Based on diplomatic practice, heads of a Mission are divided into three classes:

- ambassadors or nuncios accredited to Heads of State;
- envoys, ministers and internuncios accredited to Heads of State; and
- chargés d'affaires accredited to Ministers of Foreign Affairs.

In fact, the economic and political standing of the sending State in the international arena often requires the heads of Mission to be brought under

---

[1] See also Article 11

a specific class or category. But, of course, the class to which the heads of their Mission are to be assigned is agreed between a receiving State and a sending State. However, no differentiation is to be made between heads of Mission by reason of their class, other than in respect of precedence and etiquette[2].

Incidentally, the order of the date and time of taking up their functions is taken into account in according precedence to heads of Missions in their respective classes.

12.3 METHODS OF ESTABLISHING DIPLOMATIC RELATIONS BETWEEN STATES

Article 2 of the Convention states that:

> "The establishment of diplomatic relations between States, and of permanent diplomatic missions, takes place by mutual consent."

There are two reasons for it: (a) without the consent of the receiving State no diplomatic relations may be established; and (b) diplomatic relations should not be established by coercive means. After all, ideally, diplomatic relations should be established for mutual benefits, which, in most cases, is trade. In recent years, of course, diplomatic relations have provided military assistance too. It is to be emphasised that diplomatic relations should be kept confined to inter-state relations for mutual benefit; rendering of military assistance by one Member of the UN to another runs counter to the provisions of Article 2, paragraph 4 of the UN Charter. The primary function of diplomacy is to strengthen friendly relations between States, and where necessary, iron-out the differences between States. Incidentally, dependency on mutual trade should be a factor for ironing-out differences between States.

12.4 THE FUNCTIONS OF A DIPLOMATIC MISSION

Article 3 of the Vienna Convention states that the *"functions of a diplomatic mission consists, inter alia, in"* and thereafter details them in five paragraphs. By virtue of using the term *"inter alia"* it signifies that there may be other functions too; but they are related functions necessitated by circumstances or exigencies. Article 3 of the Convention merely itemises the most traditional functions of diplomatic missions, which are now briefly discussed.

Paragraph (6) of Article 3 states that the function of a diplomatic mission is to represent the sending State in the receiving State. The key word is *"represent"*; it means that it represents not only his/her sovereign but also the interests of that sovereign. *"Interests"* in this context predominantly stands for political and economic interests.

---

[2] Article 14(2)

Paragraph (b) Article 3 provides that a diplomatic mission is required *"to protect in the receiving State the interests of the sending State and of its nationals, within the limits permitted by international law."* The *"interests of the sending State"* would mean, inter alia, trade and investment interests, and military interests, that is, where a sending State has been assured by the receiving State of military assistance, when necessary. The phrase *"within limits permitted by international law"* means that the protection of interests, particularly, military interests, should not be contrary to the prescriptions of international law. Such prescriptions have been identified by Article 2, paragraph 4 of the UN Charter. Other principles of international law relevant to this issue would be the principles of sovereign equality and territorial integrity, that is, for example, if the sending State is militarily weaker than the receiving State, the latter should not be in violation of the principles of sovereign equality and territorial integrity. Of course, protection of the nationals of the sending State, including their business interests, residing in the receiving State is an important function of a diplomatic mission.

Paragraph (c) of Article 3 provides that it is the function of a diplomatic mission to negotiate with the government of the receiving State. *"Negotiation"* in this context would stand for negotiation of any matter, including contractual arrangements. Negotiation may be necessary for ironing-out differences on issues between the receiving State and the sending State.

Where new developments, whether political or economic in nature, may take place in a receiving State, they should be reported by the Mission to the sending State, especially developments which may have a direct effect, adverse or otherwise, in the sending State. This is particularly relevant when a change of political regime in the receiving State alters existing policies, economic, political or military, or when the security of the nationals of the sending State in the receiving State seems to be precarious. However, the conditions and developments in a receiving State must be ascertained by the Mission of the sending State by lawful means, which will include, direct enquiries, perusal of published documents, discussion in parliament or even by asking the Foreign Office in the receiving State.

Paragraph (c) of Article 3 provides that a diplomatic mission's function also consists of promoting friendly relations between the receiving State and the sending State. This may have two meanings: (a) that it is to strengthen or maintain the existing friendly relations between the two States; or (b) that where the friendly relations between the two States have to a certain extent deteriorated, it is for the Mission of the sending State to try to promote friendly relations between themselves. On the other hand, they can always develop their economic, cultural and scientific relations. In fact, relationships on these matters usually produce a *"bonding"* effect.

A diplomatic mission may also perform consular functions. In the case of larger missions, the consular division may have separate offices, but they come under the umbrella of the Mission of the sending State.

12.5 DUTIES OF A DIPLOMATIC MISSION

The duties of a mission must be benefiting the Mission, that is, to work for the mutual interests and benefits of the receiving State or the sending State. The attributes of sovereignty, respect for each other's supremacy in international relations, must be maintained. Efforts should be made to achieve everything by friendly means; including differences, if any, between the receiving State and the sending State. Special attributes are associated with the term *"mission"* – a diplomatic mission's work must entail broad ideas, like a religious mission usually does. A mission's work is not to be motivated by financial gains; development of rapport and understanding between the receiving State and the sending State should be strengthened, at all levels, political, economic, scientific and cultural. This is why the Vienna Convention of 1961 has not used any other term, such as, embassy or high commission. A mission's objectives and functions may not be limited by any ideas or conduct which is not befitting a sovereign.

The duties of a mission may be found throughout the Convention, either expressly or implicitly. A mission in a receiving State must not do anything which may be contrary to the policies, laws and regulations of the receiving State concerned[3].

Article 41 of the Convention provides, inter alia, that:

"... it is the duty of all persons enjoying such privileges and immunities to respect the laws and regulations of the receiving State. They also have a duty not to interfere in the internal affairs of that State."

The duty not interfere in the internal affairs of a receiving State is crucially important for a Mission, as otherwise, it would defeat the primary objectives of a mission in a receiving State.

Article 41, paragraph 2 of the Convention requires that *"all official business with the receiving State entrusted to the mission by the sending State shall be conducted with or through the Ministry of Foreign Affairs of the receiving State or such other ministry as may be agreed."* This is one of the means to ensure that foreign Missions in receiving States perform their official business with the receiving State's with the knowledge of the latter; and that they are in conformity with diplomatic practice. This also serves to strengthen relationship and co-operation between sending States and receiving States.

According to Article 41, paragraph 3, *"The premises of the mission must not be used in any manner incompatible with the functions of the mission"*. But, this provision has been qualified by the following provisions:

– *"as laid down in the present Convention"*; or

---

[3] For example, Article 12 of the Convention provides that: *"The sending State may not, without the prior consent of the receiving State, establish offices forming part of the mission in locations other than those in which the mission itself is established."*

- *"by other rules of general international law"*; or
- *"by any special agreements in force between the sending State and the receiving State."*

In fact, the Convention has not provided any guidelines as to how the premises of a mission must not be used *"in any manner incompatible with the functions of the mission."* This provision is based on the assumption that Missions should know what functions would be incompatible with their purposes. Generally speaking, any subversive activity or acts of espionage or any act which may jeopardise the security of the receiving State or cause harm to the nationals or citizens of the receiving State are included in it.

"Or by other rules of general international law" – would mean the principle of sovereign equality, but not rules of international law, or that premises of a mission must not be used in a manner which might be contrary to establishing friendly relations between the sending State and the receiving State.

"Or by any special agreements in force between the sending State and the receiving State" – in such a situation, the premises of the mission must be used in conformity with the provisions of those special agreements.

As regards Article 41, paragraph 3, in 1979, Libya decided that its embassies which would be run by revolutionary committees. It strained the relations between the UK and Libya and the Government of the UK insisted on Libya's nominating a person who would be the head of the Mission.[4]

In fact, if one seriously considers the connotation of the term *"mission"* it would be clear that it would be contrary to the spirit of a mission to use its premises in any manner incompatible with the functions of a mission. Incidentally, the premises of a mission in this context would include the areas appurtenant to the Mission and the vehicles owned by it too.

In dealing with the *Iran Hostage* Case (Diplomatic and Consular Staff) the International Court of Justice also pointed out that the Vienna Conventions of 1961 and 1963 contain provisions according to which members of any embassy staff, under the cover of diplomatic privileges and immunities, must not engage in such abuses of their functions as espionage and interfere in the internal affairs of the receiving State. The premises of a diplomatic mission or consular premises must not be used in any manner which would be incompatible with the functions of a mission or a consular post[5].

The Court also pointed out that:

"Thus, it is for the very purpose of providing a remedy for such possible abuses of diplomatic functions that Article 9 of the 1961 Convention on Diplomatic Relations stipulates:

---

[4] Comment by Sir Antony Acland, *Minutes of Evidence Taken Before the Foreign Affairs Committee*, Report (1979) at 20

[5] See Article 41, paragraphs 1 and 3 of the 1961 Convention, and Article 55, paragraphs 1 and 2 of the 1963 Convention

"1. The receiving State may at any time and without having to explain its decision, notify the sending State that the head of the mission or any member of the diplomatic staff of the mission is persona non grata or that any other member of the staff of the mission is not acceptable. In any such case, the sending State shall, as appropriate, either recall the person concerned or terminate his functions with the mission. A person may be declared non grata or not acceptable before arriving in the territory of the receiving State.

2. If the sending State refuses or fails within a reasonable period to carry out its obligations under paragraph 1 of this Article, the receiving State may refuse to recognize the person concerned as a member of the mission."[6]

12.6 METHODS OF ACCREDITING DIPLOMATS

The methods of accrediting diplomats have generally been embodied in Articles 4-8 of the Vienna Convention. Article 4 of the Convention provides that:

"(1) The sending State must make certain that the agreement of the receiving State has been given for the person it proposes to accredit as head of the mission to that State.

(2) The receiving State is not obliged to give reasons to the sending State for a refusal of agreement."

A receiving State, as a sovereign State, has the prerogative to refuse an agreement, without adducing any reason therefore. After giving due notification, a sending State may accredit a head of mission or assign any member of the diplomatic staff to more than one State, unless any of the receiving States concerned enters express objection to it[7]. Presumably, such objections must be entered in writing. The practice of allocating the same individual to different receiving States is based on convenience and/or economic reality. When receiving States are geographically close to each or when a sending State wishes to economise on its expenses or where the economic interests of the sending States in the receiving States are not significant, a sending State may adopt such a policy. Where a head of mission is accredited by a sending State to one or more States, the latter may establish a diplomatic mission to be headed by a *chargé d'affaires ad interim* in each State in which the head of mission has not his permanent seat[8].

"A head of mission or any member of the diplomatic staff of the mission may act as representative of the sending State to any international organisation."[9]

---

[6] *ICJ Reports*, op. cit., at 39

[7] Article 5(1)

[8] Article 5(1)

[9] Article 5(3)

This has proved to be a common practice in the world of diplomacy. Most of the diplomatic staff posted, for example, in Geneva, also represent their respective States before the UN and its specialised agencies. This practice proves to be cost effective too.

On the other hand, two or more States may accredit the same person as head of mission to another State provided of course that the receiving State does not raise any objection. Although a sending State has the freedom to recommend any individual to a foreign mission, in the final analysis, it is the receiving State which has the ultimate right to accept or reject that recommendation / nomination. In the case of military, naval or air attachés, a receiving State may require the sending State to submit their names in sufficient time, for its approval.

Although not directly related to accreditation of diplomats or heads of missions, it is worth mentioning that, according to the Convention, members of the diplomatic staff of a mission should, in principle, be of the nationals of the sending State. The term *"should"* has a specific meaning in this context. As in principle, the sovereign of the sending State is to be represented in a receiving State, it is only appropriate that the nationals of that sending sovereign should be deputised in the receiving State. The term *"should"* also indicates that exceptions to this policy have been made in the world of diplomacy. Historically, in the olden days, where an appropriate competent national could not be found in the sending State, a national of a third State could be appointed as a member of the diplomatic staff of a mission with the consent of the receiving State concerned; however such consent may be withdrawn at any time. Ideally, a receiving State should, in the main, be concerned with the national diplomats of the sending State. It is for the same reason that Article 8, paragraph 2 provides that members of the diplomatic staff of a mission may not be appointed from among the nationals of a receiving State, unless the receiving State concerned has accorded its consent to it, but its consent may be withdrawn at any time. The same restrictions apply to nationals of a third State – they do not really represent the sovereign of a sending State. Diplomacy is predominantly to be kept confined to sending States and receiving States.

The accreditation procedure is entirely controlled by the receiving State; by the same token, a receiving State, without giving any reason, may declare any head of a foreign mission or diplomatic staff *persona non grata*. In such a situation[10], the sending State concerned has no choice other than recalling the person concerned or terminate his/her position with the mission. Incidentally, a person may be declared *non grata* even before his/her arrival in the territory of the receiving State.

---

[10] Article 9

12.7 GENERAL POWERS AND DUTIES OF A SENDING STATE AND A RECEIVING STATE (ARTICLES 10-21)

The power of a receiving State to reject the nominations made by a sending State or to declare the head of a mission or any member of its diplomatic staff *persona non grata* under Article 9 has already been explained[11]. It should also be pointed out that if a sending State refuses or fails to comply with the decision of the receiving State on this matter within a reasonable period of time the receiving State may refuse to recognise the person concerned as a member of the mission[12]. It is for the receiving State to notify the Ministry of Foreign Affairs of the following:

(a) the appointment of members of the mission; the dates of arrival and departure of each member of the mission and the dates of termination of their functions;

(b) *"the arrival and final departure of a person belonging to the family of a member of the mission, and where appropriate, when a person becomes or ceases to be a member of the family of a member of the mission"*[13];

(c) the dates of arrivals and final departures of private servants in the employ of the member of the mission, and that they are leaving the employ of such persons; and

(d) *"the engagement and discharge of persons resident in the receiving State as members of the mission or private tenants entitled to privileges and immunities."*[14]

Of course, where possible, a sending State should notify the Ministry of Foreign Affairs of the receiving State, in advance, of the dates of arrival and final departures of the individuals referred to in Article 10 of the Convention.

The size of a mission is usually determined by the agreement between a receiving State and a sending State, although implicitly, the receiving State holds a stronger position than a sending State in this regard. Article 11 of the Convention provides, inter alia, that:

"In the absence of specific agreement as to the size of the mission, the receiving State may require that the size of a mission be kept within limits considered by it to be reasonable and normal, having regard to circumstances and conditions in the receiving State and to the needs of the particular mission."

---

[11] See the previous Section
[12] Article 9(2)
[13] Article 10(1)(b)
[14] Article 10(1)(d)

This provision is very broad indeed; it admits of the discretionary power of a receiving State. In reality, however, the size of a mission is very much determined by reference to the mutual commercial interest between a receiving State and a sending State.

Matters such as setting up of missions, or the size of the mission or the acceptance or rejection of officials or diplomatic staff are within the exclusive powers of a receiving State; and these powers may not be questioned by a sending State. Of course, decisions of receiving States on such matters may be retaliated by sending States, but they may prove to be counter productive.

Again, without the prior express consent of a receiving State, a sending State may not establish offices "... *forming part of the mission in locations other than those in which the mission is established*"[15]. Concern for security of the premises of mission was the primary basis for such a provision.

It is for the receiving State either to facilitate the acquisition of the premises for the mission for the sending State in it or to assist the sending State in obtaining accommodation in some other way[16]. Where necessary, a receiving State is required to assist missions in obtaining suitable accommodation for their members[17].

12.8 THE MEANING OF DIPLOMATIC PRIVILEGES AND IMMUNITIES

Satow's *Guide to Diplomatic Practice* states that:

> "In general, a privilege denotes some substantive exemption from laws and regulations such as those relating to taxation or social security, whenever an immunity does not imply any exception from substantive law but confers a procedural process of the receiving State."[18]

The simple fact is that because a diplomat is a privileged person, by virtue of representing his/her sovereign, he/she is immune from the jurisdiction of the receiving State. Satow's distinction is sustainable in that foreign diplomats cannot be treated as ordinary citizens in the receiving State; thus, the first nature of their special privileged status may be denoted by exempting them from any fiscal liability[19] under the local laws of the receiving State; they do not belong to the receiving State; but nevertheless, they deserve all kinds of protection from the receiving State however burdensome it may be for the latter. The question of applying any substantive law to these people by a receiving State would not arise; hence the issue of procedural protection from

---

[15] Article 12

[16] Article 21

[17] Article 21(2)

[18] Gore-Booth (ed), Harlow, Longman, (1979) 120

[19] See, for example, Articles 23, 26, 33, 34, 35 and 36 of the Vienna Convention on Diplomatic Relations, 1961

the enforcement process of the receiving State becomes relevant[20]. The exemption of the diplomatic agent from paying certain duties to the local jurisdiction of the receiving State has been justified by Lyons when he said that the exemptions are by no means essential for the successful functioning of a mission; however, the practice of granting them is so widespread that perhaps it has been hardened into a rule of law[21].

It must be accepted that most aspects of diplomatic law are based on long drawn State practice. But, what is the legal justification for allowing diplomats exemption from taxation? There is no conclusive answer to this question. The general assumptions have been: (a) the principle of sovereign equality whereby one sovereign cannot impose tax on the representatives of another sovereign (diplomats); (b) diplomats do not serve the receiving State; thus the question of making them liable to any tax or military service would not arise; and (c) thus, they are subject to the tax and military regimes, if any, of their sending State[22]. Hardy maintains that the basic reason for granting exemption to diplomats for taxes etc is the protection of interference by the receiving State[23]. It is not clear what *"protection of interference"* stands for. Imposition of taxes may not be regarded as an *"interference"* in the activities of a diplomat. It is maintained that the primary reason for allowing exemption from tax liability must be the principle of sovereign equality coupled with the issue that diplomats do not belong to receiving States. This does not mean however that they are exempt from the criminal law of the receiving State, but, usually, if a diplomat commits an offence (but not a high offence) he will not be amenable to the local criminal jurisdiction, but may be declared *persona non grata* as a form of punishment. Satow pointed out that if a diplomat breaks any of the laws of the receiving State, he/she cannot be arrested or detained by the executive authorities of the receiving State, and he/she cannot be sued or tried or made to testify before the judicial authorities of that State[24].

It may be inferred that the legal bases for diplomatic privileges and immunities should not be traced in law other than the legal justification provided by the principle of sovereign equality, but mostly in international comity and courtesy based on State practice.

---

[20] But see J Craig Barker who does not entirely agree with Satow's view on this matter. See J C Barker, *The Abuse of Diplomatic Privileges and Immunities: A Necessary Evil?*, Aldershot, Dartmouth (1996) 67.

[21] A B Lyons, "Personal Immunities of Diplomatic Agents", 31 *British Year Book of International Law* (1954) 326

[22] See further E Denza, *Diplomatic Law*, Dobbs Ferry, Oceana Publications (1976) 195; see also C E Wilson, *Diplomatic Privileges and Immunities*, Tucson, University of Arizona Press (1967) 101–102

[23] M Hardy, *Modern Diplomatic Law*, Manchester, Manchester University Press (1968) 71

[24] *Satow's Guide to Diplomatic Practice*, op. cit., 120

12.9 THE CONCEPT OF INVIOLABILITY

In inter-State diplomacy, the principle of *"inviolability"* is sacrosanct[25]. This is so because of the principle of sovereignty in international law, which requires every sovereign State to respect others' sovereignty. Interestingly enough, it is on the basis of a receiving State's authorisation that a mission of a sending State is allowed to be set up, and yet the receiving State cannot exercise its power over it as a superior sovereign; they are all equal. In the *United States v Iran* the International Court of Justice stated that:

> *"There is no more fundamental prerequisite for the conduct of relations between States than the inviolability of diplomatic envoys and embassies."*[26]

It is to be pointed out however that the inviolability of the person of the diplomatic agent seems to have originated first[27], and thereafter the principle of inviolability of the mission. This is because the courtesy to provide protection and to show respect to another sovereign when they were on a visit to a foreign sovereign became a form of State practice. The practice of setting up of diplomatic missions in foreign sovereign States came later. The inviolability of a mission, as an absolute principle, has been a subject of controversy: whereas at the conference of the International Law Commission certain delegates (e.g., Mexico) took a rather rigid view on this principle[28], the general consensus was that there was no legal obligation to co-operate with the receiving State even in cases of emergencies, such as fire or other extreme emergencies[29]. Perhaps, the most logical view was given by Denza: in the case of clear abuse, forcible entry could be justified *ex post facto*, and that such an entry may be justified only in the case of abuse[30]. Hardy, on the other hand, maintains that the principle of inviolability of a mission cannot be compromised[31].

The principle of inviolability is justified by the representative character of a diplomatic envoy[32]. There is no reason why the functional necessity theory may not be applied to justify the principle of inviolability of both persons of a diplomatic agent, and a diplomatic mission.

There exists at least one exception to the sacrosanct principle of inviolability however, that is, when the diplomat himself or herself commits an act of

---

[25] Brown maintains that the duty to treat a diplomatic agent with due respect is so sacred that it must preclude the entire range of law enforcement and related measures. J Brown, "Diplomatic Immunity: State Practice under the Vienna Convention on Diplomatic Relations", 37 *International and Comparative Law Quarterly* (1988) 53.

[26] ICJ Reports (1979) 7 at 19

[27] *Yearbook of International Law Commission* (1957) vol 1 at 89–90

[28] UN Doc A/CONF 20/C.1 / L.129 at 20

[29] UN Doc A/CONF 20/14 at 140–141

[30] E Denza, op. cit., at 81

[31] M Hardy, *Modern Diplomatic Law*, op. cit., at 44

[32] Bynkershoek (1721) *De Foro Legatorum*; see also Vattel (1758) *Le Droit Des Gens*

violence which disturbs the internal order of the receiving State to such an extent that the receiving State finds it necessary to restrain him/her from committing such acts, or if he/she conspires against the receiving State. Incidentally, Article 29 of the 1961 Convention does not create an absolute obligation for a receiving State to protect a diplomatic agent while within its territorial jurisdiction. Article 29 of the Vienna Convention on Diplomatic Relations, 1961 provides, *inter alia*, that:

> *"The receiving State shall treat him* [the diplomatic agent] *with due respect and shall take all appropriate steps to prevent any attack on his person, freedom, or dignity."*

The very words are *"appropriate steps"*, which signifies that it is a strict obligation; and not an absolute obligation on the part of a receiving State. Furthermore, where an unjustifiable behaviour on the part of a diplomatic agent is established, the issue of respecting inviolability in that situation would not arise[33].

12.10 DIPLOMATIC IMMUNITIES IN REGARD TO PROPERTY

Article 22 of the Vienna Convention on Diplomatic Relations provides that:

> *"1. The premises of the mission shall be inviolable. The agents of the receiving State may not enter them, except with the consent of the head of the mission.*
>
> *2. The receiving State is under a special duty to take all appropriate steps to protect the premises of the mission against any intrusion or damage and to prevent any disturbance of the peace of the mission or impairment of its dignity.*
>
> *3. The premises of the mission, their furnishings and other property thereon and the means of transport of the mission shall be immune from search, requisition, attachment or execution."*

Article 23 provides for general exemption from taxation in respect of the mission premises:

> *"1. The sending State and the head of the mission shall be exempt from all national, regional or municipal dues and taxes in respect of the premises of the mission, whether owned or leased, other than such as represent payment for specific services rendered.*
>
> *2. The exemption from taxation referred to in this Article shall not apply to such dues and taxes payable under the law of the receiving State by persons contracting with the sending State or the head of the mission."*

---

[33] See also *Oppenheim's International Law*, op. cit., at 1074–1075

In the *Philippine Embassy Bank Account* case[34] the action arose out of a tenancy agreement between the creditor (the Deutsche Bank AG) and the Republic of Philippines for providing office accommodation for its embassy in the Federal Republic of Germany. During June 1973 the tenant had moved out of the building and had placed it at the disposal of the creditor, paying the rent up to and including June 1973. The creditor claimed rent arrears up to and including May 1974 on the grounds that the contractual period of notice had not been observed as well as for repair costs.

The plaintiff obtained judgment from the Provisional Court (Landsgericht) of Bonn against the Philippines, and eventually also obtained from the District Court (Amtsgericht) of Bonn an attachment and assignment order against present and future balances of the Philippines held in its account at the Deutsche Bank in Bonn. The Philippines lodged an objection to the order before the same court on the grounds that the account which had been attached was not subject to German jurisdiction since it was designated *"Embassy of the Philippines Account"* and was used by the Philippine Government to make available to its embassy the funds necessary for its operating costs, including rent, and as a result of the attachment the embassy was no longer able to meet its current obligations.

The District Court of Bonn stayed the proceedings, and submitted the following question to the Federal Constitutional Court:

> *"Is there a rule of international law according to which forced execution under a judgment delivered against a foreign State in respect of its non-sovereign activities, on a bank account of that or of its embassy, which exists within the country and is intended to cover the official expenditure and costs of the embassy, is totally inadmissible or admissible insofar as the functioning of the embassy as a diplomatic mission is prejudiced by the attachment; is such a rule, if it exists, part of federal law?"*

The Court held, inter alia, that:

> *"There existed a general rule of international law according to which forced execution of judgment by the State of the forum under a writ of execution against a foreign State which had been issued in respect of non-sovereign acts (act jure gestionis) of that State, on property of that State which was present or situated in the territory of the State of the forum was inadmissible without the consent of the foreign State if, at the time of initiation of the measure of execution, such property served sovereign purposes of the foreign State. Claims against a general current bank account of the embassy of a foreign state which existed in the State of the forum and the purpose of which was to cover the*

---

[34] 65 *International Legal Materials*, 146

embassy's costs and expenses were not subject to forced execution by the State of the forum. This rule formed part of federal law."[35]

The Court further held that:

"Preventative measures or measures of execution against a foreign State could not, under international law, be levied on property which at the relevant time was being used by its diplomatic mission for the performance of its official functions. The principle of international law ne impediator legatio precluded such measures where they might interfere with the exercise of diplomatic duties."[36]

Of course, enforcement measures to freeze a foreign embassy funds can be taken if the money available on its bank account are not to be used for the purposes which are directly related to the functions of a diplomatic mission.

Another interesting case that raised a similar issue was *Alcom Ltd v Republic of Colombia*[37]. Sometime in 1982, the plaintiffs issued a writ against the defendant, a friendly sovereign State, which had a mission in London, claiming a sum of money in respect of goods sold and delivered. The plaintiffs obtained a default judgment (the defendant failed to give notice to defend), and sought to levy execution against moneys held with a London bank. The plaintiffs also obtained garnishee orders *nisi* against the bank accounts. The defendant applied to the High Court to discharge the orders claiming immunity from execution under the provisions of s 13(2)(b) of the State Immunity Act, 1978, according to which the property of a State may not be *"subject to any process for the enforcement of judgment"*. However, s 13(4) of the same Act provides, *inter alia*, that:

"Subsection (2)(b) above does not prevent the issue of any process in respect of property which is for the time being in use or intended for use for commercial purposes..."

The defendant's ambassador certified that the funds in the bank accounts were not used nor were being intended for use for commercial purposes, but to meet the expenditure necessarily incurred in the day-to-day running of the mission.

Section 13(5) provides, inter alia, that:

The head of a State's diplomatic mission in the United Kingdom, or the person for the time being performing his functions, shall be deemed to have authority to give on behalf of the State ... certificate to the effect that any property is not in use or intended for use by or on behalf of the State for commercial purposes shall be accepted as sufficient evidence of the fact unless contrary is proved."

---

[35] 65 *International Law Reports*, op. cit., at 147

[36] op. cit., at 148

[37] [1984] 2 ALL ER 6

The High Court held that a bank account used for an embassy was *prima facie* non-commercial, and the judge discharged the garnishee order *nisi*. The plaintiffs appealed to the Court of Appeal which held that funds in bank accounts used for the day-to-day expenditure of an embassy were used or intended for use for *"commercial transactions"*; therefore the garnishee orders must be levied. The defendant appealed to the House of Lords, which reversed the decision of the Court of Appeal. The House of Lords held that:

> "... where the bank account of a foreign State was used to meet the day-to-day running expenses a diplomatic mission it fell outside the scope of s 13(4) since it was **indivisible**[38] and would be used not only to settle liabilities incurred under contracts for the supply of goods or services to the mission but also in the exercise by the State of its sovereign authority. The immunity from process was in accordance with the rule of public international law that neither the executive nor the legal branch of government in a receiving State was entitled to act in any manner which obstructed a diplomatic mission in carrying out its functions."

The House of Lords further held that:

> "It was for the plaintiffs to show that the funds in the foreign State's bank accounts were used solely to meet liabilities incurred in commercial transactions, and since the ambassador's certificate was, in the circumstances, conclusive on that issue, the bank accounts were immune from the levying of execution."

In *Intpro Properties (UK) Ltd v Samuel*[39] the Court rendered an interpretation of s 16(1)(b) of the State Immunity Act, 1978. The plaintiffs let to the French government (represented by the French Consul General in London) certain premises for use other than that of a private dwelling house. The premises were in the occupation of a named diplomat with the French embassy in London. The French government agreed to permit the plaintiffs or their agents, with or without workmen, at reasonable times during the lease to enter into the premises for the purpose of inspecting and examining the premises and carrying out repairs, when necessary. The diplomat occupied the premises with his family as their home but also carried out his social obligations as a diplomat. Sometime during the tenure of the lease the plaintiffs instructed contractors to carry out certain remedial work, but the diplomat denied them access to the premises. The plaintiffs issued a writ against the diplomat seeking an injunction to restrain him from preventing access to the premises or interfering with the repair work.

The diplomat applied to set aside the writ on the grounds that as a member of the diplomatic staff of the French mission he was a *"diplomatic agent"* within the meaning of Article 1(e) of the Vienna Convention on Diplomatic

---

[38] Emphasis added by the author

[39] [1983] 2 ALL ER 495

Relations, 1961, as set out in Schedule 1 to the Diplomatic Privileges Act, 1964, and accordingly enjoyed diplomatic immunity.

By amending the writ, the French government was allowed to join as a party to the action, but it maintained that the writ should be set aside on the grounds that it could not be impleaded in the English courts.

According to s 6(1) of the State Immunity Act, 1978, a foreign State is not immune from proceedings relating to *"any interest of the State in or its possession or use of, immovable property in the United Kingdom"* or *"any obligation of the State arising out of its interest in, or its possession or use of, any such property"*. The question remained whether by virtue of the provisions of s 16(1)(b) of the Act that exception from immunity under s 6(1) did extend to proceedings concerning *"a State's title to or its possession of property used for the purposes of a diplomatic mission."*

The High Court held, inter alia, that the plaintiffs' action related not merely to the French government's use of the premises but also to the rights and obligations arising from its possession of the premises; therefore the action fell within the exception from immunity prescribed by s 6(1) of the Act. Furthermore, according to the Court, the premises were *"used for the purposes of a diplomatic mission"* within s 16(1)(b) of the Act; therefore, the French government was immune from proceedings.

After some time the premises fell vacant, and the plaintiffs appealed claiming that they were entitled to damages against the French government for the loss which they had sustained as a consequence of the French government's refusal to allow contractors access to the premises for repair work. They also relied on a particular covenant in the lease; which according to them came within the purview of s 6(1) of the 1978 Act.

The Court of Appeal held, inter alia, that:

Under s 16(1)(b) of the 1978 Act premises used "for the purposes of a diplomatic mission would mean premises used for the professional diplomatic purposes" of a mission, and not otherwise.

Furthermore, "the specific reference to the residence of the head of the mission in art. 1(1) of Schedule 1 to the 1964 Act made it clear that residences of other members of the mission could not form part of the premises of the mission."[40]

The Court of Appeal further held that:

"Whereas s 6(1) of the 1978 Act dealt with a State's interest in, or its possession or use of, immovable property in the United Kingdom, there was no corresponding reference to the 'use' of such property in s 16(1)(b) of the Act which dealt with proceedings concerning a State's title to or its possession of property."

---

[40] op. cit., at 496

Article 24 of the Vienna Convention on Diplomatic Relations provides that:

> "The archives and documents of the mission shall be inviolable at any time and wherever they may be."

"Wherever they may be" would mean whether they were at the mission or in transit or even outside the mission, but under the protection of the mission. As to the meaning of "archives and documents" one may like to refer to Article 1(1)(k) of the Vienna Convention on Consular Relations which provides that:

> "'Consular archives' includes all the papers, documents, correspondence, books, films, tapes and registers of the consular post, together with the ciphers and codes, the card-indexes and any article of furniture intended for their protection or safekeeping."

It is believed that the same meaning will be maintained about the similar phrase under the Vienna Convention on Diplomatic Relations too[41].

In *Shearson Lehman v MacLaine Watson Co Ltd and International Tin Council (Intervener)*[42] the House of Lords considered whether the documents that the other parties to the dispute purported to adduce in evidence were inadmissible by virtue of Article 7(1) of the International Tin Council (Immunities and Privileges) Order 1972[43] as being documents or copies of documents, in respect of which the ITC, an inter-governmental body, had a statutory inviolability akin to diplomatic privilege.

In 1985, the International Tin Council, an inter-governmental body, ran out of funds in an unsuccessful attempt to support the price of tin, and collapsed. The plaintiffs claimed against the first and second defendants damages for breach of contract. There were actions against other defendants too for alleged breach of contract.

The issue went up to the House of Lords, which held that:

> "... article 7(1) of the International Tin Council (Immunities and Privileges) Order 1972 was to be construed as conferring inviolability on the archives and documents of the ITC to the same extent as article 24 of the Vienna Convention on Diplomatic Relations set out in Schedule 1 to the Diplomatic Privileges Act 1964 conferred inviolability on the archives and documents of a diplomatic mission..."

But, the House of Lords also held that:

> "... the ITC was an entity distinct from its constituent members in the conduct of its internal affairs; and that, accordingly, once a document had been communicated by the ITC to a member or a member's representative, the protection afforded to it by article 7(1) of the Order of 1972 ceased to apply."[44]

---

[41] See further E Denza, *Diplomatic Law*, op. cit., at 162

[42] [1988] 1 WLR 16

[43] Article 7(1) of the ITC (Immunities and Privileges) Order, 1972 provides inviolability for practical reasons

[44] See also Article 14(1) of the Order of 1972

12.11 INVIOLABILITY OF A MISSION AND ITS ARTICLES AND COMMUNICATIONS

Article 22 of the Convention provides that the premises of the mission shall be inviolable. This is because the premises of a mission are to be treated as the premises of a foreign sovereign. *"Premises"* in this context stands not only for the principal premises of the mission but also other premises, if any, allocated to it. Vehicles and extra land area appurtenant to the premises are to be regarded as part of the premises. The principle of the inviolability is so sacrosanct in nature that even representatives of the receiving State may not be allowed to enter into the premises without the consent of the head of the mission[45].

Article 22(2) provides that:

> *"The receiving State is under a special duty to take all appropriate steps to protect the premises of the mission against any intrusion or damage and to prevent any disturbance of the peace of the mission or impairment of its dignity."*

To protect the premises of the mission is a very onerous task for a receiving State when a city contains a large number of missions, for commercial reasons. *"Impairment of the dignity"* is the crucial phrase in that it covers all incidents or acts which will have the effect of impairing the dignity of the sovereign (the mission is the office of a foreign sovereign).

The extent to which this rule of absolute immunity of diplomatic premises may be maintained presents controversy particularly when missions are vulnerable to terrorist attacks. In 1896, the English Courts refused to issue a writ of *habeas corpus* in respect of a Chinese refugee held against his will in the Chinese mission in London[46]. Of course, no legal guidelines could be developed by the courts as this issue was finally resolved by diplomatic means.

Neither the Vienna Convention nor customary international law provide any guidance as to whether entry into a foreign mission without the consent of the mission authorities may be allowed in certain emergencies, such as holding of hostages or in circumstances evidencing that a mission is engaged in an activity which is contrary to its functions under the Convention. Consent of the mission to enter it must be assumed, in the event of other forms of emergency, for example, fire, flood or when any emergency treatment for a staff of the mission may be necessary.

Entry into a mission premises for the kind of emergencies mentioned above is one issue; but the need for entry occasioned by the conduct of a mission staff

---

[45] This rule seems to be absolute in nature; see, for example, 767 *Third Avenue Associates v Permanent Mission of the Republic of Zaire to the United Nations* 988 F 2nd (1993): 99 *International Law Reports*, 194

[46] See further A D McNair, *International Law Opinions*, Oxford, Clarendon Press (1956) Vol 1, at 85

is an entirely different matter. Whereas consent in the former situation is not withheld for obvious reasons, in the latter situation the question of giving consent by the mission concerned would not arise[47].

The Vienna Convention does not make any provision in this regard simply because such activities are to be treated as *"unbecoming"* of a mission. The premises of a mission must not be used in a way which is incompatible with the functions of a mission[48]. According to Denza:

> *"In the last resort, however, it cannot be excluded that entry without the consent of the sending State may be justified in international law by the need to protect human life."*[49]

In 1973, a search carried out in the Iraqi embassy in Pakistan found considerable quantities of arms, in consequence of which two Iraqis, the Ambassador and an attaché, were declared *persona non grata*[50]. On the other hand, a search by US troops of the residence of the Nicaraguan ambassador in Panama in 1989 received condemnation in the form of a draft Security Council resolution by a large majority, but was vetoed by the US[51]. It should be emphasised that the receiving State is under a special obligation to protect the foreign missions within its territory; and *"protection"* in this context would include protection from *"intrusion"* or *"impairment of its dignity"*. A receiving State can also be accused of *"intrusion"* by itself, but a serious dilemma for a receiving State may arise in a situation in which the government of the United Kingdom found itself. On 17 April, 1984, during a peaceful demonstration outside the Libyan Embassy in London, shots fired from the Embassy resulted in the death of a policewoman, Yvonne Fletcher. The question arose whether the British Government should have entered into the embassy building for a search. If the Government had entered without the consent of the Libyan authorities it would have amounted to a breach of Article 22 of the Vienna Convention. If one relies on Denza's view, then entry into the mission premises would be justified. The mission was already in breach of its obligation under the Vienna Convention[52]. After a siege, the Libyans inside the mission left, and in conformity with the practice in the world of diplomacy, the building was searched in the presence of a Saudi Arabian diplomat.

Weapons were found during the search[53]. The issue remains whether the receiving State in such circumstances may enter a foreign mission on the

---

[47] When entry of police or fire safety people is allowed by the head of the mission, the issue of inviolability is irrelevant. See *Fatemi v the US* 34 *International Law Reports* (1964) 148.

[48] See *Belgium v Nicod and Another* 82 *International Law Reports* at 124

[49] E Denza, *Diplomatic Law*, at 126

[50] ibid

[51] ibid

[52] Article 41, paragraph 33

[53] See the Report of the *Foreign Affairs Committee*, at XXVI

grounds of self-defence irrespective of whether or not consent has been given by the sending State. In a situation such as that which arose in the Libyan case, one could argue that such a search would be essential for the protection of the police / nation. It was on this basis that the search of personnel leaving the Libyan embassy was justified[54]. Of course, entry into a foreign mission by a receiving State will be justified where the mission itself so requests. In 1980, Iran requested the UK government to eject militants who took over their embassy in London. The UK government maintains that Article 45(a) of the Vienna Convention does not suggest that the premises continue to be inviolable[55]. A distinction should be made between *"inviolability"* under Article 22 and *"respect and protection"* under Article 45(a)[56].

Protection of the foreign mission is a *"strict duty"* for receiving States, and not an *"absolute duty"*. This is because the capacity to provide protection varies from State to State; however, each receiving State must demonstrate that it did its best with due care and skill to protect a foreign mission.

In 1979, the US embassy in Tehran, Iran was taken over by a large number of demonstrators. Fifty diplomatic and consular staff were held hostage. The US filed an action against Iran under the Vienna Convention on Diplomatic Relations, 1961 and the Vienna Convention on Consular Relations, 1963, in addition to the Convention on the Prevention and Punishment of Crimes against Internationally Protected Persons, including Diplomatic Agents, 1973.

The International Court of Justice concluded, *inter alia*, that:

> *"By a number of provisions of the Vienna Conventions of 1961 and 1963, Iran was placed under the most categorical obligation, as a receiving State, to take appropriate steps to ensure the protection of the United States Embassy and Consulates, their staffs, their archives, their means of communication and the freedom of movement of the members of their staffs."*[57]

The obligation to protect the inviolability of the premises, documents and archives is a strict one. The receiving State must make its best efforts to provide this protection. The legal issue is whether a receiving State has actually made its best efforts to do so[58].

The Court was satisfied that there was a total inaction on the part of the Iranian authorities on the date on which demonstrations took place despite urgent and repeated requests for help. This is where obligations arose not only

---

[54] See the Memorandum of the Foreign and Commonwealth Office, Report of the Foreign Affairs Committee, at 9

[55] Memorandum of he Foreign and Commonwealth Office, op. cit., at 5

[56] See also M N Shaw *International Law*, Cambridge, Cambridge University Press (2003) at 673

[57] *ICJ Reports* (1981) at 30. See also L Gross, "The Case Governing United States Diplomatic and Consular Staff in Tehran: Phase of Provisional Measures," 74

[58] On this point, see further AAPL *American Journal of International Law* (1980) 395

under the Vienna Conventions[59], but also under the principle of state responsibility. The fault was further compounded by the fact that the government of Iran was fully aware of its obligations under the Vienna Conventions and the principle of state responsibility[60].

Even after a mission has been occupied or seized, under customary international law a receiving State has an obligation to make its efforts to bring the flagrant infringements of the inviolability of the premises, archives and the diplomatic and consular staffs to a speedy end, restore the *status quo* and to offer reparation for the damage. The Court stated that:

> *"The occupation having taken place and the diplomatic and consular personnel of the United States' mission having been taken hostage, the action required of the Iranian Government ... by general international law was manifest. Its plain duty was at once to make every effort, and to take every appropriate step, to bring these flagrant infringements of the inviolability of the premises, archives and diplomatic and consular staff of the United States Embassy to a speedy end, to restore the Consulates ... to United States control, and in general to re-establish the status quo and to offer reparation for the damage."*[61]

No such step was however taken by the Iranian authorities. The Court had evidence that at a reception in Qom on 4 November, 1979, the Ayatollah Khomeini had given his approval to the action of the militants in occupying the embassy[62].

The Iranian authorities' decision to continue the subjection of the premises of the United States Embassy to occupation by militants and of the Embassy staff to detention as hostages gave rise to multiple and repeated breaches of the applicable provisions of the Vienna Conventions even more serious than those which arose from their failure to take any steps to prevent the attacks on the inviolability of the premises and staff[63]. These multiple and repeated breaches were very clearly summarised by the Court in the following passage:

> *"In the first place, these facts constituted breaches additional to those already committed of paragraph 2 of Article 22 of the 1961 Vienna Convention on Diplomatic Relations which requires Iran to protect the premises of the mission against any intrusion or damage and to prevent any disturbance of its peace or impairment of its dignity. Paragraphs 1 and 3 of that Article have also been infringed, and continue to be infringed, since they forbid agents of a receiving State to enter the premises of a mission without consent or to undertake any search, requisition, attachment or like measure on the premises. Secondly, they*

---

[59] Articles 22(2), 24, 27 and 29 of the 1961 Convention and Articles 5 and 36 of the 1963 Convention

[60] See further *ICJ Reports*, op. cit., at 32–33

[61] *ICJ Reports*, op. cit., at 33

[62] op. cit., at 34

[63] See further *ICJ Reports*, op. cit., at 36

constitute continuing breaches of Article 29 of the same Convention which forbids any arrest or detention of a diplomatic agent and any attack on his person, freedom or dignity. Thirdly, the Iranian authorities are without doubt in continuing breach of the provisions of Articles 25, 26 and 27 of the 1961 Vienna Convention and of pertinent provisions of the 1963 Convention concerning facilities for the performance of functions, freedom of movement and communications for diplomatic and consular staff, as well as of Article 24 of the former Convention and Article 33 of the latter, which provide for the absolute inviolability of the archives and documents of diplomatic missions and consulates. This particular violation has been made manifest to the world by repeated statements by the militants occupying the Embassy, who claim to be in possession of documents from the archives, and by various government authorities, purporting to specify the contents thereof. Finally, the continued detention as hostages of the two private individuals of United States nationality entails a renewed breach of the obligations of Iran under Article II, paragraph 4, of the 1955 Treaty of Amity, Economic Relations, and Consular Rights."

The Court also reminded Iran that if their intention was to submit the hostages to any form of criminal trial or investigation that would constitute a grave breach by Iran of her obligations under Article 31, paragraph 1 of the Vienna Convention, 1961[64].

With regard to the sacrosanct nature of the principle of inviolability, the Court further pointed out that:

"The fundamental character of the principle of inviolability is, moreover, strongly underlined by the provisions of Articles 44 and 45 of the Convention of 1961 (cf. also Articles 26 and 27 of the Convention of 1963). Even in the case of armed conflict or in the case of a breach in diplomatic relations those provisions require that both the inviolability of the members of a diplomatic mission and of the premises, property and archives of the mission must be respected by the receiving State. Naturally, the observance of this principle does not mean – and this the Applicant Government expressly acknowledges – that a diplomatic agent caught in the act of committing an assault or other offence may not, on occasion, be briefly arrested by the police of the receiving State in order to prevent the commission of the particular crime. But such eventualities bear no relation at all to what occurred in the present case."[65]

Abandonment of diplomatic and consular premises by the sending State may present legal problems, but the Diplomatic and Consular Premises Act 1987 (UK) aims at resolving them. The following are the objectives of this Act:

1. to make provision as to what land is diplomatic or consular premises;

2. to give the Secretary of State power to vest certain land in himself;

---

[64] *ICJ Reports*, op. cit., at 37

[65] *ICJ Reports*, op. cit., at 40

3. to impose on him a duty to sell land vested in him in the exercise of that power;

4. to give certain provisions of the Vienna Convention on Diplomatic Relations and the Vienna Convention on Consular Relations the force of law by amending Schedule 1 to the Diplomatic Privileges Act, 1964 and Schedule 1 to the Consular Relations Act 1968; and

5. to amend Section 9(2) of the Criminal Law Act 1977.

According to s 7 of this Act where a State desires that land shall be diplomatic or consular premises, it is required to apply to the Secretary of State for his consent to the land being such premises, unless of course, the Secretary of State has already accepted it as diplomatic or consular premises immediately before the coming into force of this section. Thus, a sending State has no right in the UK to declare a plot of land as diplomatic or consular premises. The Secretary of State has also the power to withdraw his consent if he is satisfied that to do so would be permissible under international law[66].

In determining whether or not a plot of land should be so designated, the Secretary of State shall have regard to all material considerations, and, in particular:

(a) to the safety of the public;

(b) to national security; and

(c) to town and country planning[67].

If a sending State intends to cease using land as a diplomatic or consular premises, it shall give the Secretary of State notice to that effect specifying the date on which it intends to cease so using them.

If a plot of land was not designated as a diplomatic or consular premises before coming into force of s 2 of this Act, or that the land has ceased to be diplomatic or consular premises after the coming into force of this Section but not less than 12 months before he exercises power under this Section, the premises in issue may be vested in the Secretary of State. The Secretary of State shall only exercise this power if he is satisfied that to do so is permissible under international law[68]. After such land has been vested in the Secretary of State, he will have the duty to sell it[69].

In 1975, Pol Pot took over Cambodia; the Cambodian Embassy in London which represented the pre-Pol Pot regime closed down the embassy, and handed over the keys to the Foreign and Commonwealth Office. These

---

[66] S 1(4)

[67] S 1(5)

[68] S 2 of the Diplomatic and Consular Premises Act 1987

[69] S 3

premises were then decided to be governed by the provision of s 2 of the 1987 Act. However, this was the decision of the Secretary of State. The government of the United Kingdom withdrew recognition of the new Cambodian government in 1979.

However, on 6 August 1976, squatters moved into the premises of the Cambodian Embassy in London, but no attempt was made by the UK government to remove them until 1988. Under English law squatters may obtain a title to land by twelve years' adverse possession. The Foreign and Commonwealth Office maintained that to allow the squatters to obtain a title to the land would involve a violation of the UK's obligations to Cambodia. On 4 January 1988, the Secretary of State made an order providing that s 2 of the Diplomatic and Consular Premises Act 1987 would be applied to the premises.

This action was challenged by a squatter, Samuel, in the form of a judicial review, in *Secretary of State for Foreign and Commonwealth Affairs, ex parte Samuel*[70], on the grounds that the Secretary of State's action was contrary to the provisions of Article 45 of the Vienna Convention on Diplomatic Relations, 1961. The application was refused in the High Court and the applicant appealed to the Court of Appeal.

The appeal was dismissed. The Court of Appeal held, inter alia, that:

> "Section 2(2) of the 1987 Act provided that the Secretary of State had to be satisfied, before making an order under the Section, that to do so was permissible under international law. It was therefore for the Secretary of State, not the English Courts, to determine whether international law permitted the United Kingdom to act in the manner envisaged by Section 2. The Court's role was confined to determining whether the Secretary of State had satisfied himself that a proposed order was permissible under international law and whether he had acted reasonably and in good faith in reaching that conclusion. In the present case, the Secretary of State had been advised that the proposed order was permissible under international law and there was no evidence that the conclusion was reached in bad faith or was unreasonable."[71]

In this connection it would be appropriate to reproduce the Schedule to the 1987 Act which amended the 1964 and 1968 Acts. Please see Appendix 1.

Where however a previously unoccupied former embassy may be occupied by trespassers who would be in exclusive occupation of the premises, they will be required to pay rates that may be levied on them by the relevant local authority. This was decided by the Court of Appeal in *Westminster City Council v Tomlin*[72].

---

[70] 83 *International Law Reports*, at 232

[71] 83 *International Law Reports*, at 233

[72] [1990] 1ALL ER 920

Article 30 of the 1961 Convention provides that:

> "1. The private residence of a diplomatic agent shall enjoy the same inviolability and protection as the premises of the mission.
>
> 2. His papers, correspondence and, except as provided in paragraph 3 of Article 31, his property, shall likewise enjoy inviolability."

After a diplomatic mission has been closed down, the mission's premises, property and archives must be protected by the receiving State concerned for a reasonable period of time. What is a *"reasonable period"* in this context must be determined by referring to the likelihood of it being used again. In *Westminster City Council v Government of Islamic Republic of Iran*[73], the Council sought to register a land charge, but the question of immunity of the premises arose under Article 22 of the 1961 Convention. The case was concerned with the payment of expenses arising out of the repairs to the damaged and abandoned Iranian mission in London in 1980. The Court held that the premises had ceased to be diplomatic premises; they were not *"used"* for the purposes of the mission as required by Article 22 of the 1961 Convention.

In general, the receiving State is under a special duty to take all appropriate steps to protect the mission against intrusion[74] or damage.

The furnishings, other property thereon, and the means of transport of the mission are also immune from search, acquisition, attachment or execution. Attachment or execution means, no court order may be attached to a transport of a mission nor can an order be issued for the sale of it for settling the debt with the proceeds of sale.

The archives and documents of a mission must remain inviolable at all times wherever they may be. This is to be regarded as an absolute obligation. A receiving State has an obligation to permit and protect free communication for a mission in respect of official purposes. The same obligation applies to official correspondence. The characteristics of communication and correspondence are crucially important factors for determining the status of communication or correspondence.

Controversy exists however whether diplomatic bags should be opened or detained. The Convention however provides that *"The diplomatic bag shall not be opened or detained"*[75], but at the time of accepting the Convention certain States reserved their right to open such bags[76]. In this connection, the Report[77]

---

[73] [1986] 3 ALL ER 284

[74] The service of a writ upon a diplomat on diplomatic premises would be contrary to diplomatic immunity; see *Hellenic Lines Ltd v Moore* (1965) 42 *International Law Reports* at 239; see also *Oppenheim's International Law*, Vol I, op. cit., at 1077

[75] Article 27(3)

[76] For example, Bahrain, Kuwait, Libya and Saudi Arabia

[77] The Report of the Foreign Affairs Committee, op. cit.

of the Foreign Affairs Committee of the Government of the United Kingdom is worth considering.

However, the general rule has been that the packages constituting a diplomatic bag must bear visible external marks signifying that it is a diplomatic bag. Diplomatic bags may contain only diplomatic documents or articles intended for official use[78]. What is *"intended"* for official use must be determined beforehand. Though there exists a difference between *"diplomatic documents"* and *"articles intended for official use"*, whether an article is intended for *"official use"* or not can only be confirmed by the sending State or its representative. Official communication is inviolable, but controversy exists whether consent of the receiving State is required for a wireless transmission[79].

A diplomatic bag may be carried by a diplomatic courier. *"Diplomatic courier"* in this context means any individual carrying a diplomatic bag – he or she need not be a diplomat. However, a diplomatic courier is to be provided with an official document indicating his status and the number of packages constituting the diplomatic bag. Diplomatic bags shall be protected by the receiving State in the performance of the functions of the diplomatic courier.

"... in the performance of his functions" would mean carrying and delivering the diplomatic bag to the representative of the sending State in the receiving State. A diplomatic courier, by virtue of the functions he performs, shall enjoy personal inviolability, and shall not be liable to any form of arrest or detention[80]. An individual is thus allowed special treatment as he/she is temporarily engaged in activities coming under the purview of the Convention. He/she cannot proclaim to be a diplomat nor is he/she engaged in any diplomatic activity. Any form of *"arrest"* or *"detention"* would mean that a diplomatic courier must not lose his freedom of movement and may not be subject to interrogation. The provision of Article 27(5) is based on the assumption that the diplomatic bag which may be carried by a diplomatic courier may also be subject to examination by the local (receiving State) jurisdiction in certain circumstances. It is assumed that if a diplomatic courier carries a package which contains non-diplomatic articles presumably he/she can be detained, arrested, interrogated, and if the bag is found to contain non-diplomatic articles or documents, then the provisions of Article 27(5) may not apply. The legal issue remains whether in the event of any derogation by a diplomatic courier from the ethos of Article 27(5), he/she may be held liable. Although, in the main, the sending State will be held liable for abusing Article 27(5), the diplomatic courier will have difficulty in exonerating himself for liability because he acted as the courier. Unless a waiver declaration exonerating himself/herself of liability is signed by the courier, he/she as the agent of the sending State for the purpose of carrying a diplomatic bag will be held liable as an accomplice.

---

[78] Article 27(4)

[79] At the Vienna Conference, the developed States maintained that the right to install and use a wireless did not require consent; see further E Denza, op. cit., at 175–177

[80] Article 27(5)

Under the Convention, diplomatic couriers *ad hoc* may be engaged, but their immunities end as soon as these couriers have delivered to the consignee the diplomatic bags in their charge. The provisions of Article 27(5) shall also apply to a diplomatic courier *ad hoc*. However, the difference between the two types of courier is that whereas a diplomatic courier is a courier officially engaged by the sending State; a diplomatic courier *ad hoc* is appointed by a Sending State on specific occasions (ad hoc) and for that reason, he/she must be designated as such.

The captain of a commercial aircraft can also be entrusted with the carrying of a diplomatic bag, and in that event he shall be provided with an official document indicating the number of packages constituting the bag. But, he is not a diplomatic courier nor is he designated as a diplomatic courier. The bag is to be handed over to a member of the mission authorised for the purpose.

The issue of granting a special status to diplomatic bags under international law is a difficult one to resolve. On the one hand, they must be inviolable in order to protect the confidentiality of information; on the other, abuse must also be controlled; this latter issue has assumed even more importance since the current bout of terrorist activities. Article 27, paragraph 4 is based on the assumption that the inviolability of diplomatic bags is of a sacrosanct nature, and that the obligation in that provision is absolute in nature. But, then, there are examples of abuse of this privilege too: the Dikko incident (1984) or when a crate of drugs was being transported to the Moroccan embassy in London. Mr Dikko, a former Minister of the Nigerian Government, was kidnapped in London and was bundled into a crate to be flown to Nigeria. The crate claimed diplomatic status, as it was alleged to belong to a person who claimed diplomatic status, but did not contain an official seal. Thus, it was not to be regarded as a diplomatic bag, and when opened, Mr Dikko was found.

Again, in 1980, a crate bound for the Moroccan Embassy in London split open at Harwich sea port and revealed that it was carrying drugs worth US $500,000[81].

The contents of a diplomatic bag may be seen by electronic screening while the bag remains unopened. According to the government of the United Kingdom electronic screening would be permissible. The British position was stated by the Foreign Affairs Committee in the following passages:

> "*The Government had given detailed and careful study to the arguments in favour of screening and to the Committee's recommendations that we should be prepared to screen bags on specific occasion if in our judgment the need arises. There is no reference to screening in the Vienna Convention. In our view this does not rule it out, though it is arguable that any method for finding out the contents of a bag is tantamount to opening it, which is illegal.*
> ...

---

[81] See further The Times, 13 June 1980

Because screening would not be a wholly effective procedure and because of the consequences for our own bags the Government have decided against the introduction of screening as a matter of routine. We accept however the Committee's view that there may be circumstances in which it may be helpful. We will therefore be ready to screen any bag on specific occasions where the grounds for suspicion are sufficiently strong. "[82]

Other States did not accept the UK government's view on this matter. The opening/screening of bags by receiving State will always provoke controversy. What if, after screening or opening the bag no contraband is found? However, probably on humanitarian grounds[83], that in a situation such as the Dikko case presented, perhaps diplomatic bags may be allowed to be opened in the presence of an accredited diplomat from a third country (of course, in the Dikko case, the crate was not treated as a diplomatic crate/bag).

The International Law Commission studied this matter in the context of Article 27 of the 1961 Convention and analogous provisions in the 1963 Convention, the Convention on Special Missions, 1969 and the Convention on the Representation of States in their Relations with International Organisations. Article 28 of the Draft Articles on the Diplomatic Courier and the Diplomatic Bag (1989) maintains that diplomatic bags shall be inviolable; that is, they shall not be subject to any examination directly or through any technical or electronic device. Interestingly enough, in respect of consular bags the Draft Article stated that in the event of a receiving State or a transit State having serious reason to believe that a bag may contain a contraband or documents or articles not meant for official use, it may request the authorised representative of the sending State to open the bag, and if this request is refused, then the bag is to be returned to its place of origin.[84]

Article 29 of the Convention provides that the person of a diplomatic agent shall be inviolable. Consequently, he/she shall not be liable to any form of arrest or detention. From a legal standpoint, a diplomatic agent, who is the representative of a sovereign, is not answerable to any other sovereign. Each sovereign must treat any other sovereign without any discrimination and with respect. Thus, the latter part of the Article provides that:

"The receiving State shall treat him with due respect and shall take all appropriate steps to prevent any attack on his person, freedom or dignity."

Article 29 of the Vienna Convention represents the customary rule of international law. The protection due to diplomatic agents is also extended to include the members of their family, to their residences, property and correspondence.

---

[82] The First Report of the Foreign Affairs Committee in the Session 1984–85 entitled *Diplomatic Immunities and Privileges*, London, (1985) at 20–21 Cmnd 19497

[83] See further M N Shaw, op. cit. at 677

[84] See *Yearbook of the International Law Commission* (1989) Vol II, part 2 at 42–43

The need for the protection of diplomatic agents, and their staff, family etc in the light of the current spate of terrorist attacks has been recognised by the international community, and the following additional instruments were adopted:

1. The UN Convention to Prevent and Punish the Act of Terrorism Taking the Form of Crimes against Persons and Related Extortion that are of International Significance, 1971[85]; and

2. The UN Convention on Prevention and Punishment of Crimes against Internationally Protected Persons, including Diplomatic Agents, 1973[86].

Article 7 of the 1973 Convention includes as *"internationally protected person"* Heads of States, or the Head of a Government or a Minister of Foreign Affairs and members of their family accompanying them; or a representative or an official of a state or intergovernmental organisation who, at the time of the offence against him/her was entitled to special protection under international law. Offences in this context would include but not be limited to murder, kidnapping or other attack upon the person or liberty of an internationally protected person or violent attacks on his/her official premises or private accommodation or means of transport to endanger his/her person, liberty and threats, or attempts and participation in any such attack (Article 2)[87]. Each State party shall take measures as may be necessary to establish its jurisdiction over the crimes stated above, when:

(a) *"the crime is committed in the territory of that State or on board a ship or aircraft registered in that State";*

(b) *"the alleged offender is a national of that State";* and

(c) *"the crime is committed against an internationally protected person ... who enjoys his status as such by virtue of functions which he exercises on behalf of that State."*[88]

This Convention does not exclude any criminal jurisdiction in accordance with its internal law[89].

---

[85] The text of this Convention has been reproduced in 10 *International Legal Materials* (1971) at 255

[86] The text of this Convention has been reproduced in 13 *International Legal Materials* (1974) at 41

[87] See further C L Rozakis, "Terrorism and the Internationally Protected Persons in the light of the ILC's Draft Articles", 23 *International and Comparative Law Quarterly* (1974) 32; and M C Wood, "The Convention on the Prevention and Punishment of Crimes Against Internationally Protected Persons, including Diplomatic Agents", 23 *International and Comparative Law Quarterly* (1974) 791

[88] Article 3

[89] Article 3(3)

Article 6 of the Convention provides, inter alia, that *"upon being satisfied that the circumstances so warrant, the State Party in whose territory the alleged offender is present shall take appropriate measures under its internal law so as to ensure his presence for the purpose of prosecution or extradition."*[90]

Such measures shall be notified without delay directly or through the Secretary-General of the United Nations to:

> *"(c) the State or States of which the internationally protected person concerned is a national or on whose behalf he was exercising his functions; and*
>
> ...
>
> *(e) the international organization of which the internationally protected person concerned is an official or agent."*[91]

Article 12 of the Convention provides that:

> *"The provisions of this Convention shall not affect the application of the Treaties on Asylum, in force at the date of the adoption of this Convention, as between the States which are parties to those Treaties; but a State Party to this Convention may not invoke those Treaties with respect to another State Party to this Convention which is not a party to those Treaties."*

In the *Taraz Hostage* case the Court cogently summarised the essence of diplomatic law when it stated that:

> *"The rules of diplomatic law, in short, constitute a self-contained regime which, on the one hand, lays down the receiving State's obligations regarding the facilities, privileges and immunities to be accorded to diplomatic missions and, on the other, foresees their possible abuse by members of the mission and specifies the means at the disposal of the receiving State to conquer any such abuse."*[92]

However, if a diplomatic agent, for the sake of argument, commits an arrestable offence, it is for the receiving State to deal with the matter. Usually, he will be declared *persona non grata*, and asked to return to his/her country as soon as possible. However, if he/she commits a high crime (serious criminal offence – murder or kidnapping) then there may not be any reason why he/she may not be subject to the receiving State's jurisdiction, unless extradition procedure is in place between the sending State and the receiving State. There does not exist any international policy on this issue. Article 31(1) of the Convention provides, inter alia, however that:

> *"A diplomatic agent shall enjoy immunity from the criminal jurisdiction of the receiving State."*

---

[90] Article 6(1)

[91] Article 6(1)(c) and (e)

[92] *ICJ Reports*, op. cit., at 40

This provision is based on the assumption that diplomatic agents are people of dignity, and that they shall not be involved in criminal offences.

A receiving State is also required to accord full facilities for the performance of the functions of the mission[93]. The Convention has not defined the term *"full facilities"*; but it stands for the facilities that are usually required for a mission to operate effectively: these would include, in addition to the usual utility services, protection of the mission, and any other facility that the mission may reasonably ask for. Except for the zones into which entry is prohibited or regulated for reasons of national security, a receiving State must ensure that all members of a mission enjoy freedom of movement and travel in its territory[94].

Under Article 27, a receiving State undertakes the obligation to permit and protect free communication for a mission for all official purposes. The meaning of *"official purposes"* does not appear in the Convention; but it would exclude any purposes which would not relate to or promote the interest of any official business of the mission. Communications must be mission-related. A receiving State shall exempt diplomatic agents from all personal services, public services and military obligations[95]. This is because they represent a foreign sovereign; thus a diplomatic agent cannot be amenable to receiving State's regulations applicable to its nationals or residents.

Under Article 36(1) a receiving State shall grant a mission exemptions from customs duties, taxes and related charges other than charges for storage, cartage and similar services on:

- articles for official use of the mission;
- articles for the personal use of a diplomatic agent or *"members of his family forming part of his household, including articles intended for his establishment."*[96]

Article 36(2) which provides, *inter alia*, that the personal baggage of a diplomatic agent shall be exempt from inspection *"unless there are serious grounds for presuming that it contains articles not covered by the exemption mentioned in paragraph 1 of this Article ..."*[97]

12.12 TREATMENT TO BE ACCORDED TO A MISSION BY A RECEIVING STATE

In addition to treating the Mission, its archives and documents as inviolable[98], a receiving State shall abstain from charging the sending State and the head

---

[93] Article 25
[94] Article 26
[95] Article 35
[96] Article 36(1)
[97] Article 26(2)
[98] Article 24

of the mission from all national, regional or municipal dues and taxes, in respect of the premises of the mission, other than payments for specific services rendered. This is because of the respect a receiving State is required to show to a sending State; both the mission and the diplomatic agent are like guests.

Article 25 provides that:

"The receiving State shall accord full facilities for the performance of the functions of the mission."

The Convention does not state what should include the *"facilities"*; facilities must be full. *"Facilities"* would, in the main, include the following: communication, police protections, emergency services, utility services etc. The term *"full facilities"* is qualified by the phrase *for the performance of the function of the mission"*. Thus it has to be considered in the light of the general functions of a mission.

Unless laws and regulations in the receiving State prohibit entry into certain geographic areas, a receiving State shall ensure to all members of the mission freedom of movement and travel in its territory. Of course, in granting freedom of movement and travel to members of a mission, the issue of the safety and protection must be the concern of the receiving State.

Article 28 of the Convention provides that:

"The fees and charges levied by the mission in the course of official duties shall be exempt from all dues and taxes."

Recently, the Government of the United Kingdom has made missions pay council tax and this practice my be followed suit by other governments. It may be maintained that the obligations under Article 28 are not of an absolute nature, or alternatively, even if they are of an absolute nature, that all absoluteness is not being maintained any more.

Articles 44 and 45 require receiving States to perform duties of an onerous nature. Under Article 44, a receiving State, in the event of an armed conflict, is required to grant facilities in order to enable persons enjoying privileges and immunities and members of the families of such persons to leave the country at the earliest possible moment. Therefore, it is for the receiving State to provide the necessary means of transport for them and their property.

On the other hand, in the event of diplomatic relations being broken off between a receiving State and a sending State or a mission being permanently or temporarily closed, a receiving State must, even in the case of armed conflict, respect (must not, for example, allow graffiti to be written on it) and protect the premises, property and archives of the mission until a final decision on the mission has been taken. Premises will include transport owned by the mission.

A sending State may entrust the custody of the premises of the mission, its property and archives to a third State which would be acceptable to the receiving State. This is because a receiving State, for obvious reasons, would not like to choose a third State which has clear affinity with the sending State and its mission in the receiving State.

12.13 EXTENT OF IMMUNITIES TO BE ACCORDED TO A DIPLOMATIC AGENT AND WAIVER OF IMMUNITY

The issue of the immunity of a diplomatic agent from the criminal jurisdiction of a receiving State sometime provokes controversy. A diplomatic agent shall generally enjoy immunity from its civil and administrative jurisdiction except in the following cases:

> (a) action relating to private immovable property situated in the territory of the receiving State, unless the diplomatic agent *"holds it on behalf of the sending State for the purposes of the mission."*[99]

Thus, the action must relate to private immovable property, and the property must be situated in the territory (including administered areas) of the receiving State. For example, *"UK territory"* would mean the mainland and other areas administered by the UK, namely, Jersey, Guernsey, etc.

> (b) an action relating to succession in which the diplomatic agent is involved as *"executor, administrator, heir, legate as a private person and not on behalf of the sending State"*[100]; and

> (c) an action pertaining to any *"professional or commercial activity exercised by the diplomatic agent in the receiving State outside his official function."*[101]

While taking these measures, the inviolability of the person of the diplomatic agent or of his residence must not be infringed. A diplomatic agent is not obliged to give evidence as a witness[102].

A diplomatic agent is exempt from social security provisions which may be in force in the receiving State. This system of exemption also applies to private servants who are in the sole employment of a diplomatic agent, provided that: (a) they are not nationals or permanently resident in the receiving State; and (b) they are beneficiaries of the social security provisions which may be in force in the sending State. However, if the receiving State so permits, a diplomatic agent, or his servants in his sole employ, may voluntarily participate in the

---

[99] Article 31(1(a)
[100] Article 31(1(b)
[101] Article 31(1)(c)
[102] Article 31(2)

social security system in the receiving State. Of course, within the European Union, inter-State social security system operates. However, the Convention does not provide any rigid policy on this issue; Article 33, paragraph (5) of the Convention states that:

> *"The provisions of this Article shall not affect bilateral or multinational agreements concerning social security concluded previously and shall not prevent the conclusion of such agreements in the future."*

A receiving State shall allow a diplomatic agent dispensation from all dues and taxes, personal or real, regional or municipal, except:

- *indirect taxes, such as sales tax or VAT (value added tax) on goods or services;*
- *dues and taxes on private immovable property situated in the territory of the receiving State;*
- *succession or inheritance duties levied by the receiving State*[103];
- *dues and taxes on private income originated in the receiving State, and capital taxes on investments made in commercial undertakings in the receiving State;*
- *charges levied for specific services rendered; and*
- *court or record fees, mortgage dues and stamp duties with respect to immovable property in the receiving State belonging to the diplomatic agent.*

By virtue of being the representative of a sovereign, the receiving State has the duty to exempt a diplomatic agent from all personal services, public services, military obligations such as those connected with requisitioning, military contributions and billeting[104].

A receiving State may also permit entry of or grant exemption from all customs, duties, taxes, and related charges for storage, cartage and similar services on:

- *articles of official use of the mission; and*
- *"articles for the personal use of a diplomatic agent or members of his family forming part of his/her household, including articles intended for his establishment."*[105]

It is for the diplomatic agent to establish who should be regarded as members of his/her family forming part of his/her household.

The personal baggage of a diplomatic agent shall be exempt from inspection unless there exist serious grounds to believe that it contains prohibited articles or articles the import or export of which is prohibited by the law or controlled

---

[103] Exceptions to this provision have been made in paragraph 4 of Article 39
[104] Article 35
[105] Article 36(1)(b)

by the quarantine regulations of the receiving State. Inspection in such circumstances must be conducted in the presence of a diplomatic agent or his authorised representative. Presumably, the diplomatic agent or his representative will be selected by the receiving State.

When a diplomatic agent is a national or permanently resident in the receiving State, he/she shall enjoy only immunity from jurisdiction, and inviolability in respect of official acts performed in the exercise of his/her functions[106]. Of course, a receiving State has the prerogative to allow a diplomatic agent additional privileges and immunities.

Other members of the staff of the mission and private servants who are nationals of or permanently resident in the receiving State are entitled to privileges and immunities only to the extent allowed by the receiving State. Here also, a receiving State can exercise its discretion. But, the receiving State shall exercise its jurisdiction over the persons *"in such manner as not to interfere unduly with the performance of the functions of the mission."*[107]

A transit State (third State) is required to accord inviolability and necessary immunities to a diplomatic agent whilst the latter may pass through it whether for taking up or returning to his/her post or returning to his/her own country. The same is to be extended to the members of his/her family whether they accompany the diplomatic agent or travelling separately to join the diplomatic agent or to return to their country. So, their immunities are conditional upon: (a) joining the diplomatic agent; or (b) returning to their country.

A third State (transit State) shall not hinder the journey of administrative, technical or service staff of a mission, and of members of their families while they are required to pass through its territory. Ideally, the third State, in both cases, that is, whether in the case of a diplomatic agent or members of his/her family or the other members of the mission, as stated above, should be notified of their journeys in advance.

Irrespective of whoever of the actual categories and diplomatic couriers may be passing through a transit state, the latter shall accord to official correspondence and other official communications in transit, including messages in code or cipher or any other electronic means, the same inviolability and protection as is accorded by a receiving State. A transit State is under an obligation to accord privileges and immunities to those who may be entitled, and inviolability and protection to documents in whatever form when their presence in the transit State may be occasioned by *force majeure* (for fortuitous reasons). In order to remain eligible for privileges and immunities, a diplomatic agent shall not practice for personal profit any professional or commercial activity[108]. In other words, a receiving State is not obliged to accord any privileges and

---

[106] Article 38(1)
[107] Article 38(2)
[108] Article 42

immunities to a diplomatic agent when he/she may do something which is beneath his/her dignity.

12.14 EXTENSION OF PRIVILEGES AND IMMUNITIES TO MEMBERS OF THE FAMILY OF A DIPLOMATIC AGENT, PRIVATE SERVANTS, AND THE LOCAL STAFF

Privileges and immunities extended to include members of the family of a diplomatic agent forming part of his/her household, his/her private servants or members of the administrative and technical staff or members of the service staff of a mission, if they are not nationals of the receiving State, shall enjoy privileges and immunities but by different criteria. Whereas the members of the family of a diplomatic agent shall enjoy the privileges and immunities specified in Articles 29 to 36 (the scope of which has been discussed in this work) privileges and immunities specified in Articles 29 to 35 will be allowed to members of the administrative and technical staff of the mission together with members of their families forming part of their respective households, but the immunity from civil and administrative jurisdiction of the receiving State specified in paragraph 1 of Article 31 shall not extend to acts performed outside the course of their duties[109].

Members of the service staff of the mission enjoy immunity only in respect of acts performed in the course of their duties, as well as exemptions from duties and taxes on the salaries they receive[110].

Private servants of members of the mission are exempt from duties and taxes on the salaries they receive. In other respects they may enjoy privileges and immunities only to the extent admitted by the receiving State.

Privileges and immunities under Article 37 of the Convention are available to the officials mentioned above only if they are not nationals or permanently resident in the receiving State.

The other Article, Article 38, which comes under this sub-heading, has already been discussed under the previous sub-heading.

12.15 THE DURATION OF PRIVILEGES AND IMMUNITIES

Any person entitled to privileges and immunities under the Convention shall enjoy them from the moment he/she enters the territory of the receiving State for the purpose of taking up his/her post, or if already within the territory of the receiving State, from the moment when his/her appointment is notified to the Ministry of Foreign Affairs or any other Ministry allocated to such matters[111].

---

[109] Article 31 has also been discussed in this Chapter

[110] See also the discussion of Article 33

[111] Article 39

Privileges and immunities normally cease at the moment when he/she leaves the country or on expiry of a reasonable period in which to do so, which will be determined by the Ministry concerned of the receiving State. This policy applies even during armed conflict. However, even after formal termination of privileges and immunities, an individual so entitled to privileges and immunities is usually allowed to enjoy them when he/she performs acts in the exercise of his/her functions as a member of the mission[112], but always within the bounds of a *"reasonable period of time."*

In the event of the death of a member of the mission, the members of his/her family shall continue to enjoy the privileges and immunities to which they are entitled until they have left the receiving country within a reasonable period of time[113].

If however a member of a mission who is not a national nor permanently resident in the receiving state, or a member of his/her family forming part of his/her household, dies, the receiving State usually allows such person to withdraw his/her moveable property, but again these affairs must be completed within a reasonable period of time. What is a *"reasonable period of time"* is to be determined by the receiving State concerned in the circumstances of each case.

12.16 ENDING OF THE FUNCTIONS OF A DIPLOMATIC AGENT

Article 43 of the Convention states that the function of a diplomatic agent comes to an end, inter alia:

> *"(a) on notification by the sending State to the receiving State that the function of the diplomatic agent has come to an end;*
>
> *(b) on notification by the receiving State to the sending State that in accordance with paragraph 2 of Article 9, it refuses to recognise the diplomatic agent as a member of the mission."*

Whereas the provision at paragraph (a) is initiated by a sending State, implementation of the provisions of paragraph (b) proves to be necessary when a sending State fails to recall the member of a mission who has been declared *persona non grata* or unacceptable by the receiving State or to terminate his functions with the mission. Ending of the functions of a diplomatic agent under paragraph (a) is foreseeable; but not so under paragraph (b).

12.17 OTHER PROVISIONS

Of the other provisions of the Convention, Articles 47-53, only those under Article 47 deserve comments, as all other provisions except those at Article 50 and 52 (accession by States) have fallen into disuse – by virtue of the Convention being in force.

---

[112] Article 39, paragraph 2

[113] Article 39, paragraph 3

Article 47(1) clearly states that in applying the provisions of this Convention, the receiving State shall not discriminate between States; however, paragraph (2) of the same Article provides that discrimination shall not be regarded as taking place:

> "(a) where the receiving State applies any of the principles of the present Convention restrictively because of a restrictive application of that provision to its mission in the sending State;
>
> (b) where by custom or agreement States extend to each other more favourable treatment than is required by the provisions of the present Convention."

Whereas the provisions at paragraph (a) denote restricted treatment and its effect, historical ties or social ties existing between States form the basis for offering more favourable treatment by a receiving State than is required by the provisions of the Convention.

12.18 WHEN ABSOLUTE IMMUNITY MAY NOT BE CLAIMED

The doctrine of sovereign immunity which has its basis in international law maintains that a sovereign or sovereign State may not be impleaded in the Courts of another sovereign State against its will. In the Anglo-American practice the doctrine of absolute sovereign immunity was rigidly followed until the US legislation – Federal Sovereign Immunities Act, 1976 and the English legislation, the State Immunity Act, 1978 were passed.

Over a century ago, sovereigns themselves were not engaged in commercial activities; they used to perform their traditional functions: to maintain law and order; to protect their country from enemies; and to conduct foreign affairs. The sacrosanct character of sovereign immunity was clearly stated by Brett, LJ in *The Parlement Belge*[114]:

> "The exemption of the person of every sovereign from adverse suit is admitted to be a part of the law of nations [so also his property]. The universal agreement which has made these propositions part of the law of nations has been an implied agreement."[115]

The classic decision on the issues of absolute sovereign immunity was rendered by the English courts in *Compania Naviera Vascongado v SS Cristina*:

> "The courts of a country will not implead a foreign sovereign, that is, they will not by their process make him against his will a party to legal proceedings, whether the proceedings involve process against his person or to seek to recover from him specific property or damages."[116]

---

[114] (1880) 5 PD 197

[115] op. cit., at 890

[116] [1938] AC 385 at 490. See also *The Jupiter* [1924] P 236 at 244 and Lord Jowitt's speech before the House of Lords on 23 November 1949, House of Lords Debates, vol 165, col. 940.

In 1958 this doctrine was repeated by Viscount Simonds in *Rahimtoola v Nizam of Hyderabad*[117], but in the same case it was pointed out that:

> *"If the dispute brings into question, for instance, the legislative or international transactions of a foreign government, or the policy of its executive, the court should grant immunity if asked to do so, because it does offend the dignity of a foreign sovereign to have the merits of such a dispute canvassed in the domestic courts of another country; but if the dispute concerns, for instance, the commercial transactions of a foreign government (whether carried on by its own departments or agencies or by setting up separate legal entities) and it arises properly without the territorial jurisdiction of our courts, there is no ground for granting immunity."*[118]

Again, in *Thai-Europe Tapioca Service Ltd v Government of Pakistan*, Lord Denning, MR stated that:

> *"... a foreign sovereign has no immunity when it enters into a commercial transaction with a trader here and a dispute arises which is properly within the territorial jurisdiction of our courts. If a foreign government incorporates a legal entity which buys commodities on the London market, or if it has a state department which charters ships on the Baltic Exchange, it thereby enters into the market places of the world, and international comity requires that it should abide by the rules of the market."*[119]

Although in *Philippine Admiral (Owners) v Wallem Shipping (Hong Kong) Ltd*[120] the Privy Council stated that:

> *"... the trend of opinion in the world outside the Commonwealth since the last war has been increasingly against the application of the doctrine of sovereign immunity in ordinary trading transactions ... their Lordships themselves think that it is wrong that it should be applied ... Thinking as they do that the restrictive theory is more consonant with justice, they do not think that they should be deterred from applying it ..."*[121]

In *Alfred Dunhill of London Inc v Republic of Cuba*[122], the US Supreme Court stated, *inter alia*, that:

> *"... as evidenced by the* [Tate Letter] *the United States abandoned the absolute theory of sovereign immunity and embraced the restrictive view under*

---

[117] [1958] AC 379 at 394; see also F A Mann, "Sovereign Immunity" 18 *Modern Law Review* (1955) 184–187

[118] [1958] AC 379 at 422

[119] [1975] 3 ALL ER 961 at 966

[120] [1976] 1 ALL ER 78

[121] [1976] 1 ALL ER 78 at 95–96

[122] (1952) 26 Department of State Bulletin 984

which immunity in our courts should be granted only with respect to causes of action arising out of a foreign State's public or governmental activities and not with respect to those arising out of its commercial or proprietary actions. This has been the official policy of our Government since that time ..."

Lord Denning, MR also pointed out that in addition to other countries, Belgium, Germany, the Netherlands and the United States of America abandoned absolute immunity and granted only restrictive immunity[123]. The classic case in which this shift from absolute immunity to restrictive immunity was consolidated was *Trendtex*. It was a claim on a letter of credit issued by the Central Bank of Nigeria. The Bank claimed that it could not be sued in England because it was entitled to sovereign immunity. The plaintiffs disputed that this was an ordinary commercial transaction to which sovereign immunity did not apply. The Court of Appeal held that:

> *"The bank was not entitled to plead sovereign immunity as a department or organ of a foreign state because, having regard to its constitution, its functions and the control over it, it had not established that it was a department of the State of Nigeria even though it had been established by the State under statute as a separate legal entity."*

This was the case in which it was clearly established that in order to claim immunity the actual status of a government department must be established; furthermore, that the doctrine of sovereign immunity was not applicable to ordinary commercial transactions, *"as distinct from the governmental acts, of a sovereign State was part of English law and should be applied by the court."*[124] The Court further held that:

> *"The intrinsic nature of the transaction and not its purpose or object was the material consideration in determining whether the transaction was of a commercial or government nature and accordingly, the fact that the letter of credit was issued for the purpose of the purchase by the Nigerian Ministry of Defence to build army barracks did not make the transaction a government act."*[125]

In the context of this case Lord Denning, MR meticulously traced the history of sovereign immunity and its gradual erosion in the practice of a number of commercial nations. His Lordship pointed out that;

> *"International law does change, and the courts have applied the changes without the aid of any Act of Parliament."*[126]

---

[123] See *Trendtex Trading Corporation v Central Bank of Nigeria* [1977] 1 ALL ER 881 at 891
[124] op. cit., at 882
[125] ibid., see also *Czarnikow Ltd v Rolimpex* [1979] AC 315; *Kuwait Airways Corporation v Iraqi Airways Co* [1995] 1 WLR 1147
[126] op. cit., at 889

The doctrine of restrictive immunity is not altogether unknown to public international law; it was initiated by Italy by making a distinction between *jure imperii* and *jure gestionis*. Whereas the former relates to sovereign acts for which absolute immunity must be allowed, the latter can at most allow restrictive immunity when a State may be involved in a commercial activity. In fact, the distinction between *jure imperii* and *jure gestionis* was recognised by most of the States on the European Continent[127].

Over the last 80 years or so, there has been a complete transformation of the functions of a sovereign State. Nearly every country, through various legal entities, now engages in commercial activities. As many countries have departed from the rule of absolute immunity, it can no longer be considered a rule of international law. His Lordship emphasised that England should be in line with other commercial nations in this regard.

Then came the European Convention on State Immunity, 1972, the original signatories of which were: Austria, Belgium, Federal Republic of Germany, Luxembourg, the Netherlands, Switzerland and the United Kingdom[128]. This was followed by the US Foreign Sovereign Immunities Act 1976[129].

In *Trendtex* Lord Denning also raised another important legal issue, that is, if absolute immunity is to be granted to a foreign government or its department of State or any body which can be regarded as an *"alter ego or organ"* of the government, then what would be the best method of determining the real status of that body or entity. In view of the varying practice in different jurisdictions in authorising and establishing legal entities for the purpose of carrying out commercial or non-commercial activities on behalf of their State, his Lordship did not identify any particular method for determining this issue, other than suggesting that the organisational structure of the entity and the extent to which it is under the control of the government and the nature of the governmental functions it performs should be looked into[130]. In giving this opinion Lord Denning relied upon *Mellenger v New Brunswick Development Corporation*[131] in which case it was found that the corporation never pursued any ordinary trade or commerce; it was engaged only in promoting the industrial development in a way that a government department does. On the other hand, Lord Denning was mindful of the fact that:

---

[127] H Lauterpacht, "The Problem of Jurisdictional Immunities of Foreign States", 28 *British Year Book of International Law* (1951), 272; see also H Fox, *The Law of State Immunity*, Oxford, Oxford University Press (2002)

[128] For an excellent review of the Convention see I Sinclair, "The European Convention on State Immunity", 22 *International and Comparative Law Quarterly* (1973) 254

[129] The text of this legislation has been reproduced in 15 *International Legal Materials* (1976) 1437

[130] In *Krajina v Tass Agency* [1959] 2 ALL ER 274 it was decided that a certificate from the ambassador of the government claiming sovereign immunity was weighty, but not conclusive

[131] [1971] 2 ALL ER 593 at 596

"A foreign department of State ought not to lose its immunity simply because it conducts some of its activities by means of a separate legal entity."[132]

It is by applying the objective criterion of (a) the extent of governmental control; and (b) the nature of functions a so-called government entity performs that the Court of Appeal reached the conclusion that the Central Bank of Nigeria was not entitled to plead sovereign immunity in the *Trendtex* case. The Court of Appeal further held that:

> *"The rule of international law that the doctrine of sovereign immunity was not applicable to the ordinary commercial transactions, as distinct from the governmental acts of a sovereign State, was part of English law and should be applied by the court."*[133]

In 1978 the House of Lords in *Czarnikow* closely followed *Trendtex* to establish the modern judicial practice in regard to the doctrine of sovereign immunity when a sovereign or an entity of the sovereign may be engaged in commercial activities.

12.18.1 The State Immunity Act 1978

In addition to the action that was taken by the international community for consolidating the system of restrictive immunity when a State may be engaged in commercial activities, the *Trendtex* case paved the path of the State Immunity Act 1978[134]. The following are the objectives of this Act:

1. *"to make new provision with respect to proceedings in the United Kingdom by or against other States;*

2. *to provide for the effect of judgments given against the United Kingdom in the Courts of States parties to the European Convention on State Immunity;*

3. *to make new provision with respect to the immunities and privileges of heads of State; and*

4. *for connected purposes."*

The reasons for enacting this legislation have already been identified; in this section of the work only those of the provisions of the legislation which are relevant to diplomatic privileges and immunities have been examined.

It should be pointed out however that the European Convention on State Immunity is limited to the jurisdiction of civil courts and tribunals, that is, the institutions exercising judicial functions, and not otherwise, that is, it has no application to decisions of administrative or executive authorities.

---

[132] op. cit., at 894; see also *Baccus SRL v Servicio Nacional del Trigo* [1956] 3 ALL ER 715

[133] op. cit., at 882

[134] For a very good discussion of the recent developments in the law of sovereign immunity, see R Higgins, "Recent Developments in the Law of Sovereign Immunity in the United Kingdom", 71 *American Journal of International Law* (1977) 423

12.18.2 Anatomy of the Act

This Act has been developed in three Parts:

Part I:	Procedures in the United Kingdom by or against other States – Immunity from jurisdiction (Sections 7–17)	
	General Immunity from jurisdiction	(Section 1)
	Exceptions from Immunity	
	Submission to jurisdiction	(Section 2)
	Commercial transactions and contracts to be performed in the United Kingdom	(Section 3)
	Contracts of employment	(Section 4)
	Personal injuries and damage to property	(Section 5)
	Ownership, possession and use of property	(Section 6)
	Patents, trade marks etc	(Section 7)
	Membership of bodies corporate	(Section 8)
	Arbitrations	(Section 9)
	Ships used for commercial purposes	(Section 10)
	Value added tax, customs duties etc	(Section 11)
	Procedure	
	Service of process and judgments in default of appearance	(Section 12)
	Other procedural privileges	(Section 13)
	Supplementary provisions	
	States entitled to immunities and privileges	(Section 14)
	Restriction and extension of immunities and privileges	(Section 15)
	Excluded matters	(Section 16)
	Interpretation of Part I	(Section 17)
Part II	**Judgments against the United Kingdom in Convention States (Sections 18–19)**	
	Recognition of judgments against the United Kingdom	(Section 18)
	Exceptions to recognition	(Section 19)

Part III	Miscellaneous and Supplementary (Sections 20–23)	
	Heads of State	(Section 20)
	Evidence by certificate	(Section 21)
	General interpretation	(Section 22)
	Short title, repeals, commencement and extent	(Section 23)

This Act codified the law of State immunity by incorporating a major change in the law of the United Kingdom which has been preserved for a considerable period of time. After the US Foreign Sovereign Immunities Act, 1976 was enacted, the commercial and financial markets in the UK felt that unless legislation similar to that was passed, business might move to the United States[135].

12.18.3 A Brief Analysis of the Act

It is to be borne in mind that the Act does not abolish Sovereign immunity altogether; there will be no immunity however in the circumstances stated in the Act. Thus, s 2 of the Act is entitled *"Exceptions from immunity"*. A State may not claim immunity if it has submitted to the jurisdiction of the courts of the United Kingdom (s 2(1)).

In other words, immunity may not be claimed by a State if it by choice becomes a party to proceedings before the courts of the United Kingdom; submission is effective, when a court is asked to exercise jurisdiction. Submission is different from an agreement to submission[136].

A State may submit to the jurisdiction either by virtue of a prior agreement in writing; whether in the form of a contract or a treaty after a dispute giving rise to the proceedings has arisen; however, *"a provision in any agreement that is to be governed by the law of the United Kingdom is not to be regarded as submission."* (S 2(2)). Except in these cases which are identified below, a State which intervenes or takes any step in proceedings is also deemed to submit:

(a) where the intervention is exclusively for the purpose of claiming immunity; or

(b) where the intervention is for the purpose of asserting an interest in property *"in circumstances such that the State would have been entitled to immunity if the proceedings had been brought against it."* (S 2(4)(b)); or

---

[135] See further House of Commons Debate (Solicitor-General, Mr Peter Archer) vol 949, col 412

[136] *Duff Development Corporation v Kelantan Government* [1924] AC 797; this case settled the issue that an agreement to submit to arbitration does not amount to submission; see also *Baccus SRL v Servicio National del Trigo* [1957] 1 QB 438

(c) where a State has taken some steps *"in ignorance of the facts entitling it to immunity if those facts could not reasonably have been ascertained and immunity is claimed as soon as reasonably practicable."* (S2(5)).

Of course, the head of a mission or his/her alternate shall be deemed to have authority to submit on behalf of the State *"in respect of any proceedings and any person who has entered into a contract on behalf of the State or with the authority of the State shall be deemed to have authority to submit on its behalf in respect of proceedings arising out of the contract."* (S2(7)).

S 3 of the Act categorically states that a State is not immune in respect of proceedings relating to:

(a) a commercial transaction entered into by a State;

(b) an obligation under a contract (whether of a commercial nature or not) falls to be performed wholly or partly in the United Kingdom.

This section has no application if the parties to a dispute are States or agree in writing; or the contract was made in the territory of the State concerned and the obligation in question is governed by the State's administrative law.

"Commercial transaction" has been defined as:

(a) any contract for the supply of goods or services;

(b) any loan or other transaction for the provision of finance and any guarantee or indemnity in respect of any such transaction or of any other financial obligation; and

(c) any other transaction or activity (whether of a commercial, industrial, financial, professional or other similar character) into which a State enters or in which it engages otherwise than in the exercise of sovereign authority."

But this provision does not apply to contracts of employment between a State and individuals.

Section 3(3)(c) stands for an all-pervasive provision in that two particular expressions seem to cover everything: (a) *"or other similar character"*; and (b) *"in which it engages otherwise than in the exercise of sovereign authority."*

Thus, the transactions listed under paragraph (1) and (2) of Section 3 are to be regarded as being of a commercial nature to which no immunity would be allowed, whereas under sub-paragraph (3) what is to be proved is whether a transaction or dealing is in the exercise of sovereign authority. The provisions of sub-section 1(6) applies regardless of the nature of the transaction provided that the obligation arises under a contract to be performed wholly or partly in the United Kingdom.

The provisions of S 3 are subject to the following exceptions:

(a) if the parties to a dispute are States; or

(b) that they have otherwise agreed in writing that immunity is to attach to the transaction; or that courts other than those in the United Kingdom shall have jurisdiction; or that the dispute shall be submitted to arbitration; or that the provisions of this section shall not apply; or

(c) that the obligations under a contract would be governed by a State's administrative law. This practice is prevalent under French law.

According to S 4(1) *"a State is not immune as respects proceedings relating to a contract of employment between the State and an individual where the contract was made in the United Kingdom or the work is to be wholly or partly performed there."*

In the context of this work, there is no need to explain this provision because employment contracts issued by a mission for employees of the sending State are not governed by the law of the receiving State. But, it is obvious that a State will not be immune as respects proceedings relating to a contract of employment between the State and an individual where the contract was made in the United Kingdom or the work is to be entirely performed there, with the exception however that at the time of bringing proceedings the individual is a national of the foreign State concerned or that the parties to the contract otherwise agreed in writing[137].

There is no immunity however for contracts of employment where the work is for an agency maintained by a State for commercial purposes provided one of the following conditions is satisfied:

(a) that the contract was made in the United Kingdom; or

(b) that the work is to be performed wholly or in part in the United Kingdom.

S 4 should be read with s 16(1) of the Act which provides that:

> "This Part of this Act does not affect any immunity or privilege conferred by the Diplomatic Privileges Act 1964 or the Consular Relations Act, 1968; and –
>
> (a) section 4 above does not apply to proceedings concerning the employment of the members of a mission within the meaning of the Convention scheduled to the said Act of 1964 or of the members of a consular post within the meaning of the Convention scheduled to the said Act of 1968;
>
> (b) section 6(1) above does not apply to proceedings concerning a State's title to or its possession of property used for the purposes of a diplomatic mission."

S 16 further provides that this Act does not apply to proceedings relating to (a) anything done by or in relation to the armed forces of a State while present in the United Kingdom; or (b) to which s 17(6) of the Nuclear Installations Act

---

[137] S 4

1965 applies; or (c) criminal actions; or (d) taxation other than VAT, customs or excise duties or rates in respect of premises occupied by a State for commercial purposes (s 11). Under s 17(6) of the Nuclear Installations Act, 1965, in respect of claims where a foreign State is the operator, English courts will assume jurisdiction, although no execution will be levied against the property of that State to enforce a judgment obtained in such proceedings.

S 13 of the Act entitled *"Other procedural privileges"* has to take account of the different regimes that are applicable to the parties to the Brussels Convention or to the European Convention. However, according to paragraph (1) of this section, no penalty by way of committal or fine may be imposed in the event of any failure or refusal by or on behalf of a State to disclose or produce any document or other information for the purposes of proceedings to which it is a party.

The following remedies are not available against a State:

(a) injunctions; or

(b) order for specific performance; or

(c) order for the recovery of land or other property; or

(d) process against property of the State for enforcement of a judgment or an arbitration award; or

(e) in an action *in rem*, for its arrest, detention or sale.

These provisions are subject to exceptions however:

(i) any of the above mentioned remedies may be available against a State provided consent to that effect has been given in writing, whether by means of a treaty or otherwise; and

(ii) that remedies mentioned at (d) and (e) above may be available against the property of a State which is being used or intended for use for commercial purposes, but in the event of a defendant State being a party to the European Convention, and in cases which do not come within the purview of s 10 of this Act, the remedies will only be available if the process is for enforcing a judgment which is final within the purposes of s 18(1) – Recognition of judgments against the UK, or that the defendant State has made a declaration under Article 24 of the European Convention[138]; or that the process is for enforcing an arbitration award.

In relation to diplomatic immunity, the next most relevant provision may be found in s 14 which provides that:

---

[138] Article 24 of the European Convention on State Immunity

> *"(1) The immunities and privileges conferred by this Part of this Act apply to any foreign or Commonwealth State other than the United Kingdom, and references to a State included reference to –*
>
> *(a) the sovereign or other head of that State in his public capacity;*
>
> *(b) the government of that State; and*
>
> *(c) any department of that government but not to any entity (hereinafter referred to as a 'separate entity') which is distinct from the executive organs of the government of the State and capable of suing or being sued."*

This section implements Article 27 of the European Convention on State Immunity the principle of which is to establish identities of: (a) separate entities; and (b) the circumstances in which such entities enjoy immunity. The following tests are applied by the Convention:

(a) does the entity have a distinct existence separate from the executive organs of the State; and

(b) does the entity have capacity to sue and be sued?

If both these tests are satisfied, then the entity is a separate entity and will be immune when acting in the exercise of the sovereign authority.

Thus, immunity is available to:

(a) a State;

(b) the sovereign or other head of State in his public capacity;

(c) the government of that State; and

(d) any department of that government.

The term *"public capacity"* in s 14(1)(a) should not be confused with the provision of personal immunity under s 20 of the Act. Broadly speaking, the Diplomatic Privileges Act 1964 shall apply to:

(a) a sovereign or other head of State;

(b) members of his family forming part of his household; and

(c) his private servants.

> *"as it applies to the head of a diplomatic mission, to members of his family forming part of his household and to his private servants."* (s 20(1)).

Paragraph (2) of s 14 provides that:

> *"A separate entity is immune from the jurisdiction of the courts of the United Kingdom if, and only if:*

> (a) the proceedings relate to anything done by it in the exercise of sovereign authority; and
>
> (b) the circumstances are such that a State (or in the case of proceedings to which section 10 above applies[139], a State which is not a party to the Brussels Convention) would have been so immune."

The crucial issue is whether the proceedings relate to anything done by the entity in the exercise of sovereign authority. The provisions at both sub-paragraphs (a) and (b) will be subject to interpretations in such case, and the grounds for allowing immunity must be established by objective evidence.

S 14 makes special provisions in regard to central banks, presumably because of the *Trendtex* episode. Paragraph (4) of this section provides that:

> *"Property of a State's central bank or other monetary authority shall not be regarded for the purposes of subsection (4) of section 13 above as in use or intended for use for commercial purposes; and where any such bank or authority is a separate entity subsections (1) to (3) of that section shall apply to it as if references to a State were references to the bank or authority."*

Thus, based on the *Trendtex* decision it may be stated that if property and assets of a central bank or State financial institution are used or intended for use for non-commercial purposes, that is, for use in the exercise of sovereign authority, only then may immunity attach, otherwise not, and in the future, English courts will obviously rely on the *Trendtex* rules for the determination of a separate entity or non-commercial purpose.

S 15 of the Act retains the right of the government of the United Kingdom to restrict or extend privileges and immunities. This section provides that:

> *"(1) If it appears to Her Majesty that the immunities and privileges conferred by this Part of this Act in relation to any State –*
>
> > *(a) exceed those accorded by the law of that State in relation to the United Kingdom; or*
> >
> > *(b) are less than those required by any treaty, convention or other international agreement to which that State and the United Kingdom are parties;*
>
> *Her Majesty may by Order in Council provide for restricting or, as the case may be, extending those immunities and privileges to such extent as appears to Her Majesty to be appropriate."*

It must be emphasised however, that the State Immunity Act does not abolish privileges and immunities that are usually accorded to sovereigns and States. That is why s 7(1) of the Act states that *"A State is immune from the jurisdiction of the courts of the United Kingdom"*, but the Act takes away immunity when a

---

[139] S 10 relates to ships used for commercial purposes

State may be engaged in any commercial activity – this is how restrictive immunity has to be understood. However, the Act does leave a leeway in that it is for each State to establish that the department seeking immunity is genuinely a government entity, and that the transaction is not of a commercial nature. In England, judicial guidelines on these two issues are clear.

12.19 DIPLOMATIC ASYLUM

The issue of diplomatic asylum has been a matter of controversy in public international law. Diplomatic asylum has, in practice, been allowed in exceptional circumstances, based on the discretion of the ambassador. Under international law, there is no general obligation for a receiving State to grant an ambassador or a diplomatic agent asylum, nor have these offices any right to grant this privilege, it is allowed on the basis of local custom[140]. This type of asylum is allowed in derogation of the territorial sovereignty of the State where it is granted. One of the principal problems inherent in this type of asylum lies in the difficulty of reconciling the conflicting claims of humanitarian act and of State sovereignty, unless reconciliation is achieved within the framework of the law of diplomatic immunities or any relevant rule of international law[141, 142]. This type of asylum is allowed in legations or consulates or warships; thus, the grantor of this type of asylum maintains that the grant of this privilege does not interfere with the territorial sovereignty of the receiving State. Controversy exists as to the validity or viability of the practice of extra-territorial or the so-called diplomatic asylum[143]. In November 1948, when a discussion of the Draft Declaration of Human Rights began in the Third Committee of the UN General Assembly, the delegate of Uruguay suggested that a right of asylum in embassies and legations should be included, but he also admitted that the concept was not universally accepted[144]. In the twentieth century, Fauchille showed his opposition to the concept[145]. The Codification Sub-Committee on

---

[140] See also J B Scott, "The Gradual and Progressive Codification of International Law", 21 *American Journal of International Law*, (1927) 417–450 at 443–444, and McNair, A (Sir) "Extradition and Extraterritorial Asylum", 28 *British Year Book of International Law* (1951) 172–203

[141] See further F Morgenstern, "Extra-territorial Asylum", 25 *The British Year Book of International Law* (1948) 236–261 at 242; see also *United State Foreign Relation Reports* (1875) vol II, at 686–70; B Gilbert, "The Practice of Asylum in Legations and Consulates of the United States", 3 *American Journal of International Law* (1909) 562–595

[142] See further F Morgenstern, op. cit., at 236

[143] Although the concept of extra-territorial asylum existed since the seventeenth century, Bynkershoek rejected it; see further *Oppenheim's International Law*, vol 1 (Lauterpacht, ed) 1947 s. 390; see also Reale in *Recueil des cours de droit international de la Hague*, vol LXIII (1938)(i) at 514

[144] Doc. A/C.3/SR.122, at 7

[145] *Traite de droit international public*, vol 1(3) (1926) at 64 at 78

Diplomatic Privileges and Immunities of the League of Nations stated with reference to this type of asylum that:

> "... extra-territoriality is a fiction which has no foundation either in law or in fact."[146]

In 1896, the Law Officers of the Crown stated that this type of asylum does not come within the remit of the duties of an ambassador, and that no such privilege could properly be asserted by an ambassador[147]. Morgenstern maintained that no right of asylum may be inferred from the position of a diplomatic representative, and that ordinary diplomatic immunities cannot justify claims to a right which has no connection with the essential purposes of the diplomatic mission[148].

Morgenstern also pointed out that if an envoy refuses to surrender a refugee (asylee), the receiving State has the right to dismiss the envoy concerned; and that after persistent refusal of delivery, fugitive criminals may even be recovered by force from the legation building[149].

Pan American conferences advocated that the right of asylum should be a recognised principle of international law by means of treaties. Although there does not exist much evidence of such treaties, the Treaty of Montevideo of 1889 on International Penal Law imposed a direct obligation on the parties to respect the right of asylum[150]. On the other hand, the Convention on Asylum of 1928 did not create any obligation in this regard. Article 2 of this Convention provided that:

> "Asylum granted to political offenders in legations, warships, military camps or military aircraft, shall be respected to the extent in which allowed, as a right or through humanitarian toleration, by the usages, the conventions or the laws of the country in which granted ..."

Thus, the sources of obligation are custom and convention. This position was not altered by the Montevideo Convention of 1933[151]. Another Montevideo Convention was also signed in 1939[152]. The parties to this treaty were: Argentina, Bolivia, Chile, Paraguay, Peru and Uruguay. Incidentally, the United States opposed the right of asylum. The Montevideo Treaties of 1889 and 1939 were accepted by a very limited number of States; thus, it is doubtful whether these treaties have given rise to any regional international law[153].

---

[146] League Doc C 196M.70 (1927)V at 79; see also the view of the Russian delegate, Doc. A/C3/SR 122 at 3

[147] See further Morgenstern, op.cit., at 239; see also *Reports of the Law Officers of the Crown* (1896) at 8–11

[148] Morgenstern, op. cit., at 239

[149] Morgenstern, ibid.

[150] For the text of the Convention, see Bahramy, *Le Droit d'Asile* (1938) at 123–124

[151] For the text of the Convention, see Hudson, *International Legislation*, vol vi, at 608–11

[152] For the text of the Treaty, see 37 *American Journal of International Law* (1943)

[153] Morgenstern, op. cit., at 241

Despite opposition to the so-called diplomatic or extra-territorial asylum from quite a number of countries, including the United States, this type of asylum has been allowed by many States. The UK and the US, in particular, openly registered their opposition to the practice of granting diplomatic asylum. In 1895, US Secretary of State Olney condemned diplomatic asylum by saying that this kind of asylum is not derived from positive law or custom, nor is it allowed by international law[154]. In 1848, Lord Palmerston declared that a foreign minister could not *"without discredit to himself and his government, refuse to comply with it."*[155]

Asylum may be denounced unilaterally by a State. In 1867, Peru did so; in fact, all States accepted Peru's notice that she brought this privilege to an end[156]. In 1868, Paraguay abandoned the practice[157]. Some writers in Latin America justified asylum for political refugees on humanitarian grounds[158].

By the first quarter of the twentieth century, the US adopted a relaxed attitude towards asylum limiting its view that this privilege may be allowed for a temporary period only if citizens in a country are under no protection either because there is no government at all or that the government is too weak or insecure to provide them protection[159]. The US authorities did not wish to designate such acts (to provide temporary protection) as acts of asylum giving. In providing asylum to the political opponents of the Honduran government in 1919, the American Minister in Honduras declared that this was done on the basis of his *"belief of imminent peril of their lives"*.[160] In line with its contemporary practice the US Government declined to authorise asylum in Chile because *"there was no immediate danger of violence."*[161]

British practice allowed asylum within narrow limits – only when dictated by the urgent requirements of humanity. But, the British practice differed from the US practice in one major respect, that is, where local usages permitted the exercise of asylum the privilege was not denied[162].

Under international law, consulates have no right to grant asylum. This prohibition also attaches to a consul's residence. The Reports of the Law Officers of the Crown, 1896 stated, *inter alia*, that:

---

[154] See *United States Foreign Relation Reports* (1895) vol 1, at 234

[155] F.O. 72/739

[156] *Reports from the Law Officers of the Crown* (1867) at 54

[157] *Moore's Digest*, vol II at 825–831

[158] Calvo, *Le Droit International* (1896) vol II at 370; see also Nervo, *Dictionnaire Diplomatique*, vol 1 at 207

[159] See Secretary of State Hughes' instructions to the Ambassador in Chile in 1925 in the *United States Foreign Relations Reports* (1925) vol 1, at 584

[160] *United States Foreign Relations Reports* (1919) vol 2, at 378–382

[161] See Hackworth, op. cit., vol II at 630

[162] See Morgenstern, op. cit., at 249

> "*If the* [consul] *refused to give the entry* [for the purpose of arresting any person charged with crime, whether of a political nature or not] *arrest might be made without his concurrence.*"[163]

Under the British practice, shelter in consulates should be extended only to persons in imminent perils of their lives, and that it may be allowed on the grounds of humanity. The consul was to act in this regard on his own responsibility and judgment in each case and in the event of a consulate being besieged, or refugees taken, the consul would not offer any resistance[164].

The American policy for legations to allow asylum only on the grounds of humanity applied equally to consulates[165]. Asylum in warships should be governed by the principles and policies which are usually applied to legations and consulates as warships should be regarded as *"floating portion of the flag State.*[166]*"* Fauchille[167] and Westlake[168] denied extraterritoriality of warships.

What is known as the so-called diplomatic asylum[169] stands for offering and providing shelter for safety by an ambassador to a fugitive or political activist, or an individual holding a strategic position who has fallen foul with the government of the receiving State. In the eyes of the receiving State this offence must have been committed within its territorial jurisdiction. In the *Asylum* case, the International Court of Justice clearly stated some of the legal aspects of offering the so-called diplomatic asylum:

> "*A decision to grant diplomatic asylum involves a derogation from the sovereignty of the State. It withdraws the offender from the jurisdiction of the territorial State and constitutes an intervention in matters which are exclusively within the competence of that State. Such a derogation from territorial sovereignty cannot be recognised unless its legal basis is established in each particular case.*"[170]

But, of course, the point remains that in times of civil disorder it may be difficult to determine who are the legitimate territorial authorities to whom the refugees should be delivered. Unless clear custom or treaty obligations exist between a receiving State and a sending State, a receiving State can always challenge the act of an ambassador of a sending State in the receiving State concerned, which might lead to the closure of the mission. More importantly, the position in international law is not clear if and when a large number of population in a country may seek refuge in the embassy of a foreign country in

---

[163] at 8.11

[164] See further F.O. 35/122

[165] See *United States Foreign Relations Reports* (1912) at 925

[166] *Oppenheim's International Law* (Lauterpacht, edn), 6th edition, vol 1 at 764

[167] *Traité de droit international public*, vol I (2) (1926) at 9893

[168] *International Law*, 2nd edn, (1910) vol 1 at 168

[169] See *Oppenheim's International Law*, op. cit., at 1082

[170] *ICJ Reports* (1950) at 274

that receiving State, as happened to the embassies of the Federal Republic of Germany in various East European States in the 1980s, and in particular the US embassy in Prague, and in 1990 when a large number of Albanians entered into a number of embassies in Tirana seeking refuge. In the former case however the situation resolved itself when by virtue of political changes in the German Democratic Republic emigration from the latter to the Federal Republic of Germany became easier[171].

The legal issue remains whether, in such situations, the receiving State may forcibly enter into the mission of the sending State. The notable cases are the forcible entry made by the US forces on 29 December 1989 into the residence of the Nicaraguan Ambassador in Panama. Again in 1990, in order to ensure the departure of the former Panamanian leader, General Noriega, from the embassy of the Holy See in Panama City, the US forces surrounded the embassy, and controlled ingress and egress by floodlights. The US government apologised and acknowledged that this had been a mistake; Nicaragua retaliated by requesting a number of US diplomats in Managua to leave the country within days. According to *Oppenheim's International Law*, the legality of any forcible entry into a foreign embassy to remove a refugee is doubtful, and that an attack on the envoy's person would be unlawful[172].

Grant of asylum on the grounds of urgent and compelling reasons of humanity, involving *"the refugee's life being in imminent jeopardy from arbitrary action"* of the receiving State may be justified[173]. Recent examples of granting asylum in diplomatic premises on these grounds are: (a) when Cardinal Mindszenty was granted asylum by the US in Hungary; or (b) when the UK granted asylum to Geoffrey Bing in Ghana in 1966; or (c) in granting asylum to a large number of refugees by Sweden after the coup in 1973 which overthrew President Allende; or (d) when in 1975, several hundred people in Cambodia, French and non-French nationals, sought refuge in the French embassy in Phnom Penh; or (e) when the US embassy in Beijing granted asylum to Professor Fang Lizhi and his wife after the massacre by Chinese troops of protestors in Tiananmen Square in June 1989[174].

In 1950, the Institute of International Law adopted a resolution on this matter, Article 3, paragraph 2 of which provided that:

> *"... asylum may be granted to every individual whose life, person or liberty are threatened by violence emanating from local authorities or against which local authorities are manifestly not in the position to offer protection, which they tolerate or to which they incite."*

---

[171] See further *Oppenheim's International Law*, op. cit., at 3

[172] op. cit., at 1083 and 1084

[173] See further *Oppenheim's International Law*, Vol I, op. cit., at 1084

[174] These examples have been extracted from *Oppenheim's International Law*, vol I, op. cit., at 1084

But, no principle of public international law exists authorising such an act, nor does any customary rule of international law require ambassadors to grant the so-called diplomatic asylum, unless local customs require him/her to do so. It is for the diplomatic agent to justify each case of asylum granted on the ground of humanity. However, the head of a mission is under no legal obligation to grant asylum to anybody even on the ground of humanity. In this context, it would be appropriate to discuss the nature of judicial guidelines that the International Court of Justice offered in the *Asylum* case. An asylee, while under the protection of an embassy, is not, however, supposed to do anything which would be deemed to be inimical to the interest of the receiving State, nor to engage in propaganda against the same State.

In the context of this work, there is no point going into the details of all the legal aspects and political controversies pertaining to the so-called diplomatic asylum. Readers may like to consult the very instructive article on this issue by Felice Morgenstern *"Extra-territorial Asylum"*[175], particularly the historical aspects of it since the olden times.

In sum, there exists a dilemma in granting the so-called diplomatic asylum in that whereas from a government's standpoint it runs counter to the principle of sovereignty, it may, nevertheless, have to be allowed from a humanitarian standpoint.

The *Asylum* Case *(Colombia v Peru)*[176]

After an unsuccessful rebellion in Peru in 1948, a warrant was issued on a criminal charge arising out of the rebellion of one of the leaders, Haya de la Torre, a Peruvian national. He was granted asylum by the embassy of Colombia in the Peruvian capital, Lima. Despite requests by the Colombian authorities, the Government of Peru refused to allow Haya de la Torre out of the country. Colombia brought an action against Peru asking the International Court of Justice to rule, inter alia, that Colombia, as the State granting asylum, is competent to qualify the offence for the purposes of asylum *"within the limits of the obligations resulting in particular from the Bolivarian Agreement on Extradition of July 18, 1911, and the Convention on Asylum of February 20, 1928, and of American International Law in general."*[177]

Of course, Peru objected to the Colombian submission and asked the Court to declare that the grant of asylum by the Colombian Ambassador at Lima was in violation of Article 7, paragraph 1 and Article 2, paragraph 2, item I of the Convention on Asylum 1928, and that in any event the maintenance of the asylum constituted at the material time a violation of that treaty.

---

[175] Published in the 25 *British Year Book of International Law*, (1948) 236, and in a very instructive article by H Lauterpacht, op. cit.
[176] *ICJ Reports* (1950) at 266
[177] *ICJ Reports* (1950) at 270

Article 18 of the Bolivarian Agreement of 1911 provided that:

> "Aside from the stipulations of the present Agreement, the signatory States recognise the institution of asylum in conformity with the principles of international law."

The relevant part of Article 1, paragraph 1 states that:

> "It is not permissible for States to grant asylum ... to persons accused or condemned for common crimes ..."

According to Article 2, paragraph 1 of the Havana Convention 1928:

> "Asylum granted to political offenders in legations, warships, military camps or military aircraft, shall be respected to the extent in which allowed as a right or through humanitarian toleration, by the usages, the conventions or the laws of the country in which granted and in accordance with the following provisions ..."

Referring to Article 18 of the 1911 Convention, the Court observed that the expression *"the institution of asylum"* merely referred to the principles of international law, but these privileges "do not recognise any rule of unilateral and definitive qualification by the State granting diplomatic asylum." The Court also pointed out that the Colombian submission revealed a confusion between territorial asylum (extradition) on the one hand, and diplomatic asylum, on the other.

In the case of extradition, the refugee is within the territory of the State of refuge, it implies the normal exercise of the territorial sovereignty. The Court clearly stated that:

> "The refugee is outside the territory of the State where the offence was committed, and a decision to grant him asylum in no way derogates from sovereignty of that State.
>
> In the case of diplomatic asylum, the refugee is within the territory of the State where the offence was committed. A decision to grant diplomatic asylum involves a derogation from the sovereignty of that State. It withdraws the offender from the jurisdiction of the territorial State and constitutes an intervention in matters which are exclusively within the competence of that State. Such a derogation from territorial sovereignty cannot be recognised unless its legal basis was established in each particular case."[178]

The Havana Convention on Asylum of 1928, on which the Colombian government also relied, laid down rules relating to diplomatic asylum conferring on a Member State granting asylum *"a unilateral competence to qualify the*

---

[178] *ICJ Reports*, op. cit., at 274–275

offence with definitive and binding force for the territorial State. Such a competence is not inherent in the institution of diplomatic asylum."[179] Furthermore, the Havana Convention on Asylum was concluded with the manifest intention of preventing the abuses which had arisen in the previous practice. The court interpreted the provisions of Article 2, paragraph 1 of the Havana Convention in the following way:

> *"What the provision says in effect is that the State of refuge shall not exercise asylum to a larger extent than is warranted by its own usages, conventions or laws and that the asylum granted must be respected by the territorial State only where such asylum would be permitted according to the usages, conventions or laws of the State of refuge. Nothing therefore can be deduced from this provision in so far as qualification is concerned."*[180]

The Colombian government further referred to the Montevideo Conventions on Political Asylum of 1933 and 1939 and argued that by Article 2 of that Convention, the Havana Convention of 1928 would be interpreted in the sense that the qualification of a political offence would appertain to the State granting asylum[181]. But the Montevideo Convention was not ratified by Peru at the material time; thus, it could not be invoked against that State.

Finally, the Colombian Government invoked American international law in general, and on an alleged regional or local custom unique to Latin American States. But it is for the party relying on such a custom to establish that it should be regarded *"as evidence of a general practice accepted as law"* under Article 38(1)(b) of the Statute of the International Court of Justice, which Colombia failed to do. The Government of Colombia cited a number of conventions and agreements, but none of them contained any provision concerning the alleged rule of unilateral and definitive qualification. The Montevideo Convention of 1933 was at the time ratified by not more than eleven States, the Convention of 1939 by two States only.

According to the Court, the Colombian Government failed to show that:

> *"... the alleged rule of unilateral and definitive qualification was invoked or – if in some cases it was in fact invoked – that it was, apart from conventional stipulations, exercised by the States granting asylum as a right appertaining to them and respected by the territorial States as a duty incumbent on them and not merely for reasons of political expediency."*[182]

The Court by fourteen votes to two rejected the first submission of the Government of Colombia in so far as it involved a right for it, as the country

---

[179] op. cit., at 275
[180] *ICJ Reports*, op. cit., at 276
[181] *ICJ Reports*, op. cit., at 276
[182] *ICJ Reports*, op. cit., at 278

granting asylum, to qualify the nature of the offence by a unilateral and definitive decision, binding on Peru.

In his Dissenting Opinion, Judge Alvarez stated, inter alia, that:

> *"Asylum, in these countries, is regarded as a consequence of the extraterritoriality of the premises on which it is granted and not as a diplomatic protection; it is consequently considered that such asylum in no way constitutes an intervention or a limitation of the sovereignty of the territorial State, but rather that it is the legitimate exercise of a prerogative."*[183]

Incidentally, in this case the Court identified that a diplomatic representative who grants asylum has a duty to return the refugee as soon as possible. In the words of the Court:

> *"There exists undoubtedly a practice whereby the diplomatic representative who grants asylum immediately requests a safe-conduct without awaiting a request from the territorial State for the departure of the refugee. This procedure meets certain requirements: the diplomatic agent is naturally desirous that the presence of the refugee on his premises should not be prolonged, and the government for the country, for its part, desires in a great number of cases that its political opponent who has obtained asylum should depart. This concordance of views suffices to explain the practice which has been noted in this connexion, but this practice does not and cannot mean that the State to whom such a request for a safe-conduct has been addressed is legally bound to accede to it."*[184]

12.20 THE LAW GOVERNING DIPLOMACY

It has been explained before that custom regulated inter-State diplomacy. The Vienna Convention on Diplomatic Relations, 1961 and the Vienna Convention on Consular Relations, 1963 codified it. Subsequent international instruments, in particular, the Convention on the Prevention and Punishment of Crimes against Internationally Protected Persons, including Diplomatic Agents, 1973 aimed at providing protection to diplomats from terrorists and their acts. Originally, diplomacy was not governed by any law; diplomats or ambassadors were looked upon as sacrosanct; thus they were allowed privileges and protection by religion[185]. It is religious sanctity attached to diplomats and ambassadors that allowed them privileges and immunities[186]. The separation of political relationship from religion has something to do with the inception of the concept of sovereignty in the 16th century. Diplomacy and exchange of ambassadors and other diplomats between sovereign States

---

[183] *ICJ Reports*, op. cit., at 292

[184] *ICJ Reports*, op. cit., at 279

[185] *Oppenheim's International Law*, vol I, Longman (1992) op. cit.; see also Viswaratha, *International Law in Ancient India*, Bombay (1925) 29–30

[186] See further Ganshoff, F L, *The Middle Ages: A History of International Relations*, London, Harper & Row (English Translation) (1970), at 134

necessitated the international community to conceive theoretical concepts to justify the legal bases of diplomacy. These are: (a) the functional representative character concept; (b) the functional necessity concept; and (c) the extraterritoriality concept. None of these concepts, however, on its own, is complete; in fact, they often overlap in their ideas. These are now briefly discussed.

12.20.1 The Representative Character Concept

As the title suggests, this concept is based on the idea that an ambassador is a personal representative of the sovereign. The proponents of this concept were predominantly Bynkershoek[187], Grotius[188] and Vattel[189]. The representative concept, which, by analysis, admits of the *"sovereign equality"* principle, requires a receiving State to provide privileges, immunities and protection to an ambassador and his/her officers and his/her transit. States are also required to show ambassadors and their staff and family the same privileges, immunities and protection. An insult to the representative of a sovereign is an insult to the latter's personal dignity[190]. In 1707, Mr Andrei Artamonovich Matveyev, then Russian Ambassador to England was arrested. The persons who effected the arrest were prosecuted in England, but no conviction was recorded as it was not decided whether the facts made the accused guilty of an offence at law[191]. In England, the courts have consistently taken the view that diplomatic immunity existed at common law and was protected by it prior to the passing of any legislation[192].

12.20.2 The Functional Necessity Concept

The functional necessity concept is self-explanatory. In order to enable them to perform their functions without any restraint from the receiving State, whether legal or otherwise, ambassadors and their officers are required to be allowed privileges and immunities. Perhaps, the functional necessity concept provides the most sustainable justification for the inviolability of a diplomatic agent and his/her property[193]. Of course, certain aspects of the functional necessity concept overlap with those of the representative concept – a representation of a sovereign is sacrosanct; thus he/she must be allowed privileges and immunities by the receiving State to perform his/her diplomatic

---

[187] Bynkershoek, op. cit., Chapter VIII at 44

[188] Grotius, *De Jure Belli ac Pacis (Classics of International Law) Series*, Scott (ed), 1925, Book II, Chapter XVIII at 443

[189] Vattel, *Le Droit Des Gens (Classics of International Law) Series*, Scott (ed) vol. III, Chapter XXXX at 375

[190] See further M Ogdon, *Judicial Bases of Diplomatic Immunity*, Washington DC, John Byrne & Co (1936) at 105

[191] See further D C Holland, "Diplomatic Immunity in English Law", 4 *Current Legal Problems* (1851) 81–106 at 82; see also Martens *Causes célèbres des Droit des Gens* (1827) vol I at 47–77

[192] See further D C Holland, op. cit., at 83; see also *Heathfield v Chilton* (1767) 4 Burr. 2015

[193] See also Grotius, op. cit., vol II, Book II, Chapter XVIII

functions without any intervention by the receiving State. Again, it is the functional necessity concept that requires the office of a diplomatic agent (the mission) and his/her residence, property to be protected by the receiving State. It was Vattel who placed considerable emphasis on the functional necessity concept[194]. There may be reason to assume that the sacrosanct character of a diplomatic agent formed the basis for justifying the functional necessity concept. Vattel pointed out however that absolute privileges and immunities do not relieve a diplomatic agent from respecting certain of the local laws of the receiving State.

12.20.3 The Extraterritoriality Concept

This concept is based on the notion that an ambassador or a diplomatic agent can never be part of the receiving State; he/she does not belong to the receiving State. Thus, metaphorically speaking, an ambassador or a diplomatic agent, while in a receiving State, still lives in his/her sending State; the jurisdiction of the sending State is simply extended extra-territorially (beyond the boundaries of the sending State) to include the receiving State for diplomatic purposes. While an ambassador or a diplomatic agent, he still lives in his/her own country. Thus, *"missions"* and diplomatic agents' residences are treated as the territory of the sending State. The extraterritoriality concept is based on the principle of sovereign equality in international law; it also shares tenets of the *"representative concept"*. This concept also justifies why privileges and immunities should be granted to ambassadors or diplomatic agents. In both its draft Conventions of 1891 and 1929 the Institute of International Law rejected the extraterritoriality concept, and the American Institute of International Law also rejected it as a fiction[195]. The Harvard Research Draft Convention on Diplomatic Privileges and Immunities pointed out that the extraterritoriality concept was not referred to in formulating the Draft Convention[196].

It has been established that in reality it is extremely difficult to separate any of these concepts from the other. They share certain common attributes. However, it would be interesting to see the extent to which courts have relied on these concepts in dealing with cases relating to the status of ambassadors or diplomatic agents.

The Parlement Belge[197]

In this case proceedings *in rem* on behalf of the owners of the *Daring* were instituted in the Admiralty Division against *Parlement Belge* to recover redress in respect of a collision. A writ was served in the prescribed manner on board the *Parlement Belge*. The judge of the Admiralty Division allowed the warrant

---

[194] Vattel, op. cit., Book IV, Chapter VIII

[195] See the *Draft Convention of American Institute of International Law* (Article 23); Diena Report

[196] *Draft Convention on Diplomatic Privileges and Immunities*, 26 *American Journal of International Law (1932)* 26

[197] (1880) 5 PD 197

of arrest to be issued. The Attorney-General appealed. The plaintiff alleged that the *Parlement Belge* was a mail packet running between Ostend and Dover and that one of the packets was the property of His Majesty the King of the Belgians. The vessel was a public vessel of the receiving sovereign and State. The Court of Appeal held that:

> "... an unarmed packet belonging to the sovereign of a foreign state, and in the hands of officers commissioned by him, and employed in carrying mails, is not liable to be seized in a suit in rem to recover redress for a collision, and this immunity is not lost by reason of the packet's also carrying merchandise and passengers for hire."

In considering the *Parlement Belge*, Brett, LJ relied on Blackstone as an authority, who said that:

> "Our King owes no kind of subjection to any other potentate on earth. Hence it is that no suit or action can be brought against the King, even in civil matters, because no court can have jurisdiction over him."[198]

Brett, LJ also referred to the US case, *Schooner Exchange v McFadden*[199], in which it was stated, inter alia, that:

> "This perfect equality and absolute independence of sovereigns has given rise to a class of cases in which every sovereign is understood to waive the exercise of a part of the complete exclusive territorial jurisdiction which has been stated to be the attribute of very nation.
>
> One of these is the exemption of the person of the sovereign from arrest or detention within a foreign territory. Why have the whole world concurred in this? The answer cannot be mistaken. A foreign sovereign is not understood as intending to subject himself to jurisdiction incompatible with his dignity and the dignity of his nation."[200]

Brett, LJ clarified that *"dignity obviously here meant his independence of any superior authority."*[201]

In the *Duke of Brunswick v The King of Hanover*[202], the suit was against the King of Hanover. Laydele rejected the alleged doctrine of a fictitious extra-territoriality; however, he admitted that there were some reasons which might justify exemption of ambassadors, but which privilege might not necessarily apply to a sovereignty; he maintained that the sovereign character is superior to all jurisdictions[203].

---

[198] op. cit. at 206
[199] (1812) Cranch 116 (US)
[200] op. cit., at 206
[201] ibid.
[202] 6 Beav. 1
[203] op. cit., at 207

In addition to the *Schooner Exchange v McFadden* case, the Court of Appeal in the *Parlement Belge* case drew analogies with another US case, *Briggs v The Lightships*[204]. By the Massachusetts Statute it was enacted that:

> *"Any person to whom money is due for labour and materials furnished in the construction of a vessel shall have a lien upon her, which lien may be enforced by petition to the Superior Court praying for a sale of the vessel. The petition may be entered or filed, a process of attachment issued against the vessel, and notice be given to the owner thereof to appear and answer to the petition."*

In *Briggs*, the plaintiffs filed a petition and requested the Court for an attachment and sale of the vessel which order the Court issued, and also gave notice to the US by service on the attorney. The US appeared and maintained that:

> *". . . at the time of the filing of the petition the vessels were the public property of the United States and in their possession, and held and owned by them for public uses, and as instruments employed by them for the execution of their sovereign and constitutional powers, and, therefore, not subject to the process or jurisdiction of the Court."*[205]

The Court gave judgment declining the jurisdiction. Brett, LJ pointed out that:

> *"The immunity from such interference arises, not because they are instruments of war, but because they are instruments of sovereignty."*[206]

The property in issue must be regarded and seen to be as public property for the purpose of seeking waiver from jurisdiction.

With reference to the judgment in *De Haber v The Queen of Portugal*[207], Brett LJ commented that:

> *". . . that the immunity of the sovereign is at least as great as the immunity of an ambassador but as the Statute declares that the law is, and always has been, not only that an ambassador is free from present suit or but that his goods are free from such process as distress or seizure, the latter meaning seizure by process of law, it follows that the goods of every sovereign are free from any seizure by process of law."*[208]

The concept of sovereign immunity was so well-grounded even in the 19th century, that Brett, LJ further stated that:

> *"It has been held that an ambassador cannot be personally sued, although he has traded; . . . because . . . a suit would be inconsistent with the independence*

---

[204] 11 Allen, 157

[205] op. cit., at 211

[206] op. cit., at 212

[207] 17 QB 171

[208] *The Parlement Belge*, op. cit., at 214; see also *Vavasseur v Krupp* 9 Ch D 351

and equality of the State which he represents. If the remedy sought by an action in rem against public property is, as we think it is, an indirect mode of exercising the authority of the Court against the owner of the property, then the attempt to exercise such an authority is an attempt inconsistent with the independence and equality of the State which is represented by such owner."[209]

From the judgments in these cases it may be inferred that both the English and US Courts declined to assume jurisdiction over ambassadors or their properties or the properties belonging to States not necessarily on the grounds of the extraterritoriality concept, but on the representative character concept combined with the functional necessity concept.

During the negotiation stages of the Vienna Convention on Diplomatic Relations, the role of the representative character concept was discussed and questioned by the International Law Commission on the grounds that this concept was less frequently invoked[210]. It further stated that the principle of the sovereign equality of States does not necessarily provide the justification for granting ambassadors or diplomatic agents privileges and immunities[211].

The functional necessity concept received a mixed reception as a basis for the grant of privileges and immunities. Some of the members of the International Law Commission did not find it necessary to discuss the theoretical bases for diplomatic privileges and immunities in drafting the Convention, although they may be referred to or considered where relevant[212]. However, in general, in the event of any controversy or interpretational difficulty in regard to a draft article, the International Law Commission was primarily guided by the functional necessity concept presumably because, as stated above, no restraint must be placed by a receiving State on ambassadors / diplomatic agents in performing their functions. Thus they must be allowed privileges and immunities. Indeed, the Preamble to the Vienna Convention of 1961 provides that:

> *"Realising that the purpose of such privileges and immunities is not to benefit individuals but to ensure the efficient performance of the functions of diplomatic mission as representing States."*

Privileges and immunities are primarily granted for the performance of functions by ambassadors or diplomatic agents; protection of their person and property becomes necessary so that they can perform their functions. This

---

[209] *The Parlement Belge*, op. cit., at 220

[210] See UN Doc A/CN.4/98, 1956 See UN Doc A/CN.4/98, 1956 *Year Book of the International Law Commission*, vol. II at 159

[211] ibid., 160

[212] See the views of Tunkin and Yokota in the *Year Book of the International Law Commission* (1957) vol I respectively at 5 and 3. Fitzmaurice disagreed, ibid., at 2

view was advocated by the Mexican delegate[213], supported by Argentina, Panama, Portugal, Spain, Switzerland and Venezuela.

That there was a theoretical basis of diplomatic law was rejected by the Union of Soviet Socialist Republics[214]. The Federal Republic of Germany and Romania held similar views too[215]. Iraq pointed out that the Convention should be considered in the light of all the concepts on which diplomatic privileges and immunities were based, and not according to any single concept[216]. Whereas the Spanish delegate advocated an inclusion of the representative character concept in the Preamble to the Convention[217], the Irish delegate was concerned that the functional necessity concept should not be discarded[218].

By a process of elimination it may be concluded that the role of the extraterritoriality concept did receive much attention in the drafting of the Convention. Tunkin pointed out to the Conference that the International Law Commission appropriately recognised the role of the representative character concept; of course, one should appreciate that the basis for diplomatic privileges and immunities cannot solely be the *"functional necessity concept"*; thus the Vienna Convention on Diplomatic Relations, 1961 is based on both the representative character concept and the functional necessity concept. Indeed, the Preamble to the Convention has also incorporated these two concepts.

12.21 HEADS OF STATE

Although Heads of States are not governed by the Vienna Convention on Diplomatic Relations, 1961, it is opportune to briefly discuss their status and the sources of privileges and immunities in international law.

As the title suggests, the Head of State holds the most prestigious position in any State. He or she is the head of a sovereign State. The Head can be a monarch or a President or may hold some other title. A Head of a State has no international rights of his/her own; the position of a Head is derived from international rights and duties belonging to his/her State[219]. In the olden days relations between States were often conducted and managed by Heads of States. Depending upon their power, both military and economic, and influence, certain Heads of States became more popular and significant than others. But, over the last hundred years or so, certain Heads of States have

---

[213] UN Doc A / Conf 20 /CI/L.127, *UN Conference on Diplomatic Privileges and Immunities, Official Records* vol II, at 20

[214] UN Doc A/CONF.20/14, vol 1 at 131

[215] ibid., at 132

[216] ibid., at 229

[217] ibid., at 228

[218] ibid., at 230

[219] *Oppenheim's International Law*, Jennings and Watts (eds), vol 1, Harlow, Longman, (1992) at 1033

assumed a formal constitutional role, such as the Queen of Great Britain (the UK), the King of Spain, and the substantive aspects of governance are transferred to an elected government which is usually headed by a Prime Minister. However, no matter how much power a Prime Minister may have[220], he/she cannot be compared with the Head of State, the latter's international status and personality is supreme, which are governed by the customary rules of international law.

Although they are Heads of States, they must act to represent their State; they act, like Prime Ministers, on behalf of their State. One of the primary differences between these two institutions is that whereas the Head of a State is the sovereign when he/she is a monarch, the Prime Minister is not. Thus, a sovereign is required to receive, in his/her State, other sovereigns, diplomats and consuls from other friendly States; and depending upon the constitutional provisions of the State concerned, to declare war[221] or conclude peace.

Logically speaking, irrespective of the size and power of a State, there is no reason why all sovereigns should not be treated equally. They represent their State. Thus, under customary international law, the principle of the sovereign equality of States developed. They are not amenable to the jurisdiction of any other sovereign State; they enjoy full immunity in respect of all matters, except for high crimes. In practical terms, the distinction between a Head of State and monarch is becoming minimal, as both of them seem to be accorded the same privileges and immunities. Moreover, both of them are received by foreign States with equal ceremonial formalities but the modes of address remain different. It is to be borne in mind, however, that under the constitutional laws of States the constitutional position of a monarch can be different in different States[222], but international law does not make any difference between the status of monarchs. A President is not a sovereign; he is a citizen, but is elected as head of the State. Thus, the status of a monarch in international law

---

[220] A Prime Minister or whatever equivalent title he/she may have is not required to furnish any evidence of authority to negotiate or sign a document on behalf of the State he/she represents – see further Article 7(2) of the Vienna Convention on the Law of Treaties, 1969, and the Vienna Convention on the Law of Treaties between States and International Organisations, 1986

[221] The *"war power"* of the President of the United States has been subject of more controversy, particularly his right to commit US military forces abroad without the consent of the US Congress; see further *Oppenheim's International Law*, vol 1, op. cit., Congressional Joint Resolution of 7 November 1977 (War Power Resolution) 12 *International Legal* Materials (1973) 1521; see further G R Delaume, "The State Immunity of the United Kingdom" 73 *American Journal of International Law* (1979) 185; see also *Trendtex Trading Corporations Ltd v Central Bank of Nigeria* [1977] 2 WLR 356; and M B Feldman, "The United States Foreign Sovereign Immunities Act of 1976 in Perspective: a Founder's View" 35 *International and Comparative Law Quarterly* (1986) 302

[222] See further H F Rawlings, "The Malaysian Constitutional Crisis of 1983", 35 *International and Comparative Law Quarterly* (1986) 237

is different from that of a President. The distinction between monarchs and presidents was discussed in *USA v Wagner*[223]:

> *"In a monarchy all the public rights and interests of the nation are vested in, and represented by, the monarch. In a republic they are property of the State. When a foreign monarch sues in the Courts of this country it is not as the representative of his nation, but as the individual possessor of the rights which are the subject of the suit."*

As stated earlier, a sovereign's status is not governed by any specific international convention; it is based on customary international law developed by consistent State practice. This internationally recognised practice has developed, so to say, a code of practice which has provided status with certain rights of request, which are usually complied with by all States. For example, when a Head of State stays in a foreign State with the consent of its government, the government of the Head of State can:

(a) demand that certain ceremonial honours be rendered to him or her[224];

(b) insist on his/her being afforded special protection as regards personal safety and the maintenance of personal dignity. Indeed, the Convention on the Prevention and Punishment of Crimes against Internationally Protected Persons, including Diplomatic Agents, 1973[225], includes Heads of States among *"internationally protected persons"*;

(c) demand that the residence in which he/she is staying in the foreign country be granted inviolability, and inviolability must be extended to include his/her personal belongings, means of transport and other property that he/she may have with him/her;

(d) demand he/she must be allowed to perform their sovereign acts while within the jurisdiction of another sovereign State, whether they are in exile or not[226];

(e) demand that he/she must be exempt from national and local taxation, fiscal regulations, criminal and civil jurisdictions, unless he/she submits to the foreign jurisdiction[227].

It has been a matter of controversy whether the retinue of Heads of States, accompanying him/her during his/her stay abroad should be allowed the same

---

[223] (1867) LR2 Ch App 582 at 587; see also *Jimenez v Aristeguieta* (1962) ILR 33, 353

[224] See s 115 in *Oppenheim's Public International Law*, vol 1, op. cit., at 379

[225] See the text of the Convention, see 13 *International Legal Materials* (1974) 41

[226] This information has largely been drawn from *Oppenheim's International Law*, vol 1, op. cit.

[227] See further *Thakore Saheb Khanji Kashari Khanji v Gulam Rosul Chandbhai* 22 *International Legal Materials* (1955) 253

privileges and immunities including inviolability as for the Head of State himself or herself. State practice on this matter varies. In this connection it is worth pointing out that s 20(1) of the State Immunity Act 1978 does not state that the families and private servants of Heads of States may, as retinue, be fully entitled to privileges and immunities to which Heads of States are entitled.

By the same token, members of the family of a Head of State, while accompanying the latter on an official visit, will in large measure enjoy privileges similar to those accorded to the Head of State himself/herself, but of course, the home State should request the host State accordingly. In any event, the spouse of the Head of State is usually allowed the privileges and immunities to which the Head of State is entitled. As this is not based on any rule of international law, a State may deny it[228]. As to the position of the children of the Head of State, as a matter of practice they are also allowed some privileges and immunities. Furthermore, members of a Head of State's family who may accompany him/her come within the purview of the Convention on the Prevention and Punishment of Crimes Against Internationally Protected Persons, including Diplomatic Agents, 1973.

The nature of the special treatment accorded to the members of the family of a Head of State (not being accompanied by the Head of State) while on a private visit varies from State to State. It is believed that in the unfortunate event of any serious incident in which the members of the family of a Head of State were involved they would not be allowed privileges and immunities for the purposes of carrying out enquiries by the host State concerned.

International law is not clear about the nature of privileges and immunities to which a Head of State may be entitled while he/she may be visiting a foreign State in a private capacity, although, in practice, out of courtesy, special treatment is accorded to him/her by the host State concerned on a reciprocal basis. According to the International Law Commission however:

> " – *a Head of State ... is entitled to special protection whenever he is in a foreign State and whatever may be the nature of his visit – official, unofficial or private.*"[229]

This privilege or treatment may not be extended to include the President of a State. All privileges and immunities which the Head of a State usually receives last until he/she holds that position, and not beyond that[230]. Incidentally, all

---

[228] See further *Rani Kunwar v Commission of Income Tax* 22 *International Legal Materials* (1955) 73

[229] Commentary on Article 1 of the draft Articles on the Prevention and Punishment of Crimes against Diplomatic Agents and Other Internationally Protected Persons, *Yearbook of the International Law Commission* (1972), vol II, at 312–313

[230] See further *Thakore Saheb Khanji Kashari Khanji v Gulam Rosul Chandbhai*, 21 *International Legal Reports* (1955) 253; *Re Grand Jury Proceedings*, Doc No 700 (1987) 81 *International Legal Reports*, 599; and *Islamic Republic of Iran v Pahlavi* 81 *International Law Reports* (1984) 557

privileges due to a monarch are also allowed to a regent, whether at home or abroad.

12.22 CONCLUSIONS

As stated earlier, the Vienna Convention on Diplomatic Relations predominantly consolidated the State practice developed over the centuries. The Convention does present discriminatory treatment between States based either on discretion or historical and social ties. Incidentally, in reality, a strong economic tie between a receiving State and a sending State often forms the basis for more favourable bilateral treatment than that provided by the Convention.

Of course, the withdrawal of immunity from diplomatic bags by certain States has, in recent years, provoked controversy; but two issues should be borne in mind: (a) that certain States have entered reservation to Article 27 of the Convention; thus the obligations under the Convention in this regard are not of an absolute character; and (b) that if all States maintain ethics in diplomacy, the question of opening of diplomatic bags would not arise.

The inviolability of the mission is another issue which received attention in recent years, particularly after the Libyan People's Bureau episode in London, England. But, the provisions of the Convention are clear on this matter. Of course, owing to advancement of technology the inviolability of missions will remain as a matter for concern for many. Again, ethics in diplomacy may provide answers to these issues.

It is to be emphasised however that by and large States do observe the provisions of the Vienna Convention on Diplomatic Relations; infrequent derogations from its provisions by a limited number of States should not undermine the importance of this Convention.

The notion of respect for the representative of a sovereign still remains as the basis for granting privileges and immunities; furthermore, the freedom that a diplomatic agent and the mission would need to perform its functions in a receiving State is recognised by the parties to the 1961 Convention. Where however a State derogates, the provisions of the Vienna Convention coupled with the relevant principles of international law are adequate to deal with them.

The issue of whether the Vienna Convention should be amended to accommodate the new State practice of a limited nature particularly in regard to the opening of diplomatic bags should be carefully considered. Insertion of amendments might not be a prudent move on the part of the international community in that in the course of time the Convention would be subject to amendments every now and then. It is reiterated that the Convention's primary purpose was to consolidate State practice in relation to diplomatic relations, and there is no reason why the generally recognised State practice, which seems to be working well, should be changed. The international community is familiar with the new State practice that has emerged in respect of a limited number of issues, such as opening of diplomatic bags or the inviolability of the premises of a mission. If however State practice about diplomatic relations significantly changes, then there may be a case for the international community to propose amendments to the existing Convention or draft a totally new Convention.

CHAPTER 13

A Brief Analysis of the Vienna Convention on Consular Relations, 1963

A Brief Analysis of the Historical Evolution of Consular Relations

13.1 INTRODUCTION

Consular institutions have had a longer history than permanent diplomatic missions, perhaps because the necessities of international trade and commerce required sovereigns to initiate consular relations, albeit in a rudimentary form[1]. A *"Consul"* is an official appointed by a State to live in a foreign city and protect the State's citizens and interests there. Originally, this task was not as varied and complex as it is now, but the basic ethos of the appointment of consuls remains the same. The functions of consuls have varied according to the changing needs at different periods of history. The technological dimension of international trade and commerce, and the development of international relations, have made a consul's functions and responsibilities more complex.

The purpose of this chapter is not to detail the historical growth and development of consular institutions but to demonstrate how these institutions were required to adapt to the accelerating changes in international trade and commerce and how their functions changed in consequence. It should also be pointed out that in the early days consular functions developed in a piece-meal fashion, and often by means of bilateral treaties, although eventually the common elements in State practice were consolidated, which culminated in the Vienna Convention on Consular Relations, 1963.

13.2 THE HISTORY OF INTERNATIONAL TRADE AND COMMERCE AND CONSULAR RELATIONS

The early development of the consular system may be found in the Greek city-states in the form of *prostates* and *proxenos*. Whereas the *prostates* were chosen by Greek colonists living abroad to act as representatives in legal and political relations between the colony and the local government, during the first millennium B.C. *proxenoi* were appointed in the Greek city-states to protect

---

[1] See Arthur Nussbaum, *A Concise History of the Law of Nations* (1954); Oppenheim, International Law (Jenning and Watts (eds), Harlow, Longman (1992) Chapter 11 and Luke T, *Consular Law and Practice*, second edition, Oxford, Clarendon Press (1991)

the interests of the appointing State[2]. The *proxenos* held more a political than a commercial appointment, and he was chosen from the nationals of the receiving State. This was primarily because the receiving State would find it more re-assuring and convenient to work with such a person. The functions of the *proxenos* included protection of the nationals of the State he represented, promoting sales of their cargoes, proving wills, when a person died intestate, and obtaining security for their loans, where necessary. Interestingly enough, he received diplomatic officials of the sending State and assisted them generally in performing their functions.

In 242 B.C. the Roman Empire created the *praetor peregrinus* to settle disputes between foreigners (peregrini) or between foreigners and Roman citizens by applying *jus gentium* (the law of nations)[3]. The Roman Empire thus extended the scope of functions of consuls (although the *praetor peregrinus* was not totally treated as a consul) to include settlement of disputes of a commercial nature as courts were found to be most familiar with the rules of international trade and custom. It must however be stressed that the Roman Republic used the term *"consul"* for civil and military magistrates, although the essence of current consular functions could be found in their functions.

Lee maintains that with the growth of trade during and after the Crusades the consular system developed, and that the French, Italian and Spanish merchants elected their consuls in the Eastern countries to supervise their commerce, protect national interests and adjudicate disputes between merchants. This dates back to 1223 when Marseilles posted consuls in Tyre and Beirut[4]. But the Capitulations treaties between Christian and Moslem countries during the 15th and 16th centuries enlarged the functions of consuls by giving them civil and criminal jurisdiction over their nationals living in the Byzantine Empire.

By the latter part of the Middle Ages, the appointment of consuls by nationals residing abroad became a common phenomenon in the West. Foreign merchants in the commercial towns of France, Italy and Spain appointed their own *Consuls marchands* predominantly to serve as adjudicators in commercial disputes; exchange of consuls between Great Britain, Denmark, Italy, the Netherlands and Sweden also took place during the 15th century[5]. Consular officers, in their informal status (not named as consular officers as such) were posted by China hundreds of years before she officially initiated trade relationships with the West in the mid-19th century[6]. By the 15th century, the importance of the services rendered by consuls or similar officers became evident; and during the 16th century, the functions of a consul

---

[2] See further Luke T Lee, op. cit., at 4

[3] see further Luke T Lee, op. cit., at 5

[4] ibid.

[5] See further, B Sen, op. cit., at 244

[6] See further, Luke T Lee, op. cit., 16 6

underwent a rapid and radical change. Consuls were no longer elected by the local representatives in the receiving States, but were appointed by the sending States, and they became the official representatives of the sending States. They were required to perform certain diplomatic functions with regard to the protection of the sending State's interest in international trade and commerce; and they were also allowed certain privileges and immunities.

During the 17th century, the international community began to feel that it was incompatible with the territorial sovereignty of receiving States to endow consuls with judicial functions in respect of civil and criminal matters[7]. Of course, the practice of opening diplomatic missions by States gradually resulted in the division between consular offices and diplomatic missions; and the duties of the two types of diplomats were demarcated. This did not however mean that the position of consular offices was undermined – the division simply identified the functions of consuls and diplomats.

Incidentally, with the steady growth of international trade and commerce particularly during the latter part of the 18th century, the foundation of the consular offices was made stronger, primarily by means of legislation[8].

France was the first country to begin a career consular services, and other States in Europe soon followed suit; in Great Britain, a consular service was set up in 1825, as part of the civil service, which was eventually placed under the control of a special department of the Foreign and Commonwealth Office. It was not until 1906 that the United States organised a career consular service. In addition to their career consular officers, many States also now appoint honorary consuls from the local residents in the jurisdiction; such consuls need not be citizens of the State which they represent.

By the late 19th century, the separation of the consular services from diplomatic services was abolished, and States regarded them as a unified Service. For example, in France, the unification of the Service took place by the Decrees of 1880 and 1883, whereas the U.S. achieved it by the Rogers Act of 1924 and in Britain the unification did not take place until 1943.

Despite the unification of the two services by almost all countries in the world, it must be pointed out that the functions that a diplomat and a consul are required to perform are different in nature; consequently their respective privileges and immunities differ in scope. Privileges are attached to a post and not a person; therefore, the nature of the post determines the scope of privileges and immunities to which a diplomat or a consul is entitled. Furthermore, a diplomatic representative is the political agent of his government, whereas a consular officer is not normally required to perform any political functions; and it is because of this latter type of functions that a diplomatic representative is required to exercise much more secrecy of his work, and is allowed wider privileges than a consular officer.

---

[7] See further B Sen, op. cit., at 244

[8] See, for example, the French Ordinances of 1781 and 1833; the British Consular Act, 1825; the US Consular Services Acts, 1792 and 1856

However, by the 19th century, the nature of functions to be performed by consular officers became clear, and indeed, in order to utilise their services in full in international trade and commerce, consular officers were involved in implementing the commercial treaties containing, in particular, most favoured nation treatment or other trade preferences. The Franco-British Treaty of Commerce of 1860, generally known as the Cobden Treaty, was the first modern prototype which has been followed by many other States, although examples of commercial treaties containing a most-favoured nation clause were available prior to the Cobden Treaty[9]. During the 19th century, many Asian countries, China (1843), Japan (1858) and Siam (1855–56), also offered trade preferences to Western merchants in the form of most-favoured nation treatment or the open door policy. It is safe to conclude that by the 19th century, through the offices of consuls, a high degree of uniformity in international trade law and custom was developed[10].

For several centuries, consuls of Christian powers were empowered to exercise extraterritorial jurisdiction in non-Christian countries over their nationals in respect of civil and criminal matters, although exception to this practice was available[11], evidencing the fact that extraterritoriality was exercised in Christian countries too. Under this practice, the sending State's law would be applied to the citizens of that State even if they were involved in civil or criminal offences. Mutual extraterritorial arrangements were also made, for example, under the Sino-Russian Treaty of Nerchinsk of 1689 – criminals were to be handed over to the respective authorities for punishment. Other examples would be: the Franco-United States Consular Convention of 1788[12] or the Japanese-American Treaty of 1858.

The 1858 Japanese-American Treaty seems to have served as a model for many other pacts concluded by Japan with France, Great Britain, the Netherlands and Russia. Of course, the 1858 Treaty conferred extraterritorial rights upon US citizens in Japan, which privilege was abolished in 1899. The Treaty of Nerchinsk became a landmark in the system of extraterritoriality and governed the relations between China and Russia for about 170 years, until the Sino-American Treaty of Wanghia of 1844 was concluded and which

---

[9] See further S K Hornbeck and G Schwarzenberger, op. cit.

[10] For a detailed discussion of the *"most-favoured nation Clause"* and Consular conventions, see *Yearbook of International Law Commission* (1960) II, pp 19 et. seq., see also the treaties concluded between China and the following countries: Great Britain (the Treaty of Tientsin, 1858; the Chefoo Agreement, 1876); France (the Treaty of Whampoa, 1844; the Treaty of Tientsin, 1858; the Convention of Tientsin, 1886); Norway and Sweden (Treaty of 20 March 1947– 1 Hertslet, *China Treaties* No. 93, at 527); Germany (2 September 1861 – 1 Hertslet, No 56 at 331); Denmark (13 July 1863 – 1 Hertslet, No 38 at 249); Belgium (2 November 1865, 1 Hertslet, No 34 at 223); and Italy (26 October, 1866 – 1 Hertslet No 60 at 345)

[11] See S Nicholson's review of Achille Emilianides "Privileges and Concessions of Foreigners in Cyprus", 31 *American Journal of International Law* (1937) at 775

[12] Cited in Robert R Wilson, "Access to Courts Provisions in United States Commercial Treaties", 47 *American Journal of International Law* (1953) 30–31

provided for unreciprocated type of extraterritoriality in China. In other words, a degree of resentment towards extraterritoriality was shown by China. Due to the lack of any legal status as sovereign States in many cases, it was not perhaps possible for the Near East and Far East to register their support for or protest against extraterritoriality.

However, the consular court system seems to have progressed without much hindrance. US consuls in China were given the responsibility for applying US law in China on US citizens and in regard to US matters, and this system was consolidated by the Congressional Act of 1906 whereby a US court for China having the status of a Federal District Court was created.

The powers and jurisdiction of the British consular system seems to have been more extensive and developed than the corresponding US system. The judicial powers of the consuls which were originally exercised under the prerogative rights of the British Crown, were consolidated by the Foreign Jurisdiction Act 1843 by placing them on a statutory basis so as to ensure extraterritorial application of judicial powers. The China Order in Council of 1925 established a Supreme Court for China. In addition, except Shanghai, in all other consular districts, a provincial court existed in which the principal consul served as the presiding officer of the court. Both France and Japan also set up an organised system of consular courts in China.

However, with the end of the First World War, Austria[13], Germany[14], Hungary[15] and Russia[16] relinquished their extraterritorial rights in China. During the Second World War both the British[17] and US[18] governments renounced their extraterritorial rights in China. The resentment against the extraterritorial rights of foreign States became evident not only because of the legal difficulty it imports, such as the lack of justification for punishment of an offender by a foreign law, but also because that it questioned the sanctity of the principle of sovereign equality. However, the onward march of extraterritorial application of sovereignty remained unhindered as many nations became subjugated to the militarily superior nations. Extraterritoriality thus did not have much legal foundation; nevertheless it became a practice for unjusticiable and unsustainable reasons.

In other parts of the world, the Capitulatory and extraterritorial systems became unpopular, and were gradually abolished. Thus, Egypt, Iran, Lebanon, Morocco, Romania, Serbia, Syria and Tunisia terminated the system; however, the mixed courts in Egypt were, in effect, under the influence

---

[13] See the Sino-Austrian Treaty of 19 October 1925 (Article 4), 55 *League of Nations Treaty Series* 21

[14] See the Sino-German Treaty of 20 May 1921 (Article 3), *China Year Book* (1925) at 783–4

[15] See the Treaty of Trianon (Article 217) *Journal Official*, 26 August 1921, at 9887

[16] See the Sino-Soviet Agreement of 31 May 1924, *China Year Book* (1924) at 860–861

[17] See the Sino-British Treaty of 11 January 1943, *China Handbook* (1937-43) at 185–90

[18] See the US-Chinese Treaty for Relinquishment of Extraterritorial Rights in China and the Regulation of Related Matters of 11 January 1943, *US Treaty Series* at 984

of extraterritoriality in that they were heavily manned by foreign judges who virtually administered a foreign legal system[19]. By the Convention of 1937 for the Abolition of Capitulations in Morocco and Zanzibar, capitulations in these two countries were abolished; both Great Britan and France renounced their respective right of capitulations in the other's protected country. Article 10 of the Convention granted to the Signatory Powers *"most-favoured nation"* treatment save the jurisdictional privileges accorded by the Sultan of Morocco to the United States under a Treaty of 1836[20]. But in the *Case concerning Rights of Nationals of the United States of America in Morocco (France v United States)*[21] France maintained that the establishment of the French Protectorate in Morocco superseded the Capitulations Treaty of 1836 in consequence of which the United States lost its extraterritorial rights in Morocco, but the US, on the other hand, contended that by virtue of the most-favoured nation clause it was entitled to exercise consular jurisdiction over US nationals, but the Court found against the US on the ground that the broader jurisdiction emanating from treaties with Great Britain and Spain had already renounced that privilege. The US relinquished her jurisdictional rights in Morocco immediately after Morocco attained her independence in 1956[22]. In May 1952, the Government of the United Kingdom also relinquished to the Sheikh of Bahrain all extraterritorial jurisdiction it had previously exercised over the nationals of Kuwait, Muscat, Oman, Qatar, Saudi Arabia and Yemen, and the Trucial States[23].

This discussion points to the fact that proper consular relations may not be established with foreign sovereigns unless two parties are in effect and from all standpoints sovereign States. However, due to historical reasons certain foreign States, albeit by virtue of treaty relations, exercised extraterritorial jurisdiction in respect of consular matters, but opposition to that practice became manifest and, eventually, the practice of extraterritorial rights was abolished. The decision of the International Court of Justice in the *France v US* case must be regarded as a landmark in respect of the practice of extraterritoriality in that it decided against the US contention primarily on the basis of the contemporary attitude towards extraterritoriality.

In the following Section of this work, a discussion of the modern developments in regard to Consular relations has been held.

---

[19] See Sumner Lobingier's review of Brinton *Mixed Courts of Egypt*, 25 *American Journal of International Law* (1931) 170

[20] 8 Stat. 484

[21] *ICJ Reports* (1952) at 176; see also W W Bishop, Jr, "Judicial Decision", 47 *American Journal of International Law* (1953) at 136–145

[22] See 35 *Department of State Bulletin* (1956) at 844; see further 51 *American Journal of International Law* (1957) at 466

[23] See R Young, "The United Kingdom – Muscat Treaty of 1951", 46 *American Journal of International Law* (1952) at 708

13.3 MODERN DEVELOPMENTS

International consular relations between States seem to have developed in a haphazard fashion; often by means of bilateral treaties, although examples of regional treaties in this regard exist[24]. Modern developments in regard to consolidating the position of consular relations started primarily in the 19th century[25], which developments culminated in the drafting of the Vienna Convention on Consular Relations in 1963. It would be apposite to briefly discuss some of the important attempts that had been made by the international community in this regard.

The basis for developing and consolidating the position of consular relations was offered by customary rules of international law[26]. The subsequent treaties that were concluded on this subject, and the work of academics also relied on the customary rules of international law, which of course were based on the practice developed by various sovereign States. During the 19th century, three important works were published in the form of draft Codes: *Le Droit International Codifié* by J C Bluntschli, *Outlines of an International Code* by D D Field in 1876, and *International Law Codified* by P Fiore in 1898. These works must be regarded as pioneering in that they uniformly emphasised the need for a consolidated approach to the issue of consular relations and recognition of the consuls and their activities. These works were timely in that, by the 19th century, the progress in international commerce emanating from the Industrial Revolution necessitated the interaction between States in regard to commercial matters, and that the need for an identifiable international practice in regard to the consular officers and the consular offices was felt. As stated by Beckett, early customary rules of international law almost solely recognised the importance of the inviolability of archives and the immunity of consular officers in regard to their official acts, but no detailed practice nor any attempt to extend the immunity to other related activities of the consuls or the consular office was developed.

The Harvard Research Draft of 1932[27] was preceded by the works of Bluntschli, Field and Fiore. It is interesting to note that the need for developing any unified consular practice and law did not become manifest until recently. Consular practice seems to have developed in a haphazard fashion and the law relating to consular practice did not receive much attention of the international community, at least until the Harvard Research Draft of 1932 was published. This was perhaps mainly because of the perception of the

---

[24] See further, W E Beckett, "Consular Immunities", 21 *British Yearbook of International Law* (1944) at 34. As to regional treaties, see, for example, the Caracas Convention of 1911, 107 *British and Foreign State Papers* at 601, and the Havana Convention on Consular Agents, 1931, 26 *American Journal of International Law* (Supp) (1932) at 378

[25] See the works of Bluntschli, Field and Fiore

[26] See W E Beckett, op. cit. According to Beckett, the inviolability of archives and community in regard to official acts were recognised in the early days by the international community.

[27] Reproduced in 26 *American Journal of International Law* (1932) (Supp.) 189

international community that interaction between States was to be primarily developed at the diplomatic level. In other words, international trade and commerce and the related activities and matters were not given their appropriate importance, although international trade and commerce always have played a very crucial role in the economic life of the international community. Interestingly enough, some of the smaller States were engaged in consular relations too. Belgium, for example, sent 113 consuls to countries in the British Empire, but Great Britain did not reciprocate in similar numbers[28]; Denmark sent 109 consuls but received only 10[29], the Netherlands sent 134 and received only 13[30] and Norway sent 148 and received only 17[31]. Apparently, the practice developed by the smaller States contributed to the development of the institution of honorary consuls, particularly during the 1930s. The position of an honorary consul was not only prestigious but also impressive. Persons of dignity used to be employed as honorary consuls. Furthermore, by the 1930s the importance of the smaller independent States as commercial States was well established, and the honorary consuls served a significant purpose particularly in relation to issuing passports, consular invoices, legitimisation of documents or facilitating international trade and commerce in general. Honorary consuls were not required to be involved in diplomatic or political issues; they were more like notaries public, although, of course, the latter's activities are usually governed by the legislation of the home State. The institution of the honorary consul became particularly popular among the Benelux, the Scandinavian and the Spanish-speaking countries[32]. This does affirm the fact that at least for commercial reasons the smaller States used the office of the honorary consul more than many of the powerful States.

The War periods intervened, and the entire sphere of international relations placed importance to war and peace issues, rather than commercial issues. Naturally, the issue of expanding the institution of the consul did not receive much attention during this period. Nevertheless, treaty relations for the exchange of honorary consuls continued, and in these treaties emerged a pattern of consular practice. Certainly, by the end of the Second World War, the international community became more interested in developing principles and policies of international trade and commerce. Indeed, the Charter of the United Nations also made special provisions for international economic relations. The treaties that were concluded prior to the UN period served as models for developing future international treaties/conventions in relation to the institution of the consul.

---

[28] See further Luke T Lee, op. cit., at 18; see also UK *Instructions* (1949) ss 527–529

[29] ibid., ss 535–537

[30] ibid., ss 550–553

[31] ibid., ss 553–556, and s 96

[32] See further Luke T Lee, op. cit., at 19

The position of the honorary consul became a matter of controversy, among States, and in particular between the British and the US governments. Whereas the British government wanted to consolidate the position of honorary consuls, the US government remained silent on this issue. Although the US government receives honorary consuls from foreign jurisdictions, it does not send any honorary consul to any foreign jurisdiction[33]. The US government seems to have cast doubt as to the legal status of honorary consuls in international relations, primarily because they were honorary. The legal issue of the liability of both the government and their honorary consuls became a moot point.

Among the model consular treaties, mention must be made of the Anglo-American model and the Soviet model. The Soviet model is based on the treaties concluded between the Communist States, and the Anglo-American model is based on the United States – United Kingdom Consular Convention of 1951. However, the attitudes and perceptions of consuls seemed to be remarkably different between the United Kingdom and the United States. Whereas the government of the United Kingdom primarily regarded the position of a consul as that of an international attorney, an official endowed with representative and administrative functions in relation to international trade and commerce, the United States government seems to have regarded a consul primarily as an officer who would perform executory functions in estates matters. Perhaps it may be maintained that the US perception of consuls, at least prior to the conclusion of the Vienna Convention, was primarily concerned with the estate related functions; the British government took a rather broad and liberal approach, emphasising the representative character of the consul in a foreign jurisdiction in respect of non-diplomatic matters. However, the common features in the British and US approaches far outweighed their differences, whether attitudinal or otherwise[34].

As to the Soviet model, importance was placed on the political functions of consuls in protecting the rights and interests of their States; non-recognition of the institutions of honorary consuls; absolute immunity of consular premises; prior approval from the receiving States in appointing consuls; and in view of the State monopoly of industries and foreign trade, consuls were not to be entrusted with any functions in relation to these areas, which were for the trade delegations or trade agencies or trade attachés to perform. Although the Soviet model seems to be more concise and articulate than the Anglo-American model, the basic differences between the two models were minimal. Nevertheless, both the US and the Soviet Union wished to see the position of a consul more legalistic than otherwise. The Soviet model was more concerned with placing the position of a consul on the basis of reciprocity than the Anglo-American model. The issue of immunity of the consular premises and consul was more crucial for the Soviet model than the Anglo-American model,

---

[33] See the Special Paper produced by the State Department entitled *"Proposed Consular Convention with the United Kingdom"* (1946)

[34] See further Luke T Lee, op. cit., at 21

although in respect of ships and other government owned properties the Anglo-American model followed the Soviet model. It is also interesting to note that the Soviet model ascribed political functions to consuls, as they were representatives of governments which enjoy in most cases State monopoly over economic matters. Under the Soviet model, it became difficult to maintain any distinction between the political and economic functions of a consul. Necessarily, consuls were not required to discharge trade and trade-related issues. It was under the Soviet model that consuls were almost regarded as diplomats; indeed, according to the Soviet model there was no reason why consuls would not be allowed a high level of immunities. By coincidence, from a practical standpoint, the Western States did not object to this attitude, as the consuls of Western States would be eligible for a high level of immunities while posted in Communist States. There thus arose two different views as to the status of consuls in international law; but, a high level of immunities to consuls became a common practice within the Communist States.

13.4 COMMENTS

The process of growth and development of the institution of consuls has been a haphazard one, partly because of the uncertainty of the nature of the functions that the older States thought should have been ascribed to consuls, and partly because in international relations, diplomatic intercourse, rather than relations between States at any other level, was not thought to be the most important. In other words, it was the perception of the States in the contemporary world as to the basis for developing consular relations between States that seems to have hindered the progress in the consolidation of the status of consuls. Interaction between States was almost solely thought to be a matter for diplomats as representatives of their sovereigns.

Furthermore, in many cases, consuls were regarded as agents for conducting the judicial functions on behalf of the sending States. The extraterritorial activities conducted by the sending States through their consuls in the receiving States, however unsupportable, also hindered the progress in the process of consolidating the status of consuls. It has been pointed out that the purpose for which the services of consuls were utilised by the sending States in the receiving States was often questioned by the receiving States; there thus developed a degree of controversy, so to say, against the institution of consuls. Interestingly enough, even the industrialised States in the contemporary world failed in many cases to strengthen the position of consuls as agents for facilitating international trade and trade-related issues. This attitude on the part of the industrialised States also points to the fact that international relations until the UN period were largely viewed as a discipline which was almost solely concerned with diplomatic relations regarding political and military issues between States; that trade and economic relations between States might be a contributory factor for strengthening diplomatic relations between States did not seem to have received much attention of the contemporary world.

Apparently the lesser degree of importance that was ascribed to the functions of a consul was responsible for the lack of any coherent State practice in regard to the status and functions of consuls. It was only in the late 19th century that action in regard to the recognition of the status of consuls was urged by academics, culminating in the preparation of the Harvard Research Draft in 1932. During the inter-War periods, nothing of any significance in this regard took place, even though many of the rules of international trade were developed by then.

It was after the Second World War that a growing recognition became manifest that consular law should be codified. In 1949, the International Law Commission designated the subject of consular relations and immunities as part of the programme of the progressive development of international law and its codification[35]. In 1961, the International Law Commission adopted the Final Draft Articles for an international Convention on the subject[36]. Upon receipt of this Draft Articles, the General Assembly of the United Nations decided in 1962 to convene a UN Conference on Consular Relations in 1963[37], which incidentally, proved to be a natural progression of the UN Convention on Diplomatic Relations, 1961. Interestingly enough, the Conference for the Consular Convention was attended by more States than were represented at the 1961 Conference for the Convention on Diplomatic Relations[38].

By 1963, a number of newly born States joined the United Nations, and they also participated in this Conference, and their aspirations were also taken into consideration. The conclusion of the Consular Convention must be regarded as a remarkable achievement of the international community in that despite the controversy surrounding the institution of the consul, a Convention based on the consensus of States was finally adopted, and which must be regarded as the instrument to govern consular relations, and the related matters.

13.5 CLASSIFICATION OF CONSULS AND CERTAIN OTHER RELEVANT OFFICERS

Article 9 of the Vienna Convention on Consular Relations provides that: *"Heads of Consular posts are divided into four classes, namely:*

(a) Consuls-general;

(b) Consuls;

(c) Vice-consuls;

(d) Consular agents."

---

[35] UN General Assembly, *Official Records*, 4th Session, Supp No 10 (A/925), paras 16 and 20)

[36] UN General Assembly, *Official Records*, 16th Session, Supp No 9 (A/4425)

[37] See General Assembly Resolution 1685(XVI), *Official Records*, 16th Session, Supp No 17 at 61 (A/5100) (1962)

[38] For the list of States represented at the Conference adopting the Final Act, see 500 UNTS 212, para 3

But, paragraph 2 of the same Article provides that:

> *"Paragraph 1 of this article in no way restricts the right of any of the Contracting Parties to fix the designation of Consular Officer other than the heads of consular posts."*

This is because, in evaluating the institution of consuls, States have differently named consular officers[39]. The variety of titles used by States evidences the fact that they used consular officers for various purposes, commercial and commerce-related, although in certain cases the functions of such officers coincided with those of diplomats. The most common titles that are used in consular offices are: consul-general, vice-consul-general, deputy consul-general, commercial agent, junior vice-consul, adjunct consul. Although under the State practice various titles are accorded to consular officers, a receiving State, as a party to the Vienna Convention on Consular Relations, has the right to recognise only the category of consular officers listed in Article 9(1) of the Convention[40]. In other words, in the case of a dispute as to the interpretation of paragraphs (1) and (2), paragraph 1 provisions may prevail.

13.6 AN ANALYSIS OF THE VIENNA CONVENTION ON CONSULAR RELATIONS, 1963[41]

This Convention consists of 79 Articles and Optional Protocols: (a) Protocol concerning Acquisitions of Nationality[42]; and (b) Protocol concerning the Compulsory Settlement of Disputes[43]. The Convention has been developed through the following chapters:

Chapter I:	Consular Relations in General (Articles 2–27);
Chapter II:	Facilities, Privileges and Immunities Relating to Consular Posts, Career, Consular Officers and Officer Members of a Consular Post (Articles 28–57);
Chapter III:	Regime Relating to Honorary Consular Officers and Consular Posts by Such Officers (Articles 58–68);

---

[39] See, for example, UK-Norway Consular Treaty 1951, UK-Sweden Consular Treaty of 1951; and UK-Italy Consular Treaty of 1951; US-Soviet Consular Convention of 1964, see also *International Law Commission, Draft Articles on Consular Relations* and Commentaries. Report of the International Law Commission covering the works of the Thirteenth Session, 1 May–7 July 1961, UNGA *Official Records*, Supp No (A/4843) YILC, 1961 II 89–128. For some of the State practices, see Luke T Lee, op. cit., Chapter 3.

[40] In the dispute between the United States and the Federal Republic of Germany, Dept of States files No. p 81 0099-0596 and p 87 0103-0960 cited by Luke T Lee at 36; see also 75 AJIL 942–3 (1981).

[41] This Convention was signed on 24 April 1963, and came into force 19 March 1967

[42] UN Doc A/CONF.25/14 of 23 April 1963

[43] UN Doc A/CONF.25/14 of 23 April 1963

> Chapter IV: General Provisions (Articles 69–73);
> Chapter V: Final Provisions (Articles 74–79).

The important issues in these Chapters are now discussed. However, it would be appropriate first to provide the definitions of certain expressions which may be found in Article 1 of the Convention.

(a) *"Consular Post"* means *"any consular-general, consulate, vice-consulate or consular agency."* These different expressions for a consular post have evolved in State practice; thus any of these expressions would refer to a consular post.

(b) *"Consular District"* means *"the area assigned to a consular post for the exercise of consular functions"*. The assignment of an area would depend on the need for covering an area by a consular post.

(c) *"Head of Consular Post"* means "the person charged with the duty of acting in that capacity."

(d) *"Consular Officer"* means *"any person, including the head of a consular post, entrusted in that capacity with the exercise of consular functions."* In other words, any person entrusted with the exercise of consular functions is a Consular Officer.

Under the Convention, Consular Officers are of two categories: career consular officers and honorary consular officers. Whereas the provisions of Chapter II applies to consular posts led by career consular officers, consular posts headed by honorary consular officers are governed by the provisions of Chapter III. The status of the members of the consular posts who are nationals or permanent residents of the receiving State is governed by the provisions of Article 71. These officers are entitled to jurisdictional immunities and personal inviolability only in respect of official acts performed in the exercise of their functions, and the privilege provided for in paragraph 3 of Article 44[44], i.e. members of a consular post are under no obligation to give evidence, including expert evidence, nor to produce official correspondence and documents in relation to matters connected with the exercise of their functions.

If criminal proceedings are instituted against a member of the consular staff or in the event of his / her being arrested or detained, pending trial, the receiving State shall notify promptly the head of the consular post, but if the latter is the object of such measure, the receiving State shall notify the sending State through the diplomatic channel[45].

---

[44] Article 44, paragraph 3

[45] Article 42

Members of a consular post who are nationals of or permanently resident in the receiving State, and members of their families are also entitled to privileges and immunities, but only to the extent that may be granted to them by the receiving State. Article 71, paragraph 2 provides however that:

> *"The receiving State shall, however, exercise its jurisdiction over these persons in such a way as not to hinder unduly the performance of the functions of the consular post."*

13.7 CONSULAR RELATIONS IN GENERAL

Like diplomatic relations, consular relations between States take place by mutual consent; in the event of diplomatic relations being severed, consular relations shall not *ipso facto* be severed between the two States concerned. When consular functions may also be exercised by diplomatic missions, they do so in accordance with the present Convention. Consular posts are established in a receiving State only with its consent. The seat of the consular post, its classification and its district are determined with the consent of the receiving State; the same principle applies when subsequent changes to these matters may take place. The consent of the receiving State is also required when a sending State may wish to open a vice-consulate or a consular agency in a district / locality other than that in which it is established.

Article 5 of the Convention details consular functions. According to this Article, consular functions consist in:

> *"(a) protecting in the receiving State the interests of the sending State and of its nationals, both individuals and bodies corporate, within the limits permitted by international law;*
>
> *(b) furthering the development of commercial, economic, cultural and scientific relations between the sending State and the receiving State and otherwise promoting friendly relations between them in accordance with the provisions of the present Convention;*
>
> *(c) ascertaining by all lawful means conditions and developments in the commercial, economic, cultural and scientific life of the receiving State, reporting thereon to the Government of the sending State and giving information to persons interested;*
>
> *(d) issuing passports and travel documents to nationals of the sending State, and visas or appropriate documents to persons wishing to travel to the sending State;*
>
> *(e) helping and assisting nationals, both individuals and bodies corporate, of the sending State;*
>
> *(f) acting as notary and civil registrar and in capacities of a similar kind, and performing certain functions of an administrative nature, provided*

that there is nothing contrary thereto in the laws and regulations of the receiving State;

(g) safeguarding the interests of nationals, both individuals and bodies corporate, of the sending State in cases of succession mortis causa in the territory of the receiving State, in accordance with the laws and regulations of the receiving State;

(h) safeguarding, within the limits imposed by the laws and regulations of the receiving State, the interests of minors and other persons lacking full capacity who are nationals of the sending State, particularly where any guardianship or trusteeship is required with respect to such persons;

(i) subject to the practices and procedures obtaining in the receiving State, representing or arranging appropriate representation for nationals of the sending State before the tribunals and other authorities of the receiving State, for the purpose of obtaining, in accordance with the laws and regulations of the receiving State, provisional measures for the preservation of the rights and interests of these nationals, where, because of absence or any other reason, such nationals are unable at the proper time to assume the defence of their rights and interests;

(j) transmitting judicial and extrajudicial documents or executing letters rogatory or commissions to take evidence for the courts of the sending State in accordance with international agreements in force or, in the absence of such international agreements, in any other manner compatible with the laws and regulations of the receiving State;

(k) exercising rights of supervision and inspection provided for in the laws and regulations of the sending State in respect of vessels having the nationality of the sending State, and of aircraft registered in that State, and in respect of their crews;

(l) extending assistance to vessels and aircraft mentioned in sub-paragraph (k) of this Article and to their crews, taking statements regarding the voyage of a vessel, examining and stamping the ship's papers, and, without prejudice to the powers of the authorities of the receiving State, conducting investigations into any incidents which occurred during the voyage, and settling disputes of any kind between the master, the officers and the seamen in so far as this may be authorized by the laws and regulations of the sending State;

(m) performing any other functions entrusted to a consular post by the sending State which are not prohibited by the laws and regulations of the receiving State or to which no objection is taken by the receiving State or which are referred to in the international agreements in force between the sending State and the receiving State.

It is clear that a consular post essentially performs functions of a practical nature, and they are primarily addressed to issues which would protect the interests of the sending State and the interests of the nationals of the sending State living in the receiving State. In special circumstances, a consular officer may, with the consent of the receiving State, exercise his / her functions outside his / her district[46]; and unless objections are raised by a third State, it may be possible for the sending State to authorise a consular post in a second country (the first receiving State) to exercise consular functions in third countries (the other receiving State). By the same token, with the consent of the receiving State, a consular post of the sending State may exercise consular functions (in the receiving State) on behalf of a third State[47].

Heads of consular posts are divided into the following classes: (a) consular-general; (b) consuls; (c) vice-consuls; and (d) consular agents. It is possible for a Contracting Party to this Convention *"to fix the designation of consular officer other than the heads of consular posts."*[48] It is for the sending State to appoint heads of consular posts, but they are admitted to exercise their functions designated by the receiving State.

The sending State is required to provide the head of a consular post a document in the form of a commission or similar instrument[49], made out for each appointment, confirming the capacity of the incumbent, and his / her full name, category and class to which he / she will be assigned, in addition to the consular district and the seat of the consular post. The sending State sends the commission or similar instrument through the diplomatic or other appropriate channel to the government of the receiving State in which the head of a consular post is to exercise his / her functions.

The head of a consular post is admitted to the exercise of his / her functions by an *exequatur* granted by the receiving State. A refusal to grant an *exequatur* need not be justified by the receiving State. Where the head of a consular post has been admitted on a provisional basis to the exercise of his / her functions, pending delivery of the *exequatur*, the incumbent will be governed by the provisions of this Convention. Usually, the head of a consular post is not allowed to enter upon his / her duties until he / she has been granted an *exequatur*. In the event of the head of a consular post being unable to carry out his / her functions or his / her position being vacant, the acting head of the post may act provisionally as the head of the consular post[50]. The full name of the acting head of the post is to be notified to the Ministry of Foreign Affairs or to the authority that may be designated by that Ministry either by the diplomatic mission of the sending State or in the absence of a diplomatic mission in the

---

[46] Article 6

[47] Article 8

[48] Article 9, paragraph 2

[49] With the consent of the receiving State concerned, the sending State may send a notification to the receiving State instead of a commission or similar instrument (Article 11, paragraph 3)

[50] Article 15, paragraph 1

receiving State, by the head of the consular post or by any competent authority of the sending State. The receiving State has the discretion however to allow a person to act as the head of post who is neither a diplomatic agent nor a consular officer of the sending State with the consent of the State concerned (that was to be the sending State). Whereas the provisions of this Convention shall apply to the acting head of post on the same basis as to the head of the consular post concerned, and whereas the receiving State is supposed to afford assistance and protection to the acting head of post, the receiving State is not obliged however to grant an acting head of post *"any facility, privilege or immunity which the head of the consular post enjoys only subject to conditions not fulfilled by the acting head of post."*[51] If a member of the diplomatic staff of the diplomatic mission of the sending State in the receiving State is designated by the sending State as an acting head of post, he / she shall, unless the receiving State raises any objection, continue to enjoy diplomatic privileges and immunities[52].

As regards precedence between heads of consular posts, the Convention provides that *"Heads of consular posts shall rank in each class according to the date of the grant of the* exequatur."[53] Where the head of a consular post is admitted to the exercise of his functions provisionally, prior to his / her obtaining the *exequatur,* his / her precedence is determined according to the date of the provisional admission. Paragraph 3 of Article 16 provides that:

> *"The order of precedence as between two or more heads of consular posts who obtained the exequatur or provisional admission on the same date shall be determined according to the dates on which their commissions or similar instruments or the notifications ... were presented to the receiving State."*

Acting heads of posts rank after all heads of consular posts and, as between themselves, they rank according to the dates on which they assumed their functions as acting heads of posts. Honorary consular officers who are heads of consular posts rank in each class after career heads of consular posts[54]. Heads of consular posts have precedence over consular officers not having that status[55]. The order of precedence as between consular officers and any change thereof shall be notified to the Ministry of Foreign Affairs or any other authority designated by that Ministry by the diplomatic mission of the sending State, and if it has no mission in the receiving State, then by the head of the consular post.

If no diplomatic mission of a sending State exists in a receiving State, nor is the sending State represented in the receiving State by a diplomatic mission of

---

[51] Article 15(3)

[52] Article 15(4)

[53] Article 16(1)

[54] Article 16, paragraph 5

[55] Article 16, paragraph 6

a third State, a consular officer may, with the consent of the receiving State be authorised to perform diplomatic functions, but he / she shall only be allowed privileges and immunities to which he / she is entitled under the present Convention. But when a consular officer after notifying the receiving State may act as representative of the sending State to any inter-governmental organisation, he / she shall be entitled to enjoy privileges and immunities as allowed by customary international law or by international agreements. *"Two or more States may, with the consent of the receiving State, appoint the same person as a consular officer in that State."*[56]

A receiving State has the discretionary power to determine the size of the consular staff[57], and it is only after the size of the consular staff has been determined that the sending State appoints the members of the consular staff. The full names, categories and classes of all consular officers, other than the head of a consular post, must be notified by the sending State to the receiving State in sufficient time in order to enable the latter to consider whether any nomination is unacceptable, and if it is so declared, the sending State shall withdraw his / her appointment[58]. In such an event, the receiving State is not obliged to give the sending State any reason for its decision. If the laws and regulations in the receiving State so require, it may grant an *exequatur* to a consular officer other than the the head of consular post. In principle, consular officers should have the nationality of the sending State; a person having the nationality of the receiving State may be appointed as a consular officer only with the express consent of that State, which may be withdrawn at any time. The same right may be exercised by the receiving State in respect of nationals of a third State[59].

The receiving State may at any time, without giving any reasons, declare a consular officer *persona non grata*, and in that event the sending State should recall the officer within a reasonable time, otherwise the receiving State may either withdraw the *exequatur* form the officer concerned, or cease to consider him / her as a member of the consular staff[60].

The sending State is required to notify the Ministry of Foreign Affairs or the authority designated by the Ministry of:

(a) the appointment of members of a consular post, their arrival dates and final departure dates or the date of termination of their functions and *"any other changes affecting their status that may occur in the course of their service with the consular post;"*[61]

---

[56] Article 18

[57] Article 20

[58] Article 19 and Article 23, paragraph 3

[59] Article 22

[60] Article 23, paragraphs (1) and (2)

[61] Article 24(1)(a)

(b) the dates of arrival and final departures of the persons belonging to the family of a member of the consular post which must form part of his / her household or when such persons become or cease to be members of his / her family. This means that all new members that may be added to the family or if any person leaves the family, the Ministry of Foreign Affairs or its designated office must be notified of the changes;

(c) the dates of arrival and departures of the members of the private staff, where allowed, and of the termination of their service; and

(d) *"the engagement and discharge of persons resident in the receiving State as members of a consular post or as members of the private staff entitled to privileges and immunities."*[62]

The functions of a member of a consular post comes to an end in one of the following ways:

– where the sending State notifies the receiving State that his / her functions have come to an end;

– if the *exequatur* is withdrawn by the receiving State;

– when the receiving State notifies the sending State that it has ceased to consider a member part of the consular staff.

At the time of departure, even during armed conflict, the receiving State shall grant members of the consular post, private staff of the members, and members of their families forming part of their households the necessary time and facilities to enable them to prepare for their departure and to leave at the earliest possible opportunity. In case of need, the receiving State shall provide means of transport too. The obligation of a receiving State does not extend however to include the nationals of the receiving State who are members of the consular post.

In the event of the severance of consular relations between the two States, the receiving State shall, even in case of armed conflict, respect and protect the consular premises, including the property of the consular post and consular archives. The sending State has the discretion to entrust the custody of the consular premises, including its property and archives, to a third State, but only with the consent of the receiving State. By the same token, the sending State may entrust the protection of its interests and those of its nationals to a third State with the consent of the receiving State[63]. Similar provisions apply when the diplomatic mission or the consular post of the sending State may be closed temporarily or permanently.

---

[62] Article 24(1)(d)

[63] Article 27

Chapter I of the Convention is thus concerned with the establishment of consular relations between States.

13.7.1 Facilities, Privileges and Immunities Relating to Consular Posts, Career Consular Officers and Other Members of a Consular Post

The receiving State must ensure that full facilities are accorded to the consular post for the performance of its functions. The receiving State cannot object to the use of the national flag and coat-of-arms of the sending State on the building occupied by the consular post, and the residence of the head of the consular post, in addition to his / her means of transport when used on official business. The receiving State shall either facilitate or assist the sending State in the acquisition of premises in the jurisdiction of the former. The receiving State shall also assist the consular post in obtaining suitable accommodation for its members[64] or of the head of the diplomatic mission of the sending State. However, the consent of the head of the consular post may be assumed in case of fire or other disaster which requires prompt protective action. A receiving State has a special obligation to take appropriate steps to protect the consular premises against any intrusion or damage to the premises and to *"prevent any disturbance of the peace of the consular post or impairment of its dignity."*[65] *"The Consular premises, their furnishings, the property of the consular post and its means of transport for purposes of national defence or public utility;"*[66] however, if expropriation is deemed necessary, the consular functions should be allowed to be performed in their normal ways, and prompt, appropriate and effective compensation shall be paid to the sending State. Incidentally, this provision does not appear in the Vienna Convention on Diplomatic Relations, 1961.

Consular premises and residence of the career head of the consular post of which the sending State is the owner or lessee are exempt from all national, regional or municipal dues and taxes, other than those that may represent payment for specific services rendered[67]. *"The consular archives and documents shall be inviolable at all times and wherever they may be."*[68]

The consular post must be allowed freedom of movement and freedom of communication by the receiving State. Freedom of movement in this context is however subject to the receiving country's laws and regulations concerning zones entry, and for reasons of national security. According to the Convention, the consular post may install and use a wireless transmitter only with the consent of the receiving State. The official correspondence, that is, all

---

[64] Article 30

[65] Article 31(3)

[66] Article 31(4)

[67] Article 32(1)

[68] Article 33. On this issue please see the section on inviolability of diplomatic premises in Chapter 12.

correspondence relating to the consular post and its functions, shall be inviolable. By the same token, the consular bag, according to the Convention shall be neither opened nor detained. This inviolability is subject to exceptions. Article 35, paragraph 3 provides, *inter alia*, that:

> *"The consular bag shall be neither opened nor detained. Nevertheless, if the competent authorities of the receiving State have serious reason to believe that the bag contains something other than the correspondence, documents or articles referred to in paragraph 4 of this Article, they may request that the bag be opened in their presence by an authorized representative of the sending State. If this request is refused by the authorities of the sending State, the bag shall be returned to its place of origin."*

Similar kind of provisions may also be found in the Vienna Convention on Diplomatic Relations, 1961, and this issue has received attention in Chapter 12 of this work.

However, consular bags must bear visible external marks of their character and may contain only official correspondence and documents or articles intended exclusively for official use[69]. These bags are usually carried by a consular courier. A courier should ideally be a national of the sending State, unless the receiving State gives its consent to the appointment of some other. While on duty, a consular courier shall be protected by the receiving State. He / she enjoys personal inviolability and shall not be liable to any form of arrest or detention. Consular couriers *ad hoc* may also be appointed, but in respect of such couriers the immunities cease to apply when he / she delivers to the consignee the consular bag[70].

A consular bag may be entrusted to the captain of a ship or of a commercial aircraft. He is provided with an official document evidencing the number of packages constituting the bag, but he cannot be considered to be a consular courier. It is possible for the consular post to arrange collection of the bag from the captain of the ship or of the aircraft.

Article 36 of the Convention is concerned with communications and contact with nationals of the sending State, which is one of the most important functions of a consular post. Consular officers are allowed freedom to communicate with nationals of the sending State, and *vice versa*.

In the event of a national of the sending State being arrested in the receiving State or committed to prison or to custody pending trial or is detained in any other manner, the receiving State has a duty to inform the consular post without delay. The receiving State has also the duty to inform the person concerned of his rights without delay.

Consular officers will have the right to visit a national of the sending State who is in prison, custody or detention, to converse and correspond with him

---

[69] Article 35(4)

[70] Article 35(6)

and to arrange for his legal representation[71]. Consular officers cannot take action on behalf of a national of the sending State who is in the prison, custody or detention if he expressly opposes such action[72].

In the event of the death of a national of the sending State or of a guardian or trustee being appointed in the interest of a minor or any other person lacking full capacity, the competent authorities of the receiving State have a duty to inform the consular post, without delay, if this information is available to them. By the same token, if a vessel having the nationality of the sending State is wrecked or runs aground in the territorial sea of the receiving State or if an aircraft registered in the sending State suffers an accident on the territory of the receiving State, the consular post nearest to the scene of the incident must be informed of the incident by the competent authorities of the receiving State without delay, if the information is available to them[73].

In 1998, a new situation arose under Article 36, sub-paragraph 1(b) of the Consular Convention, 1963 which led to a dispute between Germany and the United States.

Case Concerning the Vienna Convention on Consular Relations: Germany v United States of America Request for the Indication of Provisional Measures Provisional Measures Order issued by ICJ on 3/3/99[74]

In 1982, the state of Arizona (US) authorities detained, tried and sentenced to death Karl and Walter LaGrand, two German nationals, without having been informed of their rights, as required under Article 36, sub-paragraph 1(b) of the Vienna Convention on Consular Relations 1963. Under the same provisions of the Convention, the competent authorities in Germany were required to be advised *"without delay"* in order to allow the nationals' right to seek consular assistance. The competent authorities in Germany alleged that the failure to notify precluded them from protecting their nationals' interests in the United States provided for by Articles 5 and 36 of the Vienna Convention at both the trial and the appeal stages in the US courts.

The State of Arizona maintained that until recently, that is prior to referring the matter to the ICJ by Germany, they were unaware of the fact that Karl and Walter LaGrand were nationals of Germany, although that was proved to be untrue, and evidence to that effect was made available to the Arizona Mercy Committee on 23 February 1999.

However, in their application for the Indication of Provisional Measures, Germany stated that the victims, eventually, with the assistance of German

---

[71] Article 36 (1)(c)
[72] Article 36(1)(c)
[73] Article 37
[74] 38 ILM 308 (1999)

Consular Officers, did claim violations of the Vienna Convention before the Federal Court of First Instance, but the said court applying the municipal doctrine of *"procedure default"* decided that by virtue of the failure of the victims to assert their rights under the Convention in the proceedings at the State level they would be barred from asserting them before the Federal *habeas corpus* proceedings. The intermediate federal appellate court affirmed this decision.

Karl LaGrand was executed by the US authorities on 24 February 1999, despite all appeals for clemency and numerous diplomatic interventions by the German Government at the highest level, and Walter LaGrand was sentenced for his execution on 3 March 1999 pursuant to Article 41 of the Statute of the Court and Articles 73, 74 and 75 of the Rules of the Court. On 2 March 1999, Germany filed an application with the Registry of the International Court of Justice requesting provisional measures in order to ensure that the execution of Walter LaGrand did not take place as scheduled.

Germany emphasised that:

> *"The importance and security of an individual human life are well established in international law. As recognised by Article 6 of the International Covenant on Civil and Political Rights, every human being has the inherent right to life and this right shall be protected by law."*[75]

Germany asked the Court to indicate that:

> *"The United States should take all measures at its disposal to ensure that Walter LaGrand is not executed pending the final decision in these proceedings, and it should inform the court of all the measures which it has taken in implementation of that Order."*[76]

In view of the extreme urgency of the matter, Germany, relying upon Article 75 of the Rules of the Court, asked the Court to indicate forthwith provisional measures, *proprio motu*, which the US opposed.

The Jurisdictional Issues

Germany based the jurisdiction of the Court on Article 36, paragraph 1 of the Statute of the ICJ and on Article 1 of the Optional Protocol concerning the Compulsory Settlement of Disputes[77] (which accompanies the Vienna Convention on Consular Relations); in addition, pointing out that the dispute between the two Governments concerned Articles 5 and 36 of the Vienna Convention and fell within the compulsory jurisdiction of the Court under

---

[75] ILM, op. cit., at 310

[76] ibid.

[77] Article 1 of the Optional Protocol provides that: "Disputes arising out of the interpretation or application of the Convention shall lie within the compulsory jurisdiction of the International Court of Justice and may accordingly be brought before the Court by an application made by any party to the dispute being a Party to the present Protocol."

Article 1 of the Optional Protocol. On 2 March 1999, the Vice-President of the Court in accordance with Articles 13 and 32 of the Rules of the Court, and acting in conformity with Article 74, paragraph 4 of the said Rules, drew the attention of the Government of the United States, in writing, *"to the need to act in such a way as to enable any Order the Court will make on the request for provisional measures to have its appropriate effects."*[78]

The Court was satisfied that, *prima facie*, it had jurisdiction under Article 1 of the Optional Protocol. The Court however reminded Germany of the requirement for submission of a request for the indication of provisional measures based on Article 73 of the Rules of the Court in good time. Having appreciated Germany's reasons for submitting her request for the indication of provisional measures at such short notice, the Court said that under Article 75, paragraph 1 of the Rules of the Court, it *"may at any time decide to examine* proprio motu *whether the circumstances of the case require the indication of provisional measures which ought to be taken or complied with by any or all of the parties,"*[79] and that in the case of an extreme emergency it may proceed without holding oral hearings. Furthermore, *"it is for the Court to decide in each case if, in the light of the particular circumstances of the case, it should make use of the said power."*[80]

The Court also defined the remit of its jurisdiction by linking its task to interim measures only, and relying upon the jurisdiction of the Court it clearly stated that it will not order interim measures in the absence of *"irreparable prejudice ... to rights which are the subject ..."*[81] and that a stay of execution would necessarily be provisional in nature and would not in any way prejudice findings of the Court or the merits of the case[82], and also that interim measures would preserve the respective rights of Germany and of the United States.

After justifying the reasons for assuming jurisdiction for an order for interim measures, the Court unanimously indicated the following provisional measures:

> "(a) The United States of America should take all measures at its disposal to ensure that Walter LaGrand is not executed pending the final decision in these proceedings, and should inform the Court of all the measures which it has taken in implementation of this Order;

---

[78] 38 ILM, op. cit., at 311

[79] 38 ILM op. cit., at 312

[80] ibid

[81] *Nuclear Tests (Australia v France), Interim Protection ICJ Report* (1973) p 103; *United States Diplomatic and Consular Staff in Tehran, Provisional Measures, ICJ Reports* (1979); *Application of the Convention on the Prevention and Punishment of the Crime of Genocide (Bosnia – Herzegovina v Yugoslavia (Serbia and Montenegro), Provisional Measures, ICJ Reports* (1993); and *The Vienna Convention on Consular Relations (Paraguay v United States of America) Provisional Measures, ICJ Reports* (1998)

[82] 38 ILM (1999), op. cit.

(b) *The Government of the United States of America should transmit this Order to the Governor of the State of Arizona.*"[83]

It is interesting to note the Declaration of Judge Oda to the Order of the Court, and the Separate Opinion of President Schwebel. Judge Oda voted in favour of the Court's Order with great hesitation on various grounds: (a) that Germany requested the restoration of the *status quo ante*; but according to Judge Oda, if consular contact had occurred initially, that is, at the time when Mr LaGrand was arrested and detained, the judicial procedure in the United States Courts relating to his case would have remained same; (b) that as a general rule, the purpose of granting provisional measures is to preserve rights of States *"exposed to an imminent breach which is irreparable and these rights of States must be those to be considered at the merits stage of the case, and must constitute the subject-matter of the application instituting proceedings or be directly related to it"*[84], which was not present in this case; (c) that there was no question of such rights of States parties, under the Vienna Convention, being exposed to an imminent irreparable breach[85]; (d) that a request for provisional measures should not be used for the purpose of obtaining interim judgment that would affirm the applicants' own rights and predetermine the main case[86]; and (e) that the use of the Court for inter-State disputes under the pretext of the prosecution of human rights must be discouraged. Judge Oda maintained that given the fundamental nature of provisional measures, those measures should not have been indicated upon Germany's request, but he voted in favour of the Court's Order solely for humanitarian reasons.

In his Separate Opinion, President Schwebel maintained that the Order indicating provisional measures was unprecedented, and was ordered *ex parte* (the other party was not heard); furthermore, as he pointed out that this was the first case in which the International Court of Justice issued an Order on its own motion (*proprio motu*) pursuant to Article 75, paragraph 1 of the Rules of the Court. This was also inconsistent with the fundamental rules of the procedure *quality of the parties*. The Court should examine this extraordinary power with utmost caution. According to the President of the Court:

"The Rule assumes that the Court may act on its own motion where a party has not made a request for the indication of provisional measures."[87]

President Schwebel did not oppose the substance of the Court's Order, but had profound reservations about the procedures followed by both the Applicant and the Court[88].

---

[83] 38 *ILM* (1999), op. cit., at 313

[84] op. cit., at 315

[85] ibid

[86] ibid

[87] 38 ILM (1999) at 316

[88] ibid

Although from a legal standpoint the decision of the International Court of Justice may provoke controversy, particularly whether the Court appropriately exercised its authority to order indication of provisional measures, the fact remains that the case arose because the United States failed to pursue the provisions of the Vienna Convention on Consular Relations, 1963.

A similar case was filed with the International Court of Justice by Paraguay against the United States of America in 1998 in respect of a Paraguayan national, Mr Angel Francisco Breard, and the Court's determination was similar. The relevant US court in this case was a Virginia court (the Circuit Court of Arlington county)[89]. The Government of Paraguay put forward arguments similar to those advanced by the Government of Germany in the LaGrand case; the defences relied upon by the Court of the United States were similar to those advanced by it in the LaGrand case. In so far as the composition of the Court was concerned, except Judge Bedjoui (who was present in the Paraguay case), the Bench consisted of the same judges.

The fees and charges that a consular post may levy in the jurisdiction of the receiving State shall be exempt from all dues and taxes in the receiving State.

The protection of consular officers, and the maintenance of their personal inviolability are two very important responsibilities of the receiving State. *"The receiving State shall also treat consular officers with due respect, and shall take all appropriate steps to prevent any attack on their person, freedom or dignity."*[90] Thus, consular officers may not be arrested or detained pending trial except in the case of a grave crime. What may be treated as a *"grave crime"* is a matter which is to be determined by the judicial authorities of the receiving State. However, if criminal proceedings are instituted against a consular officer, he / she must appear before the competent authorities of the receiving State. Where however it proves to be necessary for the receiving State to detain a consular officer, the proceedings against him / her must be instituted with the minimum delay. The Convention does not mention anything about the sentence to which a consular officer may be subject. However, consular officers and consular employees *"shall not be amenable to the jurisdiction of the judicial or administrative authorities of the receiving State in respect of acts performed in the exercise of consular functions."*[91]

Immunity from the jurisdiction of the judicial or administrative authorities are not available however in respect of civil action, or an action by a third party for damages arising from an accident caused by a vehicle, vessel or aircraft[92].

Members of a consular post may be called upon to give evidence as witnesses in the course of judicial or administrative proceedings, and indeed no member

---

[89] The details of the ICJ's determination have been reproduced in 37 ILM (1998) 810; see also the *Case Concerning America and Other Mexican Nationals (Mexico v US)* 42 *International Legal Materials* (2003) 309

[90] Article 40

[91] Article 43

[92] Article 43(2)(b)

shall decline to give evidence, unless it is a dispute connected with the exercise of their functions[93]. The authority requiring the evidence may, when possible, take evidence at the residence of a consular officer or at the consular post or they may accept a statement from him / her in writing.

The sending State may waive privileges and immunities provided for in Articles 41, 43 and 44 in respect of the consular post and in that event the receiving State must be notified accordingly, in writing. Of course, when proceedings are instituted by a consular officer, no immunity from the jurisdiction may be claimed.

Consular officers and consular employees and members of their families forming part of their household are not required to register as aliens in the receiving State or seek residence permits from it. However, this privilege applies only to consular employees who are permanent employees of the sending State.

Members of a consular post are not required to obtain work permits from a receiving State, unless the laws and regulations so require otherwise. This privilege also applies to the members of the private staff of consular officers unless they take up other gainful occupation in a receiving State. In other words, such persons are required to work solely as members of the private staff of consular officers. Individuals of both these categories are also exempt from social security provisions in a receiving State. In order to enjoy their privileges members of the private staff of consular officers are required to be nationals of the sending State. By the same token, they shall be exempt from taxation, personal, national, regional or municipal laws in a receiving State except for:

- indirect taxes, included in the price of goods and services;

- dues or taxes on private insurable property situate in the territory of the receiving State, subject to the provisions of Article 32 (exemption from taxation of consular premises);

- estate, succession or inheritance duties, and duties on transfers, levied by a receiving State[94];

- dues and taxes on private income, including capital gains earned in a receiving State, and any other tax or income from investments made in commercial or financial undertakings in a receiving State;

- charges levied for specific services rendered; and

- registration, court or record fees, mortgage and stamp duties, subject to the provisions of Article 32.

Members of the service staff are exempt from dues and taxes on their wages; but this privilege does not apply to employees who are nationals of the receiving State or who are permanently resident in such jurisdiction.

---

[93] See ante

[94] See Article 51

A receiving State shall permit entry of and grant exemption from customs duties, taxes and related charges, other than charges for storage, cartage and similar services on:

- articles for the official use of the consular post;
- *"articles for the personal use of a consular officer or members of his / her family forming part of his / her household, including articles intended for his establishment."*[95] Articles intended for consumption shall not exceed the quantity necessary for direct utilisation by the persons concerned.

Personal baggage accompanying consular officers and members of their families forming part of their household shall be exempt from inspection unless the authorities concerned in a receiving State have serious reasons to believe that the baggage contains articles the import or export of which is prohibited by the laws and regulations of the receiving State or which are subject to its quarantine laws and regulations. Inspection of baggage must be carried out in the presence of the consular officer or members of his / her family.

In the event of the death of a member of the consular post or of a member of his / her family forming part of his / her household, the receiving State is to allow the export of the movable property of the deceased other than those which were acquired in the receiving State and the export of which was prohibited at the time of his / her death. A receiving State shall not also levy any national, regional or municipal estate, succession or inheritance duties on movable property the presence of which in the receiving State was solely for the use by the consular post or as a member of the family of a member of the consular post. All members of a consular post, and members of their families forming part of their household, shall be exempt from all personal services, public service of any kind whatsoever, and from military obligations[96].

Privileges and immunities are available to every member of a consular post as from the moment he / she enters the territory of the receiving State with a view to taking up his / her post or, if he / she is already in its territory, from the moment when he / she accepts his / her duties with the consular post. Members of the family of a member of the consular post forming part of his / her household and members of his / her private staff shall be eligible for privileges and immunities from the date on which he / she becomes eligible for privileges and immunities or from the date of their entry into the territory of the receiving State or from the date of their becoming a member of such family or private staff, whichever is the latest[97].

---

[95] Transportation of goods or articles

[96] e.g. requisitioning, military contributions and billeting (a civilian house where soldiers are lodged temporarily)

[97] Article 53(2)

Privileges and immunities allowed to a member of the consular post, and to a member of his / her family forming part of his / her household or a member of his / her private staff, ceases when he / she leaves the receiving State (although officially they cease when his / her functions come to an end) or on the expiry of a reasonable period in which he / she will leave, whichever is the sooner.

Privileges and immunities of the members of the family of a member of the consular post forming part of his / her household or members of his / her private staff terminate when they cease to belong to the household or to be in the service of the member of a consular post; but privileges and immunities for all are usually allowed until their departure from the receiving State within a reasonable period of time after the functions of a member of the consular post have come to an end. In the event of the death of a member of the consular post, the members of his / her family forming part of his / her household continue to enjoy the privileges and immunities accorded to them *"until they leave the receiving State or until the expiry of a reasonable period of time enabling them to do so, whichever is sooner."*[98]

Under the Convention, third States have the following obligations in respect of a consular officer:

- when a consular officer passes through or is in the territory of a third State (which has granted him / her a visa, if a visa was necessary) while proceeding to take up or return to his post or when returning to the sending State, the third State shall accord to him / her all immunities[99] provided for by this Convention. Any member of his / her family forming part of his / her household, and who may be accompanying the consular officer or travelling separately to join him / her or to return to the sending State shall enjoy immunities too in the transit State;

- no third State shall hinder the transit of the members of a consular post or members of their families forming part of their households while they may pass through its territory;

- third states shall *"accord to official correspondence and to other official communications in transit, including messages in code or cipher, the same freedom and protection as the receiving State is bound to accord under the present Convention. They shall accord to consular couriers who have been granted a visa, if a visa was necessary, and to consular bags in transit, the same inviolability and protection as the receiving State is bound to accord under the present Convention."*[100]

---

[98] Article 53(5)
[99] Article 54(1)
[100] Article 54(3)

- these obligations for a third state remain even when a member of a consular post, and / or members of his / her family forming part of his / her household are in its territory due to *force majeure*. The same obligations also apply to official communications and consular bags.

The Convention clearly maintains that all persons enjoying privileges and immunities under it have a duty to respect the laws and regulations of the receiving State. They must not interfere in the internal affairs of that State. *"The consular premises shall not be used in any manner incompatible with the exercise of consular functions."*[101] The phrase *"in any manner"* is crucially important. Whether the premises are being used in a manner which is incompatible with the exercise of consular functions is to be determined by a receiving State. This does not mean however that other offices or agencies may not be accommodated in part of the building in which consular premises are situate provided that the premises assigned to them are separate from those used by the consular post[102]. Members of the consular post must comply with any legal requirement whereby insurance policies may have to be taken out against third party risks arising from the use of any vehicle, vessel or aircraft.

Career consular officers must not be engaged in any professional or commercial activity in the receiving State for personal profit. Indeed, privileges and immunities shall not be accorded to:

- consular employees or to members of the service staff who may be engaged in any private gainful occupation in the receiving State;

- members of the family of a person described above or to members of his private staff;

- members of the family of a member of a consular post who may be engaged in any private gainful occupation in the receiving State[103].

Chapter II of the Convention is thus primarily concerned with the issues and matters which should facilitate the functions of a consular post after it has been established in a receiving State, and the responsibility of the receiving State in relation to consular officers, members of the staff, their families forming part of their household. It also details the duties and obligations of these persons under the Convention.

13.7.2 Regime relating to Honorary Consular Officers and Consular Posts headed by such Officers

The practice of appointing honorary consular officers and consular posts headed by such officers has a long history[104]. In view of the prestige allocated

---

[101] Article 55(2)

[102] Article 55(3)

[103] Article 57

[104] See further L T Lee, op. cit.

A Brief Analysis of the Vienna Convention on Consular Relations, 1963

to these positions eminent and experienced people offered their services in an honorary capacity. Perhaps the position of honorary consular officers confirms that irrespective of whether any diplomatic relations between two States existed or not, the importance of consular posts, even to be headed by a national of the receiving State for maintaining the interests of the people living in a receiving State, could hardly be denied.

There are certain facilities and formalities which are common to a duly appointed consular officer or a consular post and an honorary consular officer and the consular post headed by him / her. For example, the following provisions of the Convention which are addressed to a consular officer and consular post duly appointed by a sending State equally apply to an honorary consular officer and the consular post headed by him / her.

Article 28	–	Facilities for the work of the consular post
Article 29	–	Use of national flag and coat-of-arms
Article 30	–	Accommodation
Article 34	–	Freedom of movement
Article 35	–	Freedom of communication
Article 36	–	Communication and contact with nationals of the sending State
Article 37	–	Information in cases of death, guardianship or trusteeship, wrecks and air accidents
Article 38	–	Communication with the authorities of the receiving State
Article 39	–	Consular fee and charges
Article 42	–	Notification of arrest, detention or prosecution
Article 43	–	Immunity from jurisdiction
Article 44, paragraph 3	–	An honorary consular officer is under no obligation to give evidence in relation to matters connected with the exercise of his / her functions or to produce official correspondence and documents relating thereto. He / she may also decline to give evidence as an expert witness with regard to the law of the sending State.
Article 45	–	Waiver of privileges and immunities by the sending State in certain circumstances.
Article 53	–	Beginning and end of consular privileges and immunities.

Article 54, paragraph 3	–	Obligations of third States to protect the inviolability of official correspondence, communication while in transit through that State as the transit State and the protection to be provided to a consular courier and consular bags while in transit through a third State.
Article 55, paragraph 1	–	Honorary consular officers have a duty to respect the laws and regulations of the receiving State, as they have a duty not to interfere in the internal affairs of that State.
Article 55, paragraphs 2 and 3	–	Respect for the laws and regulations of the receiving State, and, in particular, that the consular premises *"shall not be used in any manner incompatible with the execution of consular functions."* (paragraph 2). Where other offices of other institutions or agencies may be accommodated in part of the building in which the consular premises are situate, such premises must be separate from those used by the consular post (paragraph 3).

Like the consular premises of a duly appointed consul by the sending State, the receiving State shall take all necessary steps to protect the premises of a consular post headed by an honorary consular officer against any intrusion or damage and *"to prevent any disturbance of the peace of the consular post or impairment of its dignity."*[105]

Consular premises of a consular post led by an honorary consular officer of which the sending State is the owner or lessee are exempt from all municipal, national or regional dues and taxes whatsoever. The consular archives and documents of a consular post led by an honorary consular officer shall be inviolable at all times provided that they are kept separate from the private correspondence of the head of a consular post or of any person working with him[106]. The honorary consular officer's office is also eligible for exemption from all customs duties, taxes and related charges for storage, cartage and similar services, coats-of-arms, flags, signboards, seals and stamps, books, official printed matters, office furniture, office equipment and similar articles supplied by the sending State provided that they are for the official use of the honorary consular officer[107]. Article 63 of the Convention provides that:

---

[105] Article 59
[106] Article 60
[107] Article 62

> *"If criminal proceedings are instituted against an honorary consular officer, he must appear before the competent authorities. Nevertheless, the proceedings shall be conducted with the respect due to him by reason of his official position and, except when he is under arrest or detention, in a manner which will hamper the exercise of consular functions as little as possible. When it has become necessary to detain an honorary consular officer, the proceedings against him shall be instituted with the minimum of delay."*

The receiving State has a duty to provide protection to an honorary consular officer as may be required by him / her[108].

Honorary consular officers are exempt from registration as aliens and residence permits in a receiving State, but this privilege does not extend to them when they may be engaged in any professional or commercial activity in a receiving State for personal profits. An honorary consular officer is also exempt from all dues and taxes on the remuneration and emoluments which he / she receives from the sending State; he / she is also exempt from all personal services and public services, military obligations such as those concerned with requisitioning, military contributions and billeting. It is to be borne in mind that each State has its discretion to decide whether it will appoint or receive honorary consular officers.

13.7.3 General Provisions

It is for each State to decide whether it will establish or admit consular agencies which would be conducted by consular agents who may not be designated as head of a consular post by the sending State. The conditions under which consular agencies may be engaged and the extent of the privileges and immunities to which they may be entitled are determined by agreement between the sending State and the receiving State[109].

It is possible for a diplomatic mission to exercise consular functions; but it has to assign these functions and notify the Ministry of Foreign Affairs of the receiving State or the authority designated by that Ministry. The privileges and immunities of the members of a diplomatic mission assigned to consular functions *"shall continue to be governed by the rules of international law concerning diplomatic relations."*[110]

The receiving State has an obligation to ensure that in the application of the provisions of the present Convention it does not discriminate as between States. However, discrimination shall not be regarded as taking place:

> *"(a) where the receiving State applies any of the provisions of the present Convention restrictively because of a restrictive application of that provision to its consular posts in the sending State;*

---

[108] Article 64

[109] Article 69

[110] Article 70, paragraph (4)

(b) *where by custom or agreement States extend to each other more favourable treatment than is required by the provisions of the present Convention.* "[111]

Whereas the provisions at (a) are based on the principle of reciprocity, those at (b) are based on historical practice, and nothing much about it may be done. Indeed, two friendly States, and two trading partners may rely on Article 72, paragraph (b) to justify discriminatory treatment against other States, including their consular posts.

13.7.4 Final Provisions

These provisions relate primarily to signatures, notification, entry into force etc which have already been explained, and no comments on them would be necessary.

13.8 CONCLUSIONS

It would be unfair to undermine consular services in comparison with diplomatic services. Whereas the former is concerned primarily with the protection of interests of the nationals of a sending State living and / or doing business in a receiving State, including the protection of their commercial interests, the latter is concerned with maintenance of diplomatic relations with the receiving State concerned. These two branches of service are different. Where a sending State does not have a consular post in a receiving State, the diplomatic mission can perform consular functions, and *vice versa*.

Both Diplomatic Relations Convention, 1961 and the Convention on Consular Relations, 1963 consolidated respectively the diplomatic and consular custom. These provide the framework of relations between a sending State and a receiving State for both diplomatic and consular matters. Both the Conventions are primarily based on two principles: sovereignty and reciprocity. However, parties to both Conventions are allowed to derogate from the principle of non-discrimination on the grounds of historical relations between a sending State and a receiving State.

The States which were born after 1961 will be bound by these Conventions, if they accept them. The obligation of receiving States as to the inviolability of diplomatic or consular bags does not seem to be absolute in nature. States, in the name of national security or high suspicion, may open bags. As explained earlier, in the UK practice, this obligation is not absolute in nature. Certain countries entered reservations in relation to opening of diplomatic bags.

Sovereign States also allow non-State entities to establish their missions in their territory, for example, the mission of Northern Cyprus in the United Kingdom. Privileges and immunities to such missions are based on the discretion of the receiving State.

---

[111] Article 72, paragraphs 2(a) and (b)

A Brief Analysis of the Vienna Convention on Consular Relations, 1963

In diplomatic and consular relations, a State, as the receiving State, has a total discretion on what terms these relations may be developed. Within the European Union, for example, these must be based on the principle of non-discrimination; however, the differing trading position of a State with the receiving State seems to make differences in according facilities, and this can be justified on the grounds of historical relationship between the two countries.

CHAPTER 14

The United Nations and International Diplomacy

14.1 INTRODUCTION

With the increasing need for and growth of multilateral diplomacy, diplomats are required to familiarise themselves with the UN functional mechanics in addition to its Purposes and Principles. It is opportune to point out that the benefits that a Member State derives from the UN should not be over-emphasised. There seems to exist a perceived belief that the United Nations is primarily a forum or institution for developing countries, but the need for interdependence between developed and developing countries requires both groups of countries to meet at a common forum to discuss issues and formulate policies and principles the implementation of which might lead to a better world order, whether political, economic or legal. Nowhere can the need for interdependence be more found than in relation to economic issues; whereas the rich countries require opportunities for trade and investment, the developing countries under the current situation are the primary providers of natural resources, and they would also like to effectively participate in the international trading community and system. The needs for both groups of countries emanate from different reasons, but unless a basis for a workable international co-operation is found, neither the rich nor the poor will benefit.

Where bilateral diplomacy may fail, resolution of matters may be achieved through the initiative of the UN. It needs to be emphasised that the UN has been more involved in socio-economic and development issues than in political and military issues; in fact, the UN should not be abused by any State in achieving its socio-economic ends. Furthermore, it is elementary to point out that economic issues bring countries together; political issues culminating in military activities, simply make them apart.

If an issue, whether of a political or military or socio-economic nature, may not be resolved by diplomacy, then there can be three assumptions: (a) that effective diplomacy, with articulation in negotiation, has not been applied; or (b) that the parties are reluctant to resolve that issue; or (c) that the parties have not correctly identified the facts and issues. Many may find such assumptions difficult to accept, but what other assumptions may be made? It is from this standpoint that one may maintain that diplomacy should be broad-based with a sense of compromise and co-operation, and the UN often provides a forum for effective negotiation and compromise. Consensual diplomacy based on the need for resolution of issues and reciprocity is an essential element of international diplomacy. Training in diplomacy entails two very important components: (a) the limits to state sovereignty; and (b) the need for international co-operation. The attitude to dominate the others on the basis of economic, financial or even military strengths not only creates tension or even hatred against the state aggrandising its position, it simply recedes the prospects of resolving issues by diplomatic means. One of the problems with the current-day diplomacy is that the diplomatic world is often involved in war diplomacy even during peace-time. The distinction between diplomacy during war-time and cold-war time is in many ways artificial in nature; a war is a war, whether described as a cold or hot one. *"Hot wars"* often represent the failures of diplomacy; consequently further diplomacy is necessary for bringing such wars to an end, whereas persistence or continuity of a cold war situation, which is another version of hostility, short of arms warfare, requires an effective multilateral diplomacy. Multilateral diplomacy must therefore be conducted on a co-operative basis without presenting any threat to any party. *"Cold wars"* may turn to *"hot wars"* when diplomacy is based on weapon-based threats. If true peace-making is the primary aim of diplomatic activity during a *"cold war"* situation, then there does not seem to be any logic in procrastinating it by posing threats to each other in consequence of which the international community at large suffers. Furthermore, the issue of international responsibility is involved in it, that is, whether because of the action of a few, a large majority may suffer. All so-called *"cold wars"* are nothing but examples of threatened military might; diplomacy and diplomats should therefore be directed at freeing the world from wars, whether cold or hot. Multilateral diplomacy at multilateral *fora* should be enlarged and applied to deal with such issues.

The United Nations is a truly international forum in the world which provides the platform for multilateral diplomacy. Most of the States in the international community belong to it. If it is not utilised properly, then there seems to be two choices: (a) either to abolish it; or (b) to account for its non-utilisation. Furthermore, if the current UN system does not seem to be adequate or effective enough for dealing with international issues, then it is for the Member States to correct the system.

From a legal standpoint non-utilisation of the UN system amounts to a breach of treaty obligations of its Member States; any act contrary to the maintenance of international peace and security committed by a UN Member is an act which runs counter to the Purposes and Principles of the UN Charter. In this regard, one should only recall the circumstances and intentions which prompted the founding Members to set up the United Nations.

States may find the wealth of experience and expertise held by this organisation useful for developing their national policies, if necessary. The relationship between national diplomacy and international diplomacy is a circular one. International diplomats engaged by international organisations, primarily under the umbrella of the United Nations, devote themselves to pursue its cause; the majority of national diplomats who, on the other hand, tend to primarily concentrate on their national policies, may defeat the purposes of these organisations, and deprive themselves of the services that this organisation may render at the national level, primarily in the form of technical assistance or development of national legislation or facilitating the growth of infrastructural development process. It is through the co-operation of national governments that rules of international law may be developed, and States, in turn, are expected to follow them. On the other hand, Member States are required to follow the customary rules of international law.

A balance between national diplomacy and international diplomacy is essential. In view of the pervasiveness of issues across national borders, such as environmental issues, immigration, drugs-related matters, international crimes, sharing of international resources, international peace and security, and prohibition of wars, to name but a few, diplomats are required to pay attention to international rules and effectively participate in developing such rules. Of course, matters of exclusive national interest, such as private law related matters – marriages, divorce etc or tax matters, must be dealt with by national means; and intervention by any external body would amount to encroaching upon the sovereignty of the State concerned. But, how to determine matters of the national interest?

It would be appropriate to maintain that what used to be exclusively matters of national interest, are no longer so. In fact, the training of diplomats should entail learning of the nature of interaction between national interest and international interest. One certain way of developing an understanding of the nature of interaction between national interest and international interest, is for a diplomat to thoroughly learn the principle of international responsibility. The limits of national interest are set by the principle of international responsibility. What is to be noticed is whether any action taken in the national interest may run counter to the principle of international responsibility. For example, if any industrial act within one's own national boundaries pollutes the environment of a neighbouring country, then the matter falls to be considered by the rules of international responsibility. The instructive case on this issue is *Trail Smelter* arbitration between the United States and Canada in 1938 and 1941[1].

Even before the international convention rules in respect of the protection of the environment were developed, the arbitrator considered the issue of the pollution of the environment by reference to international tort, that is, acts based on negligence. Under international law, a State has an obligation to exercise due care and skill, when its act may adversely affect another State. In the *Corfu Channel* case[2] the Albanian government maintained that it did not

---

[1] 3 RIAA 1941

[2] *ICJ Reports* (1949) 4

have any knowledge as to who might have laid mines in the Channel bed which destroyed two British vessels. But, the onus was on the Albanian government to prove that it did not itself lay any mines, which in the circumstances of the case was difficult to establish. The court maintained that it is for the coastal State to keep the territorial waters safe and navigable particularly when a waterway is an international waterway. It is a matter of duty towards the other users of the channel. The British government, on the other hand, launched Operation Red to sweep the mines in the Albanian territorial waters. The Court unanimously accepted the Albanian contention that in so doing the British government had an obligation to seek the Albanian government's permission. International law thus protects the integrity of national sovereignty. The decision of the International Court of Justice in the *Corfu Channel* case demonstrated two very important aspects of international law: first, the binding nature of the principle of international responsibility to which all sovereign States must submit; and the limits of national sovereignty, which was exceeded by the government of the United Kingdom.

In the *Nuclear Tests* cases 1974, the French government maintained that by virtue of not being a party to the Nuclear Test Ban Treaty, France was not obliged to follow the Treaty-based law, and the principle of *res inter alios acta* (third parties are not bound by a treaty law to which treaty it does not belong) but the Court did not accept that argument, as it was a norm-making treaty which would bind all States, whether parties or not, to the Nuclear Test Ban Treaty. Furthermore, the aspirations of the members of the international community as to the prohibition of nuclear tests were demonstrated through various resolutions of the General Assembly of the United Nations, namely 1652(XVI), 1762 (XVII), 1901 (XVIII), 2032 (XX), 2033 (XX), 2663 (XXI), 2343 (XXII), 2455 (XXIII), 2064 (XXIV), 2663 (XXV), 2828 (XXVI) and 2934 (XXVII)[3].

The decision of the International Court of Justice in the *Nuclear Tests* cases clearly evidenced the fact that in relation to matters of *"international concern"* national interests and national sovereignty must submit to the international interest and the principle of international responsibility.

In the *Nicaragua v the United States*[4] the Court had an opportunity to deal with the peremptory nature of Article 2, paragraph 4 of the UN Charter. There is no need to go into the details of the principle that the International Court of Justice either developed or re-affirmed through various cases; suffice to say that, in most cases, the decisions of the Court related to the limits to national sovereignty and the duty to observe the principle of international responsibility.

---

[3] Statement made by the Australian government in the *Nuclear Test cases (Australia v France)*, ICJ Pleadings (1978) at 329

[4] *ICJ Reports* (1986) 14; See also C Gray, *International Law and the Use of Force*, Oxford, Oxford University Press (2000) Chapter 3

INTERNATIONAL LAW AND DIPLOMACY

This chapter attempts to evaluate the adequacy of the current UN machinery in dealing with matters of international concern, and to demonstrate that for multilateral diplomacy an international forum such as the United Nations is indispensable, although it requires certain changes.

14.2 THE UN SYSTEM GENERALLY

The UN system is based on the founding Treaty of the United Nations, the Charter of the United Nations. The Purposes and Principles of this institution are remarkably significant; and it is thought appropriate to append them.

14.2.1 Purposes - Article 1

"1. To maintain international peace and security, and to that end: to take effective collective measures for the prevention and removal of threats to the peace, and for the suppression of acts of aggression or other breaches of the peace, and to bring about by peaceful means, and in conformity with the principles of justice and international law, adjustment or settlement of international disputes or situations which might lead to a breach of the peace;

2. To develop friendly relations among nations based on respect for the principle of equal rights and self-determination of peoples, and to take other appropriate measures to strengthen universal peace;

3. To achieve international co-operation in solving international problems of an economic, social, cultural, or humanitarian character, and in promoting and encouraging respect for human rights and for fundamental freedoms for all without distinction as to race, sex, language, or religion; and

4. To be a centre for harmonizing the actions of nations in the attainment of these common ends."

14.2.2 Principles – Article 2

"1. The Organization is based on the principle of the sovereign equality of all its Members;

2. All Members, in order to ensure to all of them the rights and benefits resulting from membership, shall fulfil in good faith the obligations assumed by them in accordance with the present Charter;

3. All Members shall settle their international disputes by peaceful means in such a manner that international peace and security, and justice, are not endangered;

4. All Members shall refrain in their international relations from the threat or use of force against the territorial integrity or political independence of any state, or in any other manner inconsistent with the Purposes of the United Nations;

5. All Members shall give the United Nations every assistance in any action it takes in accordance with the present Charter, and shall refrain from giving assistance to any state against which the United Nations is taking preventive or enforcement action;

6. The Organization shall ensure that states which are not Members of the United Nations act in accordance with these Principles so far as may be necessary for the maintenance of international peace and security;

7. Nothing contained in the present Charter shall authorize the United Nations to intervene in matters which are essentially within the domestic jurisdiction of any state or shall require the Members to submit such matters to settlement under the present Charter; but this principle shall not prejudice the application of enforcement measures under Chapter VII."

Each of these paragraphs stands for a principle, and these Principles were adopted by the Founding Members of the United Nations in 1945, when the organisation was set up. Even after 60 years, the Principles remain valid; but unfortunately, in many instances, States have violated them, and in particular, the Principle enunciated by paragraph 4 of Article 2. Violation of a Principle does not amount to questioning the validity of the Principle; it simply affirms lawlessness on the part of the violator; in the international arena, it is for the Member States to condemn the act of the violator, rather than tacitly or expressly accepting the violation, as this latter act would encourage others to violate the Principle too. But, diplomats are required to deal with the violator in a peaceful manner, and not by resorting to wars, as by so doing they will be in violation of Article 2(4) of the Charter. Furthermore, relying upon the Purposes and Principles of the UN Charter it may easily be stated that the Charter expressly aims at achieving international peace and security by peaceful means. Hence the importance of Article 2(4), the exception to which obligation may be allowed only in the situations enunciated by Article 51 (use of force on a temporary basis in self-defence only).

The UN was set up as a peace-making body, and not as a body which should be unnecessarily involved in war efforts. On the other hand, in conformity with Article 2(4) the Member States are required to restrain themselves from any warfares outside the UN system, and once the matter has been brought to the attention of the UN, the machinery is available to genuinely deal with the matter promptly. But, the success of the UN machinery very much depends upon the promptness in which a dispute has been referred to it by a Member State. Member States should not wage wars first, and then refer the matter to the UN as a mere formality or for post-mortem, so to say.

When one thinks of the wars that have taken place since 1945, one should be able to deduce the conclusion that most of these wars were initiated by the aggressor State(s) without notifying the UN; in fact, theUN has no mandate to authorise warfares; it can only send Emergency Forces for ceasefire in appropriate cases.

The significant part of the UN's work is involved in socio-economic issues, namely socio-economic development; human rights; trade issues; health; education; labour and employment; industrial and infrastructural growth; development of human resources; management of resources, both human and natural, etc. The work of the UN in these fields should not be overshadowed by military diplomacy which has attained significant attention, particularly over the past two decades.

The UN system includes its specialised agencies. Each of these specialised agencies has been entrusted with specific tasks, when the activities of the specialised agencies may overlap, they co-ordinate between themselves. For example, in dealing with environmental issues in the workplace, both the International Labour Office (ILO) and the World Health Organisation (WHO) may be involved and co-ordinate their activities. All specialised agencies come under the Economic and Social Council, but under Article 15, the General Assembly has the authority to ask any of them to submit special reports, in addition to requiring them to submit their annual reports.

The activities of these specialised agencies and of the main organs of the United Nations have been discussed in a separate section; in this context, it should be pointed out that the UN system generally works on a consensus basis; as from a realistic standpoint, it may not be possible to attain unanimity on each issue. Diplomats are therefore required to iron out their differences if they really want to adopt internationally-recognised principles for the purposes of regulating the conduct of Members of the United Nations rather than adhering to the narrow national interests, unless the protection of such interests may be fully justified at the UN forum, as for example, the special interests of the archipelagic States; or States depending upon limited resources because of natural and/or geographical conditions or land-locked States etc. It is essential to bear in mind that as national diplomats may contribute to diplomacy at an international forum, such as the UN, the latter may also directly contribute to enriching diplomacy. Diplomacy, in this context, stands for development of ideas and principles through joint efforts at a truly international forum and implementation of them at the national level; otherwise there exists little reason for being engaged in such form of diplomacy. Training in diplomacy should entail learning of the limits of national-interest based diplomacy, and the interaction between such diplomacy and the diplomacy that should be acted upon at a world forum, with specific purpose in mind.

The following section briefly discusses the UN, including its specialised agencies, so as to allow the reader to familiarise himself/herself with the basics of the System; the purpose is not to give an entire evaluation of the activities of the organs and specialised agencies, as that will be outside the purview of this work.

14.3 THE UN SYSTEM
14.3.1 Some Preliminary Information

The UN Charter was drafted by the representatives of 50 States at the UN Conference on International Organisation, which met at San Francisco from 25 April to 26 June, 1945. The Charter was signed by these States on 26 June 1945 and came into force on 24 October 1945. The UN Charter is an international treaty and it has codified the major principles of international relations and law: promotion and maintenance of international peace and security; sovereign equality; prohibition of wars; and socio-economic progress, including progress in respect of human rights and justice. Membership of the United Nations is open to all peace-loving nations which accept the obligations of the Charter.

Article 3 Membership was open to those of the States which participated in the UN Conference on International Organisation[5], for all other States, membership is governed by Article 4. Basically, new Members are admitted by the General Assembly on the recommendation of the Security Council. Of course, the expression *"peace-loving"* provokes controversy, as the determination of it is based on value judgment; but unless the criteria of membership are changed, applicants are bound by it.

The official languages of the United Nations are: Chinese, English, French, Russian and Spanish. The Arabic language is also used as an official language of the General Assembly, the Security Council and the Economic and Social Council. Many reports and resolutions of the UN and its specialised agencies are published in Chinese, English, French and Spanish. Documents are also available in Arabic and Russian, when the subject matter of the conference requires the proceedings to be published in these languages.

The Preamble to the Charter states that:

"WE THE PEOPLES OF THE UNITED NATIONS DETERMINED
- *to save succeeding generations from the scourge of war, which twice in our lifetime has brought untold sorrow to mankind, and*
- *to reaffirm faith in fundamental human rights, in the dignity and worth of the human person, in the equal rights of men and women and of nations large and small, and*
- *to establish conditions under which justice and respect for the obligations arising from treaties and other sources of international law can be maintained, and*
- *to promote social progress and better standards of life in larger freedom,*

AND FOR THESE ENDS
- *to practise tolerance and live together in peace with one another as good neighbours, and*
- *to unite our strength to maintain international peace and security, and*

---

[5] Article 3

- to ensure, by the acceptance of principles and the institution of methods, that armed force shall not be used, save in the common interest, and

- to employ international machinery for the promotion of the economic and social advancement of all peoples,

HAVE RESOLVED TO COMBINE OUR EFFORTS TO ACCOMPLISH THESE AIMS.

Accordingly, our respective Governments, through representatives assembled in the city of San Francisco, who have exhibited their full powers found to be in good and due form, have agreed to the present Charter of the United Nations and do hereby establish an international organization to be known as the United Nations."

14.3.2 Structure of the United Nations

There are five principal organs of the United Nations: The General Assembly; the Security Council; the Economic and Social Council; the Trusteeship Council[6]; the International Court of Justice and the Secretariat. Most of these organs have the power to create subsidiary bodies. In the following section, a brief discussion of the functions and powers of these organs is held.

14.3.2.1 *General Assembly*

The title of this organ is significant; it is a *"General"* organ, it is an Assembly. In other words, all Members of the United Nations assemble at the General Assembly to discuss matters of international concern. The General Assembly is composed of all Members of the United Nations. In addition to its regular sessions, the General Assembly may meet in special sessions at the request of the Security Council, a majority of the Members of the United Nations or even at the request of any one Member provided the majority of Members concur. The Security Council can request the General Assembly on the basis of the votes of any nine members of the Council to hold emergency special sessions, and such request may also be made by a majority of the Members of the UN or by one Member if the majority concurs. Emergency special sessions are usually held within 24 hours of a request.

Each regular session elects a new President, 21 Vice-Presidents and the Chairman of the General Assembly's six principal committees, mentioned below. In order to ensure equitable geographical representation, the presidency of the Assembly rotates each year among five groups of States: African, Asian, Eastern European, Latin American, Western European and other States.

---

[6] With the independence of Palau, the last remaining trust territory, on 1 October, 1994, the Council suspended operation on 1 November 1994. A formal termination of the Trusteeship Council cannot take place without amending the UN Charter.

At the beginning of each regular session, the General Assembly holds a general debate on issues of international concern. These debates are often addressed by heads of State and Government and they express their views on these issues. This is another instance where training of diplomats is essential to learn how to articulate issues, and how an issue deserves to be regarded as an issue of international concern, and how, if at all, it may adversely affect his/her national interest. The contents of such debates must be substantive, and not value-based or emotive. Lack of substance and purpose of a debate will defeat its basic objectives. Such debates form the bases for future action, hence they must be policy- and principle-oriented. However, over the decades, a vast number of issues have been referred to the General Assembly as issues of international concern. As it is not possible for the Assembly to consider such vast number of issues, it allocates many of them to its committees:

- *Disarmament and International Security Committee (First Committee);*
- *Economic and Financial Committee (Second Committee);*
- *Social, Humanitarian and Cultural Committee (Third Committee);*
- *Special, Political and Decolonisation Committee (Fourth Committee);*
- *Administrative and Budgetary Committee (Fifth Committee); and*
- *Legal Committee (Sixth Committee).*

There also exist a General Committee (composed of the President and 21 Vice-Presidents of the Assembly and the Chairman of the Committees) and a Credential Committee (composed of the nine members appointed by the Assembly on the proposal of the President of each session). Where possible, questions are debated in plenary meetings of the Assembly; these Committees submit their draft resolution based on the debates held at its meetings, to the plenary meeting at which all questions are addressed.

Whereas a simple majority formula is followed in Committees, the plenary meeting resolutions may be adopted by acclamation, without objection or without a vote, or the vote may be taken by roll-call and may or may not be recorded.

As stated earlier, the General Assembly offers a platform for discussion of matters of international concern; it thus considers such issues which, in turn, require it to make special studies and reports. From any standpoint, it is a very important organ of the United Nations, and its success depends upon diplomats, both national and international, and the faith and confidence that its Members place in it.

The Powers and Functions of the General Assembly

The powers and functions of the General Assembly have been detailed in Articles 10–22 of the Charter. The first two articles, 10 and 11, give the General

Assembly power to take action even in respect of matters of international peace and security, provided of course the Security Council has failed to take action on such matters because of a lack of unanimity of its permanent members.

Indeed, in 1960 such a situation arose where two of the permanent members of the Security Council, France and the Soviet Union, were prepared to veto the proposal for sending emergency forces to the Congo. The General Assembly sent such forces to the aforementioned area on the basis of its resolution entitled the *"Uniting for Peace"* Resolution 377 of 1950. It can therefore assume the role of the Security Council in the event of a situation arising of the nature described above. But under the Charter the General Assembly shall exercise this power only in special circumstances. The other powers and functions of the General Assembly may be summarised as follows:

(1) to discuss any question relating to international peace and security provided of course that question is not being considered by the Security Council (Article 12);

(2) to consider principles of co-operation in the maintenance of international peace and security, including the principles governing disarmament and the regulations of armament, and make recommendations, where necessary;

(3) to discuss any other question that may come under the purview of the UN Charter or may affect the powers and functions of any organ of the United Nations. This is indeed a broad power; and it can also discuss any question that may affect or has affected the powers and functions of the Security Council;

(4) *"to initiate studies and make recommendations for the purpose of:*

    a. promoting international co-operation in the political field and encouraging the progressive development of international law and its codification;

    b. promoting international co-operation in the economic, social, cultural, educational, and health fields, and assisting in the realization of human rights and fundamental freedoms for all without distinction as to race, sex, language, or religion.

    2. The further responsibilities, functions and powers of the General Assembly with respect to matters mentioned in paragraph 1 (b) above are set forth in Chapters IX and X."

Under this provision the General Assembly has functions of an extensive nature.

(5) to make recommendations for the peaceful settlement of any situation which might impair friendly relations among nations. This point

has been further developed in a separate section to cater for diplomats;

(6) to consider and approve the budget of the United Nations and to apportion the contributions among its Members; this is an extremely important power that the General Assembly enjoys;

(7) to elect the following: non-permanent members of the Security Council; members of the Economic and Social Committee [and of the Trusteeship Council]; and jointly with the Security Council, the judges of the International Court of Justice; and to apprise the Secretary-General, on the recommendation of the Security Council; and

(8) to receive and consider reports whether annual or special from the Security Council and other organs of the United Nations. This power of the General Assembly clearly suggests that all other organs of the United Nations are accountable to it. It is the responsibility of the General Assembly to keep an overview of what the UN as an organisation is doing.

14.3.2.1 *The Security Council*

The Charter has entrusted the Security Council with the primary responsibility for the maintenance of international peace and security. The special position of the Security Council may be traced in the historical experience of the then international community. The failure of the League of Nations to prevent the Second World War from taking place seems to have made the contemporary international community entrust a particular organ with the task of the maintenance of international peace and security, which organ will be controlled by the most influential powers, who are also the permanent Members of it.

However, it is to be reiterated that the primary purpose of the Security Council must be in conformity with the basic ethos of the United Nations, which is peace-making by amicable means and not by wars. In other words, under the Charter the Security Council has no mandate to take enforcement action (Chapter VII) without exhausting the procedure available under Chapter VI. Even then, action under Chapter VII must be taken in a progressive manner.

Diplomats are required to bear in mind that no one permanent Member can under the Charter initiate any enforcement action: the wish of the other permanent Members must be pursued. Although the veto power has been vested in the permanent Members of the Security Council, there is no reason why the general feeling of the non-permanent Members should not be taken into consideration along with the recommendations of the General Assembly. The Security Council must not work as an aggressive organ of the UN; its mechanism is defensive; only in very exceptional cases may it resort to Chapter VII action. The reason for investing the permanent Members with the veto power was to ensure that checks were imposed on the undue pressure that may be brought to bear upon other Members, whether for coercive / enforcement measures or for inaction. It must be emphasised however that although the unanimity rule seems to have lost its importance in the decision-making process of the Security Council, it is still the rule. Diplomats should therefore consider whether any amendment to Article 27(3)[7] would be necessary.

The other issue that merits serious consideration by diplomats is that the Security Council, is exclusively concerned with the responsibility for the maintenance of peace and security; if a matter should have a military dimension which may require measures / action to be taken by the Security Council respectively under Chapter VI and Chapter VII, that may be considered by the Security Council, and the remaining issues are to be considered by the General Assembly. Matters meriting sanctions on a recalcitrant Member State are also to be considered by the Security Council. Again, peace-making through friendly and non-aggressive means is the primary aspect of its principal responsibility.

The Security Council has 15 members, five of which are permanent members: China, France, the Russian Federation, the United Kingdom and the United States. The ten other members are elected by the General Assembly for two years.

Each member of the Security Council has one vote. Decision on procedural matters are made by an affirmative role of at least 9 of the 15 members. Decisions on substantive matters require nine votes, including the concurring votes of all five permanent members. A new development in the voting procedure has developed outside Article 27(3) since 1965, which is when the Rhodesian situation was referred to the Security Council. In considering whether sanctions should have been imposed on Rhodesia, China and France, two permanent members, abstained. As Article 27(3) does not provide for abstention it initially presented a legal problem. However, despite abstention of two permanent members sanctions were imposed on Rhodesia and had been renewed several times. The gradual legitimisation of *"abstentions"* may only suggest two things: either abstentions may be disregarded or they may be regarded as *"affirmative"* votes to satisfy the requirements of paragraph (3) of Article 27.

The Legal Effect of UN General Assembly Resolutions

In examining the legal effect of the resolutions adopted by the UN General Assembly, attention of the reader should be drawn to the significance of the title of this organ of the United Nations – it is an Assembly, and it is a *"general"* as opposed to a *"special"* assembly. The term *"assembly"* signifies that it is a

---

[7] Article 27(3)

forum at which every member of the United Nations may assemble for discussion of matters and issues, which is, in fact, the case. Secondly, the term *"general"* signifies that it has the authority under the UN Charter to discuss generally any matter or issue, which is also the case. This would mean that it has the mandate to discuss even matters and issues of the maintenance of international peace and security.

Nowhere in the UN Charter has it been stated that the General Assembly's resolutions would not have any legally binding effect. The reason for having this notion that its resolutions are not binding is anecdotal in that, at the time the Charter was being drafted, the drafters' attention was set to the idea that military and security issues must be accorded the utmost priority, in consequence of which the importance of the Security Council and the binding nature of its resolutions were emphasised. This is the reason for making provision for the veto system in the Security Council and also the provisions in Chapter VIII of the Charter. Proponents of the view that the UN General Assembly resolutions have no binding effect maintain that the drafters of the Charters had never intended to accord the General Assembly with any such power[8]. It is true that in examining a document the intention of the drafters must be looked into. But, the UN Charter is an instrument *sui generis*; its Purposes and Principles must be referred to in examining any of its provisions; this is where the conflict between the drafters' intention and the Purposes and Principles of the organisation became evident; the latter has an overriding effect over the former, especially when the exigencies of the contemporary world are taken into consideration.

Interestingly enough, at the time the Charter was drafted, two broad issues, among others, received the attention of the drafters: (a) the issue of international peace and security; and (b) socio-economic issues, including development and human rights. In so far as the first issue is concerned, the stronger military powers, led by the United States, placed much emphasis on the Security Council and provided that it would have enforcement powers, which, in effect, stands for conferring powers on it to issue legally binding resolutions.

The General Assembly, on the other hand, was thought to be a forum for discussion generally, of all matters; thus the question of endowing it with the power to adopt binding resolutions would not arise[9]. This perception still prevails, in general, without appreciating that the General Assembly has adopted binding resolutions, namely, the Uniting for Peace Resolution, 1950 or the Resolution entitled Permanent Sovereignty over Natural Resources, 1962[10]. The controversy surrounding the legal effect of the resolutions passed by the UN General Assembly may be considered from several

---

[8] D H N Johnson, "The Effect Resolutions of the General Assembly of the United Nations:", 32 *British Year Book of International Law* (1955–56) 97

[9] For a good discussion, see Goodrich and Hambro

[10] GA Res 1803

points of view: (a) nowhere in the UN Charter has it been mentioned that the General Assembly resolutions will be devoid of any legal effect; (b) if one maintains the significance of hierarchy of institutions in law, then it may be argued that in so far as non-military or non-security issues are concerned, the General Assembly is the highest organ; furthermore, under Article 15 all other organs of the UN, including the Security Council, are required to submit their reports to the General Assembly. Article 15 of the UN Charter provides that:

> "1. *The General Assembly shall receive and consider annual and special reports from the Security Council; these reports shall include an account of the measures that the Security Council has decided upon or taken to maintain international peace and security.*
>
> 2. *The General Assembly shall receive and consider reports from the other organs of the United Nations.*"

This does evidence the fact that the other Organs of the UN are accountable to the General Assembly. This is how the hierarchy issue may be settled. In reality, however, the perception against the General Assembly's law-making power or the power to adopt legally binding resolutions remains.

At this point, it is worth looking at the legal arguments on this issue. Resolutions of the General Assembly reflect, in general, the aspirations and consensus of the international community. One should not go into the unnecessary controversy whether they give rise to any hard law or soft law[11]. In examining the issue whether resolutions of the General Assembly carry any binding force, Sloan said that[12]:

> "*There is, however, in the Charter no express undertaking to accept recommendations of the General Assembly similar to the agreement in Article 25 to accept and carry out decisions of the Security Council. On the other hand, it cannot be said that the Charter specifically negates such an obligation, and it may be possible to deduce certain obligations from the Charter as a whole which it would be impossible to establish from an express undertaking.*"

He became even more specific as to the status of the General Assembly resolutions in the following passage[13]:

---

[11] See further, S K Chatterjee, "The Charter of Economic Rights and Duties of States: An Evaluation after 15 years", 40 *International and Comparative Law Quarterly*, 669 at 681; see also the statement made by Ambassador Castañeda of Mexico as Chairman of the Working Group Meetings, UN Doc. TD/B/AC12/R4 at 2; C N Brower and J B Tepe, Jr, "The Charter of Economic Rights and Duties of States: A Reflection or Rejection of International Law", 9 *International Lawyer* (1975) 295–318; G W Haight, "The New International Economic Order and the Charter of Economic Rights and Duties of States", idem, at 591–604; and P C Rao, "Charter of Economic Rights and Duties of States", 15 *Indian Journal of International Law* (1975) 469–370

[12] F B Sloan, "The Binding Force of a 'Recommendation' of the General Assembly of the United Nations" (1948) 25 *British Year Book of International Law*, 14

[13] ibid., p 23

"It seems clearly inherent in the position of the General Assembly that Members can take steps within the Organisation to reach binding agreements. It also appears true that consent to such agreements may be expressed by a vote in the General Assembly. But when we consider the next logical step, namely, the extent to which the General Assembly possesses power to bind States that have not voted in favour of a resolution, we must abandon the firm ground of established principle and approach the realm de lege ferenda.*"*

He went on to say that:[14]

"The question whether an affirmative vote cast by a delegation to the General Assembly can itself constitute the consent necessary to give rise to a binding contractual obligation will be subject to greater controversy, but where the intention is to be so bound there is no reason why it should not be given effect."

And concluded by saying:[15]:

"The judgment by the General Assembly as a collective world conscience is itself a force external to the individual conscience of any given State. It is submitted that in view of these considerations the "moral code" of the General Assembly is in fact a nascent legal force."

Higgins maintains that:[16]

"Resolutions of the Assembly are not per se *binding: though those rules of general international law which they may embody are binding on member states, with or without the help of the resolution. But the body of resolutions as a whole, taken as indications of a general customary law, undoubtedly provide a rich source of evidence."*

14.3.3.2 *Powers and Functions of the Security Council*

The powers and functions of the Security Council have been predominantly incorporated in Chapters VI and VII of the UN Charter. However, the primary functions of the Security Council may be summarised in the following way:

(a) to maintain international peace and security in accordance with the Purposes and Principles of the United Nations;

(b) to develop a system to regulate armaments;

(c) to take enforcement action against an aggressor;

---

[14] ibid., p 22

[15] ibid., p 32

[16] R Higgins, "The Development of International Law through the Political Organs of the United Nations", Oxford, Clarendon Press, (1963), p 5; see also G Tunkin, "The Legal Nature of the United Nations" (1966) III Hague Rec. 1–68; and D H N Johnson, "The Effect of Resolutions of the General Assembly of the United Nations" (1955–56) 32 *British Year Book of International Law* L 97–122

(d) to recommend to the General Assembly admission of new members and the terms on which States may become parties to the Statute of the International Court of Justice;

(e) to recommend to the General Assembly the appointment of the Secretary-General, and in conjunction with the General Assembly to elect the Judges of the International Court of Justice; and

(f) to promote the machinery for peace-making and maintenance of international peace.

14.3.3.3 *Peace-making and Peace-keeping Functions of the Security Council*

The Security Council is engaged in two types of major functions: peace-making and peace-keeping. Ironically, after the end of the Second World War these two issues have required the United Nations to devote its attention to them significantly. Furthermore, peace and security are no longer perceived as matters solely concerned with military issues; these have impact upon the socio-economic realities, environmental issues and general welfare of humankind. The United Nations has increased its peace-keeping operations and peace-making efforts significantly. Diplomats are now required to be extremely familiar with preventative diplomacy, the ingredients of which do not yet seem to have been fully explored. As the world faces more military tensions and experiences more wars, the more is the need for the United Nations, and in particular, the Security Council, to be engaged in peace-keeping efforts. It must be emphasised that the success of the Security Council depends upon the technique of preventative diplomacy that diplomats employ, rather than resorting to the use of weapons. Diplomats may also like to create public awareness as to the ill-effects of wars. The increased peace-keeping function of the Security Council does suggest that diplomacy about the maintenance of the peace is not absolutely successful.

Chapters VI and VII of the Charter have detailed the procedure for peace-keeping operations. Peace-keeping operations are those operations that are launched to deal with conflicts that that have occurred between States, and thereby threaten international peace and security. Peace-keeping operations are supposed to be short-lived, which are to be carried out through the UN Emergency Forces. Such forces cease hostility by means of cease-fire or separation of forces and thereafter political solutions of conflicts are sought.

Peace-keeping operations may involve military observer missions (which may be made up of unarmed officers, peace-keeping forces or both). Such operations also help implement a settlement which have already been negotiated by the peacemakers. This aspect of preventative diplomacy has assumed particular significance since 1988; therefore it is to be emphasised in this connection that diplomatic studies should emphasise the role of preventative diplomacy rather than *"war-based"* diplomacy. UN peace-keeping forces which are made up of military personnel provided by the Member States also facilitate delivery of humanitarian assistance provided by governmental and non-governmental sources.

It is the Security Council that establishes peace-keeping operations. No peace-keeping operation is established without the consent of the host government(s) concerned, and usually the consent of the other party involved is also obtained. Between 1988 and 1994, 21 peace-keeping operations were launched, compared with 13 such operations undertaken during the previous 40 years[17].

The above examples also evidence the fact that if Member States refer their disputes to the UN which they are required to do in fulfilment of their obligations under Article 2(4) of the Charter, the UN machinery may be activated for attaining peaceful settlement of dispute upon their consideration by the Security Council. What however is to be ensured is that the powerful Members of the UN also utilise its available services, when necessary, so that conflict resolutions are inevitably achieved through the implementation of the UN machinery, otherwise the Purposes of the UN and the obligations under Article 2, paragraph 4 of the Charter, will be most honoured in their breach.

The Security Council often provides the test ground for preventative diplomacy. The engagement of the UN peace-keeping operations entails a considerable amount of funds and deployment of military personnel. The Security Council may not necessarily be considered as the Council at which the militarily powerful States may take decisions as to whether enforcement measures or peace-keeping operations should be taken; contemporary diplomacy requires smaller States to dissuade militarily powerful States from engaging in either enforcement actions or peace-keeping operations, as in the final analysis, any such action or operation affects all States. Peace and security may be best achieved by preventative actions rather than by enforcement actions or peace-keeping operations, and the Security Council thus should be more engaged in preventative actions by suasion by all countries, rather than exclusively leaning on it as a chamber for the militarily powerful States. If other States necessarily submit to the militarily powerful States, then the ethos of diplomacy loses its importance. The changing nature of multilateral diplomacy demands a change in the traditional diplomacy within the Security Council.

14.3.4 The Secretary-General

Although the Charter describes the Secretary-General as the *"Chief administrative officer"* of the organisation, the nature of the work that the Secretary-General is required to perform exceeds the nature of the work that a chief administrative officer of an organisation traditionally performs. The Secretary-General may be described as a diplomat and as an initiator, a conciliator and provocateur, *"who stands before the world community as the very emblem of the*

---

[17] *Basic Facts About the United Nations*, United Nations, New York (1995) at 27

United Nations. The task demands great vigour, sensitivity and imagination, to which the Secretary-General must add a tenacious sense of optimism – a belief that the ideals expressed in the Charter can be made in reality."[18] Chapter XV of the Charter entitled *the Secretariat* describes the nature of the functions that the Secretary-General is required to perform.

The Secretary-General serves the international community; he is also accountable to the Member States of the United Nations. The Charter allows an appreciable margin of flexibility in the functions of the Secretary-General, which is justifiable in the light of the activities he is required to be engaged in on behalf of the organisation. Indeed, each Secretary-General has so far used his mandate according to the exigencies of the time, but within the context of the United Nations, and sometimes taken the initiative of launching new programmes, such as An Agenda for Development, a blueprint for development in the future, promoted in 1992 by then Secretary-General Mr Boutros Boutros-Ghali.

In the same year, the Secretary-General submitted to the Member States an Agenda for Peace[19], the primary aim of which was to build peace among former adversaries in the post-war period, and to engage the UN more effectively in order to identify the real causes of political conflicts.

Perhaps the best known service for which the Secretary-General is known is the use of his *"good offices"*. This is where his knowledge, experience and personality become very important ingredients to exercising his influence. In exercising his *"good offices"* he must remain impartial and do his best for protecting the interest of all parties concerned.

The Secretary-General is a truly international diplomat with the sole aim of promoting the cause of the United Nations. Peace-making is only one aspect of his functions; the materialisation of the other Purposes of the United Nations which have been embodied in Article 1 of the Charter entails a variety of difficult functions on his part. The Secretary-General is not only the ambassador of the United Nations, but is also a pioneer of ideas and a person with vision. But, he cannot be indifferent to issues and problems at the national level; the UN resolutions and guidelines to which the Secretary-General contributes must therefore be realistic and capable of being implemented by its Member States.

"Preventative diplomacy" has always been a very important aspect of the Secretary-General's activities. Through fact-finding, an early warning system for assessing possible threats to peace is operated, and in his capacity as the Secretary-General, in 1992, Dr Boutros Boutros-Ghali suggested a new technique whereby UN forces would be deployed to deter hostilities in areas which would appear to be engaged in hostilities. He also recommended full participation of the General Assembly in supporting efforts at mediation,

---

[18] *Basic Facts About the United Nations*, op. cit., at 18

[19] *An Agenda for Peace*: Preventative Diplomacy, Peace-making and Peace-keeping, DP1/1247 (1992); see also Supplement DP1/1623/PKS E 95/115 (1995)

negotiation or arbitration. The Secretary-General represents the United Nations as the protector of the international peace and security; he has the right to suggest new ideas as to how this mission of the UN may be reviewed and/or improved. Dr Boutros-Ghali, for example, suggested the creation of specially trained *"peace-enforcement units"* which could be deployed in cases where the task of *"cease-fire"* might exceed the limits of peace-keeping.

The Secretary-General's work also entails rapport with world leaders and other influential individuals, in addition to attendance at sessions of various UN bodies. The Secretary-General of the UN may be described as peacemaker of the world, and his diplomacy relates to the entire world, but the effect of which is felt by the Members and non-members of the United Nations. The co-operation of national diplomats is needed in order to make the efforts of the Secretary-General in peace-making successful. The role of the Secretary-General in peace-keeping efforts may be described by means of a few examples.

Eritrea

Eritrea, a former Italian colony, assumed federal status with Ethiopia in 1952, and became one autonomous unit within the Federation of Ethiopia and Eritrea, which federation became a State on 14 November 1962. The integration of Eritrea with Ethiopia as a unitary State gave rise to political upheaval, and was the cause of the movement for secession of Eritrea.

The government of President Mengistu Haile Mariam fell in 1991, and the Eritrean People's Liberation Front announced a provisional government pending a UN supervised referendum to determine the political status of Ethiopia; in May 1992, the Commissioner of the Referendum Commission of Eritrea invited the Secretary-General to send a delegation to observe the referendum scheduled from July 1992 to April 1993. In June 1992, a UN Technical Team visited Eritrea to discuss with the Referendum Commission, the Provisional Government, political, social and religious organisations to improve the organisation of the referendum.

In October, the Secretary-General submitted to the UN General Assembly a proposal for an observer mission and on 16 December 1992, the General Assembly established the UN Observer Mission to verify the Referendum in Eritrea (UNOVER), with the Secretary-General as the Head of the mission. UNOVER carried out the observer mission work leading to a supervised referendum.

Eritrea was declared independent on 24 May and was admitted to the UN as a Member on 28 May 1993.

The Congo

Immediately after the former Belgian colony became independent in June 1960, civil strife broke out, and the Belgian government sent troops with a view to protecting and evacuating Europeans. On 12 July 1960, the Congolese Government asked the UN for military assistance in order to protect the country from external aggression. In less than 48 hours the UN Emergency Force was constituted and sent to the Congo; UN civilian experts were also sent to the Congo to ensure the availability of the essential public services.

Until about 1964, the UN Operation in the Congo (ONUC) continued to help the Government to restore peace, law and order and territorial integrity. The UN was required to commit significant resources to the Congo. A few times during 1961 and 1962, the secessionist forces led by the foreign mercenaries, who wanted secession by Katanga, clashed with the UN force. Eventually the UN force was able to overcome the situation, and in February 1963, after Katanga had been integrated into the Congo, the phasing out of the UN force began, and this process was completed in June 1964.

Incidentally, ONUC presented a novel situation in the early days of the UN, which expressly brought out a new dimension to the power of the General Assembly under Articles 10 and 11 of the UN Charter. During the Congo crisis it became clear that by virtue of the opposition of the Soviet Union and France in agreeing to any proposal for sending a UN Emergency Force to the Congo, the Security Council would not be able to adopt a resolution to that effect. However, as part of the UN peace-keeping function and responsibility, the Secretary-General requested the General Assembly to take action on the request made by the Congolese Government in regard to sending a UN force. The General Assembly exercised its power in relation to the maintenance of international peace and security, adopted the important resolution entitled Uniting for Peace and constituted an emergency for the Congo. UN forces, as explained, earlier, were sent into the Congo and restored peace in the country.

This example does prove the power matrix between the Security Council and the General Assembly of the UN in relation to the maintenance of international peace and security. It would be inappropriate to maintain that the responsibility for the maintenance of international peace and security and the related functions thereto, exclusively lies with the Security Council.

Lebanon

In early 1972, Israel attacked Palestinian camps in Lebanon on the alleged grounds of reprisal for raids carried out in its territory by Palestinian commandos. Soon after that at the Lebanese Government's request, the Security Council took a decision to set up the UN Truce Supervision Organisation (UNTSO) for observing the cease-fire operation in the affected area.

Raids and counter-raids became an almost regular phenomenon between the two sides. In 1978, another UN peace-keeping force, UN Interim Force in Lebanon (UNIFIL) was set up to ensure the withdrawal of Israeli forces, and to restore international peace and security in the area.

The Israeli forces, having completed their withdrawal from Lebanon in June 1978, handed over their positions in the border area not to UNIFIL but to

Lebanese irregular forces (Christian and associated militias). This caused frequent exchanges of conflicts between the irregular forces and the Israel Defence Forces (IDF) on the one hand, and the armed forces predominantly of the PLO, and Lebanese National Movement on the other.

However, in July 1981, a *de facto* cease-fire came into effect, and the area generally remained quiet until mid-1982.

But, in June 1982, the Israeli forces moved into Lebanese territory, UNFIL was by-passed, and they surrounded Beirut. As hostilities continued, the UN Security Council intervened, and called for a cease-fire and demanded that Israel withdrew to the internationally recognised boundaries of Lebanon. In August, the Security Council authorised the deployment of UN military observers (the Observer Group Beirut) to monitor the situation in and around Beirut. A cease-fire was effected on 12 August. In the same month, France, Italy and the United States concluded an agreement with Lebanon for participation of their troops in a multinational force to assist Lebanon in carrying out an orderly departure from Lebanon of Palestinian armed forces in the Beirut area. The Palestinian armed forces left Lebanon on 1 September, and the multinational force withdrew on 13 September 1982.

However, tension continued to increase leading to the killing of President elect Bashir Gemayel, and the following day, IDF Units took up new positions in the area. The Security Council condemned the Israeli attacks in Beirut and demanded that they returned to pre-15 September positions. The Security Council advised Israel to respect Lebanon's sovereignty and territorial integrity. On 16 September, Lebanese Christian militias entered the Sabra and Chatila Palestinian refugee camps in the suburbs of Beirut and killed large numbers of refugees. Both the General Assembly and the Security Council condemned the massacre referring to the Fourth Geneva Convention on the Protection of Civilian Persons in Time of War. Shortly afterwards, at the request of the Lebanese Government, British, French, Italian and the US contingents of the multinational force returned to Beirut.

In July 1983, the withdrawal of the IDF from Beirut began, but it led to fighting between the Lebanese Government forces and Christian Phalangists, and Shi'ite and Druse militias in which the French and US contingents of the multinational forces were involved in the fighting. The multinational force suffered heavy casualties; France, Italy, the UK and US withdrew their forces in early 1984.

In 1984, the Secretary-General of the United Nations convened a conference of military representatives of Lebanon and Israel (at UNIFIL headquarters), which met at various times between November 1984 and January 1985, the primary purpose of which was to expedite the withdrawal of the Israeli forces, and the three-phase withdrawal plan was completed by 1985. But soon after the withdrawal of the forces attacks by Lebanese resistance groups against Israeli forces continued.

The Secretary-General's efforts to persuade Israel to leave the security zone met with no success. Israel maintained that the Lebanese Government did not have any authority to control the security zone, and that UNIFIL being a peace-keeping force was not mandated to action to control cross-border attacks. Lebanon, of course, insisted on Israel's withdrawal from the area maintaining that the occupation was illegal and contrary to the UN resolutions. UNIFIL however continued providing humanitarian assistance.

In 1988, fighting started again, and in August 1989, the intensity of hostilities reached such a level that the Secretary-General notified the situation to the Security Council, and the latter appealed for an immediate cease-fire. On the basis of a peace formula rendered in October 1989 at an Arab League meeting held in Ta'if, Saudi Arabia (the Ta'if accord), in November, the Lebanese members of parliament elected a new President, René Mouawad, who was assassinated soon after his election, and succeeded by Elias Hrawi. The Security Council expressed its support for the new government elected under the Ta'if accord.

A year later (October 1990) President Hrawi invited Syrian forces to take control of Beirut, and the President started implementing the security plan for Beirut which was part of the peace formula revealed by the Ta'if accord. By December 1990, with the Syrian support, the Lebanese army was in control of Beirut.

In 1991, the United Nations adopted a special plan for the reconstruction and development of Lebanon, and in July of the same year various UN agencies and programmes concluded a mission for the assessment of the needs of Lebanon. In December, the UN General Assembly invited the international community to provide financial and technical assistance to Lebanon. Also, in the same year, the diplomacy of the Secretary-General and his envoys led to the release of several hostages and prisoners.

During 1992-94, the situation along the Israel-Lebanon border remained tense. In July 1993, for example, the Lebanese forces launched attacks against Northern Israel, and the IDF responded to it by massive air strikes against South Lebanon causing death and destruction of villages, houses and displacement of thousands of civilian Lebanese people.

At the request of the government, the UN dispatched a needs-assessment mission to Lebanon. In August 1994, on the basis of the mission's findings, the Secretary-General launched an appeal for humanitarian assistance to Lebanon. Meanwhile, UNIFIL continued to work to bring stability in the area[20].

Democratic Republic of the Congo
As a result of the genocide in Rwanda in 1994 and the establishment of a new government there, some 1.2 million Hutus, a tribe in Rwanda, fled to the Kivu province of Zaire, an area inhabited by ethnic Tutsis and others. In 1996, a

---

[20] The primary source of information on all these events is the UN publication entitled *Basic Facts About the United Nations*, New York, United Nations (1995)

rebellion led by Laurent D Kabila against the army of President Mobutu Sese Seko took place. Kabila's forces, aided by Rwanda and Uganda, took the capital city of Kinshasa in 1997, and the country's name was changed to the Democratic Republic of the Congo (DRC).

In 1998, a rebellion against the Kabila government started in the Kivu, and over a short period of time seized large areas of the country. Whereas Rwanda and Uganda supported the rebel government, the Congolese Rally for Democracy (RCD), Angola, Chad, Namibia and Zimbabwe promised President Kabila military support. As the situation in the Congo further deteriorated the UN Security Council called for a ceasefire and the withdrawal of foreign forces. In May 1999, the RCD split into two factions.

In July 1999, the Lusaka Ceasefire Agreement which was initiated by the UN Secretary-General, and the South African Development Community, was signed by DRC, on the one hand, and Angola, Namibia, Rwanda, Uganda and Zimbabwe, on the other, in order to bring the hostilities to an end. In an attempt to implement the Lusaka Ceasefire Agreement, the Security Council decided to deploy 90 UN military liaison officer to strategic areas in the countries concerned, including their capital towns. In November 1999, the United Nations Mission in the Democratic Republic of the Congo (MONUC) was established to facilitate the implementation of the agreement, and monitor security conditions.

On 16 January 2001, President Kabila was assassinated, and was succeeded by his son, Joseph Kabila.

It was revealed by experts appointed by the Security Council that DRC was also interested in the minerals in the Republic of the Congo. Although President Joseph Kabila decided to relax the ban on political parties in the DRC, fighting continued with the involvement of Burundi, Rwanda and the local Congolese militia known as Mai-Mai and the RCD. In October 2001 the Security Council authorised the deployment of UN troops and military observers to that region. Although Agreements were concluded for withdrawal of Rwandan troops from the DRC, fighting still continued. Diplomatic efforts to bring peace into the area also continued and in December 2002, under the UN and South African mediation, the parties concerned agreed to form a transitional government. The Security Council enlarged MONUC to 8,700 military personnel. Unfortunately, new fighting erupted in the South Kivu region, and the UN-led ceasefire agreement signed in March 2003 in Ituri failed. Major violence resumed in Bunia.

In May 2003, the parties signed another ceasefire agreement for the Ituri region but the ethnic tensions and fighting continued. On 30 May 2003, the Security Council authorised the deployment of an Interim Emergency Multi-national Force (IEMF) to Bunia until 1 September to help stabilise the situation.

On 29 June 2003, the government and the country's opposition factions, including RCD and the Movement for the Liberation of the Congo (MLC) signed an agreement on military and security arrangements. On 17 July 2003, the DRC's new power-sharing transitional government led by President Kabila was established. The Security Council extended MONUC's mandate until 30 July 2004, and increased the military strength to 10,800 in preparation for the transfer of security responsibilities from the IEMF.

MONUC was authorised by the Security Council to take necessary measures to protect civilians, humanitarian workers and UN personnel. On 5 September 2003, the responsibilities were handed over from the IEMF to MONUC, but unfortunately sporadic fighting went on in Ituri, in particular, and the exploitation of DRC's natural resources remained unabated. The Security Council condemned the practice, but preparations were being made for holding elections in 2005.

Cambodia

Before the implementation of the Paris Peace Agreement, 1991, internal conflicts in Cambodia, since the days of the Viet-Nam war until the 1970s became a regular phenomenon. During the *"Khmer Rouge"* regime from 1975 through 1979, nearly 2 million people perished of murder, disease and starvation.

In 1993, with the assistance of the United Nations Transitional Authority in Cambodia (UNTAC), democratic elections took place in Cambodia. The Office of the High Commissioner for Human Rights, which supports the work of the special representative of the Secretary-General for human rights in Cambodia, provides help to the government and people of Cambodia to promote and protect human rights.

In 2003, the Government of Cambodia and the UN reached an agreement whereby the country would be helped by the latter to set up and operate a special court to prosecute crimes committed during the regime of the Khmer Rouge[21].

14.3.5 The Economic and Social Council

The Economic and Social Council (ECOSOC) is an extremely important organ of the United Nations through which socio-economic development activities of the UN are co-ordinated. In order to help governments develop and establish a sustainable infrastructure for development, the United Nations and its specialised agencies offer support in various ways for national development with a view to their achieving balanced economic and social progress by best utilising their available human, financial and physical resources which should increase their export earnings and inward flow of foreign direct investment. But development programmes for individual countries are carried out by the United Nations at the request of the government concerned; although

---

[21] In detailing these facts and events the author has referred to the UN publication entitled *Basic Facts About the United Nations*, New York, United Nations (2004)

regional programmes are implemented by ECOSOC. The Economic and Social Council is also the principal forum for discussing international socio-economic issues and for formulating policies and recommending them to the UN Members States through the General Assembly.

Articles 61–72 describe the powers and functions of the Economic and Social Council. The mandate given to the ECOSOC is very broad; indeed the nature of activities it has already undertaken is varied and extremely useful, especially in relation to developing guidelines and legislation at the national level.

If one believes that diplomacy is also significantly concerned with socio-economic issues, then one must admit that the ECOSOC provides the platform for learning and utilising that aspect of diplomacy. The ECOSOC generally holds one five-week long substantive session each year, and at least two organisational seminars. These seminars discuss major economic and social issues and are attended by ministers and other high officials. Without thorough familiarity with these issues national diplomats will not be able to effectively participate in these seminars; in many ways, their familiarity with these issues including the issue of their national interest in certain cases, gives them the real bargaining power; their economic strength is not of paramount importance.

Throughout the year, the work of the ECOSOC is carried out by its subsidiary bodies, namely, committees and commissions, which are accountable to the ECOSOC. There are a large number of subsidiaries and related bodies under the ECOSOC: for example, *functional commissions*: e.g. Commission for Social Development, Statistical Commission, Commission on the Status of Women, Commission on Population and Development, Commission on Crime Prevention and Criminal Justice, Commission on Sustainable Development; *regional commissions:* Economic Commission for Africa (Addis Ababa, Ethiopia), Economic and Social Commission for Asia and the Pacific (Bangkok, Thailand), Economic Commission for Europe (Geneva, Switzerland), Economic Commission for Latin America and the Caribbean (Santiago, Chile); and Economic and Social Commission for Western Asia (Amman, Jordan); *standing committees:* Committee for Programme and Co-ordination, Commission on Human Settlements, Committee on Non-Governmental Organizations, and Committee on Negotiations with Intergovernmental Agencies; *expert bodies:* on various subjects, e.g. natural resources, development planning; the *related bodies:* e.g. the UN Children's Fund, the Office of UN High Commissioner for Refugees, the United Nations Development Programmes (UNDP), and the World Food Programme.

Under the Charter, the ECOSOC has the mandate to consult non-governmental organisations (NGOs) in connection with matters that come under its purview. Interaction between the ECOSOC and the NGOs (over 1,500) provides an opportunity to both parties to understand the nature of the problems and issues on which the ECOSOC may make special studies and issue recommendations.

Of course, the nature of interaction between the ECOSOC and the NGOs depends upon the status of the latter. NGOs are classified into four categories: NGOs of category I are those that are concerned with most of the ECOSOC's activities; organisations with special competence in specific areas, and which can make contributions to the ECOSOC's activities are included in category II; NGOs with consultative status are placed in category III; such NGOs can only send observers to public meetings of the ECOSOC and its subsidiary bodies and submit written statements to the Council's work.

The economic and social development programmes of the UN are largely carried out under the responsibility of the ECOSOC. The needs of programmes and their strategies are determined through the expertise of the ECOSOC. Various UN organisations facilitate the economic and social development programmes under the overall co-ordination of the ECOSOC. Article 62(1) of the UN charter provides that:

> *"The Economic and Social Council may make or initiate studies and reports with respect to international economic, social, cultural, educational, health, and related matters and may make recommendations with respect to any such matters to the General Assembly to the Members of the United Nations, and to the specialized agencies concerned."*

The ECOSOC is also the central forum for considering international economic and social issues and for adopting recommendations. The Council has the authority to establish functional commissions in order to be advised by such expert bodies. An example of such expert bodies is the Commission for Social Development. Although the ECOSOC has a particular role to play in setting development priorities and co-ordinating activities within the UN family of organisations, the Council may receive mandates for various socio-economic programmes from other sources, such as the Secretary-General (An Agenda for Development 1994), the General Assembly (UN Development Decade 1961–70; International Development Strategies – 1971–80; 1981–90; 1991–2000; Declaration and Programme of Action on the Establishment of a New International Economic Order (NIEO) 1974).

The specialised agencies, a list of which is given below, are accountable to the ECOSOC.

- International Labour Organization (ILO);

- Food and Agriculture Organization of the United Nations (FAO);

- UN Educational, Scientific and Cultural Organization (UNESCO);

- World Health Organization

- World Bank (including the International Bank for Reconstruction and Development, the International Development Association, International Finance Corporation and the Multinational Investment Guarantee Agency);

- International Monetary Fund (IMF);
- International Civil Aviation Organization (ICAO);
- Universal Postal Union (UPU);
- International Telecommunication Union (ITU);
- World Meteorological Organization (WMO);
- International Maritime Organization (IMO);
- World Intellectual Property Organization (WIPO);
- International Fund for Agricultural Development (IFAD);
- United Nations Industrial Development Organization (UNIDO).

The International Atomic Energy Agency (IAEA) which is an inter-governmental body with the status of a specialised agency submits its reports annually to the General Assembly, and where appropriate, to the Security Council and the ECOSOC.

The World Trade Organization (WTO) which was established in 1995 is the principal inter-governmental organisation which deals with policies, principles and related issues concerning international trade. Then there are other programmes and organisations, such as the United Nations Development Programme (UNDP) or the UN Conference on Trade and Development (UNCTAD), which work closely with the ECOSOC and submit reports to the Council. ECOSOC can establish subordinate bodies, when necessary.

Development programmes for individual countries are carried out at the request of the Member State concerned. Their socio-economic and development programmes are implemented on a regional basis by the UN Economic and Social Commissions for various regions, namely, Africa, Asia and the Pacific, Western Asia, Latin America and the Caribbean, and Europe.

National diplomats have a significant constructive role to play in regard to the programmes with which ECOSOC may be concerned. Policy making and adoption of recommendations are done on a consensus basis. Diplomats should be sufficiently familiar with the issues and try to adopt such policies which may be implemented at the national level.

The Trusteeship Council

The Trusteeship Council, which was one of the principal organs of the United Nations, was entrusted with the task of supervising the administration of the Trust Territories (eleven in number) placed under the Trusteeship System, and to promote the advancement of the inhabitants of those territories towards self-government or independence[22].

---

[22] See further UN General Assembly's Declaration on the Granting of Independence to Colonial Countries and Peoples (Resolution 1514(xv) of 14 December 1960)

14.3.6 The Secretariat

Article 97 of the UN Charter provides that:

> *The Secretariat shall comprise a Secretary-General and such staff as the Organization may require. The Secretary-General shall be appointed by the General Assembly upon the recommendation of the Security Council. He shall be the chief administrative officer of the Organization.*

The Secretariat carries out the day-to-day work of the Organization. The Secretary-General who is appointed by the General Assembly on the recommendation of the Security Council is the head of the Secretariat. Other principal organs of the UN are serviced by the Secretariat and it also administers the policies and programmes adopted by them. It is thus involved in the variety of work that the UN undertakes, that is, peace-keeping, preparation of studies on various subjects, viz., human rights, socio-economic issues, organisation of international conferences on issues of international concern, even interpreting speeches and translating documents into the official languages of the UN. It is also the function of the Secretariat to study the progress made by the Member States as regards the implementation of UN resolutions and declarations. The Secretariat may be described as the central nerve centre of the UN with which all other organs must liaise and work.

14.3.7 The International Court of Justice

The International Court of Justice (ICJ) is the principal judicial organ of the United Nations. The Court is open to all Members of the United Nations. As subjects of international law are States, the ICJ is not open to private individuals. However, a non-member state may become a party to the Statute on conditions determined in each case by the General Assembly on the recommendation of the Security Council.

The Court consists of 15 judges elected independently by the General Assembly and the Security Council. The judges serve for nine-year terms and may be re-elected. No two judges can be nationals of the same State. The judges are chosen on the basis of their nationality and in selecting them it is ensured that the principal legal systems are represented in the Court.

The Court may deal with (jurisdiction of the Court) (a) all legal questions which States may refer to it, (b) all issues arising under treaties and conventions, including the UN Charter. The basic system of conferring jurisdiction on the Court may be described in the following way: (a) States by a signing a treaty or convention which provides for the jurisdiction of the Court may bind themselves in advance to accept the jurisdiction of the Court; or (b) by making a declaration accepting the compulsory jurisdiction in respect of certain classes of cases.

As to the applicable law, Article 38(1) of the Statutes provides that:

> *"The Court, whose function is to decide in accordance with international law such disputes as are submitted to it, shall apply:*

a. international conventions, whether general or particular, establishing rules expressly recognized by the contesting states;

b. international custom, as evidence of a general practice accepted as law;

c. the general principles of law recognized by civilized nations;

d. subject to the provisions of Article 59, judicial decisions and the teachings of the most highly qualified publicists of the various nations, as subsidiary means for the determination of rules of law."

The ICJ has two types of jurisdiction: advisory and optional. When the General Assembly or the Security Council or a specialised agency, the latter with the authorisation of the General Assembly, seeks an advice of the Court on a legal issue, the Court exercises its advisory jurisdiction. A sovereign State has the *"option"* to confer jurisdiction on the Court by the processes stated above; hence it is called the *"optional"* jurisdiction, which is also described as the *"compulsory jurisdiction"*. Once the option has been exercised by a sovereign State, it becomes compulsory for that State to bind itself to accept the jurisdiction when the Court renders judgments.

14.4 CONCLUSIONS

This Chapter attempts to explain the basic objectives of the UN, whether expressed through its principal organs or through the activities of its specialised agencies. It is not possible nor is it advisable to detail all the functions of the UN family through one Chapter. However, the above discussion only attempts to illustrate the basic purposes and functions of the UN family.

A national diplomat should find it useful to learn the UN machinery, particularly because many of the so-called national issues are no longer to be treated as such. International co-operation is essential for dealing with many national issues. Often, the guidelines issued by the UN and its agencies are useful for States to follow, particularly in respect of developing legislation at the national level or for attaining national development, whether socio-economic or otherwise. Of course, in order to take advantage of the contributions made by the UN family, States are required to appreciate that a rigid treatment of and notion towards sovereignty will hinder progress and indeed international co-operation.

Conclusions

It has been stated in this work that diplomacy dates back to antiquity; there is no need to emphasise the necessity of diplomatic relations between States. However, one should pay attention to the new dimensions to diplomacy. Owing to a variety of politico-economic issues that have arisen over the past four or five decades, one is required to consider whether all aspects of classical diplomacy may still be applied to resolve these issues. By the same token it may be stated that in order to be able to deal with these critical and unprecedented issues, diplomats should develop a new kind of skills in negotiating terms and conditions, a more comprehensive idea of the complex world in which we live, and the capacity to deal with issues at an international level.

The days of war-based diplomacy should be numbered. Poverty and the lack of the application of democracy is one of the fundamental reasons why governments in most of the developing countries are unstable. Diplomats may find it useful to take a united approach to resolve this problem. With economic progress, the need for peace-keeping will be much reduced. This is an issue which should receive the urgent attention of diplomats. Action in this regard will also reduce the need for what may be described as diplomacy of dependency.

The perception of bargaining power should be reviewed; if diplomacy is based on the bargaining power of the stronger, then there is no need for diplomatic intercourse.

Incidentally, the true meaning of *"bargaining power"* is the power to negotiate and, from this standpoint, there is no reason why developing countries may not use their bargaining power.

Aid/loan-based diplomacy is no diplomacy. It gives rise to diplomacy of dependency, which cannot be the principal function of diplomatic relations. Diplomatic relations become effective when each party can offer something to the other. In a world which is divided between the *"haves"* and *"have-nots"* proper diplomacy can never take place; hence the need for strengthening the trading position and economies of developing countries. This is an area in which diplomats are required to do much work. This aspect of diplomacy will embrace issues such as the policies currently operated by the World Trade Organisation (WTO) to establish commercial equality or to allow market access to every State or to consider the effect of regional integrations comprised of rich countries and of developing countries. It is emphasised that economic prosperity of a country automatically provides it with more negotiating power.

Abuse of sovereignty has always been an issue in contemporary diplomatic relations. This again is founded on the perception of the power-game. Modern-day diplomacy should not be perceived as a diplomacy of power-game; co-operative diplomacy for the protection of interests of all should receive much attention. This is why this work has placed emphasis on economic diplomacy, and the importance of truly international organisations which should be directed at creative work by means of new principles and experience.

The underlying policy of the setting up of the UN was clearly to indicate that there was a need for a shift from pre-1945 diplomacy to a new type of diplomacy in which socio-economic issues would receive priority. Indeed, two chapters in the Charter of the United Nations, Chapters IX and X, are exclusively devoted to such issues. Unfortunately, in many instances power-based diplomacy has remained evident. When one studies the origins of international diplomacy, one will find that diplomatic relations between States were found to be necessary for commercial and business purposes. Furthermore, however emotional it may sound, the fact remains that various chapters of the UN Charter rightly placed emphasis on the issue of abolition of warfares, and the use of force. Article 2, paragraph 4 of the UN Charter provides that:

All Members shall refrain in their international relations from the threat or use of force against the territorial integrity or political independence of any state, or in any manner inconsistent with the Purposes of the United Nations.

Member States have failed the UN. There is hardly any justification to maintain that the Security Council or the General Assembly are not effective enough institutions. It is precisely the duty of diplomats to make them effective by changing their membership, policies and functional mechanism. It is regrettable that the current international diplomacy has predominantly returned to the diplomacy of the pre-1945 days which was often characterised by the violation of the principle of the political integrity of States.

The new dimensions to diplomacy, e.g. protection of the environment, apportionment of natural resources between States (common heritage of mankind), rights of minorities, multilateral trade policies, require diplomats to have comprehensive knowledge of most of the complex contemporary issues.

International diplomacy cannot be totally dissociated from international law; diplomats are thus required to be familiar with the basic principles of international law. In view of the current nature of international relations, diplomats are required to be extremely familiar with the current developments of international affairs and international law in order to be able to participate effectively in matters of international concern. Contemporary diplomacy goes beyond the narrow bounds of national interests, although the latter may not be disregarded altogether.

Contemporary diplomats are also required to develop international norms, through international Conventions, with a view to protecting the interests of the international community.

Finally, diplomacy should be ethics-based, as this has a direct bearing upon the use of force by a strong State over the weak. Humanitarian diplomacy is more sustainable than war-based diplomacy. Contemporary diplomacy should be directed at socio-economic development whether in the developed or developing world.

APPENDIX I

Vienna Convention on Diplomatic Relations and Optional Protocols

Done at Vienna, on 18 April 1961

The States Parties to the present Convention,

Recalling that peoples of all nations from ancient times have recognized the status of diplomatic agents,

Having in mind the purposes and principles of the Charter of the United Nations concerning the sovereign equality of States, the maintenance of international peace and security, and the promotion of friendly relations among nations,

Believing that an international convention on diplomatic intercourse, privileges and immunities would contribute to the development of friendly relations among nations, irrespective of their differing constitutional and social systems,

Realizing that the purpose of such privileges and immunities is not to benefit individuals but to ensure the efficient performance of the functions of diplomatic missions as representing States,

Affirming that the rules of customary international law should continue to govern questions not expressly regulated by the provisions of the present Convention,

Have agreed as follows:

Article 1

For the purpose of the present Convention, the following expressions shall have the meanings hereunder assigned to them:

(a) the "head of the mission" is the person charged by the sending State with the duty of acting in that capacity;
(b) the "members of the mission" are the head of the mission and the members of the staff of the mission;
(c) the "members of the staff of the mission" are the members of the diplomatic staff, of the administrative and technical staff and of the service staff of the mission;

(d) the "members of the diplomatic staff" are the members of the staff of the mission having diplomatic rank;
(e) a "diplomatic agent" is the head of the mission or a member of the diplomatic staff of the mission;
(f) the "members of the administrative and technical staff" are the members of the staff of the mission employed in the administrative and technical service of the mission;
(g) the "members of the service staff" are the members of the staff of the mission in the domestic service of the mission;
(h) a "private servant" is a person who is in the domestic service of a member of the mission and who is not an employee of the sending State;
(i) the "premises of the mission" are the buildings or parts of buildings and the land ancillary thereto, irrespective of ownership, used for the purposes of the mission including the residence of the head of the mission.

Article 2

The establishment of diplomatic relations between States, and of permanent diplomatic missions, takes place by mutual consent.

Article 3

1. The functions of a diplomatic mission consist inter alia in:

(a) representing the sending State in the receiving State;
(b) protecting in the receiving State the interests of the sending State and of its nationals, within the limits permitted by international law;
(c) negotiating with the Government of the receiving State;
(d) ascertaining by all lawful means conditions and developments in the receiving State, and reporting thereon to the Government of the sending State;
(e) promoting friendly relations between the sending State and the receiving State, and developing their economic, cultural and scientific relations.

2. Nothing in the present Convention shall be construed as preventing the performance of consular functions by a diplomatic mission.

Article 4

1. The sending State must make certain that the agreement of the receiving State has been given for the person it proposes to accredit as head of the mission to that State.

2. The receiving State is not obliged to give reasons to the sending State for a refusal of agreement.

Article 5

1. The sending State may, after it has given due notification to the receiving States concerned, accredit a head of mission or assign any member of the diplomatic staff, as the case may be, to more than one State, unless there is express objection by any of the receiving States.

2. If the sending State accredits a head of mission to one or more other States it may establish a diplomatic mission headed by a charge d'affaires ad interim in each State where the head of mission has not his permanent seat.

3. A head of mission or any member of the diplomatic staff of the mission may act as representative of the sending State to any international organization.

Article 6

Two or more States may accredit the same person as head of mission to another State, unless objection is offered by the receiving State.

Article 7

Subject to the provisions of Articles 5, 8, 9 and 11, the sending State may freely appoint the members of the staff of the mission. In the case of military, naval or air attaches, the receiving State may require their names to be submitted beforehand, for its approval.

Article 8

1. Members of the diplomatic staff of the mission should in principle be of the nationality of the sending State.

2. Members of the diplomatic staff of the mission may not be appointed from among persons having the nationality of the receiving State, except with the consent of that State which may be withdrawn at any time.

3. The receiving State may reserve the same right with regard to nationals of a third State who are not also nationals of the sending State.

Article 9

1. The receiving State may at any time and without having to explain its decision, notify the sending State that the head of the mission or any member of the diplomatic staff of the mission is persona non grata or that any other member of the staff of the mission is not acceptable. In any such case, the sending State shall, as appropriate, either recall the person concerned or terminate his functions with the mission. A person may be declared non grata or not acceptable before arriving in the territory of the receiving State.

2. If the sending State refuses or fails within a reasonable period to carry out its obligations under paragraph 1 of this Article, the receiving State may refuse to recognize the person concerned as a member of the mission.

Article 10

1. The Ministry for Foreign Affairs of the receiving State, or such other ministry as may be agreed, shall be notified of:

(a) the appointment of members of the mission, their arrival and their final departure or the termination of their functions with the mission;
(b) the arrival and final departure of a person belonging to the family of a member of the mission and, where appropriate, the fact that a person becomes or ceases to be a member of the family of a member of the mission;
(c) the arrival and final departure of private servants in the employ of persons referred to in sub-paragraph (a) of this paragraph and, where appropriate, the fact that they are leaving the employ of such persons;
(d) the engagement and discharge of persons resident in the receiving State as members of the mission or private servants entitled to privileges and immunities.

2. Where possible, prior notification of arrival and final departure shall also be given.

Article 11

1. In the absence of specific agreement as to the size of the mission, the receiving State may require that the size of a mission be kept within limits considered by it to be reasonable and normal, having regard to circumstances and conditions in the receiving State and to the needs of the particular mission.

2. The receiving State may equally, within similar bounds and on a non-discriminatory basis, refuse to accept officials of a particular category.

Article 12

The sending State may not, without the prior express consent of the receiving State, establish offices forming part of the mission in localities other than those in which the mission itself is established.

Article 13

1. The head of the mission is considered as having taken up his functions in the receiving State either when he has presented his credentials or when he has notified his arrival and a true copy of his credentials has been presented to the Ministry for Foreign Affairs of the receiving State, or such other ministry as may be agreed, in accordance with the practice prevailing in the receiving State which shall be applied in a uniform manner.

2. The order of presentation of credentials or of a true copy thereof will be determined by the date and time of the arrival of the head of the mission.

Article 14

1. Heads of mission are divided into three classes, namely:

(a) that of ambassadors or nuncios accredited to Heads of State, and other heads of mission of equivalent rank;
(b) that of envoys, ministers and internuncios accredited to Heads of State;
(c) that of charges d'affaires accredited to Ministers for Foreign Affairs.

2. Except as concerns precedence and etiquette, there shall be no differentiation between heads of mission by reason of their class.

Article 15

The class to which the heads of their missions are to be assigned shall be agreed between States.

Article 16

1. Heads of mission shall take precedence in their respective classes in the order of the date and time of taking up their functions in accordance with Article 13.

2. Alterations in the credentials of a head of mission not involving any change of class shall not affect his precedence.

3. This Article is without prejudice to any practice accepted by the receiving State regarding the precedence of the representative of the Holy See.

Article 17

The precedence of the members of the diplomatic staff of the mission shall be notified by the head of the mission to the Ministry for Foreign Affairs or such other ministry as may be agreed.

Article 18

The procedure to be observed in each State for the reception of heads of mission shall be uniform in respect of each class.

Article 19

1. If the post of head of the mission is vacant, or if the head of the mission is unable to perform his functions, a charge d'affaires ad interim shall act provisionally as head of the mission. The name of the charge d'affaires ad interim shall be notified, either by the head of the mission or, in case he is

unable to do so, by the Ministry for Foreign Affairs of the sending State to the Ministry for Foreign Affairs of the receiving State or such other ministry as may be agreed.

2. In cases where no member of the diplomatic staff of the mission is present in the receiving State, a member of the administrative and technical staff may, with the consent of the receiving State, be designated by the sending State to be in charge of the current administrative affairs of the mission.

Article 20

The mission and its head shall have the right to use the flag and emblem of the sending State on the premises of the mission, including the residence of the head of the mission, and on his means of transport.

Article 21

1. The receiving State shall either facilitate the acquisition on its territory, in accordance with its laws, by the sending State of premises necessary for its mission or assist the latter in obtaining accommodation in some other way.

2. It shall also, where necessary, assist missions in obtaining suitable accommodation for their members.

Article 22

1. The premises of the mission shall be inviolable. The agents of the receiving State may not enter them, except with the consent of the head of the mission.

2. The receiving State is under a special duty to take all appropriate steps to protect the premises of the mission against any intrusion or damage and to prevent any disturbance of the peace of the mission or impairment of its dignity.

3. The premises of the mission, their furnishings and other property thereon and the means of transport of the mission shall be immune from search, requisition, attachment or execution.

Article 23

1. The sending State and the head of the mission shall be exempt from all national, regional or municipal dues and taxes in respect of the premises of the mission, whether owned or leased, other than such as represent payment for specific services rendered.

2. The exemption from taxation referred to in this Article shall not apply to such dues and taxes payable under the law of the receiving State by persons contracting with the sending State or the head of the mission.

Article 24

The archives and documents of the mission shall be inviolable at any time and wherever they may be.

Article 25

The receiving State shall accord full facilities for the performance of the functions of the mission.

Article 26

Subject to its laws and regulations concerning zones entry into which is prohibited or regulated for reasons of national security, the receiving State shall ensure to all members of the mission freedom of movement and travel in its territory.

Article 27

1. The receiving State shall permit and protect free communication on the part of the mission for all official purposes. In communicating with the Government and the other missions and consulates of the sending State, wherever situated, the mission may employ all appropriate means, including diplomatic couriers and messages in code or cipher. However, the mission may install and use a wireless transmitter only with the consent of the receiving State.

2. The official correspondence of the mission shall be inviolable. Official correspondence means all correspondence relating to the mission and its functions.

3. The diplomatic bag shall not be opened or detained.

4. The packages constituting the diplomatic bag must bear visible external marks of their character and may contain only diplomatic documents or Articles intended for official use.

5. The diplomatic courier, who shall be provided with an official document indicating his status and the number of packages constituting the diplomatic bag, shall be protected by the receiving State in the performance of his functions. He shall enjoy personal inviolability and shall not be liable to any form of arrest or detention.

6. The sending State or the mission may designate diplomatic couriers ad hoc. In such cases the provisions of paragraph 5 of this Article shall also apply, except that the immunities therein mentioned shall cease to apply when such a courier has delivered to the consignee the diplomatic bag in his charge.

7. A diplomatic bag may be entrusted to the captain of a commercial aircraft scheduled to land at an authorized port of entry. He shall be provided with an

official document indicating the number of packages constituting the bag but he shall not be considered to be a diplomatic courier. The mission may send one of its members to take possession of the diplomatic bag directly and freely from the captain of the aircraft.

Article 28

The fees and charges levied by the mission in the course of its official duties shall be exempt from all dues and taxes.

Article 29

The person of a diplomatic agent shall be inviolable. He shall not be liable to any form of arrest or detention. The receiving State shall treat him with due respect and shall take all appropriate steps to prevent any attack on his person, freedom or dignity.

Article 30

1. The private residence of a diplomatic agent shall enjoy the same inviolability and protection as the premises of the mission.

2. His papers, correspondence and, except as provided in paragraph 3 of Article 31, his property, shall likewise enjoy inviolability.

Article 31

1. A diplomatic agent shall enjoy immunity from the criminal jurisdiction of the receiving State. He shall also enjoy immunity from its civil and administrative jurisdiction, except in the case of:

(a) a real action relating to private immovable property situated in the territory of the receiving State, unless he holds it on behalf of the sending State for the purposes of the mission;
(b) an action relating to succession in which the diplomatic agent is involved as executor, administrator, heir or legatee as a private person and not on behalf of the sending State;
(c) an action relating to any professional or commercial activity exercised by the diplomatic agent in the receiving State outside his official functions.

2. A diplomatic agent is not obliged to give evidence as a witness.

3. No measures of execution may be taken in respect of a diplomatic agent except in the cases coming under sub-paragraphs (a), (b) and (c) of paragraph 1 of this Article, and provided that the measures concerned can be taken without infringing the inviolability of his person or of his residence.

4. The immunity of a diplomatic agent from the jurisdiction of the receiving State does not exempt him from the jurisdiction of the sending State.

Article 32

1. The immunity from jurisdiction of diplomatic agents and of persons enjoying immunity under Article 37 may be waived by the sending State.

2. Waiver must always be express.

3. The initiation of proceedings by a diplomatic agent or by a person enjoying immunity from jurisdiction under Article 37 shall preclude him from invoking immunity from jurisdiction in respect of any counter-claim directly connected with the principal claim.

4. Waiver of immunity from jurisdiction in respect of civil or administrative proceedings shall not be held to imply waiver of immunity in respect of the execution of the judgment, for which a separate waiver shall be necessary.

Article 33

1. Subject to the provisions of paragraph 3 of this Article, a diplomatic agent shall with respect to services rendered for the sending State be exempt from social security provisions which may be in force in the receiving State.

2. The exemption provided for in paragraph 1 of this Article shall also apply to private servants who are in the sole employ of a diplomatic agent, on condition:

(a) that they are not nationals of or permanently resident in the receiving State; and
(b) that they are covered by the social security provisions which may be in force in the sending State or a third State.

3. A diplomatic agent who employs persons to whom the exemption provided for in paragraph 2 of this Article does not apply shall observe the obligations which the social security provisions of the receiving State impose upon employers.

4. The exemption provided for in paragraphs 1 and 2 of this Article shall not preclude voluntary participation in the social security system of the receiving State provided that such participation is permitted by that State.

5. The provisions of this Article shall not affect bilateral or multilateral agreements concerning social security concluded previously and shall not prevent the conclusion of such agreements in the future.

Article 34

A diplomatic agent shall be exempt from all dues and taxes, personal or real, national, regional or municipal, except:

(a) indirect taxes of a kind which are normally incorporated in the price of goods or services;

(b) dues and taxes on private immovable property situated in the territory of the receiving State, unless he holds it on behalf of the sending State for the purposes of the mission;
(c) estate, succession or inheritance duties levied by the receiving State, subject to the provisions of paragraph 4 of Article 39;
(d) dues and taxes on private income having its source in the receiving State and capital taxes on investments made in commercial undertakings in the receiving State;
(e) charges levied for specific services rendered;
(f) registration, court or record fees, mortgage dues and stamp duty, with respect to immovable property, subject to the provisions of Article 23.

Article 35

The receiving State shall exempt diplomatic agents from all personal services, from all public service of any kind whatsoever, and from military obligations such as those connected with requisitioning, military contributions and billeting.

Article 36

1. The receiving State shall, in accordance with such laws and regulations as it may adopt, permit entry of and grant exemption from all customs duties, taxes, and related charges other than charges for storage, cartage and similar services, on:

(a) Articles for the official use of the mission;
(b) Articles for the personal use of a diplomatic agent or members of his family forming part of his household, including Articles intended for his establishment.

2. The personal baggage of a diplomatic agent shall be exempt from inspection, unless there are serious grounds for presuming that it contains Articles not covered by the exemptions mentioned in paragraph 1 of this Article, or Articles the import or export of which is prohibited by the law or controlled by the quarantine regulations of the receiving State. Such inspection shall be conducted only in the presence of the diplomatic agent or of his authorized representative.

Article 37

1. The members of the family of a diplomatic agent forming part of his household shall, if they are not nationals of the receiving State, enjoy the privileges and immunities specified in Articles 29 to 36.

2. Members of the administrative and technical staff of the mission, together with members of their families forming part of their respective households,

shall, if they are not nationals of or permanently resident in the receiving State, enjoy the privileges and immunities specified in Articles 29 to 35, except that the immunity from civil and administrative jurisdiction of the receiving State specified in paragraph 1 of Article 31 shall not extend to acts performed outside the course of their duties. They shall also enjoy the privileges specified in Article 36, paragraph 1, in respect of Articles imported at the time of first installation.

3. Members of the service staff of the mission who are not nationals of or permanently resident in the receiving State shall enjoy immunity in respect of acts performed in the course of their duties, exemption from dues and taxes on the emoluments they receive by reason of their employment and the exemption contained in Article 33.

4. Private servants of members of the mission shall, if they are not nationals of or permanently resident in the receiving State, be exempt from dues and taxes on the emoluments they receive by reason of their employment. In other respects, they may enjoy privileges and immunities only to the extent admitted by the receiving State. However, the receiving State must exercise its jurisdiction over those persons in such a manner as not to interfere unduly with the performance of the functions of the mission.

Article 38

1. Except insofar as additional privileges and immunities may be granted by the receiving State, a diplomatic agent who is a national of or permanently resident in that State shall enjoy only immunity from jurisdiction, and inviolability, in respect of official acts performed in the exercise of his functions.

2. Other members of the staff of the mission and private servants who are nationals of or permanently resident in the receiving State shall enjoy privileges and immunities only to the extent admitted by the receiving State. However, the receiving State must exercise its jurisdiction over those persons in such a manner as not to interfere unduly with the performance of the functions of the mission.

Article 39

1. Every person entitled to privileges and immunities shall enjoy them from the moment he enters the territory of the receiving State on proceeding to take up his post or, if already in its territory, from the moment when his appointment is notified to the Ministry for Foreign Affairs or such other ministry as may be agreed.

2. When the functions of a person enjoying privileges and immunities have come to an end, such privileges and immunities shall normally cease at the moment when he leaves the country, or on expiry of a reasonable period in

which to do so, but shall subsist until that time, even in case of armed conflict. However, with respect to acts performed by such a person in the exercise of his functions as a member of the mission, immunity shall continue to subsist.

3. In case of the death of a member of the mission, the members of his family shall continue to enjoy the privileges and immunities to which they are entitled until the expiry of a reasonable period in which to leave the country.

4. In the event of the death of a member of the mission not a national of or permanently resident in the receiving State or a member of his family forming part of his household, the receiving State shall permit the withdrawal of the movable property of the deceased, with the exception of any property acquired in the country the export of which was prohibited at the time of his death. Estate, succession and inheritance duties shall not be levied on movable property the presence of which in the receiving State was due solely to the presence there of the deceased as a member of the mission or as a member of the family of a member of the mission.

Article 40

1. If a diplomatic agent passes through or is in the territory of a third State, which has granted him a passport visa if such visa was necessary, while proceeding to take up or to return to his post, or when returning to his own country, the third State shall accord him inviolability and such other immunities as may be required to ensure his transit or return. The same shall apply in the case of any members of his family enjoying privileges or immunities who are accompanying the diplomatic agent, or travelling separately to join him or to return to their country.

2. In circumstances similar to those specified in paragraph 1 of this Article, third States shall not hinder the passage of members of the administrative and technical or service staff of a mission, and of members of their families, through their territories.

3. Third States shall accord to official correspondence and other official communications in transit, including messages in code or cipher, the same freedom and protection as is accorded by the receiving State. They shall accord to diplomatic couriers, who have been granted a passport visa if such visa was necessary, and diplomatic bags in transit the same inviolability and protection as the receiving State is bound to accord.

4. The obligations of third States under paragraphs 1, 2 and 3 of this Article shall also apply to the persons mentioned respectively in those paragraphs, and to official communications and diplomatic bags, whose

presence in the territory of the third State is due to force majeure.

Article 41

1. Without prejudice to their privileges and immunities, it is the duty of all persons enjoying such privileges and immunities to respect the laws and regulations of the receiving State. They also have a duty not to interfere in the internal affairs of that State.

2. All official business with the receiving State entrusted to the mission by the sending State shall be conducted with or through the Ministry for Foreign Affairs of the receiving State or such other ministry as may be agreed.

3. The premises of the mission must not be used in any manner incompatible with the functions of the mission as laid down in the present Convention or by other rules of general international law or by any special agreements in force between the sending and the receiving State.

Article 42

A diplomatic agent shall not in the receiving State practise for personal profit any professional or commercial activity.

Article 43

The function of a diplomatic agent comes to an end, inter alia:

(a) on notification by the sending State to the receiving State that the function of the diplomatic agent has come to an end;
(b) on notification by the receiving State to the sending State that, in accordance with paragraph 2 of Article 9, it refuses to recognize the diplomatic agent as a member of the mission.

Article 44

The receiving State must, even in case of armed conflict, grant facilities in order to enable persons enjoying privileges and immunities, other than nationals of the receiving State, and members of the families of such persons irrespective of their nationality, to leave at the earliest possible moment. It must, in particular, in case of need, place at their disposal the necessary means of transport for themselves and their property.

Article 45

If diplomatic relations are broken off between two States, or if a mission is permanently or temporarily recalled:

(a) the receiving State must, even in case of armed conflict, respect and protect the premises of the mission, together with its property and archives;

(b) the sending State may entrust the custody of the premises of the mission, together with its property and archives, to a third State acceptable to the receiving State;

(c) the sending State may entrust the protection of its interests and those of its nationals to a third State acceptable to the receiving State.

Article 46

A sending State may with the prior consent of a receiving State, and at the request of a third State not represented in the receiving State, undertake the temporary protection of the interests of the third State and of its nationals.

Article 47

1. In the application of the provisions of the present Convention, the receiving State shall not discriminate as between States.

2. However, discrimination shall not be regarded as taking place:

(a) where the receiving State applies any of the provisions of the present Convention restrictively because of a restrictive application of that provision to its mission in the sending State;

(b) where by custom or agreement States extend to each other more favourable treatment than is required by the provisions of the present Convention.

Article 48

The present Convention shall be open for signature by all States Members of the United Nations or of any of the specialized agencies or Parties to the Statute of the International Court of Justice, and by any other State invited by the General Assembly of the United Nations to become a Party to the Convention, as follows: until 31 October 1961 at the Federal Ministry for Foreign Affairs of Austria and subsequently, until 31 March 1962, at the United Nations Headquarters in New York.

Article 49

The present Convention is subject to ratification. The instruments of ratification shall be deposited with the Secretary-General of the United Nations.

Article 50

The present Convention shall remain open for accession by any State belonging to any of the four categories mentioned in Article 48. The instruments of accession shall be deposited with the Secretary-General of the United Nations.

Article 51

1. The present Convention shall enter into force on the thirtieth day following the date of deposit of the twenty-second instrument of ratification or accession with the Secretary-General of the United Nations.

2. For each State ratifying or acceding to the Convention after the deposit of the twenty-second instrument of ratification or accession, the Convention shall enter into force on the thirtieth day after deposit by such State of its instrument of ratification or accession.

Article 52

The Secretary-General of the United Nations shall inform all States belonging to any of the four categories mentioned in Article 48:

(a) of signatures to the present Convention and of the deposit of instruments of ratification or accession, in accordance with Articles 48, 49 and 50;
(b) of the date on which the present Convention will enter into force, in accordance with Article 51.

Article 53

The original of the present Convention, of which the Chinese, English, French, Russian and Spanish texts are equally authentic, shall be deposited with the Secretary-General of the United Nations, who shall send certified copies thereof to all States belonging to any of the four categories mentioned in Article 48.

IN WITNESS WHEREOF the undersigned Plenipotentiaries, being duly authorized thereto by their respective Governments, have signed the present Convention.

DONE at Vienna, this eighteenth day of April one thousand nine hundred and sixty-one.

Optional Protocol to the Vienna Convention on Diplomatic Relations Concerning Acquisition of Nationality

DONE at Vienna, on 18 April 1961

The States Parties to the present Protocol and to the Vienna Convention on Diplomatic Relations, hereinafter referred to as "the Convention", adopted by the United Nations Conference held at Vienna from 2 March to 14 April 1961,

Expressing their wish to establish rules between them concerning acquisition of nationality by the members of their diplomatic missions and of the families forming part of the household of those members,

Have agreed as follows:

Article I

For the purpose of the present Protocol, the expression "members of the mission" shall have the meaning assigned to it in Article 1, sub-paragraph (b), of the Convention, namely "the head of the mission and the members of the staff of the mission".

Article II

Members of the mission not being nationals of the receiving State, and members of their families forming part of their household, shall not, solely by the operation of the law of the receiving State, acquire the nationality of that State.

Article III

The present Protocol shall be open for signature by all States which may become Parties to the Convention, as follows: until 31 October 1961 at the Federal Ministry for Foreign Affairs of Austria and subsequently, until 31 March 1962, at the United Nations Headquarters in New York.

Article IV

The present Protocol is subject to ratification. The instruments of ratification shall be deposited with the Secretary-General of the United Nations.

Article V

The present Protocol shall remain open for accession by all States which may become Parties to the Convention. The instruments of accession shall be deposited with the Secretary-General of the United Nations.

Article VI

1. The present Protocol shall enter into force on the same day as the Convention or on the thirtieth day following the date of deposit of the second instrument of ratification or accession to the Protocol with the Secretary-General of the United Nations, whichever date is the later.

2. For each State ratifying or acceding to the present Protocol after its entry into force in accordance with paragraph 1 of this Article, the Protocol shall enter into force on the thirtieth day after deposit by such State of its instrument of ratification or accession.

Article VII

The Secretary-General of the United Nations shall inform all States which may become Parties to the Convention:

(a) of signatures to the present Protocol and of the deposit of instruments of ratification or accession, in accordance with Articles III, IV and V;
(b) of the date on which the present Protocol will enter into force, in accordance with Article VI.

Article VIII

The original of the present Protocol, of which the Chinese, English, French, Russian and Spanish texts are equally authentic, shall be deposited with the Secretary-General of the United Nations, who shall send certified copies thereof to all States referred to in Article III.

IN WITNESS WHEREOF the undersigned Plenipotentiaries, being duly authorized thereto by their respective Governments, have signed the present Protocol.

DONE at Vienna, this eighteenth day of April one thousand nine hundred and sixty-one.

Optional Protocol to the Vienna Convention on Diplomatic Relations, Concerning the Compulsory Settlement of Disputes

DONE at Vienna, on 18 April 1961

The States Parties to the present Protocol and to the Vienna Convention on Diplomatic Relations, hereinafter referred to as "the Convention", adopted by the United Nations Conference held at Vienna from 2 March to 14 April 1961,

Expressing their wish to resort in all matters concerning them in respect of any dispute arising out of the interpretation or application of the Convention to the compulsory jurisdiction of the International Court of Justice, unless some other form of settlement has been agreed upon by the parties within a reasonable period,

Have agreed as follows:

Article I

Disputes arising out of the interpretation or application of the Convention shall lie within the compulsory jurisdiction of the International Court of Justice and may accordingly be brought before the Court by an application made by any party to the dispute being a Party to the present Protocol.

Article II

The parties may agree, within a period of two months after one party has notified its opinion to the other that a dispute exists, to resort not to the International Court of Justice but to an arbitral tribunal. After the expiry of the said period, either party may bring the dispute before the Court by an application.

Article III

1. Within the same period of two months, the parties may agree to adopt a conciliation procedure before resorting to the International Court of Justice.

2. The conciliation commission shall make its recommendations within five months after its appointment. If its recommendations are not accepted by the parties to the dispute within two months after they have been delivered, either party may bring the dispute before the Court by an application.

Article IV

States Parties to the Convention, to the Optional Protocol concerning Acquisition of Nationality, and to the present Protocol may at any time declare that they will extend the provisions of the present Protocol to disputes arising out of the interpretation or application of the Optional Protocol concerning Acquisition of Nationality. Such declarations shall be notified to the Secretary-General of the United Nations.

Article V

The present Protocol shall be open for signature by all States which may become Parties to the Convention, as follows: until 31 October 1961 at the Federal Ministry for Foreign Affairs of Austria and subsequently, until 31 March 1962, at the United Nations Headquarters in New York.

Article VI

The present Protocol is subject to ratification. The instruments of ratification shall be deposited with the Secretary-General of the United Nations.

Article VII

The present Protocol shall remain open for accession by all States which may become Parties to the Convention. The instruments of accession shall be deposited with the Secretary-General of the United Nations.

Article VIII

1. The present Protocol shall enter into force on the same day as the Convention or on the thirtieth day following the date of deposit of the second instrument of ratification or accession to the Protocol with the Secretary-General of the United Nations, whichever day is the later.

2. For each State ratifying or acceding to the present Protocol after its entry into force in accordance with paragraph 1 of this Article, the Protocol shall enter into force on the thirtieth day after deposit by such State of its instrument of ratification or accession.

Article IX

The Secretary-General of the United Nations shall inform all States which may become Parties to the Convention:

(a) of signatures to the present Protocol and of the deposit of instruments of ratification or accession, in accordance with Articles V, VI and VII;
(b) of declarations made in accordance with Article IV of the present Protocol;
(c) of the date on which the present Protocol will enter into force, in accordance with Article VIII.

Article X

The original of the present Protocol, of which the Chinese, English, French, Russian and Spanish texts are equally authentic, shall be deposited with the Secretary-General of the United Nations, who shall send certified copies thereof to all States referred to in Article V.

IN WITNESS WHEREOF the undersigned Plenipotentiaries, being duly authorized thereto by their respective Governments, have signed the present Protocol.

DONE at Vienna, this eighteenth day of April one thousand nine hundred and sixty-one.

APPENDIX II

Vienna Convention on Consular Relations and Optional Protocols

Done at Vienna, on 24 April 1963

The States Parties to the present Convention,

Recalling that consular relations have been established between peoples since ancient times,

Having in mind the Purposes and Principles of the Charter of the United Nation concerning the sovereign equality of States, the maintenance of international peace and security, and the promotion of friendly relations among nations,

Considering that the United Nations Conference on Diplomatic Intercourse and Immunities adopted the Vienna Convention on Diplomatic Relations which was opened for signature on 18 April 1961,

Believing that an international convention on consular relations, privileges and immunities would also contribute to the development of friendly relations among nations, irrespective of their differing constitutional and social systems,

Realizing that the purpose of such privileges and immunities is not to benefit individuals but to ensure the efficient performance of functions by consular posts on behalf of their respective States,

Affirming that the rules of customary international law continue to govern matters not expressly regulated by the provisions of the present Convention,

Have agreed as follows:

Article 1: Definitions

1. For the purposes of the present Convention, the following expressions shall have the meanings hereunder assigned to them:

(a) "consular post" means any consulate-general, consulate, vice-consulate or consular agency;
(b) "consular district" means the area assigned to a consular post for the exercise of consular functions;
(c) "head of consular post" means the person charged with the duty of acting in that capacity;

(d) "consular officer" means any person, including the head of a consular post, entrusted in that capacity with the exercise of consular functions;
(e) "consular employee" means any person employed in the administrative or technical service of a consular post;
(f) "member of the service staff" means any person employed in the domestic service of a consular post;
(g) "members of the consular post" means consular officers, consular employees and members of the service staff;
(h) "members of the consular staff" means consular officers, other than the head of a consular post, consular employees and members of the service staff;
(i) "member of the private staff" means a person who is employed exclusively in the private service of a member of the consular post;
(j) "consular premises" means the buildings or parts of buildings and the land ancillary thereto, irrespective of ownership, used exclusively for the purposes of the consular post;
(k) "consular archives" includes all the papers, documents, correspondence, books, films, tapes and registers of the consular post, together with the ciphers and codes, the card-indexes and any article of furniture intended for their protection or safekeeping.

2. Consular officers are of two categories, namely career consular officers and honorary consular officers. The provisions of Chapter II of the present Convention apply to consular posts headed by career consular officers; the provisions of Chapter III govern consular posts headed by honorary consular officers.

3. The particular status of members of the consular posts who are nationals or permanent residents of the receiving State is governed by Article 71 of the present Convention.

Chapter 1

Consular Relations in General

Section 1: ESTABLISHMENT AND CONDUCT OF CONSULAR RELATIONS

Article 2: Establishment of Consular Relations

1. The establishment of consular relations between States takes place by mutual consent.

2. The consent given to the establishment of diplomatic relations between two States implies, unless otherwise stated, consent to the establishment of consular relations.

3. The severance of diplomatic relations shall not ipso facto involve the severance of consular relations.

Article 3: Exercise of Consular Functions

Consular functions are exercised by consular posts. They are also exercised by diplomatic missions in accordance with the provisions of the present Convention.

Article 4: Establishment of a Consular Post

1. A consular post may be established in the territory of the receiving State only with that State's consent.

2. The seat of the consular post, its classification and the consular district shall be established by the sending State and shall be subject to the approval of the receiving State.

3. Subsequent changes in the seat of the consular post, its classification or the consular district may be made by the sending State only with the consent of the receiving State.

4. The consent of the receiving State shall also be required if a consulate-general or a consulate desires to open a vice-consulate or a consular agency in a locality other than that in which it is itself established.

5. The prior express consent of the receiving State shall also be required for the opening of an office forming part of an existing consular post elsewhere than at the seat thereof.

Article 5: Consular Functions

Consular functions consist in:
(a) protecting in the receiving State the interests of the sending State and of its nationals, both individuals and bodies corporate, within the limits permitted by international law;
(b) furthering the development of commercial, economic, cultural and scientific relations between the sending State and the receiving State and otherwise promoting friendly relations between them in accordance with the provisions of the present Convention;
(c) ascertaining by all lawful means conditions and developments in the commercial, economic, cultural and scientific life of the receiving State, reporting thereon to the Government of the sending State and giving information to persons interested;
(d) issuing passports and travel documents to nationals of the sending State, and visas or appropriate documents to persons wishing to travel to the sending State;
(e) helping and assisting nationals, both individuals and bodies corporate, of the sending State;

(f) acting as notary and civil registrar and in capacities of a similar kind, and performing certain functions of an administrative nature, provided that there is nothing contrary thereto in the laws and regulations of the receiving State;

(g) safeguarding the interests of nationals, both individuals and bodies corporate, of the sending State in cases of succession mortis causa in the territory of the receiving State, in accordance with the laws and regulations of the receiving State;

(h) safeguarding, within the limits imposed by the laws and regulations of the receiving State, the interests of minors and other persons lacking full capacity who are nationals of the sending State, particularly where any guardianship or trusteeship is required with respect to such persons;

(i) subject to the practices and procedures obtaining in the receiving State, representing or arranging appropriate representation for nationals of the sending State before the tribunals and other authorities of the receiving State, for the purpose of obtaining, in accordance with the laws and regulations of the receiving State, provisional measures for the preservation of the rights and interests of these nationals, where, because of absence or any other reason, such nationals are unable at the proper time to assume the defence of their rights and interests;

(j) transmitting judicial and extrajudicial documents or executing letters rogatory or commissions to take evidence for the courts of the sending State in accordance with international agreements in force or, in the absence of such international agreements, in any other manner compatible with the laws and regulations of the receiving State;

(k) exercising rights of supervision and inspection provided for in the laws and regulations of the sending State in respect of vessels having the nationality of the sending State, and of aircraft registered in that State, and in respect of their crews;

(l) extending assistance to vessels and aircraft mentioned in sub-paragraph (k) of this Article and to their crews, taking statements regarding the voyage of a vessel, examining and stamping the ship's papers, and, without prejudice to the powers of the authorities of the receiving State, conducting investigations into any incidents which occurred during the voyage, and settling disputes of any kind between the master, the officers and the seamen in so far as this may be authorized by the laws and regulations of the sending State;

(m) performing any other functions entrusted to a consular post by the sending State which are not prohibited by the laws and regulations of the receiving State or to which no objection is taken by the receiving State or which are referred to in the international agreements in force between the sending State and the receiving State.

Article 6: Exercise of Consular Functions outside the Consular District

A consular officer may, in special circumstances, with the consent of the receiving State, exercise his functions outside his consular district.

Article 7: Exercise of Consular Functions in a Third State

The sending State may, after notifying the States concerned, entrust a consular post established in a particular State with the exercise of consular functions in another State, unless there is express objection by one of the States concerned.

Article 8: Exercise of Consular Functions on Behalf of a Third State

Upon appropriate notification to the receiving State, a consular post of the sending State may, unless the receiving State objects, exercise consular functions in the receiving State on behalf of a third State.

Article 9: Classes of Heads of Consular Posts

1. Heads of consular posts are divided into four classes, namely:

(a) consuls-general;
(b) consuls;
(c) vice-consuls;
(d) consular agents.

2. Paragraph 1 of this Article in no way restricts the right of any of the Contracting Parties to fix the designation of consular officers other than the heads of consular posts.

Article 10: Appointment and Admission of Heads of Consular Posts

1. Heads of consular posts are appointed by the sending State and are admitted to the exercise of their functions by the receiving State.

2. Subject to the provisions of the present Convention, the formalities for the appointment and for the admission of the head of a consular post are determined by the laws, regulations and usages of the sending State and of the receiving State respectively.

Article 11: The Consular Commission of Notification of Appointment

1. The head of a consular post shall be provided by the sending State with a document, in the form of a commission or similar instrument, made out for each appointment, certifying his capacity and showing, as a general rule, his full name, his category and class, the consular district and the seat of the consular post.

2. The sending State shall transmit the commission or similar instrument through the diplomatic or other appropriate channel to the Government of the State in whose territory the head of a consular post is to exercise his functions.

3. If the receiving State agrees, the sending State may, instead of a commission or similar instrument, send to the receiving State a notification containing the particulars required by paragraph 1 of this Article.

Article 12: The Exequatur

1. The head of a consular post is admitted to the exercise of his functions by an authorization from the receiving State termed an exequatur, whatever the form of this authorization.

2. A State which refuses to grant an exequatur is not obliged to give to the sending State reasons for such refusal.

3. Subject to the provisions of Articles 13 and 15, the head of a consular post shall not enter upon his duties until he has received an exequatur.

Article 13: Provisional Admission of Heads of Consular Posts

Pending delivery of the exequatur, the head of a consular post may be admitted on a provisional basis to the exercise of his functions. In that case, the provisions of the present Convention shall apply.

Article 14: Notification to the Authorities of the Consular District

As soon as the head of a consular post is admitted even provisionally to the exercise of his functions, the receiving State shall immediately notify the competent authorities of the consular district. It shall also ensure that the necessary measures are taken to enable the head of a consular post to carry out the duties of his office and to have the benefit of the provisions of the present Convention.

Article 15: Temporary Exercise of the Functions of the Head of a Consular Post

1. If the head of a consular post is unable to carry out his functions or the position of head of consular post is vacant, an acting head of post may act provisionally as head of the consular post.

2. The full name of the acting head of post shall be notified either by the diplomatic mission of the sending State or, if that State has no such mission in the receiving State, by the head of the consular post, or, if he is unable to do so, by any competent authority of the sending State, to the Ministry for Foreign Affairs of the receiving State or to the authority designated by that Ministry. As a general rule, this notification shall be given in advance. The receiving State may make the admission as acting head of post of a person who is neither a diplomatic agent nor a consular officer of the sending State in the receiving State conditional on its consent.

3. The competent authorities of the receiving State shall afford assistance and protection to the acting head of post. While he is in charge of the post, the provisions of the present Convention shall apply to him on the same basis as to the head of the consular post concerned. The receiving State shall not, however, be obliged to grant to an acting head of post any facility, privilege or immunity which the head of the consular post enjoys only subject to conditions not fulfilled by the acting head of post.

4. When, in the circumstances referred to in paragraph 1 of this Article, a member of the diplomatic staff of the diplomatic mission of the sending State in the receiving State is designated by the sending State as an acting head of post, he shall, if the receiving State does not object thereto, continue to enjoy diplomatic privileges and immunities.

Article 16: Precedence as between Heads of Consular Posts

1. Heads of consular posts shall rank in each class according to the date of the grant of the exequatur.

2. If, however, the head of a consular post before obtaining the exequatur is admitted to the exercise of his functions provisionally, his precedence shall be determined according to the date of the provisional admission; this precedence shall be maintained after the granting of the exequatur.

3. The order of precedence as between two or more heads of consular posts who obtained the exequatur or provisional admission on the same date shall be determined according to the dates on which their commissions or similar instruments or the notifications referred to in paragraph 3 of Article 11 were presented to the receiving State.

4. Acting heads of posts shall rank after all heads of consular posts and, as between themselves, they shall rank according to the dates on which they assumed their functions as acting heads of posts as indicated in the notifications given under paragraph 2 of Article 15.

5. Honorary consular officers who are heads of consular posts shall rank in each class after career heads of consular posts, in the order and according to the rules laid down in the foregoing paragraphs.

6. Heads of consular posts shall have precedence over consular officers not having that status.

Article 17: Performance of Diplomatic Acts by Consular Officers

1. In a State where the sending State has no diplomatic mission and is not represented by a diplomatic mission of a third State, a consular officer may, with the consent of the receiving State, and without affecting his consular

status, be authorized to perform diplomatic acts. The performance of such acts by a consular officer shall not confer upon him any right to claim diplomatic privileges and immunities.

2. A consular officer may, after notification addressed to the receiving State, act as representative of the sending State to any inter-governmental organization. When so acting, he shall be entitled to enjoy any privileges and immunities accorded to such a representative by customary international law or by international agreements; however, in respect of the performance by him of any consular function, he shall not be entitled to any greater immunity from jurisdiction than that to which a consular officer is entitled under the present Convention.

Article 18: Appointment of the Same Person by Two of More States as a Consular Officer

Two or more States may, with the consent of the receiving State, appoint the same person as a consular officer in that State.

Article 19: Appointment of Members of Consular Staff

1. Subject to the provisions of Articles 20, 22 and 23, the sending State may freely appoint the members of the consular staff.

2. The full name, category and class of all consular officers, other than the head of a consular post, shall be notified by the sending State to the receiving State in sufficient time for the receiving State, if it so wishes, to exercise its rights under paragraph 3 of Article 23.

3. The sending State may, if required by its laws and regulations, request the receiving State to grant an exequatur to a consular officer other than the head of a consular post.

4. The receiving State may, if required by its laws and regulations, grant an exequatur to a consular officer other than the head of a consular post.

Article 20: Size of the Consular Staff

In the absence of an express agreement as to the size of the consular staff, the receiving State may require that the size of the staff be kept within limits considered by it to be reasonable and normal, having regard to circumstances and conditions in the consular district and to the needs of the particular post.

Article 21: Precedence as between Consular Officers of a Consular Post

The order of precedence as between the consular officers of a consular post and any change thereof shall be notified by the diplomatic mission of the sending State or, if that State has no such mission in the receiving State, by the head of the consular post, to the Ministry for Foreign Affairs of the receiving State or to the authority designated by that Ministry.

Article 22: Nationality of Consular Officers

1. Consular officers should, in principle, have the nationality of the sending State.

2. Consular officers may not be appointed from among persons having the nationality of the receiving State except with the express consent of that State which may be withdrawn at any time.

3. The receiving State may reserve the same right with regard to nationals of a third State who are not also nationals of the sending State.

Article 23: Persons Declared "Non Grata"

1. The receiving State may at any time notify the sending State that a consular officer is persona non grata or that any other member of the consular staff is not acceptable. In that event, the sending State shall, as the case may be, either recall the person concerned or terminate his functions with the consular post.

2. If the sending State refuses or fails within a reasonable time to carry out its obligations under paragraph 1 of this Article, the receiving State may, as the case may be, either withdraw the exequatur from the person concerned or cease to consider him as a member of the consular staff.

3. A person appointed as a member of a consular post may be declared unacceptable before arriving in the territory of the receiving State or, if already in the receiving State, before entering on his duties with the consular post. In any such case, the sending State shall withdraw his appointment.

4. In the cases mentioned in paragraphs 1 and 3 of this Article, the receiving State is not obliged to give to the sending State reasons for its decision.

Article 24: Notification to the Receiving State of Appointments, Arrivals and Departures

1. The Ministry for Foreign Affairs of the receiving State or the authority designated by that Ministry shall be notified of:

(a) the appointment of members of a consular post, their arrival after appointment to the consular post, their final departure or the termination of their functions and any other changes affecting their status that may occur in the course of their service with the consular post;

(b) the arrival and final departure of a person belonging to the family of a member of a consular post forming part of his household and, where appro-

priate, the fact that a person becomes or ceases to be such a member of the family;
(c) the arrival and final departure of members of the private staff and, where appropriate, the termination of their service as such;
(d) the engagement and discharge of persons resident in the receiving State as members of a consular post or as members of the private staff entitled to privileges and immunities.

2. When possible, prior notification of arrival and final departure shall also be given.

SECTION II: END OF CONSULAR FUNCTIONS

Article 25: Termination of the Functions of a Member of a Consular Post

The functions of a member of a consular post shall come to an end inter alia:

(a) on notification by the sending State to the receiving State that his functions have come to an end; (b) on withdrawal of the exequatur; (c) on notification by the receiving State to the sending State that the receiving State has ceased to consider him as a member of the consular staff.

Article 26: Departure from the Territory of the Receiving State

The receiving State shall, even in case of armed conflict, grant to members of the consular post and members of the private staff, other than nationals of the receiving State, and to members of their families forming part of their households irrespective of nationality, the necessary time and facilities to enable them to prepare their departure and to leave at the earliest possible moment after the termination of the functions of the members concerned. In particular, it shall, in case of need, place at their disposal the necessary means of transport for themselves and their property other than property acquired in the receiving State the export of which is prohibited at the time of departure.

Article 27: Protection of Consular Premises and Archives and of the Interests of the Sending State in Exceptional Circumstances

1. In the event of the severance of consular relations between two States:

(a) the receiving State shall, even in case of armed conflict, respect and protect the consular premises, together with the property of the consular post and the consular archives;
(b) the sending State may entrust the custody of the consular premises, together with the property contained therein and the consular archives, to a third State acceptable to the receiving State;

(c) the sending State may entrust the protection of its interests and those of its nationals to a third State acceptable to the receiving State.

2. In the event of the temporary or permanent closure of a consular post, the provisions of sub-paragraph (a) of paragraph 1 of this Article shall apply. In addition,

(a) if the sending State, although not represented in the receiving State by a diplomatic mission, has another consular post in the territory of that State, that consular post may be entrusted with the custody of the premises of the consular post which has been closed, together with the property contained therein and the consular archives, and, with the consent of the receiving State, with the exercise of consular functions in the district of that consular post; or
(b) if the sending State has no diplomatic mission and no other consular post in the receiving State, the provisions of sub-paragraphs
(b) and
(c) of paragraph 1 of this Article shall apply.

Chapter II

Facilities, Privileges and Immunities Relating to Consular Posts, Career Consular Officers and Other Members of a Consular Post

Section I: FACILITIES, PRIVILEGES AND IMMUNITIES RELATING TO A CONSULAR POST

Article 28: Facilities for the Work of the Consular Post

The receiving State shall accord full facilities for the performance of the functions of the consular post.

Article 29: Use of National Flag and Coat-of-Arms

1. The sending State shall have the right to the use of its national flag and coat-of-arms in the receiving State in accordance with the provisions of this Article.

2. The national flag of the sending State may be flown and its coat-of-arms displayed on the building occupied by the consular post and at the entrance door thereof, on the residence of the head of the consular post and on his means of transport when used on official business.

3. In the exercise of the right accorded by this Article regard shall be had to the laws, regulations and usages of the receiving State.

Article 30: Accommodation

1. The receiving State shall either facilitate the acquisition on its territory, in accordance with its laws and regulations, by the sending State of premises necessary for its consular post or assist the latter in obtaining accommodation in some other way.

2. It shall also, where necessary, assist the consular post in obtaining suitable accommodation for its members.

Article 31: Inviolability of the Consular Premises

1. Consular premises shall be inviolable to the extent provided in this Article.

2. The authorities of the receiving State shall not enter that part of the consular premises which is used exclusively for the purpose of the work of the consular post except with the consent of the head of the consular post or of his designee or of the head of the diplomatic mission of the sending State. The consent of the head of the consular post may, however, be assumed in case of fire or other disaster requiring prompt protective action.

3. Subject to the provisions of paragraph 2 of this Article, the receiving State is under a special duty to take all appropriate steps to protect the consular premises against any intrusion or damage and to prevent any disturbance of the peace of the consular post or impairment of its dignity.

4. The consular premises, their furnishings, the property of the consular post and its means of transport shall be immune from any form of requisition for purposes of national defence or public utility. If expropriation is necessary for such purposes, all possible steps shall be taken to avoid impeding the performance of consular functions, and prompt, adequate and effective compensation shall be paid to the sending State.

Article 32: Exemption from Taxation of Consular Premises

1. Consular premises and the residence of the career head of consular post of which the sending State or any person acting on its behalf is the owner or lessee shall be exempt from all national, regional or municipal dues and taxes whatsoever, other than such as represent payment for specific services rendered.

2. The exemption from taxation referred to in paragraph 1 of this Article shall not apply to such dues and taxes if, under the law of the receiving State, they are payable by the person who contracted with the sending State or with the person acting on its behalf.

Article 33: Inviolability of the Consular Archives and Documents

The consular archives and documents shall be inviolable at all times and wherever they may be.

Article 34: Freedom of Movement

Subject to its laws and regulations concerning zones entry into which is prohibited or regulated for reasons of national security, the receiving State shall ensure freedom of movement and travel in its territory to all members of the consular post.

Article 35: Freedom of Communication

1. The receiving State shall permit and protect freedom of communication on the part of the consular post for all official purposes. In communicating with the Government, the diplomatic missions and other consular posts, wherever situated, of the sending State, the consular post may employ all appropriate means, including diplomatic or consular couriers, diplomatic or consular bags and messages in code or cipher. However, the consular post may install and use a wireless transmitter only with the consent of the receiving State.

2. The official correspondence of the consular post shall be inviolable. Official correspondence means all correspondence relating to the consular post and its functions.

3. The consular bag shall be neither opened nor detained. Nevertheless, if the competent authorities of the receiving State have serious reason to believe that the bag contains something other than the correspondence, documents or articles referred to in paragraph 4 of this Article, they may request that the bag be opened in their presence by an authorized representative of the sending State. If this request is refused by the authorities of the sending State, the bag shall be returned to its place of origin.

4. The packages constituting the consular bag shall bear visible external marks of their character and may contain only official correspondence and documents or articles intended exclusively for official use.

5. The consular courier shall be provided with an official document indicating his status and the number of packages constituting the consular bag. Except with the consent of the receiving State he shall be neither a national of the receiving State, nor, unless he is a national of the sending State, a permanent resident of the receiving State. In the performance of his functions he shall be protected by the receiving State. He shall enjoy personal inviolability and shall not be liable to any form of arrest or detention.

6. The sending State, its diplomatic missions and its consular posts may designate consular couriers ad hoc. In such cases the provisions of paragraph 5 of this Article shall also apply except that the immunities therein mentioned shall cease to apply when such a courier has delivered to the consignee the consular bag in his charge.

7. A consular bag may be entrusted to the captain of a ship or of a commercial aircraft scheduled to land at an authorized port of entry. He shall be provided with an official document indicating the number of packages constituting the bag, but he shall not be considered to be a consular courier. By arrangement with the appropriate local authorities, the consular post may send one of its members to take possession of the bag directly and freely from the captain of the ship or of the aircraft.

Article 36: Communication and Contact with Nationals of the Sending State

1. With a view to facilitating the exercise of consular functions relating to nationals of the sending State:

(a) consular officers shall be free to communicate with nationals of the sending State and to have access to them. Nationals of the sending State shall have the same freedom with respect to communication with and access to consular officers of the sending State;
(b) if he so requests, the competent authorities of the receiving State shall, without delay, inform the consular post of the sending State if, within its consular district, a national of that State is arrested or committed to prison or to custody pending trial or is detained in any other manner. Any communication addressed to the consular post by the person arrested, in prison, custody or detention shall also be forwarded by the said authorities without delay. The said authorities shall inform the person concerned without delay of his rights under this sub-paragraph;
(c) consular officers shall have the right to visit a national of the sending State who is in prison, custody or detention, to converse and correspond with him and to arrange for his legal representation. They shall also have the right to visit any national of the sending State who is in prison, custody or detention in their district in pursuance of a judgment. Nevertheless, consular officers shall refrain from taking action on behalf of a national who is in prison, custody or detention if he expressly opposes such action.

2. The rights referred to in paragraph 1 of this Article shall be exercised in conformity with the laws and regulations of the receiving State, subject to the proviso, however, that the said laws and regulations must enable full effect to be given to the purposes for which the rights accorded under this Article are intended.

Article 37: Information in Cases of Deaths, Guardianship or Trusteeship, Wrecks and Air Accidents

If the relevant information is available to the competent authorities of the receiving State, such authorities shall have the duty:

(a) in the case of the death of a national of the sending State, to inform without delay the consular post in whose district the death occurred;
(b) to inform the competent consular post without delay of any case where the appointment of a guardian or trustee appears to be in the interests of a minor or other person lacking full capacity who is a national of the sending State. The giving of this information shall, however, be without prejudice to the operation of the laws and regulations of the receiving State concerning such appointments;
(c) if a vessel, having the nationality of the sending State, is wrecked or runs aground in the territorial sea or internal waters of the receiving State, or if an aircraft registered in the sending State suffers an accident on the territory of the receiving State, to inform without delay the consular post nearest to the scene of the occurrence.

Article 38: Communication with the Authorities of the Receiving State

In the exercise of their functions, consular officers may address:

(a) the competent local authorities of their consular district;
(b) the competent central authorities of the receiving State if and to the extent that this is allowed by the laws, regulations and usages of the receiving State or by the relevant international agreements.

Article 39: Consular Fees and Charges

1. The consular post may levy in the territory of the receiving State the fees and charges provided by the laws and regulations of the sending State for consular acts.

2. The sums collected in the form of the fees and charges referred to in paragraph 1 of this Article, and the receipts for such fees and charges, shall be exempt from all dues and taxes in the receiving State.

Section II: FACILITIES, PRIVILEGES AND IMMUNITIES RELATING TO CAREER CONSULAR OFFICERS AND OTHER MEMBERS OF A CONSULAR POST

Article 40: Protection of Consular Officers

The receiving State shall treat consular officers with due respect and shall take all appropriate steps to prevent any attack on their person, freedom or dignity.

Article 41: Personal Inviolability of Consular Officers

1. Consular officers shall not be liable to arrest or detention pending trial, except in the case of a grave crime and pursuant to a decision by the competent judicial authority.

2. Except in the case specified in paragraph 1 of this Article, consular officers shall not be committed to prison or liable to any other form of restriction on their personal freedom save in execution of a judicial decision of final effect.

3. If criminal proceedings are instituted against a consular officer, he must appear before the competent authorities. Nevertheless, the proceedings shall be conducted with the respect due to him by reason of his official position and, except in the case specified in paragraph 1 of this Article, in a manner which will hamper the exercise of consular functions as little as possible. When, in the circumstances mentioned in paragraph 1 of this Article, it has become necessary to detain a consular officer, the proceedings against him shall be instituted with the minimum of delay.

Article 42: Notification of Arrest, Detention or Prosecution

In the event of the arrest or detention, pending trial, of a member of the consular staff, or of criminal proceedings being instituted against him, the receiving State shall promptly notify the head of the consular post. Should the latter be himself the object of any such measure, the receiving State shall notify the sending State through the diplomatic channel.

Article 43: Immunity from Jurisdiction

1. Consular officers and consular employees shall not be amenable to the jurisdiction of the judicial or administrative authorities of the receiving State in respect of acts performed in the exercise of consular functions.

2. The provisions of paragraph 1 of this Article shall not, however, apply in respect of a civil action either:

(a) arising out of a contract concluded by a consular officer or a consular employee in which he did not contract expressly or impliedly as an agent of the sending State; or
(b) by a third party for damage arising from an accident in the receiving State caused by a vehicle, vessel or aircraft.

Article 44: Liability to Give Evidence

1. Members of a consular post may be called upon to attend as witnesses in the course of judicial or administrative proceedings. A consular employee or a member of the service staff shall not, except in the cases mentioned in

paragraph 3 of this Article, decline to give evidence. If a consular officer should decline to do so, no coercive measure or penalty may be applied to him.

2. The authority requiring the evidence of a consular officer shall avoid interference with the performance of his functions. It may, when possible, take such evidence at his residence or at the consular post or accept a statement from him in writing.

3. Members of a consular post are under no obligation to give evidence concerning matters connected with the exercise of their functions or to produce official correspondence and documents relating thereto. They are also entitled to decline to give evidence as expert witnesses with regard to the law of the sending State.

Article 45: Waiver of Privileges and Immunities

1. The sending State may waive, with regard to a member of the consular post, any of the privileges and immunities provided for in Articles 41, 43 and 44.

2. The waiver shall in all cases be express, except as provided in paragraph 3 of this Article, and shall be communicated to the receiving State in writing.

3. The initiation of proceedings by a consular officer or a consular employee in a matter where he might enjoy immunity from jurisdiction under Article 43 shall preclude him from invoking immunity from jurisdiction in respect of any counter-claim directly connected with the principal claim.

4. The waiver of immunity from jurisdiction for the purposes of civil or administrative proceedings shall not be deemed to imply the waiver of immunity from the measures of execution resulting from the judicial decisio n; in respect of such measures, a separate waiver shall be necessary.

Article 46: Exemption from Registration of Aliens and Residence Permits

1. Consular officers and consular employees and members of their families forming part of their households shall be exempt from all obligations under the laws and regulations of the receiving State in regard to the registration of aliens and residence permits.

2. The provisions of paragraph 1 of this Article shall not, however, apply to any consular employee who is not a permanent employee of the sending State or who carries on any private gainful occupation in the receiving State or to any member of the family of any such employee.

Article 47: Exemption from Work Permits

1. Members of the consular post shall, with respect to services rendered for the sending State, be exempt from any obligations in regard to work permits

imposed by the laws and regulations of the receiving State concerning the employment of foreign labour.

2. Members of the private staff of consular officers and of consular employees shall, if they do not carry on any other gainful occupation in the receiving State, be exempt from the obligations referred to in paragraph 1 of this Article.

Article 48: Social Security Exemption

1. Subject to the provisions of paragraph 3 of this Article, members of the consular post with respect to services rendered by them for the sending State, and members of their families forming part of their households, shall be exempt from social security provisions which may be in force in the receiving State.

2. The exemption provided for in paragraph 1 of this Article shall apply also to members of the private staff who are in the sole employ of members of the consular post, on condition:

(a) that they are not nationals of or permanently resident in the receiving State; and
(b) that they are covered by the social security provisions which are in force in the sending State or a third State.

3. Members of the consular post who employ persons to whom the exemption provided for in paragraph 2 of this Article does not apply shall observe the obligations which the social security provisions of the receiving State impose upon employers.

4. The exemption provided for in paragraphs 1 and 2 of this Article shall not preclude voluntary participation in the social security system of the receiving State, provided that such participation is permitted by that State.

Article 49: Exemption from Taxation

1. Consular officers and consular employees and members of their families forming part of their households shall be exempt from all dues and taxes,n personal or real, national, regional or municipal, except:

(a) indirect taxes of a kind which are normally incorporated in the price of goods or services;
(b) dues or taxes on private immovable property situated in the territory of the receiving State, subject to the provisions of Article 32;
(c) estate, succession or inheritance duties, and duties on transfers, levied by the receiving State, subject to the provisions of paragraph (b) of Article 51;
(d) dues and taxes on private income, including capital gains, having its source in the receiving State and capital taxes relating to investments made in commercial or financial undertakings in the receiving State;

(e) charges levied for specific services rendered;

(f) registration, court or record fees, mortgage dues and stamp duties, subject to the provisions of Article 32.

2. Members of the service staff shall be exempt from dues and taxes on the wages which they receive for their services.

3. Members of the consular post who employ persons whose wages or salaries are not exempt from income tax in the receiving State shall observe the obligations which the laws and regulations of that State impose upon employers concerning the levying of income tax.

Article 50: Exemption from Customs Duties and Inspection

1. The receiving State shall, in accordance with such laws and regulations as it may adopt, permit entry of and grant exemption from all customs duties, taxes, and related charges other than charges for storage, cartage and similar services, on:

(a) articles for the official use of the consular post;
(b) articles for the personal use of a consular officer or members of his family forming part of his household, including articles intended for his establishment. The articles intended for consumption shall not exceed the quantities necessary for direct utilization by the persons concerned.

2. Consular employees shall enjoy the privileges and exemptions specified in paragraph 1 of this Article in respect of articles imported at the time of first installation.

3. Personal baggage accompanying consular officers and members of their families forming part of their households shall be exempt from inspection. It may be inspected only if there is serious reason to believe that it contains articles other than those referred to in sub-paragraph (b) of paragraph 1 of this Article, or articles the import or export of which is prohibited by the laws and regulations of the receiving State or which are subject to its quarantine laws and regulations. Such inspection shall be carried out in the presence of the consular officer or member of his family concerned.

Article 51: Estate of a Member of the Consular Post or of a Member of his Family

In the event of the death of a member of the consular post or of a member of his family forming part of his household, the receiving State:

(a) shall permit the export of the movable property of the deceased, with the exception of any such property acquired in the receiving State the export of which was prohibited at the time of his death; (b) shall not levy national, regional or municipal estate, succession or inheritance duties, and duties on transfers, on movable property the presence of which in the receiving State was due solely to the presence in that State of the deceased as a member of the consular post or as a member of the family of a member of the consular post.

Article 52: Exemption from Personal Services and Contributions

The receiving State shall exempt members of the consular post and members of their families forming part of their households from all personal services, from all public service of any kind whatsoever, and from military obligations such as those connected with requisitioning, military contributions and billeting.

Article 53: Beginning and End of Consular Privileges and Immunities

1. Every member of the consular post shall enjoy the privileges and immunities provided in the present Convention from the moment he enters the territory of the receiving State on proceeding to take up his post or, if already in its territory, from the moment when he enters on his duties with the consular post.

2. Members of the family of a member of the consular post forming part of his household and members of his private staff shall receive the privileges and immunities provided in the present Convention from the date from which he enjoys privileges and immunities in accordance with paragraph 1 of this Article or from the date of their entry into the territory of the receiving State or from the date of their becoming a member of such family or private staff, whichever is the latest.

3. When the functions of a member of the consular post have come to an end, his privileges and immunities and those of a member of his family forming part of his household or a member of his private staff shall normally cease at the moment when the person concerned leaves the receiving State or on the expiry of a reasonable period in which to do so, whichever is the sooner, but shall subsist until that time, even in case of armed conflict. In the case of the persons referred to in paragraph 2 of this Article, their privileges and immunities shall come to an end when they cease to belong to the household or to be in the service of a member of the consular post provided, however, that if such persons intend leaving the receiving State within a reasonable period thereafter, their privileges and immunities shall subsist until the time of their departure.

4. However, with respect to acts performed by a consular officer or a consular employee in the exercise of his functions, immunity from jurisdiction shall continue to subsist without limitation of time.

5. In the event of the death of a member of the consular post, the members of his family forming part of his household shall continue to enjoy the privileges and immunities accorded to them until they leave the receiving State or until the expiry of a reasonable period enabling them to do so, whichever is the sooner.

Article 54: Obligations of Third States

1. If a consular officer passes through or is in the territory of a third State, which has granted him a visa if a visa was necessary, while proceeding to take up or return to his post or when returning to the sending State, the third State shall accord to him all immunities provided for by the other Articles of the present Convention as may be required to ensure his transit or return. The same shall apply in the case of any member of his family forming part of his household enjoying such privileges and immunities who are accompanying the consular officer or travelling separately to join him or to return to the sending State.

2. In circumstances similar to those specified in paragraph 1 of this Article, third States shall not hinder the transit through their territory of other members of the consular post or of members of their families forming part of their households.

3. Third States shall accord to official correspondence and to other official communications in transit, including messages in code or cipher, the same freedom and protection as the receiving State is bound to accord under the present Convention. They shall accord to consular couriers who have been granted a visa, if a visa was necessary, and to consular bags in transit, the same inviolability and protection as the receiving State is bound to accord under the present Convention.

4. The obligations of third States under paragraphs 1, 2 and 3 of this Article shall also apply to the persons mentioned respectively in those paragraphs, and to official communications and to consular bags, whose presence in the territory of the third State is due to force majeure.

Article 55: Respect for the Laws and Regulations of the Receiving State

1. Without prejudice to their privileges and immunities, it is the duty of all persons enjoying such privileges and immunities to respect the laws and regulations of the receiving State. They also have a duty not to interfere in the internal affairs of that State.

2. The consular premises shall not be used in any manner incompatible with the exercise of consular functions.

3. The provisions of paragraph 2 of this Article shall not exclude the possibility of offices of other institutions or agencies being installed in part of the building in which the consular premises are situated, provided that the premises assigned to them are separate from those used by the consular post. In that event, the said offices shall not, for the purposes of the present Convention, be considered to form part of the consular premises.

Article 56: Insurance against Third Party Risks

Members of the consular post shall comply with any requirement imposed by the laws and regulations of the receiving State in respect of insurance against third party risks arising from the use of any vehicle, vessel or aircraft.

Article 57: Special Provisions Concerning Private Gainful Occupation

1. Career consular officers shall not carry on for personal profit any professional or commercial activity in the receiving State.

2. Privileges and immunities provided in this Chapter shall not be accorded:

(a) to consular employees or to members of the service staff who carry on any private gainful occupation in the receiving State; (b) to members of the family of a person referred to in sub-paragraph (a) of this paragraph or to members of his private staff; (c) to members of the family of a member of a consular post who themselves carry on any private gainful occupation in the receiving State.

Chapter III

Regime Relating to Honorary Consular Officers and Consular Posts Headed by Such Officers

Article 58: General Provisions Relating to Facilities, Privileges and Immunities

1. Articles 28, 29, 30, 34, 35, 36, 37, 38 and 39, paragraph 3 of Article 54 and paragraphs 2 and 3 of Article 55 shall apply to consular posts headed by an honorary consular officer. In addition, the facilities, privileges and immunities of such consular posts shall be governed by Articles 59, 60, 61 and 62.

2. Articles 42 and 43, paragraph 3 of Article 44, Articles 45 and 53 and paragraph 1 of Article 55 shall apply to honorary consular officers. In addition, the facilities, privileges and immunities of such consular officers shall be governed by Articles 63, 64, 65, 66 and 67.

3. Privileges and immunities provided in the present Convention shall not be accorded to members of the family of an honorary consular officer or of a consular employee employed at a consular post headed by an honorary consular officer.

4. The exchange of consular bags between two consular posts headed by honorary consular officers in different States shall not be allowed without the consent of the two receiving States concerned.

Article 59: Protection of the Consular Premises

The receiving State shall take such steps as may be necessary to protect the consular premises of a consular post headed by an honorary consular officer against any intrusion or damage and to prevent any disturbance of the peace of the consular post or impairment of its dignity.

Article 60: Exemption from Taxation of Consular Premises

1. Consular premises of a consular post headed by an honorary consular officer of which the sending State is the owner or lessee shall be exempt from all national, regional or municipal dues and taxes whatsoever, other than such as represent payment for specific services rendered.

2. The exemption from taxation referred to in paragraph 1 of this Article shall not apply to such dues and taxes if, under the laws and regulations of the receiving State, they are payable by the person who contracted with the sending State.

Article 61: Inviolability of Consular Archives and Documents

The consular archives and documents of a consular post headed by an honorary consular officer shall be inviolable at all times and wherever they may be, provided that they are kept separate from other papers and documents and, in particular, from the private correspondence of the head of a consular post and of any person working with him, and from the materials, books or documents relating to their profession or trade.

Article 62: Exemption from Customs Duties

The receiving State shall, in accordance with such laws and regulations as it may adopt, permit entry of, and grant exemption from all customs duties, taxes, and related charges other than charges for storage, cartage and similar services on the following articles, provided that they are for the official use of a consular post headed by an honorary consular officer: coats-of-arms, flags, signboards, seals and stamps, books, official printed matter, office furniture, office equipment and similar articles supplied by or at the instance of the sending State to the consular post.

Article 63: Criminal Proceedings

If criminal proceedings are instituted against an honorary consular officer, he must appear before the competent authorities. Nevertheless, the proceedings shall be conducted with the respect due to him by reason of his official position and, except when he is under arrest or detention, in a manner which will hamper the exercise of consular functions as little as possible. When it has become necessary to detain an honorary consular officer, the proceedings against him shall be instituted with the minimum of delay.

Article 64: Protection of Honorary Consular Officers

The receiving State is under a duty to accord to an honorary consular officer such protection as may be required by reason of his official position.

Article 65: Exemption from Registration of Aliens and Residence Permits

Honorary consular officers, with the exception of those who carry on for personal profit any professional or commercial activity in the receiving State, shall be exempt from all obligations under the laws and regulations of the receiving State in regard to the registration of aliens and residence permits.

Article 66: Exemption from Taxation

An honorary consular officer shall be exempt from all dues and taxes on the remuneration and emoluments which he receives from the sending State in respect of the exercise of consular functions.

Article 67: Exemption from Personal Services and Contributions

The receiving State shall exempt honorary consular officers from all personal services and from all public services of any kind whatsoever and from military obligations such as those connected with requisitioning, military contributions and billeting.

Article 68: Optional Character of the Institution of Honorary Consular Officers

Each State is free to decide whether it will appoint or receive honorary consular officers.

Chapter IV

General Provisions

Article 69: Consular Agents Who Are Not Heads of Consular Posts

1. Each State is free to decide whether it will establish or admit consular agencies conducted by consular agents not designated as heads of consular post by the sending State.

2. The conditions under which the consular agencies referred to in paragraph 1 of this Article may carry on their activities and the privileges and immunities which may be enjoyed by the consular agents in charge of them shall be determined by agreement between the sending State and the receiving State.

Article 70: Exercise of Consular Functions by Diplomatic Missions

1. The provisions of the present Convention apply also, so far as the context permits, to the exercise of consular functions by a diplomatic mission.

2. The names of members of a diplomatic mission assigned to the consular section or otherwise charged with the exercise of the consular functions of the mission shall be notified to the Ministry for Foreign Affairs of the receiving State or to the authority designated by that Ministry.

3. In the exercise of consular functions a diplomatic mission may address:

(a) the local authorities of the consular district; (b) the central authorities of the receiving State if this is allowed by the laws, regulations and usages of the receiving State or by relevant international agreements.

4. The privileges and immunities of the members of a diplomatic mission referred to in paragraph 2 of this Article shall continue to be governed by the rules of international law concerning diplomatic relations.

Article 71: Nationals or Permanent Residents of the Receiving State

1. Except in so far as additional facilities, privileges and immunities may be granted by the receiving State, consular officers who are nationals of or permanently resident in the receiving State shall enjoy only immunity from jurisdiction and personal inviolability in respect of official acts performed in the exercise of their functions, and the privilege provided in paragraph 3 of Article 44. So far as these consular officers are concerned, the receiving State shall likewise be bound by the obligation laid down in Article 42. If criminal proceedings are instituted against such a consular officer, the proceedings

shall, except when he is under arrest or detention, be conducted in a manner which will hamper the exercise of consular functions as little as possible.

2. Other members of the consular post who are nationals of or permanently resident in the receiving State and members of their families, as well as members of the families of consular officers referred to in paragraph 1 of this Article, shall enjoy facilities, privileges and immunities only in so far as these are granted to them by the receiving State. Those members of the families of members of the consular post and those members of the private staff who are themselves nationals of or permanently resident in the receiving State shall likewise enjoy facilities, privileges and immunit ies only in so far as these are granted to them by the receiving State. The receiving State shall, however, exercise its jurisdiction over those persons in such a way as not to hinder unduly the performance of the functions of the consular post.

Article 72: Non-Discrimination

1. In the application of the provisions of the present Convention the receiving State shall not discriminate as between States.

2. However, discrimination shall not be regarded as taking place:

(a) where the receiving State applies any of the provisions of the present Convention restrictively because of a restrictive application of that provision to its consular posts in the sending State; (b) where by custom or agreement States extend to each other more favourable treatment than is required by the provisions of the present Convention.

Article 73: Relationship Between the Present Convention and Other International Agreements

1. The provisions of the present Convention shall not affect other international agreements in force as between States parties to them.

2. Nothing in the present Convention shall preclude States from concluding international agreements confirming or supplementing or extending or amplifying the provisions thereof.

Chapter V

Final Provisions

Article 74: Signature

The present Convention shall be open for signature by all States Members of the United Nations or of any of the specialized agencies or Parties to the

Statute of the International Court of Justice, and by any other State invited by the General Assembly of the United Nations to become a Party to the Convention, as follows until 31 October 1963 at the Federal Ministry for Foreign Affairs of the Republic of Austria and subsequently, until 31 March 1964, at the United Nations Headquarters in New York.

Article 75: Ratification

The present Convention is subject to ratification. The instruments of ratification shall be deposited with the Secretary-General of the United Nations.

Article 76: Accession

The present Convention shall remain open for accession by any State belongi ng to any of the four categories mentioned in Article 74. The instruments of accession shall be deposited with the Secretary-General of the United Nations.

Article 77: Entry into Force

1. The present Convention shall enter into force on the thirtieth day following the date of deposit of the twenty-second instrument of ratification or accession with the Secretary-General of the United Nations.

2. For each State ratifying or acceding to the Convention after the deposit of the twenty-second instrument of ratification or accession, the Convention shall enter into force on the thirtieth day after deposit by such State of its instrument of ratification or accession.

Article 78: Notifications by the Secretary-General

The Secretary-General of the United Nations shall inform all States belonging to any of the four categories mentioned in Article 74:

(a) of signatures to the present Convention and of the deposit of instruments of ratification or accession, in accordance with Articles 74, 75 and 76; (b) of the date on which the present Convention will enter into force, in accordance with Article 77.

Article 79: Authentic Texts

The original of the present Convention, of which the Chinese, English, French, Russian and Spanish texts are equally authentic, shall be deposited with the Secretary-General of the United Nations, who shall send certified copies thereof to all States belonging to any of the four categories mentioned in Article 74.

IN WITNESS WHEREOF the undersigned Plenipotentiaries, being duly authorized thereto by their respective Governments, have signed the present Convention.

DONE at Vienna, this twenty-fourth day of April, one thousand nine hundred and sixty-three.

Optional Protocol to the Vienna Convention on Consular Relations Concerning Acquisition of Nationality

DONE at Vienna, on 24 April 1963

The States Parties to the present Protocol and to the Vienna Convention on Consular Relations, hereinafter referred to as "the Convention", adopted by the United Nations Conference held at Vienna from 4 March to 22 April 1963,

Expressing their wish to establish rules between them concerning acquisition of nationality by members of the consular post and by members of their families forming part of their households,

Have agreed as follows:

Article I

For the purposes of the present Protocol, the expression "members of the consular post" shall have the meaning assigned to it in sub-paragraph (g) of paragraph 1 of Article 1 of the Convention, namely, "consular officers, consular employees and members of the service staff".

Article II

Members of the consular post not being nationals of the receiving State, and members of their families forming part of their households, shall not, solely by the operation of the law of the receiving State, acquire the nationality of that State.

Article III

The present Protocol shall be open for signature by all States which may become Parties to the Convention, as follows: until 31 October 1963 at the Federal Ministry for Foreign Affairs of the Republic of Austria and, subsequently, until 31 March 1964, at the United Nations Headquarters in New York.

Article IV

The present Protocol is subject to ratification. The instruments of ratification shall be deposited with the Secretary-General of the United Nations.

Article V

The present Protocol shall remain open for accession by all States which may become Parties to the Convention. The instruments of accession shall be deposited with the Secretary-General of the United Nations.

Article VI

1. The present Protocol shall enter into force on the same day as the Convention or on the thirtieth day following the date of deposit of the second instrument of ratification of or accession to the Protocol with the Secretary-General of the United Nations, whichever date is the later.

2. For each State ratifying or acceding to the present Protocol after its entry into force in accordance with paragraph 1 of this Article, the Protocol shall enter into force on the thirtieth day after deposit by such State of its instrument of ratification or accession.

Article VII

The Secretary-General of the United Nations shall inform all States which may become Parties to the Convention:

(a) of signatures to the present Protocol and of the deposit of instruments of ratification or accession, in accordance with Articles III, IV and V; (b) of the date on which the present Protocol will enter into force, in accordance with Article VI.

Article VIII

The original of the present Protocol, of which the Chinese, English, French, Russian and Spanish texts are equally authentic, shall be deposited with the Secretary-General of the United Nations, who shall send certified copies thereof to all States referred to in Article III.

IN WITNESS WHEREOF the undersigned plenipotentiaries, being duly authorized thereto by their respective Governments, have signed the present Protocol.

DONE at Vienna, this twenty-fourth day of April, one thousand nine hundred and sixty-three.

Optional Protocol to the Vienna Convention on Consular Relations Concerning the Compulsory Settlement of Disputes

DONE at Vienna, on 24 April 1963

The States Parties to the present Protocol and to the Vienna Convention on Consular Relations, hereinafter referred to as "the Convention", adopted by the United Nations Conference held at Vienna from 4 March to 22 April 1963,

Expressing their wish to resort in all matters concerning them in respect of any dispute arising out of the interpretation or application of the Convention to the compulsory jurisdiction of the International Court of Justice, unless some other form of settlement has been agreed upon by the parties within a reasonable period,

Have agreed as follows:

Article I

Disputes arising out of the interpretation or application of the Convention shall lie within the compulsory jurisdiction of the International Court of Justice and may accordingly be brought before the Court by an application made by any party to the dispute being a Party to the present Protocol.

Article II

The parties may agree, within a period of two months after one party has notified its opinion to the other that a dispute exists, to resort not to the International Court of Justice but to an arbitral tribunal. After the expiry of the said period, either party may bring the dispute before the Court by an application.

Article III

1. Within the same period of two months, the parties may agree to adopt a conciliation procedure before resorting to the International Court of Justice.

2. The conciliation commission shall make its recommendations within five months after its appointment. If its recommendations are not accepted by the parties to the dispute within two months after they have been delivered, either party may bring the dispute before the Court by an application.

Article IV

States Parties to the Convention, to the Optional Protocol concerning Acquisition of Nationality, and to the present Protocol may at any time declare that they will extend the provisions of the present Protocol to disputes arising out of the interpretation or application of the Optional Protocol concerning

Acquisition of Nationality. Such declarations shall be notified to the Secretary-General of the United Nations.

Article V

The present Protocol shall be open for signature by all States which may become Parties to the Convention as follows: until 31 October 1963 at the Federal Ministry for Foreign Affairs of the Republic of Austria and, subsequently, until 31 March 1964, at the United Nations Headquarters in New York.

Article VI

The present Protocol is subject to ratification. The instruments of ratification shall be deposited with the Secretary-General of the United Nations.

Article VII

The present Protocol shall remain open for accession by all States which may become Parties to the Convention. The instruments of accession shall be deposited with the Secretary-General of the United Nations.

Article VIII

1. The present Protocol shall enter into force on the same day as the Convention or on the thirtieth day following the date of deposit of the second instrument of ratification or accession to the Protocol with the Secretary-General of the United Nations, whichever date is the later.

2. For each State ratifying or acceding to the present Protocol after its entry into force in accordance with paragraph 1 of this Article, the Protocol shall enter into force on the thirtieth day after deposit by such State of its instrument of ratification or accession.

Article IX

The Secretary-General of the United Nations shall inform all States which may become Parties to the Convention:

(a) of signatures to the present Protocol and of the deposit of instruments of ratification or accession, in accordance with Articles V, VI and VII;
(b) of declarations made in accordance with Article IV of the present Protocol;
(c) of the date on which the present Protocol will enter into force, in accordance with Article VIII.

Article X

The original of the present Protocol, of which the Chinese, English, French, Russian and Spanish texts are equally authentic, shall be deposited with the Secretary-General of the United Nations, who shall send certified copies thereof to all States referred to in Article V.

IN WITNESS WHEREOF the undersigned plenipotentiaries, being duly authorised thereto by their respective Governments, have signed the present Protocol.

DONE at Vienna, this twenty-fourth day of April, one thousand nine hundred and sixty-three.

Table of Statutes

1792 and 1856	US Consular Services Acts
1781 and 1833	French Ordinances
1870	Extradition Act (United Kingdom)
1978	State Immunity Act
1980	Protection of the Trading Interests Act
1989	Extradition Act
1945	Statute of International Court of Justice
1974	Federal Sovereign Immunities Act
1976	State Immunity Act

Table of International Conventions

Caracas Convention of 1911, 107 *British and Foreign State Papers*

Charter of Economic Rights and Duties of States 1974

Convention on Asylum 1928

Convention of Saint-Germain-en-Laye, 10 September 1919

Convention on the Prevention and Punishment of the Crime of Genocide, 1948

Convention on the Prevention and Punishment of Crimes against Internationally Protected Persons, including Diplomatic Agents 1973

Convention on the Provisional Administration of European Colonies, and Possessions in America

Convention on Psychotropic Substances, 1971

Council of Europe Convention on Extradition, 1957

Covenant of the League of Nations

Draft Convention of American Institute of International Law; Diena Report

Draft Convention on Diplomatic Privileges and Immunities, 26 *American Journal of International Law* (1932)

European Convention on Extradition, 1947

European Convention on State Immunity, 1972

Franco-Italian Consular Convention, 1955

Havana Convention on Asylum 1928

Havana Convention on Consular Agents, 1931, 26 *American Journal of International Law* (Supp) (1932)

ILO Convention entitled "Elimination of the Worst Forms of Child Labour" the text of which has been reproduced in 38 *International Legal Materials* (1949) 1207

Inter-American Convention on Extradition, 1987

International Tin Council (Immunities and Privileges) Order 1972

Montevideo Convention, 1933

Rio Declaration on Environment and Development, 1992

Stockholm Declaration on Human Environment, 1972

Tokyo Convention on Offences and Certain Other Acts Committed on Board Aircraft, 1963

United Nations Convention on the Law of the Sea, 1982

United Nations General Assembly Resolution 2631 of 1974

Table of International Conventions

United Nations General Assembly Resolution entitled The Declaration on the Granting of Independence to Colonial Countries and Peoples, (1960) Resolution No 1514 (XV)

United Nations General Assembly Resolution 3218

Vienna Convention on Diplomatic Relations, 1961

Vienna Convention on Consular Relations, 1963

Vienna Convention on the Law of Treaties, 1969

Other Primary Sources

Abuse of Diplomatic Immunities and Privileges (The), First Report of the Foreign Affairs Committee of the House of Commons, (1984)

Act of Chapultepec of 3 March 1945

Advisory Opinion of the International Court of Justice in *Certain Expenses of the UN* case (1962), ICJ Report 151

Advisory Opinion of the International Court of Justice in *Restrictions to the Death Penalty* (1983), 70 *International Law* Reports

Aide Memoire submitted by the UK government to the ECJ following the Commission's decision in the *Dyestuffs* case. The text of the *Aide Memoire* has been produced in Lowe at 144–147

An Agenda for Peace: Preventative Diplomacy, Peace-making and Peace-keeping, DP1/1247 (1992); see also Supplement DP1/1623/PKS E 95/115 (1995)

Annex to United Nations General Assembly Resolution 2625 (XXV)

Basic Facts About the United Nations, United Nations, New York (1995)

Bolivian Agreement on Extradition, 18 July 1911

Cairo Resolution of the Organisation of African States of 21 July 1964

Caracas Declaration of 1954

Comment by Sir Antony Acland, *Minutes of Evidence Taken Before the Foreign Affairs Committee*, Report (1979)

Declaration of the Principles of Solidarity of America, 1938

Diplomatic Immunities and Privileges: Government Report on Review of Vienna Convention on Diplomatic Relations. Reply to "The Abuse of Diplomatic Immunities and Privileges", Cmnd 1419 (1985)

Doha Declaration, 41 *International Legal Materials* (2002)

Eleventh Report on Competition Policy (1987)

First Report of the Foreign Affairs Committee in the Session 1984–85 entitled *Diplomatic Immunities and Privileges*, London (1985), Cmnd 19497

Geneva Agreement

Harvard Research Draft Convention on Diplomatic Privileges and Immunities, 1979, 26 *American Journal of International Law* (Supp 1932) 26

House of Commons Debate (Solicitor-General, Mr Peter Archer) vol 949

Lateran Treaty, 1929

League Doc C 196M.70 (1927) V

Memorandum by the Secretariat of the International Law Commission on "Diplomatic Intercourse and Immunities", UN Doc A/CN/4.98, 1956 *Yearbook of the International Law Commission*, Vol II, 129

Moore's Digest vol II

Proceedings of the International Law Commission on the subject of "The Status of the Diplomatic Courier and the Diplomatic Bag, not accompanied by Diplomatic Courier", *Yearbook of the International Law Commission*, 1980, Vol II; 1982, Vols I & II; 1984, Vols I & II; 1985, Vols I & II; 1986, Vols I & II; 1989, Vols I & II

Report of the *Foreign Affairs Committee* – The Abuse of Diplomatic Privileges, and the UK Government Response to the Report (1984), Cmnd 7497

Reports of the Law Officers of the Crown (1896)

Reservations to the Convention on the Prevention and Punishment of the Crime of Genocide, ICJ Reports (1951)

Security Council Resolutions of 14 July 1960 and 9 August 1960

Sino-Austrian Treaty of 19 October 1925 (Article 4), 55 *League of Nations Treaty Series* 21

Sino-British Treaty of 11 January 1943, *China Handbook* (1937–43)

Sino-German Treaty of 20 May 1921 (Article 3), *China Year Book* (1925)

Sino-Soviet Agreement of 31 May 1924, *China Year Book* (1924)

Special Paper produced by the State Department entitled *"Proposed Consular Convention with the United Kingdom"* (1946)

Tehran Agreement

Traité de droit international public, vol I(2) (1926)

Treaties concluded between China and:

- Belgium *(2 November 1865, 1 Hertslet, No 34 at 223);*
- Denmark *(13 July 1863 – 1 Hertslet, No 38);*
- France *(the Treaty of Whampoa, 1844; the Treaty of Tientsin, 1858; the Convention of Tientsin, 1886);*
- Germany *(2 September 1861 – 1 Hertslet, No 56);*
- Great Britain *(the Treaty of Tientsin, 1858; the Chefoo Agreement, 1876);*
- Italy *(26 October, 1866 – 1 Hertslet No 60);*
- Norway and Sweden *(Treaty of 20 March 1947- 1 Hertslet, China Treaties No 93)*

Treaty of Montevideo of 1889 on International Penal Law

Treaty of Trianon (Article 217), *Journal Official*, 26 August 1921

UK *Instructions* (1949)

UN Charter 1945

UN Conference on Diplomatic Intercourse and Immunities, Official Records, Vol I, Summary Records, UN DocA/Conf.20/14

UN Conference on Diplomatic Intercourse and Immunities, Official Records, Vol II, Annexes etc., UN Doc A/Conf.20/C.1

UN Doc A/CONF 20/C.1 / L.

UN Doc A/CONF 20/14, vol 1

UN Doc A/CONF 20/14

UN Doc A/CONF 20 /CI/L.127, *UN Conference on Diplomatic Privileges and Immunities, Official Records* vol II

UN Doc A/CN.4/98, 1956 See UN Doc A/CN.4/98, 1956 *Yearbook of the International Law Commission*, vol. II

UN Doc A/CONF.25/14 of 23 April 1963

UN Doc. TD/B/AC12/R4 – statement made by Ambassador Castañeda of Mexico as Chairman of the Working Group Meetings

UN General Assembly, *Official Records*, 4th Session, Supp No 10 (A/925)

UN General Assembly, *Official Records*, 16th Session, Supp No 9 (A/4425)

UN General Assembly's Declaration on the Granting of Independence to Colonial Countries and Peoples (Resolution 1514(xv) of 14 December 1960).

UN General Assembly Resolution 1685(XVI), *Official Records*, 16th Session, Supp No 17 at 61 (A/5100) (1962)

UN General Assembly Resolution entitled *Declaration on the Granting of Independence to Colonial Countries and Peoples*, 1960

UN General Assembly Resolution No. 1803 of 1962 entitled *Permanent Sovereignty over Natural Resources*

UN General Assembly Resolution, entitled *Uniting for Peace* 3 November 1950, Res 377(v)

UN Report entitled: *Transnational Corporations in World Development*, New York (1985)

UN Resolution on the Right of Self-determination

Universal Declaration of Human Rights 1948

US-Chinese Treaty for Relinquishment of Extraterritorial Rights in China and the Regulation of Related Matters of 11 January 1943, *US Treaty Series*

US Department of Justice and Federal Trade Commission: Antitrust Enforcement – Guidelines for International Operations, April 1995, vol 1

US Federal Sovereign Immunities Act, 1976

United States Foreign Relation Reports (1875) vol II

United States Foreign Relation Reports (1895) vol I

United States Foreign Relations Reports (1912)

United States Foreign Relations Reports (1919) vol II

United States Foreign Relations Reports (1925) vol I

Yearbook of International Law Commission (1957) vol I

Yearbook of the International Law Commission (1966)

Yearbook of the International Law Commission (1989) Vol II, part 2

Other Sources

Abbott, K W	"Trust but verify: The Production of Information in Arms Control Treaties and Other International Agreements", 26 *Current International Journal* (1993) 1
Acheson, D	"Morality, Moralism and Diplomacy", *The Yale Review*, Yale University Press (1959) 488
Amstunz, M R	*International Ethics: Concepts, Theories and Cases in Global Politics*, Rowman & Littlefield (1999)
Baker, C D	"Tolerance of International Espionage: A Functional Approval", 19 *American University International Law Review* (2004) 1091
Barker, J C	*The Abuse of Diplomatic Privileges and Immunities: Necessary Evil?* Aldershot, Dartmouth (1996)
Beckett, W E	"The Exercise of Criminal Jurisdiction over Foreigners", 6 *British Year Book of International Law* (1925) 44
—	"Consular Immunities", 21 *British Year Book of International Law* (1944) 34
Bowett, D W	"Collective Self-Defence under the Charter of the United Nations", 32 *British Year Book of International Law* (1955–56) 130
Brower, C N and Tepe, J B Jr	"The Charter of Economic Rights and Duties of States: A Reflection on Rejection of International Law", 9 *International Lawyer* (1975) 295
Brown, J	"Diplomatic Immunity: State Practice under the Vienna Convention on Diplomatic Relations", 37 *International and Comparative Law Quarterly* (1988) 53
Brownlie, I	"Humanitarian Intervention" in *Law and Civil War in the Modern World*, J Moore (ed), (1974)
—	"Recognition in Theory and Practice", 53 *British Year Book of International Law* (1982) 197
—	*Basic Documents in International Law*, Oxford, Clarendon Press (1984)
Bynkershoek	*De Foro Legatorum* (1721)
Calvo, C	*Le Droit International* (1896) vol ii
Cameron, I	"First Report of the Foreign Affairs Committee of the House of Commons," 34 *International and Comparative Law Quarterly* 610

Chatterjee, C	"From Doha to Cancún: A Multilateral Trading System?" 54 *Amicus Curiae* (2004) 22
Chatterjee, H	*International Law and Inter-State Relations in Ancient India* (1958)
Chatterjee, S K	"Some Legal Problems of Support Role in International Law: Tanzania and Uganda", 30 *International and Comparative Law Quarterly* (1981) 755
—	"Forty Years of International Action for Trade Liberalization", 23 *Journal of World Trade* (1989) 45
—	"The Charter of Economic Rights and Duties of States: An Evaluation After 15 years", 40 *International and Comparative Law Quarterly* (1991) 669
Crawford, J	"The Criteria for Statehood in International Law", *The British Year Book of International Law* (1976–77)
—	*The Creation of States in International Law*, Oxford, Clarendon Press (1979)
—	"Execution of Foreign Judgments and Foreign Sovereign Immunity", 75 *American Journal of International Law* (1981) 870
—	"International Law of Foreign Sovereign: Distinguishing Immune Transactions", 54 *British Year Book of International Law* (1983) 55
—	"Decisions of British Courts during 1985 involving questions of Public International Law", 56 *British Year Book of International Law* (1985) 311
Delaume, G R	"The State Immunity of the United Kingdom" 73 *American Journal of International Law* (1979) 185
Demarest, G B	"Espionage in International Law", 24 *Denver Journal of International Law and Policy* (1996) 321
Denza, E	*Diplomatic Law*, Dobbs Ferry, Oceana Publications (1976)
—	*Diplomatic Law*, Oxford, Oxford University Press (1998)
Dinstein, Y	"Diplomatic Immunity from Jurisdiction *Rationae Material*", 15 *International and Comparative Law Quarterly* (1966) 76

Donaldson, T	*Traditions of International Ethics in Kant's Global Rationalism*, Cambridge, Cambridge University Press (1992)
Feldman, M B	"The United States Foreign Sovereign Immunities Act of 1976 in Perspective: a Founder's View" 35 *International and Comparative Law Quarterly* (1986) 302
Feltham, R G	*Diplomatic Handbook*, Harlow, Longman (1993)
Frey, L S and Frey, M L	*The History of Diplomatic Immunity*, Ohio, Ohio State University (1999)
Fox, H	*The Law of State Immunity*, Oxford, Oxford University Press (2002)
Fugate, W	*Foreign Commerce and Antitrust Laws* (1973)
Ganshoff, F L	*The Middle Ages: A History of International Relations*, London, Harper & Row (English Translation) (1970)
Gilbert, B	"The Practice of Asylum in Legations and Consulates of the United States", 3 *American Journal of International Law* (1909) 502
Goodrich & Hambro	*Charter of the UN*, London, Stevens (1949)
Gore-Both, I (ed)	*Satow's Guide to Diplomatic Practice*, Harlow, Longman, (1979)
Graham, G	*Ethics and International Relations*, Oxford, Blackwell (1997)
Gray, C	*International Law and the Use of Force*, Oxford, Oxford University Press (2000)
Gross, L	"The Case Concerning United States Diplomatic and Consular Staff in Tehran: Phase of Provisional Measures", 74 *American Journal of International Law* (1980) 395
Grzybowski, K	"The Regime of Diplomacy and the Teheran Hostages", 30 *International and Comparative Law Quarterly* (1981) 42
Haight, G W	"The New International Economic Order and the Charter of Economic Rights and Duties of States", *International Lawyer* (1975), 591–604
Hardy, M	*Modern Diplomatic Law*, Manchester, Manchester University Press (1968)

Harvard Research Draft of 1932	26 *American Journal of International Law* (1932) (Supp.) 189
Higgins, R	*The Development of International Law through the Political Organs of the United Nations*, Oxford, Oxford University Press (1963)
—	"Recent Developments in the Law of Sovereign Immunity in the United Kingdom", 71 *American Journal of International Law* (1977) 423
—	"Certain Unresolved Aspects of the Law of State Immunity", 29 *Netherlands International Law Review* (1982) 265
—	"The Abuse of Diplomatic Privileges and Immunities: Recent United Kingdom Experience", 79 *American Journal of International Law* (1985) 641
Hill, D J	*A History of Diplomacy in the International Development of Europe*, London, Green & Co (1905)
Holland, D L	"Diplomatic Immunity in English Law", 4 *Current Legal Problems* (1951) 81
Hornbeck, S K	"The Most-favoured Nation Clause" (Part I) 3 *American Journal of International Law* (1909) 395–422
James, A	"Diplomatic Relations and Contacts", 62 *British Year Book of International Law* (1991) 347
Jennings, R Y	"The Caroline and MacLeod Cases", 32 *American Journal of International Law* (1938) 82
—	"Extraterritorial Jurisdiction and the United States' Antitrust Laws", 33 *British Year Book of International Law* (1957) 146
Jennings R Y (Sir) and Watts, A (Sir) (eds)	*Oppenheim's International Law*, Harlow, Longman (1996)
Johnson, D H N	"The Effect of Resolutions of the General Assembly of the United Nations" (1955–56) 32 *British Year Book of International Law* (1955–56) 57–122
Kelson, H	"Recognition in International Law", 25 *American Journal of International Law* (1941) 605
Kerley, E L	"Some Aspects of the Vienna Conference on Diplomatic Intercourse and Immunities," 56 *American Journal of International Law* 88
Koul, A K	*The Legal Framework of UNCTAD in World Trade*, Leiden, Sijthoff (1977)

Kunz, J	"Critical Remarks on Lauterpacht's Recognition in International Law", 44 *American Journal of International Law* (1950) 713
Lauterpacht, H	"Recognition of Insurgents as a *de facto* Government", 3 *Modern Law Review* (1939) 1
—	*Recognition in International Law*, Cambridge, Cambridge University Press (1947)
—	"The Problem of Jurisdictional Immunities of Foreign States", 28 *British Year Book of International Law* (1951) 220
Lauterpacht, H (ed)	Oppenheim's International Law: a Treatise, Vol. I (Peace) (1958)
Lee, L T	Consular Law and Practice, Oxford, Clarendon Press (1991)
Lillich, R B and Newman, F C	*International Human Rights: Problems of Law and Policy* (1979)
Lowe, A V	*Extraterritorial Jurisdiction: an Annotated Collection of Legal Materials*, Cambridge, Griffin (1983)
—	"Jurisdiction" in *International Law*, M Evans (ed), Cambridge, Cambridge University Press (2003) 329
Lyons, A B	"The Conclusiveness of the Foreign Office Certificate", 23 *British Year Book of International Law* (1946) 240
—	"Conclusiveness of the Statements of the Executive: Continental and Latin American Practices", 25 *British Year Book of International Law* (1948) 180
—	"Personal Immunities of Diplomatic Agents", 31 *British Year Book of International Law* (1954) 299
Lyons, F S	*Internationalism in Europe, 1815–1914*, Leiden, A W Sijthoff (1963)
Machiavelli, N	*The Prince*, Oxford, Oxford University Press (1998)
Mann, F A	"Sovereign Immunity", 18 *Modern Law Review* (1955)
—	"The Dyestuffs case in the Court of Justice of the European Communities", 22 *International and Comparative Law Quarterly* (1973) 35
Martens, K von	*Causes célèbres du Droit des Gens* (1827) vol I

McNair, A (Sir)	"Extradition and Extraterritorial Asylum", 28 *British Year Book of International Law* (1951) 172
Merrills, J	"Recognition and Construction", 20 *International and Comparative Law Quarterly* (1971) 476
Miller, J	"Extraterritorial Effects of Trade Regulation" 111 *University of Pennsylvania, Law Review* (1963) 1092
Moore, J B	*Digest of International Law*, 1906
Morgenstern, F	"Extra-territorial Asylum", 25 *The British Year Book of International Law* (1948) 236
Nervo	*Dictionnaire Diplomatique*, vol 1
Nicolson, H	*Diplomacy*, Oxford, Oxford University Press (1949)
—	*The Evolution of Diplomatic Method*, Constable & Co Ltd (1954)
Nussbaum, A	*A Concise History of the Law of Nations*, New York, Macmillan (1954)
Ogdon, M	*Judicial Bases of Diplomatic Immunity*, Washington DC, John Byrne & Co (1936)
—	"The Growth of Purpose in the Law of Diplomatic Immunity", 31 *American Journal of International Law* (1937) 449
Olmstead, C (ed)	*Extraterritorial Applications of Laws and Responses Thereto*, Oxford, Oxford University Press (1984)
Phillipson, Coleman	*The International Law and Custom of Ancient Greece and Rome*, London, MacMillan & Co Ltd (1911)
Preuss, L	"Diplomatic Privileges and Immunities of International Agents", 25 *American Journal of International Law* (1931) 694
—	"Capacity for Legation and the Theoretical Basis of Diplomatic Immunity", 10 *New York University Law Quarterly Review* (1932) 170
Rojaz, M	*The United Nations and Domestic Jurisdiction* (1961)
Rao, P C	"Charter of Economic Rights and Duties of States", 15 *Indian Journal of International Law* (1975) 469–370
Rawlings, H F	"The Malaysian Constitutional Crisis of 1983", 35 *International and Comparative Law Quarterly* (1986) 237

Reale	*Recucil des cours de droit international de la Hague*, vol XIII (1938)
Rozakis, C L	"Terrorism and the Internationally Protected Persons in the light of the ILC's Draft Articles", 23 *International and Comparative Law Quarterly* (1974) 32
Schreuer, C H	*State Immunity: Some Recent Developments*, Cambridge, Cambridge University Press (1988)
Schwarzenberger, G	"The Most-favoured Nation Standard in British State Practice" 22 *British Year Book of International Law* (1945) 96–121
Scott, J B	"The Gradual and Progressive Codification of International Law" 21 *American Journal of International Law* (1927) 417
Sen, B	*A Diplomatic Handbook of International Law and Practice*, The Hague, Martinus Nijhoff, (1988)
Shearer (ed), I A	*Starke's International Law*, London, Butterworth
Shaw, M N	*International Law*, Cambridge, Cambridge University Press (2003)
Simmonds, K R	"The Rationale of Diplomatic Immunity," 12 *International and Comparative Law Quarterly* (1962) 1204
Sloan, F B	"The Binding Force of a 'Recommendation' of the General Assembly of the United Nations", 25 *British Year Book of International Law* (1948) 14
Stearns, M	"*The Achille Lauro Affair and Co-operation in Combating International Terrorism*", 24 *International Legal Materials* (1985) 1509
—	"*Talking to Strangers: Improving American Diplomacy at Home and Abroad*", New Jersey, Princeton University Press, (1996)
Sucharitkul, S	*State Immunities and Trading Activities in International Law*, Leiden, Sijthoff (1959)
Talmon, S	"Recognition of Governments: An Analysis of the New British Policy and Practice", 63 *British Year Book of International Law* (1982) 231
Tunkin, G	"The Legal Nature of the United Nations" (1966) III Hag. Rec. 1–68
Vattel	*Le Droit Des Gens* (1758)

Warbrick, C	"Kampuchea: Representation and Recognition", 30 *International and Comparative Law Quarterly* (1981) 234
—	"The New British Policy on Recognition of Governments", 30 *International and Comparative Law Quarterly* (1981) 568
—	"Executive Certificates in Foreign Affairs: Prospects for Review and Control", 35 *International and Comparative Law Quarterly* (1986) 138
Watts, A	"The Legal Position in International Law of Heads of State, Heads of Governments and Foreign Ministers", 247 *Hague Recueil* (1994) III 13
Whish, R	*Competition Law*, London, Butterworth (2001)
White, RC	"The State Immunity Act 1978," 42 *Modern Law Review* (1979) 72
Whiteman, M	*Digest of International Law*, Washington, DC (1970) vol VII
Williams, M	*International Economic Organisations and the Third World*, New York, Harvester Wheatsheaf (1994)
Wilmshurst, E	"Executive Certificate in Foreign Affairs: The United Kingdom" 35 *International and Comparative Law Quarterly* (1986) 157
Wilson, C E	*Diplomatic Privileges and Immunities*, Tucson, University of Arizona Press (1967)
Wilson, Robert R	"Access to Courts Provisions in United States Commercial Treaties", 47 *American Journal of International Law* (1953) 20
Wood, M C	"The Convention on the Prevention and Punishment of Crimes Against Internationally Protected Persons, including Diplomatic Agents", 23 *International and Comparative Law Quarterly* (1974) 791
Wright, Q	"Matters of Domestic Jurisdiction", 74 *Hague Recueil* (1949) I
—	"Is Discussion Intervention?", 50 *American Journal of International Law* (1956) 102
Young, E	"The Development of the Law of Diplomatic Relations" 40 *British Year Book of International Law* (1964) 141

Author Index

Abbott, K W   115
Acheson, D   67
Alexandrowicz   31
Amstutz, M R   69

Baker, L D   115
Barker, J C   30, 31, 189
Barnston, R   122
Beckett, W E   55, 150, 255
Bilder, R B   150
Bluntschli   255
Brower, C   298
Brown, J   190
Brownlie, I   46, 72–3, 147, 166
Bynkershoek   32, 33, 48, 190, 229, 238

Calvo, C   231
Chatterjee, C   127
Chatterjee, H   48
Chatterjee, S K   39, 46, 73, 99, 123, 133, 298
Crawford, J   30, 147, 152

Delaume, G R   244
Demarest, G B   115
Denza, E   189, 190, 196, 198, 205
Donaldson, T   67

Fauchille   229, 232
Feldman, M B   244
Feltham, R G   169
Field, D D   255
Fiore, P   255
Fitzmaurice, G (Sir)   150, 242
Fox, H (Lady)   220

Ganshoff, F L   31, 237
Gentili   32, 48
Gilbert, B   188
Goodrich, L   40, 73, 297
Gore-Booth   188
Graham, G   70, 73

Gray, C   287
Grotins   2, 32, 33, 49, 238

Haight, G W   298
Hambro, E   40, 73, 297
Hardy, M   189, 190
Higgins, R   40, 108, 109, 111, 221, 299
Hill, D J   30, 31, 32
Holland, D C   238
Hornbeck, S K   71, 39, 123, 252
Hudson   230

Jennings, R Y   8, 30, 49, 53, 54, 58, 243
Johnson, D H N   297, 299

Koul, A K   98
Kelsen, H   104
Kunz, J   104

Lauterpacht, H   40, 104, 147, 148, 151, 220
Lee, T   250, 256, 257, 260, 278
Lillich, R   46, 72
Locke   69
Lowe, A V   57, 61, 63
Lyons, A B   151, 153, 189
Lyons, F S   128

Machiavelli, N   48, 67, 68
Malkin, W (Sir)   150
Mann, F A   58, 62, 218
Martens   48, 238
McNair, A D   197, 229
Merrills, J   152
Morgenstern, F   229, 230, 231, 234

Newman, F C   46, 72
Nicholson, S   252
Nicolson, S   30, 31, 32, 33
Nussbaum, A   48, 249

Ogdon, M   238

Oppenheim, L H   8, 30, 31, 32, 49, 150, 152, 153, 191, 204, 229, 232, 233, 237, 243, 244, 245, 249

Pufendorf   48

Rao, P C   298
Rawlings, H F   244
Rozakis, C L   208

Satow   188, 189
Schwarzenberger, G   39, 73, 123, 252
Scott, J B   229
Sen, B   250, 251
Shaw, M N   199, 207
Sinclair, I   220
Sloan, F B   298
Stears, M   69

Talmon, S   147

Tepe, J B   298
Tunkin, G   242, 243, 299

Vallat, F A   150
Vattel   32, 33, 48, 190, 238, 239
Vitoria   48

Warbrick, C   147, 151
Westlake   232
Whish, R   62
Williams, M   99
Wilmshurst, E   151
Wilson, C E   189
Wilson, R   252
Wood, M C   208
Wright, Q   40

Yokota   242
Young, E   30
Young, R   254

Index

Aaland Islands 1920   24
   1856 Treaty   24
Abdul Rahman Baker v Ashford
   (1960)   153n
Acheson, Dean, US Secretary of
   State   67
Achille Lauro Affair and Co-operation in
   Combating International
   Terrorism   56
Acland, Sir Antony   184n
ACP Group   127–8
Act jure gestionis   192–3
Admiralty Division (British Court)   239
Aerial Incidents case   17n, 26
Afghanistan   46, 128
African Union   128
Agenda for Development, An (UN
   document)   302, 310
Agenda for Peace, An (UN Secretary
   General Boutros Boutros-Ghali
   document)   302
Aggression
   see belligerency
Agreement on Subsidies   125
Agrément, diplomatic   157, 158, 159
Agricultural sector   96
Aide memoire (diplomatic)   144
Aircraft captains and diplomatic
   bags   206
Airspace   36, 47n
Albania   118ff, 233, 286–7
Albanian National Assembly   118–9
Alcoa case   51n, 61
Alcom Ltd v Republic of Colombia   193
Al-Fin Corporation's Patent (1969)   152n
Alfred Dunhill of London Inc v Republic of
   Cuba 1952   218–9
Algeria   15
Allende, President Salvador   233
Alliance, treaties   2–3
Altamira, Judge, Permanent Court of
   International Justice   44

Alvarez, Judge, International Court of
   Justice   237
Ambassadeur, L' (Hotman, 1603)   32
Ambassadors   33, 141, 142, 159, 161,
   180, 220n, 237, 239, 240, 241, 242
   appointment   157
   and asylum   232
   and diplomatic asylum   229, 234
   as head of diplomatic mission   173
American Banana Co v United Fruit Co
   1909   61n
American Institute of International
   Law   239
Amity, Economic Relations, and
   Consular Rights, Treaty of
   1955   201
ANDEAN Pact   124
Angola   307
Anti-Terrorism, Crime and Security Act
   (UK 2001)   55, 56
Anti-trust legislation   51, 62
Anzilotti, Judge, Permanent Court of
   International Justice   44
Apartheid   99, 130
Apostolic Nuncio   142
Application of the Convention on the
   Prevention and Punishment of the
   Crime of Genocide (Bosnia-
   Herzegovina v Yugoslavia (Serbia-
   Montenegro)), Provisional Measures
   ICJ Reports   272n
Arab Bank Ltd v Barclays Bank DCO
   (1954)   152n
Arab League   306
Arab-Israeli conflict   xvii, 128
Archer, Peter, MP, Solicitor
   General   223n
Argentina   4, 230, 243
Arizona Mercy Committee   270
Arizona, US   270, 272
Armament   294, 299
Armed forces   225

387

Armenia 282
Assistant Marshal of the Diplomatic
 Corps 157, 163
Association of South East Asian Nations
 (ASEAN) 122, 124
Asylum case (ICJ) (Colombia v Peru) 8,
 232, 234ff
Asylum Convention (Convention on the
 Status of Refugees) 1951 13, 25–6
Asylum:
 asylum seekers 13
 political asylum 25
 territorial asylum 25–6, 235
 see also diplomatic asylum
Attaché (embassy) 142, 172, 173
 ranking of 155
Attachment 204
Attorney-General (UK legal
 official) 240
Attorney-General, UK 240
Australia 75, 92n, 96, 150, 287
Austria 220, 253
Aut dedere aut judicare 11

Baccus SRL v Servicio Nacional del Trigo
 (1956) 221n, 223n
Bahrain 204n, 254
Baltic Exchange 218
*Barcelona Traction, Light and Power
 Company* 53n, 54
Bargaining power xviii, Chapter 6, 117,
 314
 definition 91ff
 considered at various levels 95ff
*Beagle Channel Arbitration (Argentina v
 Chile)* (1979) 150n
Beckett, W E 255
Bedjoui, Judge, ICJ 274
Beirut 250, 305
Belgium 219, 220, 255, 256
 as a colonial power 41ff
 Government of 42ff
 King of 240
 see also Congo, Belgian
Belgium v Nicod and Another 198n
Belli 48
Belligerency 1
Beneficiaries, rights of 24

Benelux Convention on Extradition and
 Judicial Assistance in Penal
 Matters 12
Benelux 256
Berlin, General Act of 1885 41, 45
Billeting 276n
Bing, Geoffrey 233
Blackstone (UK legal publication) 240
Bluntschli, J C 255
*Board of Accountancy, The and
 Ferguson* 3n
Bodin, Jean 48
Bolivarian Agreement on Extradition
 1911 234, 235
Bolivia 124n, 230
*Bosnia-Herzegovina v Yugoslavia (Serbia
 and Montenegro) Provisional
 Measures*, ICJ Reports 272n
Boundaries, state 80
Boutros-Ghali, Boutros (UN Secretary
 General) 302–3
Bowett, D W 109
Brandt Commission, 1977 123
Brazil 3, 4
Breard, Angel Francisco 274
Brett LJ 217, 240, 241–2
Brezhnev Doctrine 19
Brierly 73
Briggs v The Lightships (US case) 241
Briggs 73
British Channel 152n
British Government 152, 161, 211
British Nationality and Status of Aliens
 Act 1914 152n
*British Nylon Spinners Ltd v Imperial
 Chemicals Industries Ltd* 59
*British Yearbook of International Law,
 The* 30n
Brownlie, I 72–3
Brunei Darussalam 124n
Brussels Convention 226, 228
Brussels, General Act of 1890 41
Bunia, DR Congo 307
*Burkina Faso and Mali Frontier
 Dispute* 27
Bynkershoek, Cornelius van 32, 33, 68,
 238
Byzantine Empire 31–2, 250

Index

Cairo Resolution of Organisation of African States, 21 July 1964   27
Calvo Doctrine   2
Calvo, Carlos   2
Cambodia   124n, 202–3, 233, 308
Cambodian Embassy, London, 1975 incident   202–3
Canada and *Trail Smelter Arbitration*   47n, 286
Cancún Round   *see* WTO
Capacity building   125, 126
Capitulations treaties, 15th century   250
Capitulations Treaty 1836   254
Capitulatory system   253, 254
Caracas Declaration of Solidarity 1954   19
Caribbean states   72
Carl-Zeiss-Stiftung v Rayner & Keeler (No 2) (1967)   152n
Caroline, The, case   108
Cartelisation of commodities   76, 133
Case Concerning America and Other Mexican Nationals (Mexico v US) International Legal Materials   274
Case concerning Rights of Nationals of the United States of America in Morocco (France v United States) ICJ, 1952   254
Casus Belli   2
Casus Foederis   2–3
Central America   27
Central Bank of Nigeria   219, 221
Central Bank   228
Certain Expenses of the UN case 1962 110n
Chad   307
Chancellor of the Exchequer, UK   147n
Chancery of a Mission   170–1
Channel Islands   56
Chapultepec, Act of (3 March 1945)   19
Chargé d'affaires   33, 141, 142, 160, 161, 162, 173, 180, 185
    appointment   156
Charter of Economic Rights and Duties of States 1974 (UN Resolution)   76, 79, 91–2, 99, 133
Child labour   64
Chile   230, 231, 233
China Order in Council, 1925, UK   253

China   32, 252–3, 296, 304
    and consuls   250
    extra-territoriality and   252–3
Christendom   48, 73
Christianity   48
Christian states   67, 252
    non-Christian states   67
Church of England   73
Circuit Court of Arlington, Virginia, USA   274
Ciskei, Republic of, status of   152
Civil law system   53
Coat of Arms, State, salute to   13
Cobden Treaty   252
Cold War   3, 8
Collective bargaining   65
Collective self-defence   107–9, 111
College of Fetials   31
Colombia   4, 8, 124n, 193–4, 234ff
Colonial powers   78, 94–5, 105–6
Colonialism and colonisation   33, 77, 93, 94, 120
Colonies   93
Colonies, Secretary of State for (UK)   153n
Comity   3
Commerce, freedom of   42, 45–6
Commercial disputes   18
Commercial equality   120–1
Commercial Solvents case (1974)   57n, 63
Commercial transactions in state context, defined   224
Common Agricultural Policy, EU   64, 71–2, 124
Common heritage of mankind   106
Common law system   53
Commonwealth Law Ministers meeting 1966   12
Commonwealth, British   156, 218, 256
    countries   12, 157, 160, 161
    preference   88
Commonwealth Law Ministers meeting 1966   11
Communications networks, development of   106–7
Communications, development of   113
Communism   103
Communist States   258

see also Soviet Union
Compania Naviera Vascongado v SS Cristina (1974) 217
Companies 59–60
  entity doctrine 57
  independent legal personality 62–3
  multinational as single-economic entity 57, 62–3
  nationality of 53–4, 57–8
  personalities 62–3
  transnational 94, 97–8
Competition Act UK 1998 63
Competition, commercial 42–3
Concert of Europe 33
Conciliation 115
Concordat 3
  with Italy 1984 19
Condolence, book of 145, 163
Condominium 3–4, 40n
Conferences Chapter 8
  areas of concern 135
  bilateral and multilateral 132
  bloc voting 138
  chair/president of conference 139
  classification 130–1
  conference management 138–9
  Conference Secretariat 134, 135, 136
  and conventions 136, 140
  credentials 137
  delegates to 134, 135, 136
  delegations to 136, 137–8, 140
  diplomacy 133–4
  diplomats and 133
  languages 140
  observers and 137
  organisation 134–5
  participating governments and 136
  pressure groups 135
  procedure 135–40
  procedures 135ff
  proposals and decision making 137–8
  quorum of 138
  rapporteurs 134, 136, 139–40,
  reasons for holding 131–3
  records 140
  Rules of Procedure 137, 139
  UN and 136, 137
  UN procedure 136

Conflict resolution 111
Congo, Belgian 41ff, 303–5
  post-independence civil war in 109–10, 294
Congo, Democratic Republic of 306–8
Congolese Rally for Democracy (RCD) 307
Congress of Vienna 32–3
Congressional Act, 1906, US 253
Connection theory 55
Constitutive theory 148
Consul 11, 35, chapter 13
  and armed conflict 267
  baggage inspection 276
  circumstances of arrest 274, 279
  classification of consuls and other offices 259–60, 261
  common aspects between consuls and honorary consuls 279–20
  compared with diplomats 282
  consular baggage 276
  consular courier 269
  consular functions defined 262–3
  consular officers and gainful employment 275
  consular relations 262ff
  and courts 261
  as court witnesses 274–5
  criminal activities 261, 274
  departure 267
  and detained nationals 269–70
  diplomatic functions 265–6
  diplomatic immunity and 261, 266, 274
  distinction from diplomats 251
  exemption from taxation 275, 281
  exemptions from local permits and taxation etc 275–6, 280
  functions of 249, 252, 258, 260ff
  historical development of 249ff, 255
  honorary consul 163, 256, 257, 260, 261, 278–80, 281
  honorary consul and criminal proceedings 274–5, 281
  and immunity 258
  and imprisonment of nationals 269–70
  inviolability of 261, 268, 269, 279

judicial functions of 251
models of consular activity 257–8
official correspondence 277
as official representatives 251
operating in or for two states 264, 267
order of precedence 265
privileges and immunities 274ff
and ships and planes 270
Soviet model of consular relations 257–8
and trustees 270
and UN 256, 258
and working in non-official roles 278
see also Vienna Convention on Consular Relations, diplomat, extraterritoriality
Consular Act, 1825, UK 251n
Consular agencies 281
Consular Invoice 4
Consular List 144
Consular offices and premises 10–11, 268, 278, 280
abandonment of premises 201–2
and wireless transmitters 268
as site of inappropriate activity 278
charges imposed by 274
consular archives, and inviolability of 196, 267, 268, 269, 280
consular bag 269, 277, 278, 282
consular law codification 259
consular relations 81
correspondence, inviolability of 268
death of consular staff 276, 277
emergencies and access to consular buildings 268
exemption from taxation 275
facilities available to consular staff 268
faculties provided to posts 268
and granting asylum 231–2
privileges and immunities of staff 276–7
and Soviet model 257–8
transit and third States 277, 280,
see also Vienna Convention on Consular Relations, diplomatic missions
Consular Relations Act 1968 202, 225
Consuls Marchands 18, 250

Contadora Group 4
Continental shelf 15, 80
Convention for the Abolition of Capitulations in Morocco and Zanzibar, 1937 254
Convention for the Suppression of Unlawful Acts against the Safety of Civil Aviation 1971 13
Convention for the Suppression of Unlawful Seizure of Aircraft 1970 13
Convention of Saint-Germain-en-Laye, 10 September 1919 41, 42, 44, 45
Convention on Asylum 1928 230, 234
Convention on Psychotropic Substances 11
Convention on Special Missions 1969 207
Convention on the Law of the Sea and Freedom of Transit 25
Convention on the Prevention and Punishment of Crimes Against Internationally Protected Persons, including Diplomatic Agents, 1973 151, 199, 237, 245
Convention on the Prevention and Punishment of the Crime of Genocide 1948 11, 13, 24, 47n, 68
Convention on the Provisional Administration of European Colonies and Possessions in America 19
Convention on the Representation of States in their Relations with International Organisations 207
Convention on the Status of Refugees 1951 (Asylum Convention) 13
Conventions 115, 130
Co-operative sovereignty 47
Corfu Channel case 286–7
Cost-benefit analysis 126
Council of Europe Convention on Extradition 1957 11, 13
Councillor (embassy) 141, 142
Country assessment papers 156
Coup d'état 4
Courier, consular 277

Court of Appeal 37, 42, 59–60, 153n, 194, 195, 203, 219, 221, 240, 241
Court of First Instance 42
Court of St James's 157–9
Court 184–5, 194, 241
Crawford, J 30n
Crime 51
Crime:
  continuing 56
  political 12, 13
Crimes against humanity 55
Crimes, conduct 57
grave crimes and consular office 274
Crimes, result 57
Criminal jurisdiction and international law 208
Criminal Law Act 1977 202
Criminal law 57
Criminality, double 12, 53
Criminals, political 12, 13
Cuba 19
  US military base on 50, 51
Cutting case 54
Cyprus, Northern 282
Czarnikow Ltd v Rolimpex (1978) 219n, 221
Czechoslovakia 19

Dadra, India 25
Dallal v Bank Mellat 1986 3n
Danish West Indies 151
Daring (ship) 239
De Foro Legatorum (Cornelius Van Bynkershoek) 32
De Haber v The Queen of Portugal 241
De Jure Belli ac Pacis (Grotius, 1625) 32, 49
De Legationibus Libri Tres (Gentili, 1585) 32
Death penalty 12, 56, 74
Declaration and Programme of Action on the Establishment of a New International Economic Order (NIEO) (UN programme) 310
Declaration of the Ministers of Foreign Affairs of the American Republics, Havana, July 1940 19
Declaration on Principles of International Law Concerning Friendly Relations and Co-operation among States in accordance with the Charter of United Nations, 1970, (UN Resolution) 166
Declaration on the Granting of Independence to Colonial Counties and Peoples (UN General Assembly Resolution 1960) 78n, 103n
Declaration on the Granting of Independence to Colonial Countries and Peoples, 1960 103n
Declarations of the Principles of Solidarity of America Lima, Peru (24 December 1938) 19
Declaratory theory (Lauterpacht) 148
Decolonisation 40, 64, 78, 95, 103, 106
Defence, Ministry of, Nigeria 219
Delegates 20, 134, 135, 140
Démarche 5
Democratic Republic of Congo v Belgium, ICJ Reports 2002 55n
Denmark 150–1, 250, 256
Denning, Lord, MR 218, 220–1
and definition of sovereign immunity 219
Denunciation of a treaty 5
Denza, E 190, 198
Depositories 6–7
Détente 7–8
Deutsche Bank AG 192
Developed countries 72, 76, 95, 96, 99, 106, 115, 123, 125, 126, 127, 128
Developing countries 4, 76, 95, 106, 115, 122, 123, 125, 126, 127, 128, 133
  and acquisition of technology 97–8, 125–7
  development of infrastructure in 106
  diplomats from 86, 106, 128
  and international relations 95
  lack of bargaining power 99
Dictator 46
Dikko incident 1984 206, 207
Diplomacy xvii, 3, 33, 165–6, 314
  definition 80, chapter 5
  definition of terms used chapter 1
  aid based 65, 314
  attitudes towards diplomacy 117ff

and bargaining power 90ff, 130
bilateral 66, 71, 74, 75, 77, 78, 79, 85, 88, 106, 111, 115, 130, 148, 284
and boundary between national and international aspects 115
changing nature of 107, 111ff, 301
and communications 113
concerted 58
consensual 284–5
coercive 65
conference diplomacy 131
conflict between ethics and politics of diplomacy 73–5
and conflict resolution xvii
and court/legal solutions 80
covert 148
creative 112, 165
democratic 105, 106
and developing and developed countries 115
diplomacy between developed and developing countries 106
different bases for diplomacy 105–6
diplomacy of dependency 129
economic xvii, 82, 34, 48, 130
economic/commercial issues 66, 114, 116
effects of improved communications 106–7
and ethics chapter 4, 247
ethics and multilateral diplomacy 66, 75–7, 78, 79
ethos of 129
and foreign Missions 165
functions of 85ff
and governments in exile 15
humanitarian 315
and ideology 64
international 34, 64, 108, 113, 114, 115, 75, 131, 147, 148, chapter 8, 285–6
and international community 115
and international development 34
and international law xvii, 84–5
and international trade 117ff
inter-state 34, 237
issues 130

just diplomacy 67
and knowledge 115
law governing diplomacy 237ff
limitations on military and power diplomacy 103–4
and might xvii
and military power 114
military aspects 116, 148–9
multilateral 66, 67, 76, 78, 79, 106, 112, 115, 116, 130, 285, 301
multilateral and ethics 75ff
and mutuality 117
national diplomacy 86
and nationalism 8, 106
negative diplomacy 112
and negotiation xvii
neighbourly democracy 116
non-power based 68
and North-South dialogue 122
operating at different levels 83
participatory 65
of peace xvii
polarised 105, 107
political 49
politics of 70–2
power-based 65, 111, 129
power-orientated 68
predictable 105
preferential 105
preventative diplomacy 112, 300, 302
purposes and remit of diplomacy 106, 112ff
quality of 106
and reciprocity 88, 117–8, 127
re-appraisal of diplomacy 90
regional 9–10, 83, 117
relationship with sovereign 63–5
and socio-economic issues 130, 284
and sovereignty 46–7, 63ff, 68, 75
and State size determining scope 86
stricto sensu 129
and technology 112, 113, 114, 247
training in diplomacy 111, 114, 115, 285
transitional 33–4
and UN 9–10, 87, 116, 290, 293
and the use of force 103–4

war diplomacy xvii, 34, 80–1, 102, 106, 285, 300, 314
Western form 116
see also ethics in diplomacy, Vienna Convention on Diplomatic Relations
Diplomat xvii, xviii, 1, 8, 9, 28, 35, 43, 63–5, Chapter 5, 117, 237
  accrediting of 178, 185–6
  as amiable compositeur 113
  and asylum 237
  attributes defined 82–3, 112
  and bargaining power 86
  classification of 141
  committing offences 17
  and consular service 251, 282
  and criminal activity 190–1
  and criminal jurisdiction 189
  and dispute resolution 80–1
  diplomacy and peace making 89, 285
  distinction from consuls 251
  exemption from fiscal liability 188
  functions of 85–7
  international 290
  and international law 84
  language requirements 85, 88
  Lassez-passer 18
  and sovereigns 106, 111, 247
  and taxation 189
  and UN 295, 296, 313
  and unbecoming behaviour 197–8
  and war and peace 104
  see also consul, inviolability, United Nations, Vienna Convention on Diplomatic Relations
Diplomatic Agent 168, 178, 179, 180, 194, 201ff, 210
  and taxation 213
  as representative of sovereign 207
  baggage of 213–4
  compared with consuls 282
  criminal activities of 209
  ending of functions of 216
  family membership 213, 215
  immunity of 209, 212ff
  inviolability of 207

see also diplomatic bag, Vienna Convention on Diplomatic Relations
Diplomatic and Consular List 144
Diplomatic and Consular Premises Act 1987 201–2, 203
Diplomatic Asylum 8, 14, 229–36
renunciation of 231
Diplomatic bag 204–7, 210, 247, 282
  electronic screening and 206–7
  inviolability 205ff
  withdrawal of immunity of 247
Diplomatic Corps 142, 143, 145
  Dean of the Diplomatic Corps 174
  UK Officers of 157, 159, 160
Diplomatic courier 205–6
inviolability of 205
Diplomatic credentials 141, 159–60, 161
Diplomatic envoys injurious acts 17
Diplomatic Immunities and Privileges 1985 207n
Diplomatic Immunity Act 1964 225
Diplomatic immunity 51, 143, 178, 188–91, 191ff, 212ff
  doctrine of restrictive immunity 219–20
  duration of 215–6
  exemptions from immunity 223
  and heads of diplomatic Missions 175
  limitations on 217ff
  and property 191–6
  restrictive immunity 218–20
  states and 50
  and taxation 191
  waiver of 178
Diplomatic law 33, 209
Diplomatic List 142, 143–4, 155
Diplomatic and Consular List 144
Diplomatic Missions 35, 141ff, 157, Chapter 11, 178, 179, 180
  archives and documents of 196, 201, 210, 255n
  assignment to several states 185
  and briefing 172
  British Missions 157, 158, 162, 163
  Chancery 170–1
  Commercial Section 171

communications with receiving state
    government   144
consular functions   168, 182
Consular Section   171
duties of   183–5
and entry without consent in
    emergencies   197
full facilities accorded to   209
and extra-territoriality   239
functions   181–2
Head of Mission   141, 142, 145, 155,
    157, 161–2, 164–5, 168–70, 173,
    174–5, 178, 179, 185, 224
functions   169–70
and UN   169
Vienna Convention on Diplomatic
    Missions   169
and incompatible functions   183–4
and information   171
and international organisations
    185–6
inviolability of missions   178, 197ff,
    210, 247, 248
and local staff   171
nationality of staff   186
non-resident   163
official mourning   144–5
premises of the mission   180
Press and Information Section   171–2
principal officers   141–2, 167–8, 185,
    210, 239, 264–5
protocol   143, 145, 146
and respect for law   183
and sending and receiving
    states   181ff, 187–8
staff of   179–80
state ceremonies   142–3
use of flags   142, 143
and Vienna Convention on Diplomatic
    Relations   167–8, 169, 173–5
see also attaché, consular offices, Vienna
    Convention on Diplomatic
    Missions
Diplomatic Notes   144, 156
Diplomatic premises   197ff
  abandonment of premises   201–2
  and emergencies   197
  inviolability of   14, 197f

Diplomatic Privileges Act 1964   195,
    196, 202, 227–8
Diplomatic privileges   178, 188–91,
    245–6
  duration of   215–6
Diplomatic protection   2
Diplomatic protocol and
    procedures   Chapter 9
Diplomatic rank   168
Diplomatic relations   8–10, Chapter 2,
    Chapter 12, 258
  breaking of   211
  means of establishing diplomatic
    relations   181
  see also Vienna Convention on
    Diplomatic Relations
Diplomatic Studies   10, 83–5
Diplomatic wireless transmissions,
    inviolability of   205
Disarmament   294
Discrimination   119
Dispute settlement   260
District Court (Amstgericht),
    Bonn   192
Diversion of the Waters of the River Meuse
    (1937)   17n
Documentary credits mechanism   95
Doha Declaration   124ff
Domestic legislation   96
Domino theory   9
Double criminality   12
Doyen   142, 174
DPP v Doot (1973)   51n, 57n
DPP v Stonehouse (1978)   51n, 57n
Draft Articles on the Diplomatic Courier
    and the Diplomatic Bag
    (1989)   207
Draft Declaration of Human Rights (UN
    document)   229
Droit De Gens, Le (Vattel)   32
Droit International Codifié, Le
    (Bluntschli)   255
Drug manufacture   75
Drug trafficking   113
Drugs-related problems   64, 286
*Duff Development Co v Government of
    Kelantan*   153n, 223n

395

Duke of Brunswick v The King of Hanover 240
Dyestuffs Cartel (1969) 58n, 62

Eastern Europe 19
Eastern Greenland 150
Economic and Social Council, The (UN) 123
Economic relations between states 112, 166
Economic self sufficiency 96
ECOSOC
   see United Nations Economic and Social Council
Ecuador 124n
EEC Commission Decisions 57n
Effects doctrine 55
Egypt 3, 48, 253
   mixed courts in 253–4
Eichmann trial 55
Eichmann, Adolf 55
El Salvador xvii, 78, 128
Elizabeth II, Queen
   constitutional role 244
   and diplomatic immunity 228
   and diplomatic representatives 155, 156, 157–9, 160, 161, 162, 163
Embassy 182
Enforcement jurisdiction 58
English:
   and Chinese mission London 197
   contracts in foreign courts 60
   courts 57, 151–3, 203, 219, 221, 229, 238
   law 12–13, 219, 221
Entity doctrine 57
Environmental issues 64, 80, 88, 106, 114, 286
Envoy extraordinary 141
Envoys 10, 180
Equality in law and equality in fact 119, 120
Equality, commercial 120
Eritrea 303
Eritrean People's Liberation Front 303
Espionage 184
Estrada Doctrine 10

Ethics:
   in diplomacy xviii, Chapter 4, 247
   just ethics 67
   and morality 70
   societal 66
   and war 77
Ethiopia 303
Ethnic cleansing 113
Euro 71
European Convention for the Suppression of Terrorism 1977 13
European Convention on Extradition 1947 12
European Convention on State Immunity 220, 221
   Article 24 226
   Article 27 227
European Court of Justice 62
European Union (and European Community) 4, 9–10, 62, 71–2, 74, 83, 124, 133, 213, 283
   agreement with Caribbean countries 72
   bloc voting in UN 138n
   Commission of the European Union on the Competition Policy 63, 133
   Competition Law 62ff
   economic integration 72
   Member States of 71, 133
   and regional diplomacy 64
   and US 117
   see also Common Agricultural Policy
Evidence (Proceedings in Other Jurisdictions) Act 1975 60n
Ex parte Mwenya (1959) 153n
Exclusive economic zone (maritime) 15, 16
Exclusive economic zone 16
Exequatur 10–11, 264, 265, 266, 267
Expatriation, right of 24
Export credits 123
External Relations and Trade, Ministry of, Australia 150
Extradition Act 1870 (UK) 12
Extradition Act 1989 (UK) 12, 13
Extradition treaties, bilateral 12
Extradition Treaty, US-Italy, 1983 56
Extradition 11–13, 56, 235

Extra-territorial Asylum
  (Morgenstein) 234
Extra-territoriality 50–2, 58ff, 239, 252,
  253, 254, 258
  ambassadors and 239
  and asylum 229f
  and China 252–3
  Christian states exercising in non-
    Christian states 252
  and EC/EU Competition Law 62ff
  fictitious 240
  League of Nations and 230
  mutual extraterritoriality 252
  and US Sherman Act 62
Eysinga, van, Judge, Permanent Court of
  International Justice 44, 45–6

Fagernes case, 1927 152n, 153n
Fang Lizhi, Professor 233
Fatemi v the US 198n
Fauchille 229, 232
Federal Constitutional Court, Federal
  Republic of Germany 192–3
Federal Court of First Instance 270–1
Federal District Court, US 253
Federal Sovereign Immunities Act 1976
  (US) 37–8, 217
Feltham, R G 169
Fetials, College of (Ancient Rome) 31
Field, D D 255
Fiji 75
Fiore, P 255
Flags, national, use of 142, 143, 145,
  268, 280
  salute to 13
Fletcher, Yvonne 198
Food and Agricultural Organisation
  (FAO) 310
Force majeure 214, 278
Force, use of 2
Foreign Affairs Committee, UK 206
First Report 207n
Foreign Affairs, Ministry of 141, 142,
  144, 145, 146, 149, Chapter 10, 171,
  174, 183, 187, 208, 215, 266–7
  and chargé d'affaires 173
  composition of 153ff
  and consuls 11, 264, 265, 266–7, 281

  and creative diplomacy 165–6
  and diplomats 88–9
  and envoys 180
  and foreign Missions 163–4, 183–4,
    187
  and International Law
    Commission 154
  legal department 154
  Minister of 143, 208
  and Missions abroad 164–5
  Political Affairs Section 154
  Protocol Department 155, 173
  and training of diplomats 166
  and treaties and legal matters 154
  and UN 154
Foreign and Commonwealth Office
  (FCO), UK xviii, 143, 150, 151–2,
  155, 156, 157–9, 161–2, 202–3, 251
  and Cambodian Embassy, London
    incident, 1975 202–3
  and chargés d'affaires 156–7
  Defence Advisers 155
  and diplomatic premises 201–3
  Geographical Department 157,
    158–9, 160, 161, 162, 163
  and International Law 154
  and Letters of Commission and
    Recall 156
  and treaties 154
  legal section 154
  News Department 158
  political relations 154
  Protocol Department 153, 155ff,
    160, 161, 162, 163
  Secretary of State of 151–2, 157, 160,
    161–2, 201–2, 203
Foreign Jurisdiction Act, 1843, UK 253
Foreign policy 8, 121, 149, 166
Foreign Sovereign Immunities Act, 1976,
  US 220
Formal Apology 13–14
Foster v Globe Venture Syndicate
  (1900) 153n
Fourteen Points (Woodrow
  Wilson) 103
Fourth Geneva Convention on the
  Protection of Civilian Persons in
  Time of War 305

France 18, 24, 31, 32, 51, 194–5, 253, 254, 296
  and the Congo 110, 294, 304
  diplomatic and consular services 250, 251
  embassy in Phnom Penh 233
  French Embassy, London 194–5
  and Lebanon 305
  and the Middle East 110
  and nuclear testing in Pacific 75
  and *Nuclear Tests* case 287
  and Rhodesia 138, 296
  treaty with Japan 252
  and UN 110, 294, 296
Franchise du quartier 14
Francisco de Vitoria 48
Franco, General Francisco 10
Franco-British Treaty of Commerce (Cobden Treaty) 252
Franco-Italian Consular Convention 1955 11n
Franco-United States Consular Convention, 1788 252
Free movement of goods 116
  freedom of commerce 43, 44, 45, 46
  freedom of navigation 43, 44, 45, 46
Friedmann 73
Frontier between Turkey and Iraq (1925) 17
Fugitive Offenders Act 1967 13
Fugitives 11
Full Powers (treaty making) 14
Functional Necessity Concept 238–9, 243

Gagara, The (1919) 152n
Galbraith, Prof J K 169
Garnishee order 194
GATT (General Agreement on Tariffs and Trade) 66, 98, 117–8, 122, 127
  see also WTO
Geigy v Commission 63
Geigy 62
Gemayel, Bashir, President elect of Lebanon 305
General Act of Berlin, 26 February 1885 41, 43

Generalised System of Preferences (GSP) 98, 121
Geneva Agreement 1971 128n
Geneva Convention on the Protection of Civilian Persons in Time of War, Fourth 305
Geneva Conventions 109
Geneva 186
Genocide case 29n
Genocide Convention 1948 11, 13, 24, 47n, 68
Genocide 70
Gentili (author) 32, 48
German Democratic Republic 233
German Settlers in Poland (Permanent Court of International Justice Opinion) 119
Germany v United States, Case Concerning the Vienna Convention on Consular Relations 270ff
Germany 31, 40n, 55, 57, 192–3, 219, 253, 270ff
Germany, Federal Republic of 192, 220, 233, 243, 260n, 270
Good faith 33, 166
Goodrich 40, 73
Government:
  and asylum 25–6
  de facto 4, 37, 151n, 152
  de jure 4, 11, 152
  dictatorial 128
  quality of 106
  receiving, and diplomatic missions 144, 147
  recognition of 147, 148
  undemocratic 148
  unrecognised 147
Governments in exile 15
Government departments, agreements between 14
Governmental ships and warships, distinction between 29
  status and immunity 219
Great Britain
  see United Kingdom
Greece 2–3, 118
Greece-Serbian Treaty 1913 3
Greek City States 30, 249–50

Index

Greenland 150–1
Grenada xvii, 78
Grotius, Hugo 2, 32, 33, 49, 238
Group of 77 105, 138n
GUR Corporation v Trust Bank of Africa Ltd 152

Habeas corpus, writ of 197, 271
Hambro 40, 73
Hammarskjöld, Dag 110
Hanover, King of 240
Hardy, M 189, 190
Harvard Research Draft Convention on Diplomatic Privileges and Immunities 1932 239, 255, 259
Havana Convention on Asylum 1928 235–6
Haya de la Torre case
  see The Asylum case
Haya de la Torre 234
Head of State 11, 22, 141, 150, 159, 173, 208, 223, 243ff
  capacities of 244
  and court jurisdiction 227
  deposed 8
  and envoys 10, 180
  and Full Powers 14–5
  immunity of 244
  and inviolability 245
  as an internationally protected person 245
  and international law 243
  retinue and family of Head of State 245–6
  travelling incognito or in private capacity 16–17, 246–7
  and treaty making 14
  and Vienna Convention on Diplomatic Relations 243
Heavily Indebted Poor Countries' Trust Fund (World Bank, 1992) 78
Hellenic Lines Ltd v Moore (1965) 204n
Hertford Fire Insurance Co v California 62
Hierarchy of institutions 298
Higgins, R 108–9, 299
High Commission 183
High Commissioner for Human Rights, Office of 308

High Commissioner 141, 142, 156, 158–9, 161
  Acting High Commissioner 156, 161, 162
  Deputy High Commissioner 156–7
  Interim High Commissioner 161
High Court, UK 193, 194, 195, 203
High Seas 15–16, 22, 51
Hijacking 55
Hill, D J 32
Hitler, Adolf 102–3
Hobbes, Thomas 48, 69
Holy See 3, 18, 27, 36, 141, 233
  Nunciate, Panama 233
  see also Vatican City
Honduras 231
Hot Pursuit 15–16, 29n
Hotman (author) 32
House of Lords, UK 60, 194, 196, 217n, 221
Hrawi, Elias, Resident of Lebanon 306
Huber, Max, Arbitrator 46
Human rights 49, 88, 106, 115, 133, 148
Humanitarian intervention 46, 68, 72, 74, 229, 234, 273, 306
Hungary 233, 253
Hurst, Sir Cecil, Judge, Permanent Court of International Justice 44, 45, 120
Hussain, Saddam 103–4

ICC v Commission (1972) 62n
ICI 59, 62
Idealism 66–7
Ideology 80–1
Ihlen, Mr, Norwegian Minister for Foreign Affairs 150
Immigration 40, 68, 286
Immunity: of warships 28
  jurisdictional 29n
Imperial Chemicals Industries Ltd
  see ICI, *British Nylon Spinners Ltd*
Import restrictions 123
In Dubio Mitius 17
Incognito travelling (by a Head of State) 16–17
Independence days, celebration of 142–3

India   25, 31, 33, 48
  and *Union Carbide* case   50
Indication of Provisional Measures   270
Indonesia   96, 124n
Industrial Policy, EU   124
Industrial Revolution   255
Innocent passage, right of   29n
Institute of International Law   33, 239
  and asylum   233–4
Insurgents   151n
Inter-American Conference on War and Peace   19
Inter-American Convention on Extradition   11
Inter-dependence   8, 106
Interest, international and domestic, areas of   75
Inter-governmental organisations   111, 131, 135, 208
Interim Emergency Multinational Force (IEMF) DR Congo, (UN)   307
International affairs   69
International Antitrust Enforcement Assistance Act 1994   62
International Atomic Energy Agency (IAEA)   311
International Bank for Reconstruction and Development (IBRD) (World Bank)   20, 78, 99, 100, 310, 311
International Civil Aviation Organization (ICAO)   311
International Commission of Jurists   24
International community   11, 56, 74
  and bargaining power   90
  and conferences   135ff
  consensus of   74
  diplomacy and   115
  and UN   298
International concern, areas of   75
International Convention Against the Taking of Hostages, 1979   55–6
International co-operation   75, 129, 285, 288
International cooperation, need for   64
International Court of Justice (ICJ)   23, 24, 76, 84, 200–1, 243, 292, 295, 312–3
  Aerial Incident case   26

Asylum Case   234ff
Barcelona Traction case   54
and *Burkina Faso v Mali* case   27
and *Corfu Channel* case   51–3, 286–7
and diplomatic asylum   232
and extraterritoriality   254
and *Germany v United States, Case Concerning the Vienna Convention on Consular Relations*   270ff
and *Iran Hostage* case   184
and LaGrand brothers case   271ff
Nicaragua v the United States   287
and 1960 war in the Congo   110
North Sea Continental Shelf case   26n
Nottebohm   54
and *Nuclear Tests* case   287
Optional Protocol concerning the Compulsory Settlement of Disputes   271, 272
and *Reservations to the Convention on the Prevention and Punishment of the Crime of Genocide*   23
Rights of Passage over Indian Territory case   25
Case concerning Rights of Nationals of the United States of America in Morocco (France v United States) 1952   254
South West Africa case   26n
and travaux preparatoires   26
United States v Iran   190
and US Embassy Iran   199–200
  Asylum Case   234ff
  Western Sahara case   27n
see *also* United Nations, Permanent Court of Justice
International Covenant on Civil and Political Rights   271
International crime   286
International dependency   106
International Development Association   310
International Development Strategies (UN programme)   310
International diplomacy   Chapter 7, Chapter 14
  see *also* diplomacy
International disputes   166

International Economic and Social Co-operation (UN)   123
International economics   8, 256
International ethics   77
   standards of   75
International Finance Corporation   310
International Fund for Agricultural Development (IFAD)   311
International history   8
International issues   8ff
   see also Conferences
International justice, concept of   69
International Labour Office   74n, 290
International Labour Organization (ILO)   310
International Law (Oppenheim)   152, 153
International Law Codified (Fiore)   255
International Law Commission   26, 132, 154, 138, 190, 242, 243, 247, 259
International law   70, 76, 99, 203, 208, 219, 252
   and bargaining power   86
   and belligerency   1
   and consuls   255
   and cooperation of governments   286
   and customary procedures   47, 54, 76
   and diplomacy   xvii, 182, 184
   and diplomatic asylum   229, 230
   and diplomatic activity   266
   and diplomatic bags   206, 207
   and diplomatic immunity   192–3, 219, 220
   diplomatic mission   183–4, 192
   and diplomatic premises   202–3
   and diplomats   256
   and extradition   11–13
   and extraterritorial principle   59
   general   18
   and Heads of State   243, 246
   and jurisdiction over crime   56
   and Jus Cogens   18
   Ministry of Foreign Affairs and   154
   and monarchs   244–5
   and power   90
   public international law   116, 220
   and refugees   232
   regional international law   230
   and Reservations to treaties   23
   and revolutionary government in exile   15
   and sovereign immunity   217
   and UN   299
   and universality principle   56
   and the Vatican   27
   and Vienna Convention on Diplomatic Relations   177
   and warships   28–9
   see also International Court of Justice
International Maritime Organization (IMO)   311
International Monetary Fund (IMF)   78, 99, 100, 137, 311
   see also Asylum Case, diplomatic asylum
International morality   68–70
International norms   92
International organisations and fora   7, 47, 78, 104, 114, 121, 135, 143, 185, 286
   and holding conferences   130–1
   and rapporteurs   140
   see also EU, League of Nations, United Nations
International peace and security   92, 286, 297
International responsibilities   2
International standards   2
International relations   3, 70, 80, 82, 111
   and bargaining power   80, 92, 100–1
   pre-1945 system   92–5
   post-1945 period   92, 93
   and religion   105
International responsibility   286
International Telecommunication Union (ITU)   311
International Tin Council (Immunities and Privileges) Order 1972   196
International Tin Council   196
International trading system   95, 120–1, 123–4, 126–7, 252, 255, 256
   international trade and diplomacy   117–8, 153, 251, 258
Internationally Injurious Acts of Diplomatic Envoys   17

401

INTERNATIONAL LAW AND DIPLOMACY

Internationally protected persons 151, 208
Inter-state relations
    see diplomatic relations
Inter-temporal Law 17–18
Interventionism 72, 166
Intpro Properties (UK) Ltd v Samuel 194
Investment relations between states 147
Investment, foreign 96ff
Inviolability
    consular 261, 268, 269
    diplomatic 178, 190–1, 196, 197ff
    of Head of State 245, 246
Iran Hostage case (Diplomatic and Consular Staff) 184
    Libyan People's Bureau Incident and inviolability 247
Iran 35, 199–201, 253
Iranian Embassy, London, 1980 incident 199, 204
Iraq xvii, 46, 65, 67, 111, 128, 244
    1990 intervention 78, 107–8, 111
    2003 intervention in 103–4
Iraqi Embassy, Pakistan, 1973 incident 198
Iraq-Kuwait War 149
Ireland 11, 244
Islamic Republic of Iran v Pahlavi 246n
Island of Dalwas Arbitration (1928) 30n
Island of Palmas Arbitration 46
Isle of Man 56
Israel Defence Forces (IDF) 305
Israel 55
    and Lebanon 304–6
Italy 18, 30–1, 32, 219, 250
    and Lebanon 305
Ituri, DR Congo 307

Japan 253
    Treaties with various states 252
Japanese-American Treaty, 1858 252
Jennings, R Y 58
Jessup 73
Jimenez v Aristeguieta 245
Joyce v DPP 54
Juges Consuls 18
Jupiter, The 217n
Jure gestionis 219

Jure imperii 219
Jurisdiction 49ff, 64
    types of 49ff
    absolute aspect of jurisdiction 49–50
    extension of 55–8
    enforcement jurisdiction 58
    local 2
    and sovereignty 49, 57
    territoriality of 50
    and treaties 54
Jus cogens 18
Jus fetiale 31
Jus gentium (Roman Empire) 250
Jus quarteriorum 14
Jus Sanguinis 53
Jus soli principle 53n
Justice, US Department of 60

Kabila, Joseph, President of the Democratic Republic of the Congo 307, 308
Kabila, Laurent D, President of the Democratic Republic of the Congo 307
Kant, Immanuel 66
Kasavubu, Joseph 109
Katanga (Congo) 304
Khmer Rouge 308
Khomeini, Ayatollah 200
Kinshasa 307
Kosovo xvii, 46, 111, 113
Koul, Dr A K 98
Krajina v Tass Agency (1959) 220n
Kuwait Airways Corporation v Iraqi Airways Co (1995) 219n
Kuwait 4, 46, 102, 204n, 254,
    and oil politics 149
    and 1990 war 107, 108
Kuwait-Saudi Arabia neutral zone 4
Kyoto Protocol (11 December 1997) 122

LaGrand, Karl and Walter 270ff
Laissez-passer 18
Languages:
    languages used in diplomacy 32, 88
    and treaties 20

Index

working 140
Laos 124n
Lateran Treaty 1929 18–19, 27
Latin American states 2, 8, 14, 230, 231
Lauterpacht, Sir Hirsch 40, 148
Law of nature (Grotius) 49
Law of the Sea 15, 79, 88
  1982 convention 131
Law Officers of the Crown 230, 231–2
Law, domestic 17, 286
Law, governing diplomacy 237ff
  of nations 217
Law, inter-temporal 17–8
Law, private international 50, 286
Laydele 240
League of Nations xvii, 33–4, 85, 109
  Aaland Islands case 24
  and commercial equality 120–1
  Council of the League 13, 93–4
  Diplomatic Privileges and Immunities Codification Sub-Committee 229–30
  dispute resolution process 93–4
  League of Nations Covenant 1, 77, 92n, 93–4
    Article 12 94
    Article 13 93
    Article 15 93–4
    Article 23(e) 34, 92n, 120
    Article 125(1) 77
  and Saar 40n
  and warfare 77, 93–4
  and WWII 295
Least developed countries 125, 128
Lebanese National Movement 305
Lebanon 253, 304–6
Lee, Luke T 250
Legal Status of Eastern Greenland 150–1
Legal title 27
Legations, permanent 8n, 30–1
Leopoldville, Congo (now Kinshasa) 41
Letters of Commission 156, 159, 160
Letters of Credence 159, 160, 173
Letters of Recall 156, 159–60, 173, 174
Letters Rogatory 263
Liangsiriprasert v Government of the United States of America (1991) 57
Libya 102, 184, 204n 282

Libyan People's Bureau incident, London 35, 198–9, 247
Lillich, R B and F C Newman 72
Lima, Peru 234
List of the Representatives in London of Foreign States and Commonwealth Countries in Order of Precedence (Precedence List) 161
Location and jurisdiction 56
Locke, John 69
Lockerbie, Scotland 50, 51
London Diplomatic Corps 157ff, 174
  Officers of the London Diplomatic Corps 157
London 157, 161, 162, 174
Lord Chamberlain's Office, UK 163
Lotus, The, case 51–3
Louis XIV of France 32
Luigi Monza of Genoa v Cechofracht Co Ltd (1956) 152n
Lumumba, Patrice 109
Lusaka Ceasefire Agreement 307
Luther v Sagor 1919 36, 152n
Luxembourg 220, 256
Lyons, AB 189

Machiavelli, Niccolò 48, 67, 68
Malaysia 124n
Malta 51
Managua, Nicaragua 233
Mann, F A 58
Mare Liberum (Grotius) 1, 49
Maritime Drug Law Enforcement Act (US, 1986) 54
Maritime lien 38
Market, world 130
Markets, bilateral 123
Marseilles 250
Marshal of the Diplomatic Corps, UK 157, 159, 160, 161, 162, 163
Massachusetts Statute 241
Matveyev, Andrei Artamonovich, Russian Ambassador to England 238
Mellenger v New Brunswick Development Corporation 220
Mengistu Haile Mariam, President, Ethiopia 303
Mexico 4, 10, 54, 190, 243

MFN Standard   123
Middle Ages   250
Middle East   91, 109–10, 250, 294
Mighell v Sultan of Jahore (1894)   153n
Might/power as a concept   100–1
Military alliance   2
Military policy   122
Military regime   4
Milosevic, Slobodan   46
Mindszenty, Cardinal Joseph, of Hungary   233
Minister Counsellor (embassy)   33, 141, 142, 180
Minister plenipotentiary   141
Minorities, rights of   118ff
Minority Schools in Albania (Permanent Court of International Justice, 1935)   118ff
Minutes of Evidence Taken Before the Foreign Affairs Committee Report 1979   184
Moawad, René, President of Lebanon   306
Mobuto Sese Seko, President, Zaire   307
Monarch, as an office   244–5, 246–7
Money laundering   64, 75
Monroe Doctrine   19, 37n
Monroe, James, US President   19
Montevideo Convention:
   of 1933   30n, 230, 236
   of 1939   230, 236
Montevideo on International Penal Law, Treaty of 1889   230
Moralism as a concept   69
Morality, standards of   68, 70, 74
Morgenstern, Felice   230, 234
Moroccan Embassy, London incident   206
Morocco   253, 254
Morocco-US treaty 1836   254
Most favoured nation (MFN) status   21, 39, 123, 252, 254
Mourning, official   144–6
Movement for the Liberation of Congo (MLC)   307
Multinational Investment Guarantee Agency   310

Murray v Parkes (1942)   152n
Muscat (now Oman)   254
Mutual co-operation   8
Mutuality   117
Mwenya (inhabitant of Northern Rhodesia)   153n
Myanmar   124n

Nagar Avali, India   25
Namibia   307
National anthems   143
National interests   9, 28, 40, 67, 79, 115, 286
National issues and international aspects   88
National self-sufficiency   97
National sovereignty, limits to   287
Nationalisation   133
Nationalistic attitudes and nationalism   8, 92
Nationality principle   53–4, 56, 63, 260
   nationality, dual   53
   of companies   53
Nationals, foreign   40
NATO   113
Natural resources   130
Nature, law of   49
Navigation, freedom of   42, 43, 45–6
Ne impediator legatio   193
Negligence   50
Negulesco, M, PCJ   120
Nemo Plus Juris Transferre Potest Quam Ipse Habet   19–20
Nerchinsk, Treaty of (Russia-China), 1689   252
Netherlands, The   219, 220, 250, 256
   Treaty with Japan   252
Neutrality, military   116
New Deal, US   103
New Delhi, India   174
New Zealand   75
Nicaragua v the United States   287
Nicaragua   xvii, 78, 128
Nicaraguan ambassador, Panama, US search 1989   198, 233
Niger River   41
Nigeria   219

Non-governmental organisations (NGOs) and institutions 111, 309–10
Non-paper (diplomatic) 144
Noriega, President Manuel, of Panama 26, 233
North American Free Trade Area (NAFTA) 122
North Atlantic Fisheries Arbitration 1910 24
North Charterland Exploration Co (1910) Ltd v The King (1931) 153n
North Sea Continental Shelf case 26n
North-North relations 149
North-South divide, dialogue 64, 104, 123, 124, 127, 149
Norway 96, 150–1, 256
Notarial Act 20
Note verbale (diplomatic) 144
Nottebohn case 54
Nuclear Installations Act 1965 225–6
Nuclear proliferation 133
Nuclear Test Ban Treaty 1963 7, 76, 287
Nuclear testing 75–6, 225–6
Nuclear Tests (Australia v France) Interim Protection ICJ Report (1973) 272n
Nuclear Tests case 287
Nuclear warfare and weapons 75
Nuncios and internuncios, Papal 141, 180

Objective territoriality principle 57
Oda, Judge, ICJ 273
Official mourning 144–6
Oil crisis of 1973 91, 128
Oil, politics of 102, 104, 149
Olney, US Secretary of State 231
Oman 254
OPEC (Organisation for Petroleum Exporting Countries) 91, 99, 128
Open door policy 252
Oppenheim 49, 152
Oppenheim's International Law 30, 49, 152, 153, 233
Optional Protocol concerning the Compulsory Settlement of Disputes 271, 272

Order in Council, UK 56, 228, 253
Organisation of African States 27
Organisation of American States and exclusion of Cuba 19
Oscar Chinn case 1934 41ff
Ottoman Empire 31
Outlines of an International Code (Field) 255

Pacific 75
Pacta sunt servanda 9
Palau 292n
Palestinian forces in Lebanon 305
Palestinian refugee camps 305
Palmerstone 231
Pan American Conferences 230
Panama River, 1973 Treaty between Brazil and Paraguay 3
Panama 4, 26, 128, 233, 243
Papal States 105
Paraguay v United States of America Provisional Measures ICJ Reports (1998) 472n
Paraguay 3, 4, 230, 231
Paraguay, ICJ case against USA 274
Paris Peace Agreement 1991 (Cambodia) 308
Paris 174
Parlement Belge, The 1860 217, 239–40, 241, 242n
Parliament, Act of 219
Partial Test Ban Treaty 1963 76
Passive Personality Principle 54
Passports 262
Peace-making and keeping 34, 314
Peremptory norm 76
Permanent Court of International Justice 42–3, 51–2, 287
  concept of equality in law and equality in fact 119, 120
  and extraterritoriality 52
  and *Frontier between Turkey and Iraq* case 17
  German Settlers in Poland case 119
  Legal Status of Eastern Greenland case 150–1
  Minority Schools in Albania case 118ff
  Oscar Chinn case 41ff

and *Territorial Jurisdiction of the International Commission of the River Oder* 26
and travaux preparatoires 26
and *Treatment of Polish Nationals in Danzig* case 26n
see also International Court of Justice
Permanent Sovereignty over Natural Resources (UN General Assembly Resolution, 1962) 40n, 133, 117, 297
Persecution 25
Persona non grata declaration of 17, 175, 158, 186, 187, 189, 198, 209, 216, 266
and granting diplomatic asylum 230
Peru 4, 8, 124n, 230, 231, 234ff
Philippine Admiral (Owners) v Wallem Shipping (Hong Kong) Ltd 218
Philippine Embassy Bank Account case 192–3
Philippines, the Republic of the 124n, 192–3
Piracy 29n, 55
Plenipotentiary 20
Plenipotentiary Conference 20
PLO 305
Pol Pot (Cambodian dictator) 202–3
Poland 4, 55
Political criminals 12, 13
Political independence 288
Pollution 70, 286
Port regulation 29
Portugal, and India enclaves 25
Possession of territory, effective 27
Post Office v Estuary Radio Ltd (1968) 153n
Poverty 64
Power politics 82, 112, 114, 117
Praetor peregrinus (office, Roman Empire) 250
Precedence List 161
order of precedence 265
President, as an office 156, 243, 244, 245, 246
Price fixing 123
Prime Minister: office 161, 244
UK 156, 159, 160, 161

Prince, The (Machiavelli) 68
Principle of aut dedere aut judicare 11
Privileges, attached to office 251
see also diplomatic privilege
Privy Council, UK 218
Procedure default, German municipal doctrine 270–1
Procès-verbal 20, 134
Proprio motu 271
Prostates (ancient Greece) 249
Protection of Trading Interests Act 1980, UK 60–1
Protective principle 54
Protocol 21, 33, 146, 155ff
Protocol Department and Division 143, 145, 155, 159, 160, 162, 163, 173, 175
Provisional Court (Landsgericht), Bonn 192
Proxenos/proxenoi (ancient Greece) 249–50
Public international law xvii, 84–5, 115, 116, 118
Pufendorf, Samuel von 48
Punctationes 21

Qatar 254

R Governor of Pentonville Prison ex parte Teya [1971] 153n
R v Bottrill [1947] 153n
Rahimtoola v Nizam of Hyderabad 218
Rani Kunwar v Commission of Income Tax 246
Rapporteur 21, 134, 136, 139–40
Rapproachment 21
Ratification of treaty process 15
Re (P (GE) (an Infant) 53n
Re Grand Jury Proceedings 246n
Realism as a concept 69
Reciprocity 10, 47, 88, 117, 282
Reel v Holder (1981) 152n
Recognition, act of 10
denial of 148
Recognition:
de facto 22, 105, 148
de jure 22, 148
implied 147–8

Referendum Commission of Eritrea   303
Refugees   232, 237
Regents   22, 247
Regime change   65, 72, 104–5
Regime, authoritarian   104
  regime, unacceptable   104–5
Regional economic integration and trading blocs   124, 128
Regionalism   104
Regulation of Cambridge   33
Religion   73
  and international relations   105
Religious establishments   25, 26
Report of the Foreign Affairs Committee of the Government of the United Kingdom   204–5
Report of the Law Officers of the Crown (1896)   230, 231–2
Reports of International Arbitral Awards   30n
Representative character concept   238, 239
Representatives, state   14–15
  powers of   14–15
Requisition   276n
Res Extra Commercium   22
Res inter alios acta doctrine   76, 109, 287
Reservations to the Convention on the Prevention and Punishment of the Crime of Genocide (ICJ)   23, 26n
Reservations to treaties   22–4
Restrictions to the Death Penalty (ICJ)   23n
Revolutionary government   15
Rhodesia, Northern (now Zambia)   153n
Rhodesia, UN vote on   138, 296
Richelieu, Armand, Cardinal and Duc de   32
Right erga omnes   24
Right of innocent passage   79
Rights of Passage over Indian Territory 1963   24, 25
Rights of United States Nationals in Morocco (1952)   17n
Rio Declaration on Environment and Development 1992   78n

Rio Tinto Zinc Corporation and Others v. Westinghouse Electric Corporation   59, 60
River Oder Commission case   47
Rogers Act, 1924, US   251
Roman Law   22
Romania   243, 253
Rome, classic period, diplomatic relations of   30, 31, 250
Rostworowski, Count, PCJ   120
Rousseau, Jean-Jacques   66
Russia   252, 253
  Russian Empire   24
  Russian Soviet Federative Socialist Republic   36–7
  Russian Federation   296
  Treaty with Japan   252
  see also Soviet Union
Rwanda   306, 307

Saar   40n
San Francisco   291, 292
Sandoz   62
Satow's Guide to Diplomatic Practice   188
Saudi Arabia   4, 102, 198, 204n, 254
  and Taif Accord   306
Schooner Exchange v McFadden (1812) (US)   240, 241
Schwarzenberger   73
Schwebel, President, ICJ   273
Sea, resources of the   133
Secretaries, First, Second and Third (embassy)   141, 142
Secretary of State for Foreign and Commonwealth Affairs, ex parte Samuel   203
Sectorisation of an economy   95–6
Self-defence   2, 289
  collective   107–9, 111
Self-determination, right of   27, 166, 288
Self-incrimination and privilege   60
Self-incrimination   60
Self-interest   70
Serbia   3, 113, 253
Servitudes   24–5
  tacit renunciation of servitude   25

407

Shanghai, China 253
Shearson Lehman v MacLaine Watson Co Ltd and International Tin Council (Intervener) 196
Sherman Act 62
Shoshone Indians v United States 17
Siam (Thailand) 252
Simonds, Viscount 218
Singapore 124n
Sino-American Treaty of Wanghia, 1844 252–3
Sino-Austrian Treaty 1925 253n
Sino-British Treaty 1943 253n
Sino-German Treaty 1921 253n
Sino-Russian Treaty of Nerchinsk, 1689 252
Sino-Soviet Agreement 1924 253n
Skills, transfer of 76
Sloan, F B 298–9
South Africa 58, 130, 152, 308
South African Development Community 307
South America 27
South Kivu region, DR Congo 307
South West Africa cases (1961 and 1966) 17n
South-South relations 149
Sovereign 36, 39, 49, 51, 58, 59, 85, 213, 240, 244, 245
  and consuls 249
  despotic 58
  and diplomats 63–5, 86, 106, 190
  and envoys 10, 238–9
  equality of sovereigns 86, 182, 184, 189, 238, 207, 239, 244, 253, 288
  and extra-territoriality 50, 58
  impairment of dignity of a sovereign 197, 218
  jurisdiction 57
  popularity of 74
  sovereign acts 245
  sovereign and courts 217
  sovereign authority 224
  sovereign immunity 217ff
  sovereign right and sovereignty 65
  and trade 218

Sovereignty 3–4, Chapter 3, 74–5, 84, 94, 117, 123–4, 130, 232, 237, 240, 313
  abuse of 58ff, 63, 64, 120, 166, 314
  attitudes towards 117ff
  co-operative 47
  definition and extent of 36ff
  indivisibility of 40
  over-use of 68
  relationship with diplomacy 63–5, 75
  and sovereign right 65
  and UN 131
Soviet Union (USSR) 3, 103, 243, 294
  and the Congo 110
  and Brezhnev Doctrine 19
  dismantling 128
  and Rhodesia 138
  Soviet model of consular relations 257–8
  and UN 111
  see also Russia
Spain 10, 18, 31, 243, 250, 254
  King of 244
Spanish-American states, independence of 27
State 1, 146, 179
  and areas of jurisdiction 56, 57, 58
  and bargaining power chapter 6
  buffer states 1
  categories of and diplomacy 131–2
  and casus belli 2
  causes of differences between 80
  change of political regime in 182
  changing functions of 230
  coastal 28, 29
  commercial transactions of 224
  conflicts between 111
  and consular arrangements 249ff, 263
  and consuls 249, 256, 258–9, 274
  and co-operation 47
  and defence treaties 108
  and diplomatic asylum 229
  and diplomatic immunity 50, 221ff
  and diplomatic missions 179, 210ff
  diplomatic relations between 102
  and diplomats involved in injurious acts 17

economic relations between 82, 121–2
equality of States 59
and ethics and morality 73
flag 28, 142, 232
and foreign Missions 165
foreign policy 121
foreign relations between 148–9
Greek City States 30, 249–50
history 77
immunity 37–39
interdependence between 8
land-locked 25, 76, 131, 280
limits of jurisdiction 49, 50, 57, 61
military interests of 122, 148–9
and morality 69–70
need to treat other states without preference 115
new States 105
polarisation of States 106
and propagation of ethics 73
recognition of 148
and relative strength 90
and sale of weapons 74
and separate entities 227–7
small and large 130
small states and diplomacy 130
sovereign 46, 47–8, 148
sovereign equality of 166
state ceremonies 142–3
state practice 84
state responsibility 76, 84, 198–200
state sovereignty 285
state trading 218ff
statehood 148
transit State 214, 277–8, 280
and trade 148–9
and territoriality 50ff
types of state 131
and UK Courts *see* State Immunity Act
and UN Chapter 14
see also diplomatic asylum, Vienna Convention on Diplomatic Relations, Vienna Convention on Consular Relations
State Department, US 147, 150
State Immunity Act, 1978 (UK) 38–9, 193–4, 195, 217, 221ff
analysis 223–9
objectives 221
privileges and immunities 228
Section 2(b) 193
Section 13(2)(b) 193
Section 13(4) 193
Section 13(5) 193
table on 222–3
Section 1 224
Section 2 223–4
Section 2(1) 223
Section 2(5) 224
Section 3 224–5
Section 3(3)(c) 224
Section 4 225
Section 7 228–9
Section 10 226, 228
Section 11 226
Section 13 226
Section 14 226–7
Section 15 228
Section 16 225
Section 18 226
Section 20 227, 246
States of America 19
State-to-State negotiation 47
Stockholm Declaration on Human Environment 1972 78n
Strategies, development of 91
Stricto sensu 65
Suárez 48
Sudan 3
Supreme Court for China (UK construct) 253
Supreme Court, US 218–9
Supreme Pontiff 18
Sweden 233, 250
Switzerland 220, 243
Syria 253, 282, 306

Taif Accord 305
Taiwan 102, 148
Taraz Hostage case 209
Tariff concession 123
Tate Letter (US) 218
Taxation 226, 275
Technical assistance 125–6
Technological development 112, 125ff

Technological requirements 125–7
Technology:
  acquisition of   97ff
  bargaining for   97
  and code of conduct   115
  and diplomacy   113, 114
Technology transfer   76, 78, 125–6
Tehran Agreement 1972   128n
Tehran Hostage case   200ff
Terra nullius   27
Territorial asylum   25–6, 235
Territorial integrity, principle of   182, 288
Territorial Jurisdiction of the International Commission of the River Oder   126
Territorial jurisdiction   36, 50, 57
Territorial sea   16, 50
Territorial waters   36
  territorial integrity   94
Territoriality principle   50–3, 56, 57, 63
Territory, cession of   19–20
  acquisition of   94
Terrorism, international   55, 64, 197
Textile War, China-EU   124
Thai-Europe Tapioca Service Ltd v Government of Pakistan   218
Thailand   124n, 252
Thakor Saheb Khanji Kashari Khanji v Gulam Rasol Chandbhai   245n, 246n
Third Avenue Associates v Permanent Mission of the Republic of Zaire to the United Nations 1993   197n
Threat to life   25
Tiananmen Square   233
Timberlane LBR Co v Bank of America   62
Tirana   233
Tokyo Convention on Offences and Certain Other Acts committed on Board Aircraft 1963   11
Trade and diplomacy   81, 181
Trade Negotiations Rounds   66
  see also GATT, WTO
Trade, aspects of, Doha Declaration and   124ff
Trade:
  freedom of   42–3
  and diplomacy   181
Trading agreements, regional   124
Trail Smelter Arbitration, The   47n, 286
Transparency in government   125
Travaux Préparatoires   26–7
Treason   54
Treasury, The, UK   147n
Treaties: 130, 154
  bilateral   5, 26, 36, 47, 51, 71, 96–7, 255
  bilateral and ethics   70
  defence treaties   108
  denunciation of   5
  and depositories   6–7
  establishment   6–7
  In Dubio Mitius   17
  and inter-temporal aspects   17–8
  and jurisdiction   55ff
  language   7
  multilateral   5, 77
  plurilingual   20–1
  and powers of representatives involved   14
  protocol   21
  punctationes   21
  ratification   14, 15
  reservations to   22–4
  Travaux Preparatoires   26
  treaty law   116
  For individual treaties, see under defining term
Treatment of Polish Nationals in Danzig (1932)   26n
Treaty law   115, 116
Treaty of Amity, Economic Relations, and Consular Rights, 1955   201
Trendtex Trading Corporation v Central Bank of Nigeria (1977)   219, 220, 221, 228, 244n
Trespassers and diplomatic premises   202–3
Trianon, Treaty of 1921   253n
TRIPS (WTO)   122
Trucial States (now United Arab Emirates)   254
Trusteeship Council, UN   292, 295, 311
Tunisia   15, 253
Tunkin   243

Index

Turkey 51–3
Tyre, Middle East 250

Uganda 307
UK law 38
UK-Italy Consular Treaty 260n
UK-Norway Consular Treaty 260n
UK-Sweden Consular Treaty 260n
UN Centre for Transnational Corporations 97–8
UN Conference for the Convention on Diplomatic Relations 259
UN Conference on Consular Relations, 1963 259
UN Conference on Diplomatic Privileges and Immunities 243
UN Conference on International Organisation, San Francisco, 1945 291
UN Conference on Trade and Development (UNCTAD) 98, 105, 122, 311
   Kennedy, Nixon Rounds 123
   Tokyo and Uruguay Rounds 98, 123
UN Convention on Prevention and Punishment of Crimes against Internationally Protected Persons, including Diplomatic Agents, 1973 208–9, 245, 246
UN Convention to Prevent and Punish the Act of Terrorism Taking the Form of Crimes against Persons and Related Extortion that are of International Significance, 1971 208
UN Development Decade (UN programme) 310
UN Educational, Scientific and Cultural Organization (UNESCO) 310
UN Emergency Force to the Congo 304
UN General Assembly's declaration on the Granting of Independence to Colonial Countries and Peoples 311n
UN Interim Force in Lebanon (UNIFIL) 304–6

UN Observer Mission to verify the Referendum in Eritrea (UNOVER) 303
UN Operation in the Congo (ONUC) 304
UN Truce Supervision Organisation (UNTSO) (Lebanon) 304
Underhill v Hernandez 61
Union Carbide case 50
Union Nationale des transports fluviaux (Unatra) 42ff
United Kingdom 3, 10, 11, 12, 13, 88, 116, 141, 143, 147, 153, 193, 212, 220, 225, 253, 254, 282
   British Nylon Spinners Ltd case 59
   and chargés d'affaires 156–7
   and consuls 250, 251, 253, 256
   and *Corfu Channel* case 286–7
   dealings with other states 221
   and diplomatic immunity 231–2
   and diplomatic representation 155, 156–7
   and effects doctrine 63
   England 31, 73
   Government of 42, 254
   Government, missions and council tax 211
   growth of consular service 251
   and honorary consuls 257
   and jurisdiction 51
   and Lebanon 305
   and Libya 102, 198
   and Libya mission, London 35, 184, 198–9, 247
   and Oscar Chinn case 42–4
   and Portuguese enclaves in India 25
   recognition of governments of other states 148
   and servitude 24
   State Immunity Act 221ff
   and Taiwan 102, 148
   territoriality and 50, 51, 55, 56, 58
   Treaty with Japan 252
   and UN 296
   see also Court of Appeal, English Law and courts, Foreign and Commonwealth Office, House of Lords, State Immunity Act

INTERNATIONAL LAW AND DIPLOMACY

United Nations Convention on the Law of the Sea 1982 (UNCLOS III) 29, 64, 76, 98
 and land-locked states 25, 64, 131
 and hot pursuit 15–16
 Articles 29–32 29n
 Article 95 29n
 Article 96 29n
 Article 107 29c
 Article 111(1) 15n
 Article 111(3) 16
 Article 111(4) 16
 Article III(b) 16
 Article 111(5) 16, 29n
 Article 125(1) 77
United Nations Development Programmes (UNDP) 309, 311
United Nations Industrial Development Organization (UNIDO) 311
United Nations Mission in the Democratic Republic of the Congo (MONUC) 307, 308
United Nations Transitional Authority in Cambodia (UNTAC) 308
United Nations xvii, 9, 34, 35, 40, 41, 49, 58, 65, 69, 77–9, 84, 87, 91–2, 97–8, 103, 104, 107ff, 112, 114, 130, 131, 132, 143, 148, 149, 154, 258, Chapter 14, 315
 abstention in votes 138, 296
 action against aggressors 299
 activities of the UN 290, 295
 An Agenda for Development (UN programme) 302
 An Agenda for Peace 302
 bloc voting and 138
 and Cambodia 308
 and collective self-defence 111
 and commercial relations 256
 and Conferences 9, 136
 and the Congo crisis 109–10, 303–4
 Declaration and Programme of Action on the Establishment of a New International Economic Order (NIEO) (UN programme) 310
 delegates and 137, 186
 and Democratic Republic of the Congo 306–8
 derogation from the UN Charter 133
 development of 116–7, 315
 diplomacy outside the UN 108
 diplomats and 9, 84, 116
 and Diplomatic List 143
 and domestic affairs 166
 Draft Declaration on Human Rights 1948 229
 Economic and Social Council (ECOSOC) 132, 138, 280, 291, 292, 295, 308–11
 and Eritrea 303
 establishment of 77, 291, 288–9
 as a forum for negotiation and compromise 284
 functions 288–9
 General Assembly 37, 75, 132, 229–30, 259 291, 292ff, 297, 298, 299, 302–3, 304, 315
 General Assembly officers 292
 General Assembly Resolutions 76, 103n, 110, 116, 133, 166, 287, 298–9
  legal aspects 296ff
 General Assembly Rule 92 137
 General Assembly special sessions 292
 General Assembly and UN Charter 297, 298
 General Assembly committees listed 293
 UN General Assembly's declaration on the Granting of Independence to Colonial Countries and Peoples 311n
 General Assembly powers and functions 293ff
 goals of 69, 297
 handling matters of international concern 288ff
 and International Court of Justice 312–3
 and international diplomacy 116–7
 and international trade 117
 and Iraq-Kuwait War (1990) 107–8
 and issue resolution 284
 languages of 291
 and law creation 298

Index

and Lebanon 304–6
legal effect of UN Resolutions 296ff
Member States 2, 9, 65, 74, 83, 116, 166, 259, 285, 286, 288–9, 292, 295, 296, 299, 300–1, 303, 309, 315
membership and limits to foreign policy 165
and the Middle East 110
Non-permanent members 295
Observers and 137
Observer Group Beirut 305
origins of the UN 292ff
peace-keeping operations 300, 301
peacemaking intent of the UN 295, 296, 297, 299–301
Permanent Members of Security Council 28, 294, 295–6
Permanent Members' veto 296
Permanent Representatives to 157
Permanent Sovereignty over Natural Resources (UN General Assembly Resolution, 1962) 40n, 133, 117, 297
Presidency of 292
Purposes and Principles of the UN Charter 114, 116, 134, 284, 285, 288–9, 297, 299
and Rhodesia 296
Rules of Procedure 137
Secretariat 7, 132, 302, 312
Secretary General 209, 301ff
Secretary General and good offices 302
Security Council 28, 81, 107, 108, 110–1, 137, 198, 291, 292, 294, 295–6, 298ff, 307, 315
  and abstentions 296
  peace making and keeping functions 300–1
  powers and functions 295, 296, 299–300
  veto 294, 295, 296
and socio-economic development 290, 297
Special Assembly 296
Specialised agencies 290ff
and States' foreign policy 165

Structure of 291ff
Trusteeship Council 292, 295, 311
UN Archives 20
UN Children's Fund 309,
UN Commissions (listed) 309
UN Emergency Forces 290
UN Emergency Group (Congo crisis) 304
UN expert bodies 309
UN Standing Committees (listed) 309
UN High Commissioner for Refugees 309
UN resolutions 116–7, 287
United Nations System 89, 108, 288ff
Uniting for Peace Resolution 110, 294, 297
violation of principles 289
and wars 81, 108–111, 289–90, 295
UN Charter 1, 107, 108, 166, 256, 288ff, 295, 297, 298, 315
Preamble 291–2
Article 1 288, 302
Article 2 288–9
Article 2(1) 37n
Article 2(4) 1, 2, 64, 74, 77, 81, 107–8, 111, 117, 122, 149, 181, 182, 287, 289, 301, 315
Article 2(7) 40
Article 2(11) 1
Article 3 291
Article 4 291
Article 5 92n
Article 10 110, 293–4, 304
Article 11 110, 293–4, 304
Article 12 294
Article 13 132
Article 15 298
Article 25 298
Article 27(3) 28n, 138, 296
Article 38 312–3
Article 41(33) 198n
Article 51 81, 107, 109, 111, 289
Article 59 313
Article 62(1) 310
Article 97 312
Article 102 7, 109

413

Chapter VI   295, 296, 299
Chapter VII   40, 289, 295, 296, 299, 300
Chapter VIII   297, 300
Chapter IX   121, 123, 294, 315
Chapter X   121, 123, 294, 315
Chapter XIV   291
Chapter XV   302
see also various conventions, International Court of Justice, General Agreement on Tariffs and Trade, World Trade Organisation
United States   3, 10, 19, 35, 37–8, 54, 92, 103, 116, 147, 198, 241, 253, 270
and Cambodia   202–3
and China   252–3
consular service   251, 257
and Denmark   151
development of consular service   251
and Embassy in Iran incident   199–200
and EU   117
and FR Germany   260n
and honorary consuls   257
and International Court of Justice   270ff
judiciary   61, 62
and jurisdiction   50, 51
and LaGrande case   270–4
and Lebanon   305
and Libya   102
and Morocco   254
President and declaration of war   244n
recognition of governments of other states   148
and right of asylum   230, 231, 232
and servitude   25
and sovereign immunity   218–9
Supreme Court   17
and territoriality   51
and *Trail Smelter* case   47n, 286
and *Union Carbide* case   50
and United Nations   296, 297
United States Diplomatic and Consular Staff in Tehran Provisional Measures, ICJ Reports   272n

United States v Iran   190
United States v Pilkington   62
United States-United Kingdom Consular Convention, 1951   257
Uniting for Peace (UN General Assembly Resolution)   110, 294, 297
Uniting for Peace initiative (UN)   292
Universal Declaration of Human Rights 1948   24, 77
Universal Postal Union   311
Universality Principle   55, 56
Uqair Convention (2 December 1922)   4
Uruguay   229, 230
US Department of Justice   60
US Embassy:
  Tehran, Iran, 1979 incident   35, 199–201
  Embassy Peking (now Beijing)   233
  American Minister Honduras   231
US v Aluminium Co of America (Alcoa)   51n, 61
US-China Treaty for Relinquishing of Extraterritorial Rights in China and the Regulation of Related Matters 1943   253
US v Gonzalez   54
US-Soviet Consular Convention   260n
US v Watchmakers of Switzerland Information Center Inc   61
US v Yunis   55n
USA v Wagner   245
Uti Possidetis Juris   27

VAT   213, 226
Vatican City   18, 25, 105
status in international law   27
  see also Holy See, nuncios
Vattel (author)   32, 33, 48
Vavasseur v Krupp   241n
Venezuela   4, 243
Venice, as a city state   30, 32
Versailles, Treaty of   33–4, 102
Veto   28
Vice-Marshal of the Diplomatic Corps   157, 160, 161, 163
Vienna Convention Article 41 paragraph 2   150

Index

Vienna Convention on Consular Relations
  (*Paraguay v United States of America*)
  Provisional Measures, ICJ Reports
  (1998)   272n
Vienna Convention on Consular
  Relations 1963   xvii-xviii, 35, 36,
  39, 71, 84, 171, 184, 196, 199–200,
  201, 202, 237, Chapter 13, 274
  analysis of   260ff
  Article 1(1)(k)   196
  Article 5   262–3, 271
  Article 6   264n
  Article 8   264n
  Article 9   259–60, 264n
  Article 11   264n
  Article 15   264n, 265n
  Article 16   265n
  Article 18   266n
  Article 19   10–11, 266n
  Article 20   266n
  Article 22   266n
  Article 23   266n
  Article 24   11, 196, 266n, 267n
  Article 26   201
  Article 27   201, 267n
  Article 28   279
  Article 29   279
  Article 30   268n, 279
  Article 31   268n
  Article 32   268n, 275
  Article 33   201, 268n
  Article 34   279
  Article 35   269, 279
  Article 36   269, 270, 271, 279
  Article 37   270n, 279
  Article 38   279
  Article 39   279
  Article 40   274n
  Article 41   184n, 275
  Article 42   261n, 279
  Article 43   274n, 275, 279
  Article 44   261, 275, 279
  Article 45   279
  Article 51   275n
  Article 53   276n, 277n, 279
  Article 54   277n, 280
  Article 55   278n, 280
  Article 57   278n
  Article 59   280n
  Article 60   280n
  Article 62   280n
  Article 63   280–1
  Article 64   281n
  Article 69   281n
  Article 70   281n
  Article 71   261, 262
  Article 72   39, 282n
  initiating conference   259
  and third states   277–8
  US and   257
  see also consuls, consular offices,
    *Germany v United States, Case
    Concerning the Vienna Convention
    on Consular Relations*
Vienna Convention on Diplomatic
  Relations 1961   xvii, 33, 35, 36, 39,
  50, 51, 68–9, 71, 84, 85, 111, 128,
  162, 163, Chapter 12, 199–200, 202,
  237, 242, 243, 268, 269, 282
  Articles listed   178
  Article 1   167–8
  Article 1(e)   194–5, 200
  Article 2   181
  Article 3   85, 168, 181–2, 200
  Article 3(2)   168
  Article 3(6)   181–2
  Article 3(b)   182
  Article 3(c)   182
  Article 4   185
  Article 5   185n
  Article 6   209
  Article 8(2)   186
  Article 9   184–5, 186n, 187, 216
  Article 10   187
  Article 11   180n, 187–8
  Article 12   183n, 188n, 209
  Article 13   161
  Article 14(2)   181
  Article 16   161
  Article 19   156, 162
  Article 21   188
  Article 22   191, 197, 198, 200, 204
  Article 23   188n, 191
  Article 24   196, 201, 210n
  Article 25   201, 210n, 211
  Article 26   188n, 201, 210n

415

Article 27   201, 207, 210, 247
Article 27(5)   205–6
Article 28   211
Article 29   191, 201, 207, 215
Article 30   204, 215
Article 31   201, 203, 209, 212n
Article 31 Paragraph 1   215
Articles 33   188n, 213, 215
Article 34   188n, 215
Article 35   188n, 210n, 213n, 215
Article 36   188n, 210, 213n, 215
Article 37   215
Article 38   214n, 215
Article 39   213n, 215n, 216n
Article 41   183–4
Article 41(3)   183–4
Article 42   214n
Article 44   201, 211
Article 45(a)   199, 201, 303, 211
Article 47   216
Article 47(1) and (2)   217
Article 47 paragraph 2(a)   39
Articles 49–53   216
Article 50   216–7
Article 52   217
Article 55   184n
and declaration of persona non grata   184–5, 187
defining functions of a diplomatic Mission   168
defining head of Mission   167
diplomatic missions and consular function   168
and entry without consent in emergencies   197
and existing state practice   247
Foreign Ministries and diplomatic Missions   164, 173–5
and Heads of State   243
initiating conference   259
not covering incompatible use of missions   184
Preamble   177, 242, 243
taxation   191
table of analysis of convention   178–80
see also Diplomat, Diplomatic immunity, diplomatic mission

Vienna Convention on the Law of Treaties 1969   71, 244n
Article 2(1)(d)   22
Article 2(7)   40
Article 7   15
Article 7(1)(a)   14n
Article 7(1)b   14
Article 7 paragraph 2   151n, 244n
Article 8   15
Article 11   180n
Article 14(2)   181n
Article 15   6
Article 16   6
Article 19   10–11, 23
Article 20   23
Article 21   23
Article 22   191
Article 23   23, 191
Article 23(1)   22
Article 24   196
Article 33(1)   20
Article 33(2)   20–1
Article 43   216
Article 51   2
Article 53   18
Article 56   5
Article 59   5–6
Article 76(2)   7n
Article 77(1)   6–7
Article 77(2)   7n
Jus Cogens   18
relations between states   47
reservations   22–4
Vienna Convention on the Law of Treaties between States and International Organisations 1986   244n
Vienna, Congress of   32–3
Viet-Nam   xvii, 20, 65, 78, 81, 103, 124n
 North Viet-Nam   110, 128
Virginia court, US   274
Visas   262, 274
Vitoria, Francisco de   48
Volte face   28

Wanghia, Treaty of, China-US, 1844   252–3

War crimes   55
War   1, 2, 80, 286, 300
  cold war   2, 285
  declaration of   244
  hot war   3, 285
  laws of war   109
  and League of Nations   77, 93–4
  and UN   107–111, 289
  warfare   34, 77, 106, 108, 110, 111, 113, 114
Warrington LJ   37
Warships and asylum   232
Warships in foreign waters and jurisdiction   28–9
Washington DC   174
Watchmakers of Switzerland case   61
Weapons of mass destruction (WMD)   75, 104
Weapons, sale of   74
Western Sahara case   27n
Westlake   232
Westminster City Council v Government of Islamic Republic of Iran (1986)   204
Westminster City Council v Tomlin   203
Westphalia, Treaty of, 1648   150
Wilson, Woodrow   103
Withdrawal from a treaty   5
Wolff   48
Wood Pulp case   63
World Bank
  see International Bank for Reconstruction and Development
World Court
  see Permanent Court of International Justice, International Court of Justice
World Food Programme   309
World Health Organisation (WHO)   280, 310
World Intellectual Property Organization (WIPO)   311
World Meteorological Organization (WMO)   311
World Trade Organisation (WTO)   66, 77, 117–8, 121, 122, 122, 126, 127, 314
  and agriculture   127
  Cancún Round   76, 79, 124, 127, 128
  and TRIPS   122
  and UN   311
  see also GATT
World War I   33, 34, 92–3, 112, 121, 253
World War II   34, 54, 80, 102, 109, 116, 256, 259, 295
  Post-1945 period   109, 117, 218, 259
  wars in post-1945 period   110, 289–90

Yemen   254
Yugoslavia   46, 67

Zanzibar   254
Zanzibar Declaration July 2001   126
Zimbabwe   307
Zones of Upper Savoy, The, and the District of Gex (1932)   25